SOLIDWORKS 201[illegible] in 5 Hours with Video Instruction

David C. Planchard
CSWP & SOLIDWORKS Accredited Educator

SolidWorks Solution Partner

SDC Publications

SDC Publications
P.O. Box 1334
Mission, KS 66222
913-262-2664
www.SDCpublications.com
Publisher: Stephen Schroff

ISBN-13: 978-1-63057-072-9
ISBN-10: 1-63057-072-9

Printed and bound in the United States of America.

INTRODUCTION

SOLIDWORKS® 2017 in 5 Hours with video instruction introduces the new user to the basics of using SOLIDWORKS 3D CAD software in 5 easy lessons with a bonus chapter on Additive Manufacturing (3D printing).

The book is intended for the student or designer that needs to learn SOLIDWORKS quickly and effectively for senior capstone, machine design, kinematics, dynamics and other engineering and technology projects that use SOLIDWORKS as a tool. Engineers in industry who are expected to have SOLIDWORKS skills for their company's next project. Students who need to learn SOLIDWORKS without taking a formal CAD course.

SOLIDWORKS 2017 in 5 Hours was written based on years of teaching SOLIDWORKS to engineering students, and concentrates on the areas where the new user improves efficiency in the design modeling process. By learning the correct SOLIDWORKS skills and file management techniques, you gain the most knowledge in the shortest period of time.

You develop a mini Stirling Engine and investigate the proper design intent and constraints. The mini Stirling Engine is based on the external combustion, closed cycle engine of Scottish inventor, Robert Stirling. In addition to 3D modeling, the engine can be used to teach and connect many engineering and physics principles.

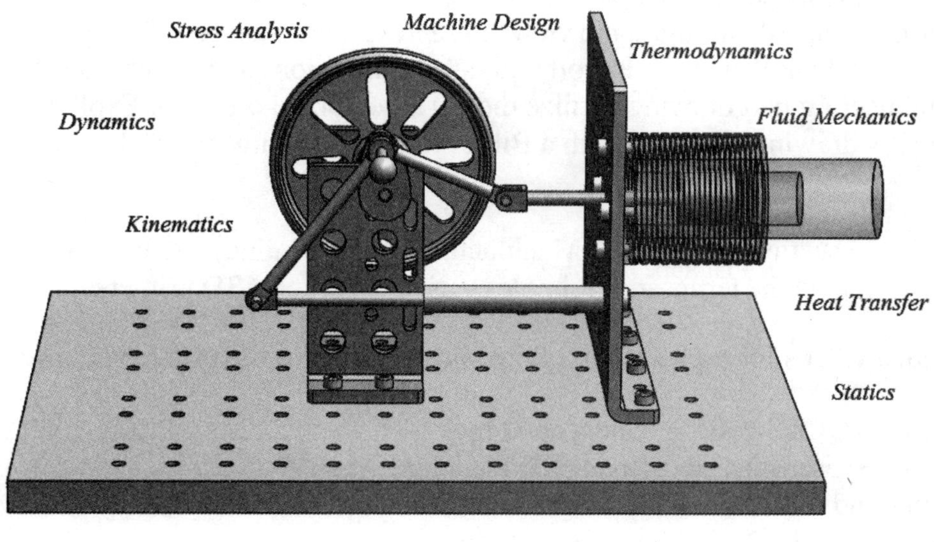

You begin with an overview of SOLIDWORKS and the User Interface (UI), its menus, toolbars and commands. With a quick pace, you learn the essentials of 2D sketching to create a profile.

Investigate view orientation based on the Front, Top and Right planes. As you sketch, use tools such as the circle, line, centerline, slot and mirror. Modify sketches and sketch planes. Learn to set document properties, identify sketch states and insert geometric relations and dimensions along with applying proper design intent and technique.

Parts are made up of features. With features you add or remove material. You apply and edit the Extruded Boss/Base, Revolved Boss/Base, Extruded Cut, Circular Pattern and Fillet feature. You explore the Hole Wizard feature with manufacturing parameters and the Mass Properties, Measure and Appearance tool.

Assemblies are made up of components and sub-assemblies. Incorporate a series of provided parts and your own part to create two assemblies utilizing the Bottom-up approach.

Utilize the following assembly tools: Insert Component, Mate, Hide, Show, Rotate, Move, Modify, Flexible, Ridge, Multiple mate and more. Learn how to add constraints that result in dynamic behavior of the assembly such as linear translation and rotation.

Before you machine or create a rapid prototype of a part or assembly, you should verify the model for clearance, interference, static and dynamic behavior. Verify behavior between the Power Piston, Power Clevis, Connecting Rod and Handle with design modifications using the Stirling Engine Modified assembly.

Apply the Assembly Visualization tool to sort components by mass while creating a motion study (animation) for a formal presentation.

Drawings are 2D representations of a part or assembly. Develop a 2D detailed part drawing and insert standard Orthographic views to represent the features of the part using the Model Items and Task Pane tool. Import and insert dimensions and annotations to complete an engineering part drawing. Utilize the 3D assembly to create an Exploded Isometric assembly drawing complete with a Bill of Materials, Balloons and Revision table.

Chapter 6 provides a section on Additive Manufacturing (3D printing) and its benefits and features. Understand the terms and technology used in low cost 3D printers.

View the provided videos for each section of the book to enhance the user experience.

- Start a SOLIDWORKS session, Understand the SOLIDWORKS User Interface, Create 2D Sketches, Sketch Planes and use various Sketch tools, Create 3D Features and apply Design Intent, Create an Assembly and Create fundamental Drawings Part 1 & Part 2.

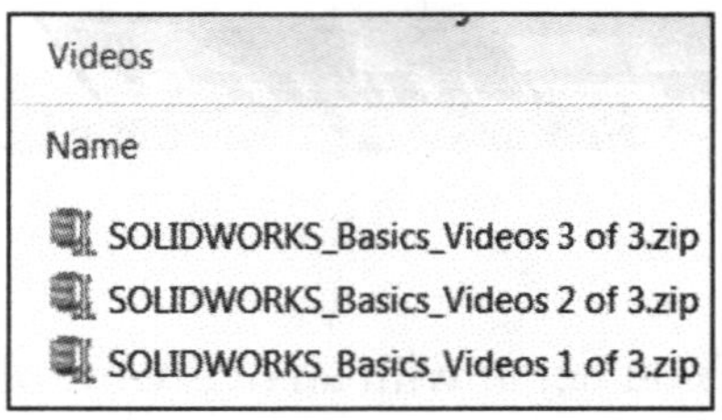

About the Author

David Planchard is the founder of D&M Education LLC. Before starting D&M Education, he spent over 27 years in industry and academia holding various engineering, marketing, and teaching positions. He holds five U.S. patents. He has published and authored numerous papers on Machine Design, Product Design, Mechanics of Materials, and Solid Modeling. He is an active member of the SOLIDWORKS Users Group and the American Society of Engineering Education (ASEE). David holds a BSME, MS with the following professional certifications: CCAI, CCNP, CSDA, CSWSA-FEA, CSWP, CSWP-DRWT and SOLIDWORKS Accredited Educator. David is a SOLIDWORKS Solution Partner, an Adjunct Faculty member and the SAE advisor at Worcester Polytechnic Institute in the Mechanical Engineering department. In 2012, David's senior Major Qualifying Project team (senior capstone) won first place in the Mechanical Engineering department at WPI. In 2014, 2015 and 2016, David's senior Major Qualifying Project team won the Provost award in Mechanical Engineering for design excellence.

David Planchard is the author of the following books:

- **SOLIDWORKS® 2017 Reference Guide with video instruction**, 2016, 2015, 2014, 2013, 2012, 2011, 2010 and 2009
- **Engineering Design with SOLIDWORKS® 2017 and video instruction**, 2016, 2015, 2014, 2013, 2012, 2011, 2010, 2009, 2008, 2007, 2006, 2005, 2004, and 2003
- **Engineering Graphics with SOLIDWORKS® 2017 and video instruction**, 2016, 2015, 2014, 2013, 2012 and 2011
- **SOLIDWORKS® 2017 in 5 Hours with video instruction**, 2016, 2015, 2014
- **SOLIDWORKS® 2017 Tutorial with video instruction**, 2016, 2015, 2014, 2013, 2012, 2011, 2010, 2009, 2008, 2007, 2006, 2005, 2004 and 2003
- **Drawing and Detailing with SOLIDWORKS® 2014**, 2012, 2010, 2009, 2008, 2007, 2006, 2005, 2004, 2003, and 2002
- **Official Certified SOLIDWORKS® Professional (CSWP) Certification Guide with video instruction, Version 4: 2017 - 2015**, Version 3: 2014 - 2012, Version 2: 2013 - 2012, Version 1: 2011, 2010
- **Official Guide to Certified SOLIDWORKS® Associate Exams: CSWA, CSDA, CSWSA-FEA Version 3: 2017 - 2015**, Version 2: 2015 - 2012, Version 1: 2013, 2012
- **Assembly Modeling with SOLIDWORKS® 2012**, 2010, 2008, 2006, 2005-2004, 2003 and 2001Plus

- **Applications in Sheet Metal Using Pro/SHEETMETAL & Pro/ENGINEER**

Acknowledgements

Writing this book was a substantial effort that would not have been possible without the help and support of my loving family and of my professional colleagues. I would like to thank Professor John M. Sullivan Jr., Professor Jack Hall and the community of scholars at Worcester Polytechnic Institute who have enhanced my life, my knowledge and helped to shape the approach and content to this text.

The author is greatly indebted to my colleagues from Dassault Systèmes SOLIDWORKS Corporation for their help and continuous support: Avelino Rochino and Mike Puckett.

Thanks also to Professor Richard L. Roberts of Wentworth Institute of Technology, Professor Dennis Hance of Wright State University, Professor Jason Durfess of Eastern Washington University and Professor Aaron Schellenberg of Brigham Young University - Idaho who provided vision and invaluable suggestions.

SOLIDWORKS certification has enhanced my skills and knowledge and that of my students. Thank you to Ian Matthew Jutras (CSWE) who is a technical contributor and the creator of the videos and Stephanie Planchard, technical procedure consultant.

Contact the Author

We realize that keeping software application books current is imperative to our customers. We value the hundreds of professors, students, designers, and engineers that have provided us input to enhance our book. We value your suggestions and comments. Please contact me or visit our website www.dmeducation.net with any comments, questions or suggestions on this book or any of our other SOLIDWORKS books. David Planchard, D & M Education, LLC, dplanchard@msn.com or planchard@wpi.edu.

Note to Instructors

Please contact the publisher **www.SDCpublications.com** for additional classroom support materials: PowerPoint presentations, Adobe files along with avi files, additional design projects, quizzes with initial and final SOLIDWORKS models and tips that support the usage of this text in a classroom environment.

Trademarks, Disclaimer and Copyrighted Material

The publisher and the author make no representations or warranties with respect to the accuracy or completeness of the contents of this work and specifically disclaim all warranties, including without limitation warranties of fitness for a particular purpose.

No warranty may be created or extended by sales or promotional materials. Dimensions of parts are modified for illustration purposes. Every effort is made to provide an accurate text. The author and the manufacturers shall not be held liable for any parts, components, assemblies or drawings developed or designed with this book or any responsibility for inaccuracies that appear in the book. Web and company information was valid at the time of this printing.

References

- SOLIDWORKS Users Guide, SOLIDWORKS Corporation, 2017
- ASME Y14 Engineering Drawing and Related Documentation Practices
- Beers & Johnson, Vector Mechanics for Engineers, 6th ed. McGraw Hill, Boston, MA
- Betoline, Wiebe, Miller, Fundamentals of Graphics Communication, Irwin, 1995
- Hibbler, R.C, Engineering Mechanics Statics and Dynamics, 8th ed, Prentice Hall, Saddle River, NJ
- Hoelscher, Springer, Dobrovolny, Graphics for Engineers, John Wiley, 1968
- Jensen, Cecil, Interpreting Engineering Drawings, Glencoe, 2002
- Jensen & Helsel, Engineering Drawing and Design, Glencoe, 1990
- Lockhart & Johnson, Engineering Design Communications, Addison Wesley, 1999
- Olivo C., Payne, Olivo, T, Basic Blueprint Reading and Sketching, Delmar, 1988
- Planchard & Planchard, Drawing and Detailing with SOLIDWORKS, SDC Publications, Mission, KS 2014

During the initial SOLIDWORKS installation, you are requested to select either the ISO or ANSI drafting standard. ISO is typically a European drafting standard and uses First Angle Projection. The book is written using the ANSI (US) overall drafting standard and Third Angle Projection for drawings.

TABLE OF CONTENTS

View the provided videos in the book to enhance the user experience.

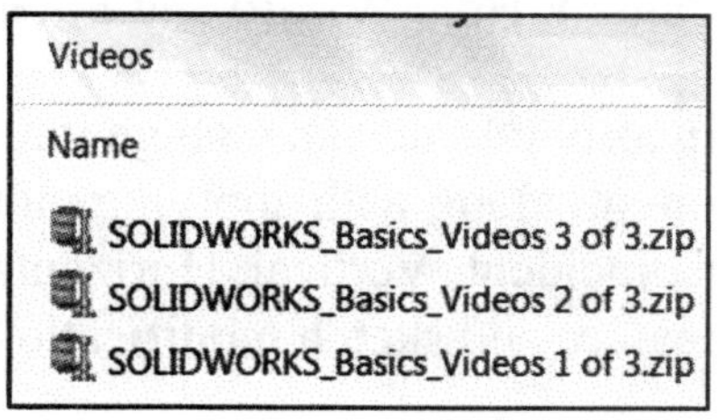

- Start a SOLIDWORKS session.
- Understand the SOLIDWORKS User Interface.
- Create 2D Sketches, Sketch Planes and use various Sketch tools.
- Create 3D Features and apply Design Intent.
- Create an Assembly.
- Create fundamental Drawings Part 1 & Part 2.

Overview of Chapters

Chapter 1: Overview of SOLIDWORKS and the User Interface

SOLIDWORKS is a design software application used to create 2D and 3D sketches, 3D parts and assemblies and 2D drawings.

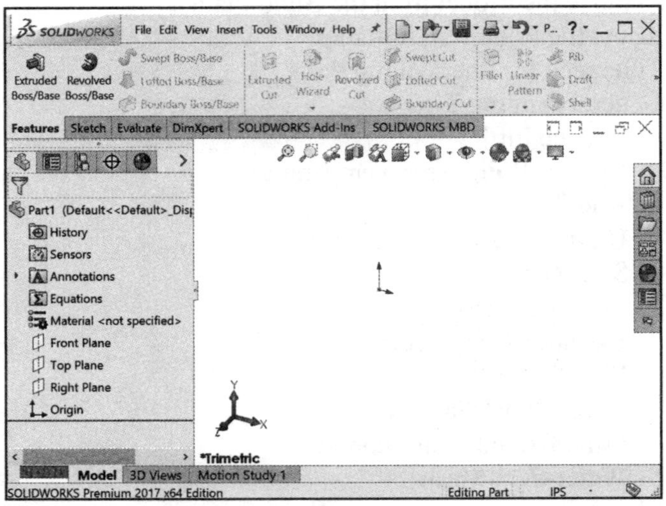

Chapter 1 introduces the user to the SOLIDWORKS User Interface (UI) and CommandManager: Menu bar toolbar, Menu bar menu, Drop-down menus, Context toolbars, Consolidated drop-down toolbars, System feedback icons, Confirmation Corner, Heads-up View toolbar, Document Properties and more.

How do you start a SOLIDWORKS session? How do you open a new or existing part? How do you start a model in SOLIDWORKS? What is design intent?

Chapter 2: 2D Sketching, Features and Parts

Learn about 2D Sketching and 3D features. Create a new part called Wheel with user defined document properties.

Create the Wheel for the Fly Wheel sub-assembly. Utilize the Fly Wheel sub-assembly in the final Stirling Engine assembly.

Apply the following sketch and feature tools: Circle, Line Centerline, Centerpoint Straight Slot, Mirror Entities, Extruded Boss, Extruded Cut, Revolved Boss, Circular Pattern, Hole Wizard and Fillet.

Incorporate design change into a part using proper design intent, along with applying multiple geometric relations: Coincident, Vertical, Horizontal, Tangent and Midpoint and feature and sketch modifications.

Utilize the Material, Mass Properties and Appearance tool on the Wheel.

Chapter 3: Assembly Modeling - Bottom-up method

Learn about the Bottom-up assembly method and create two new assemblies with user defined document properties:

- Fly Wheel.
- Stirling Engine.

Insert the following Standard and Quick mate types: Coincident, Concentric, Distance and Tangent.

Utilize the following assembly tools: Insert Component, Suppress, Un-suppress, Mate, Move Component, Rotate Component, Interference Detection, Hide, Show, Flexible, Ridge and Multiple mate mode.

Create an Exploded View with animation.

Apply the Measure and Mass Properties tool to modify a component in the Stirling Engine assembly.

Chapter 4: Design Modifications

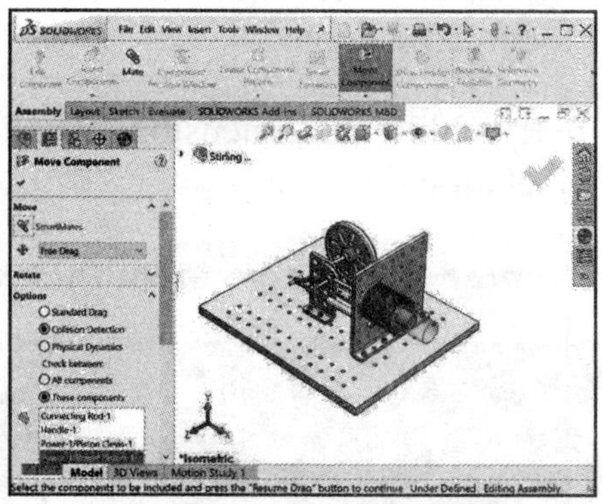

Address clearance, interference, static and dynamic behavior of the Stirling Engine Modified assembly.

Verify the behavior between the following components: Power Piston, Power Clevis, Connecting Rod and Handle in the assembly.

Apply the following assembly tools: Move, Rotate, Collision Detection, Interference Detection, Selected Components, Edit Feature and Center of Mass.

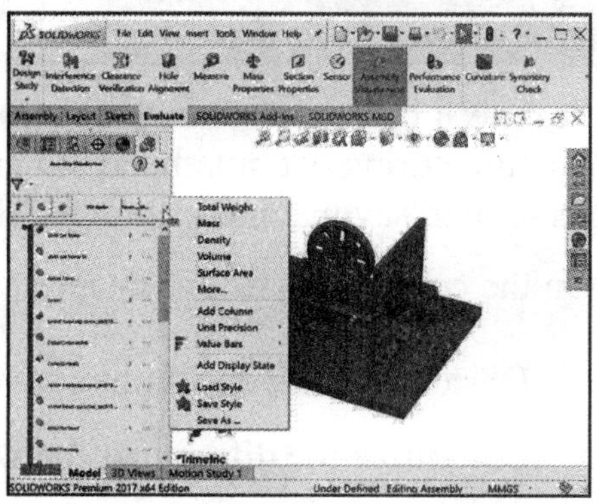

Utilize the Assembly Visualization tool on the Stirling Engine assembly and sort by component mass.

Create a new Coordinate System on the Stirling Engine assembly relative to the default origin.

Run a Motion Study and save the Motion Study AVI file.

Chapter 5: Drawing and Dimensioning Fundamentals

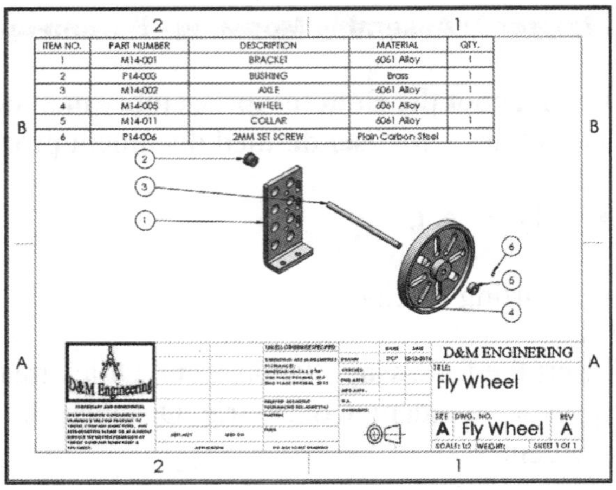

Learn about Drawing and Dimension Fundamentals and create two new drawings with user defined document properties:

- Fly Wheel Assembly.
- Bushing.

Create the Fly Wheel Assembly drawing with an Exploded Isometric view.

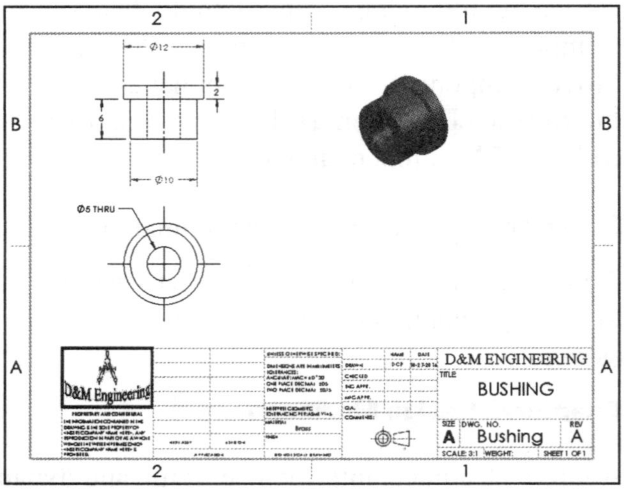

Utilize a Bill of Materials, Magnetic lines and Balloons.

Learn about Custom Properties and the Title Block.

Create the Bushing Part drawing utilizing Third Angle Projection with two standard Orthographic views: Front, Top and an Isometric view.

Address imported dimensions from the Model Items tool.

Insert additional dimensions using the Smart Dimension tool along with all needed annotations.

Chapter 6: Additive Manufacturing - 3D Printing

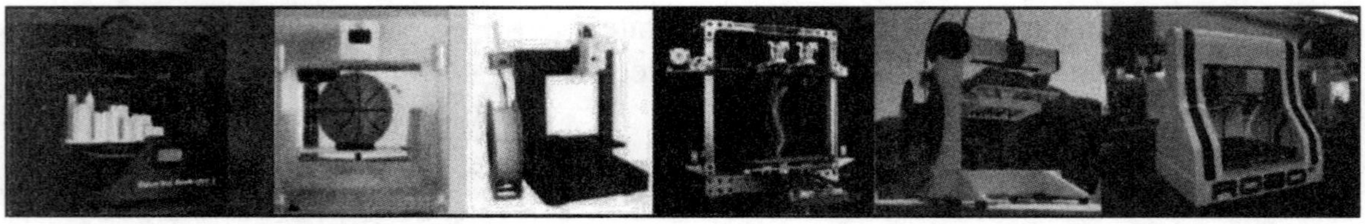

Provide a basic understanding between the differences of Additive vs. Subtractive Manufacturing. Comprehend 3D printer terminology along with a working knowledge of preparing, saving, and printing a 3D CAD model on a low cost ($500 - $2,000) printer.

On the completion of this chapter, you will be able to:

- Discuss Additive vs Subtractive Manufacturing.
- Determine the differences between a Cartesian printer and a Delta printer.

- Create a STereoLithography (STL) file in SOLIDWORKS.
- 3D print directly from SOLIDWORKS using an Add-In.
  - o Save an STL file to G-code.
- Discuss printer hardware.
- Select the correct filament type:
  - o PLA (Polylactic acid), ABS (Acrylonitrile butadiene styrene) or Nylon.
- Prepare the G-code.
  - o Address model setup, print orientation, extruder temperature, and bed temperature.
- Comprehend the following 3D printer terminology:
  - o (STereoLithography) file - STL.
  - o Fused Filament Fabrication - FFF.
  - o Fused Deposition Model - FDM.
  - o Digital Light Process - DLP.
  - o Dissolvable Support System - DDS.
  - o Fast Layer Deposition - FLD.
  - o Raft, Skirt and Brim.
  - o Support and Touching Buildplate.
  - o Slicer, G-code.
- Address fit tolerance for interlocking parts.
- Define general 3D Printing tips.

Book Layout

The following conventions are used throughout this book:

- The term document is used to refer to a SOLIDWORKS part, drawing or assembly file.

- The list of items across the top of the SOLIDWORKS interface is the Menu bar menu or the Menu bar toolbar. Each item in the Menu bar has a pull-down menu. When you need to select a series of commands from these menus, the following format is used: Click **View**, **Hide/Show**, check **Origins** from the Menu bar. The Origins are displayed in the Graphics window.

- The ANSI overall drafting standard and Third Angle projection is used as the default setting in this text. MMGS (millimeter, gram, second) unit system is used.

- The book is organized into various chapters. Each chapter is focused on a specific subject or feature.

- All templates, logos and needed model documents for this book are provided. Redeem your code on the inside cover of the book. View the videos and models to enhance the user experience. Download the **SOLIDWORKS in 5 Hours** folder to your local hard drive. Work from your local hard drive.

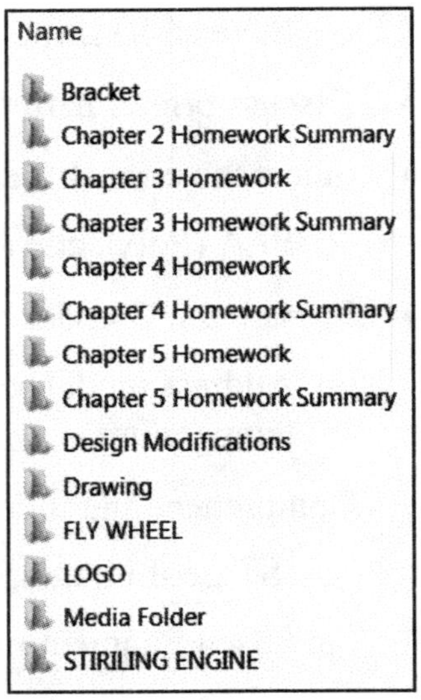

- Additional exercises are provided. Download the **SOLIDWORKS in 5 Hours** folder to your hard drive. Work from your hard drive.

- Screen shots in the book were made using SOLIDWORKS 2017 SP0 running Windows® 10.

View the provided videos in this book to enhance the user experience.

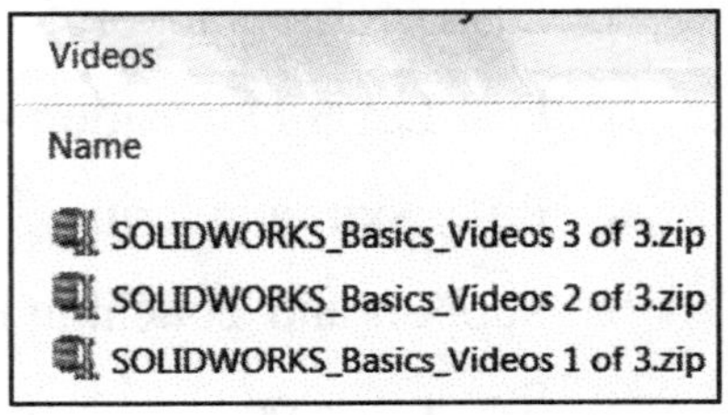

- Start a SOLIDWORKS session.
- Understand the SOLIDWORKS Interface.
- Create 2D Sketches, Sketch Planes and utilize various Sketch tools.
- Create 3D Features and apply Design Intent.
- Create an Assembly.
- Create fundamental Drawings Part 1 & Part 2.

The following command syntax is used throughout the text. Commands that require you to perform an action are displayed in **Bold** text.

Format:	Convention:	Example:
Bold	• All commands actions. • Selected icon button. • Selected geometry: line, circle. • Value entries.	• Click **Options** from the Menu bar toolbar. • Click **Corner Rectangle** from the Sketch toolbar. • Click **Sketch** from the Context toolbar. • Select the **centerpoint**. • Enter **3.0** for Radius.
Capitalized	• Filenames. • First letter in a feature name.	• Save the **FLATBAR** assembly. • Click the **Fillet** feature.

Windows Terminology in SOLIDWORKS

The mouse buttons provide an integral role in executing SOLIDWORKS commands. The mouse buttons execute commands, select geometry, display Shortcut menus and provide information feedback.

A summary of mouse button terminology is displayed below:

Item:	Description:
Click	Press and release the left mouse button.
Double-click	Double press and release the left mouse button.
Click inside	Press the left mouse button. Wait a second, and then press the left mouse button inside the text box. Use this technique to modify Feature names in the FeatureManager design tree.
Drag	Point to an object, press and hold the left mouse button down. Move the mouse pointer to a new location. Release the left mouse button.
Right-click	Press and release the right mouse button. A Shortcut menu is displayed. Use the left mouse button to select a menu command.
Tool Tip	Position the mouse pointer over an Icon (button). The tool name is displayed below the mouse pointer.
Large Tool Tip	Position the mouse pointer over an Icon (button). The tool name and a description of its functionality are displayed below the mouse pointer.
Mouse pointer feedback	Position the mouse pointer over various areas of the sketch, part, assembly or drawing. The cursor provides feedback depending on the geometry.

A mouse with a center wheel provides additional functionality in SOLIDWORKS. Roll the center wheel downward to enlarge the model in the Graphics window. Hold the center wheel down. Drag the mouse in the Graphics window to rotate the model.

Visit SOLIDWORKS website: http://www.SOLIDWORKS.com/sw/support/hardware.html to view their supported operating systems and hardware requirements.

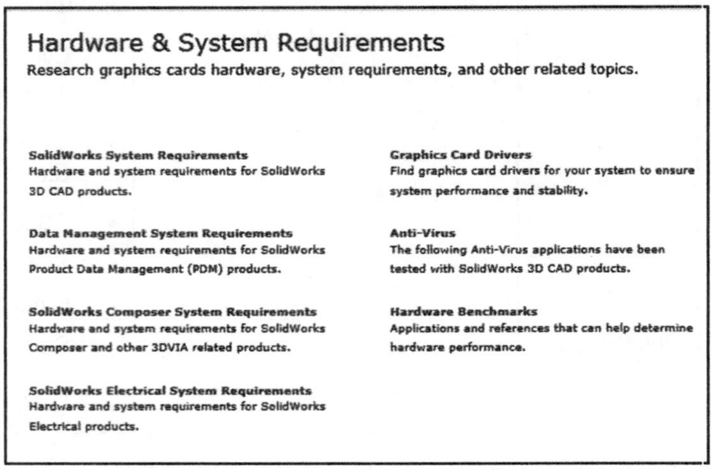

The Instructor's DVD contains over 45 classroom presentations, along with helpful hints, What's new, sample quizzes, avi files of assemblies, projects and all initial and final SOLIDWORKS models.

The book is designed to expose the new user to numerous tools and procedures. It may not always use the simplest and most direct process.

The book does not cover starting a SOLIDWORKS session in detail for the first time. A default SOLIDWORKS installation presents you with several options. For additional information for an Education Edition, visit the following site: http://www.SOLIDWORKS.com/sw/engineering-education-software.htm.

Chapter 1

Overview of SOLIDWORKS 2017 and the User Interface

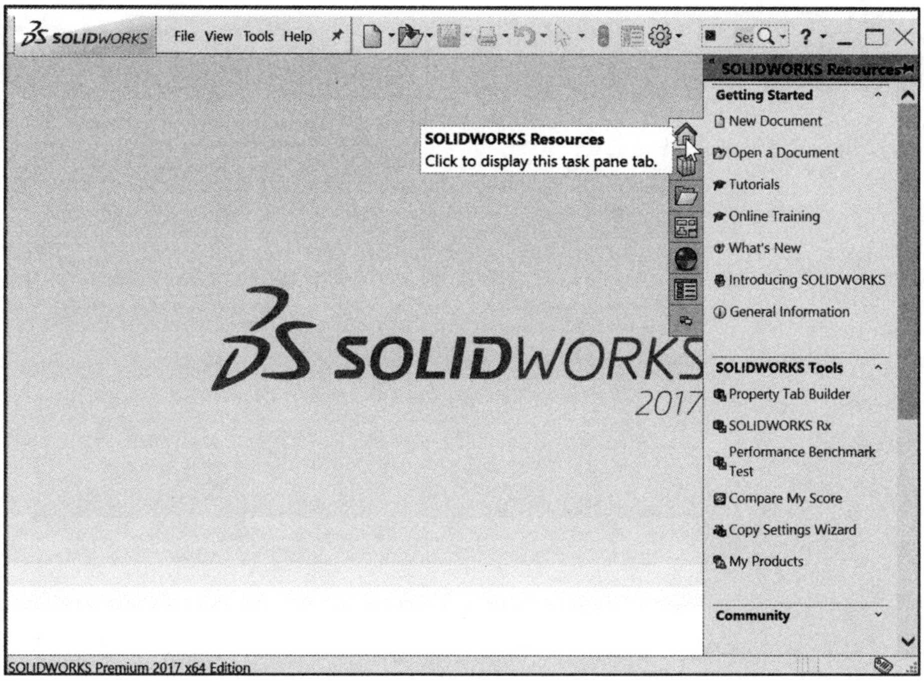

Below are the desired outcomes and usage competencies based on the completion of Chapter 1.

Desired Outcomes:	Usage Competencies:
• A comprehensive understanding of the SOLIDWORKS 2017 User Interface (UI) and CommandManager.	• Ability to establish a SOLIDWORKS session. • Aptitude to utilize the following items: Menu bar toolbar, Menu bar menu, Drop-down menus, Context toolbars, Consolidated drop-down toolbars, System feedback icons, Confirmation Corner, Heads-up View toolbar, Document Properties and more. • Knowledge to zoom, rotate and maneuver a three button mouse in the SOLIDWORKS Graphics window.

Notes:

Chapter 1 - Overview of SOLIDWORKS 2017 and the User Interface

Chapter Objective

Provide a comprehensive understanding of the SOLIDWORKS default User Interface and CommandManager: Menu bar toolbar, Menu bar menu, Drop-down menu, Right-click Pop-up menus, Context toolbars/menus, Fly-out tool button, System feedback icons, Confirmation Corner, Heads-up View toolbar and an understanding of System Options, Document Properties, Part templates, File management and more.

On the completion of this chapter, you will be able to:

- Establish a SOLIDWORKS 2017session.
- Comprehend the SOLIDWORKS User Interface.
- Recognize the default Reference Planes in the FeatureManager.
- Utilize SOLIDWORKS Help and SOLIDWORKS Tutorials.
- Zoom, rotate and maneuver a three button mouse in the SOLIDWORKS Graphics window.

What is SOLIDWORKS?

- SOLIDWORKS® is a mechanical design automation software package used to build parts, assemblies and drawings that takes advantage of the familiar Microsoft® Windows graphical user interface.
- SOLIDWORKS is an easy to learn design and analysis tool (SOLIDWORKS Simulation, SOLIDWORKS Motion, SOLIDWORKS Flow Simulation, Sustainability, etc.), which makes it possible for designers to quickly sketch 2D and 3D concepts, create 3D parts and assemblies and detailed 2D drawings.
- Model dimensions in SOLIDWORKS are associative between parts, assemblies and drawings. Reference dimensions are one-way associative from the part to the drawing or from the part to the assembly.

Start a SOLIDWORKS Session

Start a SOLIDWORKS session and familiarize yourself with the SOLIDWORKS User Interface. As you read and perform the tasks in this chapter, you will obtain a sense of how to use the book and the structure. Actual input commands or required actions in the chapter are displayed in bold.

The book does not cover starting a SOLIDWORKS session in detail for the first time. A default SOLIDWORKS installation presents you with several options. For additional information, visit http://www.SOLIDWORKS.com.

Redeem your code on the inside cover of the book. View the provided videos and models to enhance the user experience.

Activity: Start a SOLIDWORKS 2017 Session

Start a SOLIDWORKS 2017 session.

1) Click **Start** on the Windows Taskbar.

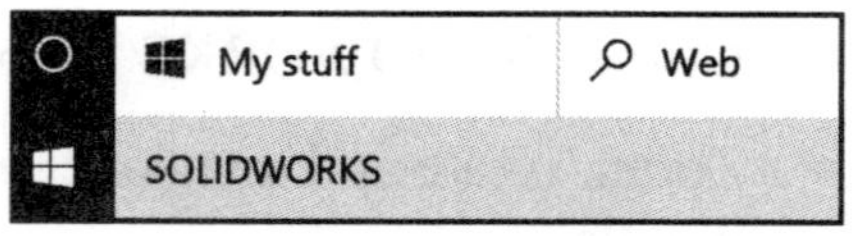

2) Click **All Programs**.
3) Click the **SOLIDWORKS 2017** folder.
4) Click **SOLIDWORKS 2017** application. The SOLIDWORKS program window opens. Do not open a document at this time.

If available, double-click the SOLIDWORKS 2017 icon on your Desktop to start a SOLIDWORKS session.

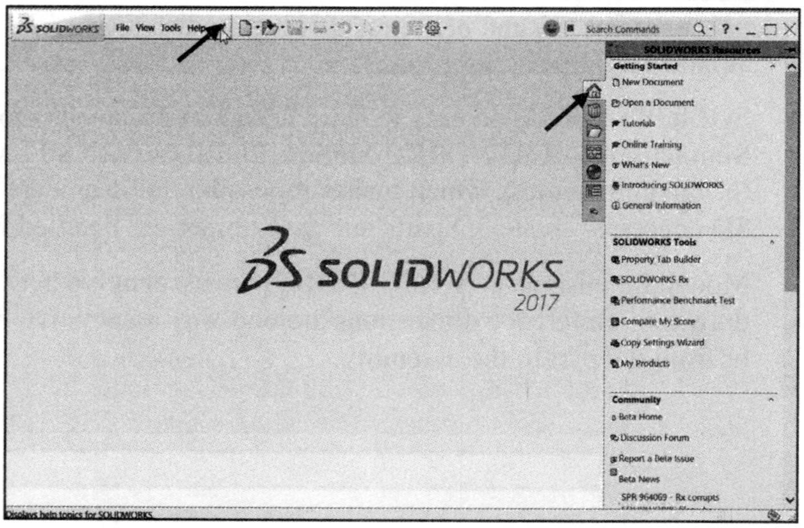

Read the Tip of the Day dialog box.

If you do not see this screen, click the SOLIDWORKS Resources icon on the right side of the Graphics window located in the Task Pane.

5) **Hover** the mouse pointer over the SOLIDWORKS icon as illustrated.

6) **Pin** the Menu Bar toolbar. View your options.

Menu Bar toolbar

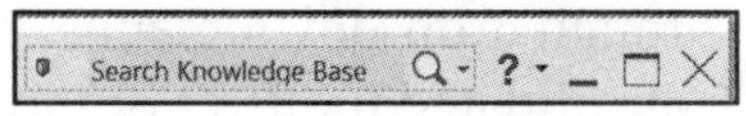

The SOLIDWORKS 2017 (UI) is designed to make maximum use of the Graphics window. The Menu Bar toolbar contains a set of the most frequently used tool buttons from the Standard toolbar.

These are the available default tools:

- **New** - Creates a new document; **Open** - Opens an existing document, **Save** - Saves an active document; **Print** - Prints an active document; **Undo** - Reverses the last action; **Select** - Selects Sketch entities, components and more; **Rebuild** - Rebuilds the active part, assembly or drawing; **File Properties** - Shows the summary information on the active document; and **Options** - Changes system options and Add-Ins for SOLIDWORKS.

Menu Bar menu

Click SOLIDWORKS in the Menu Bar toolbar to display the Menu Bar menu. SOLIDWORKS provides a context-sensitive menu structure. The menu titles remain the same for all three types of documents, but the menu items change depending on which type of document is active.

Example: The Insert menu includes features in part documents, mates in assembly documents, and drawing views in drawing documents. The display of the menu is also dependent on the workflow customization that you have selected. The default menu items for an active document are *File*, *Edit*, *View*, *Insert*, *Tools*, *Window*, *Help* and *Pin*.

The Pin option displays the Menu bar toolbar and the Menu bar menu as illustrated. Throughout the book, the Menu bar menu and the Menu bar toolbar are referred to as the Menu bar.

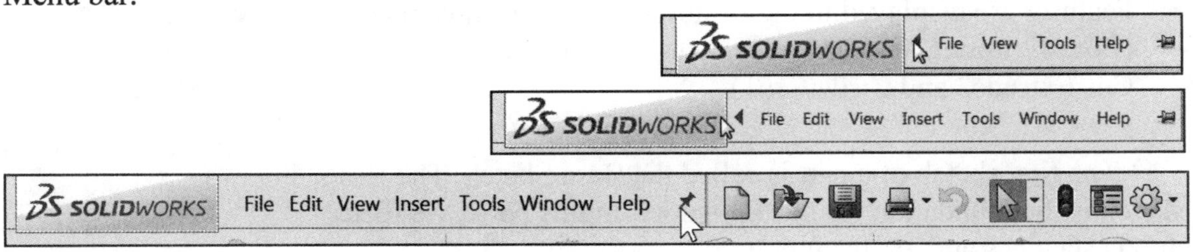

Drop-down menu

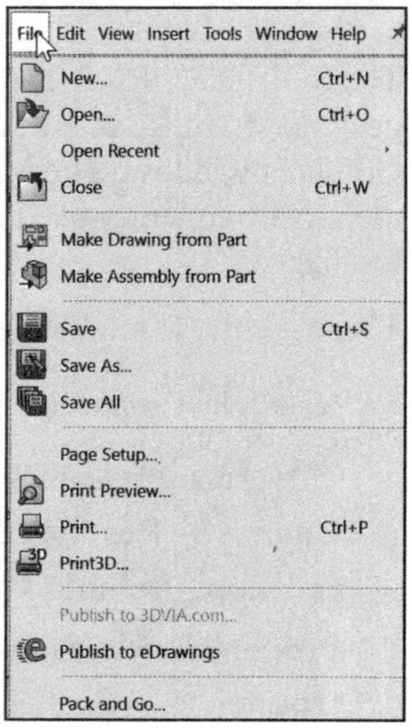

SOLIDWORKS takes advantage of the familiar Microsoft® Windows user interface. Communicate with SOLIDWORKS through drop-down menus, Context sensitive toolbars, Consolidated toolbars or the CommandManager tabs.

A command is an instruction that informs SOLIDWORKS to perform a task.

To close a SOLIDWORKS drop-down menu, press the Esc key. You can also click any other part of the SOLIDWORKS Graphics window or click another drop-down menu.

Create a New Part Document

In the next section create a new part document.

Activity: Create a New Part Document

A part is a 3D model which consists of features. What are features?

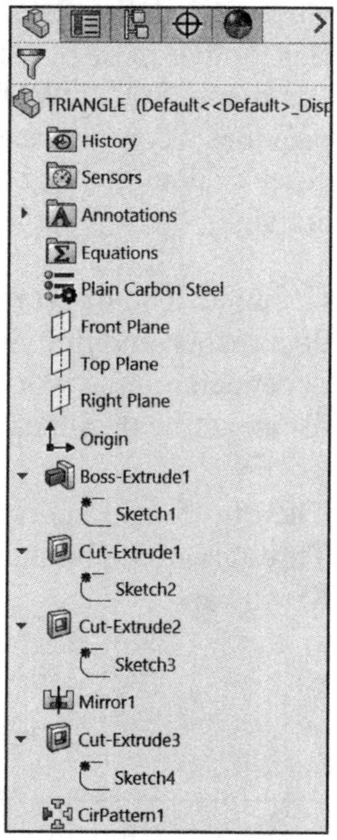

- Features are geometry building blocks.
- Most features either add or remove material.
- Some features do not affect material (Cosmetic Thread).
- Features are created either from 2D or 3D sketched profiles or from edges and faces of existing geometry.
- Features are an individual shape that combined with other features make up a part or assembly. Some features, such as bosses and cuts, originate as sketches. Other features, such as shells and fillets, modify a feature's geometry.
- Features are displayed in the FeatureManager as illustrated (Boss-Extrude1, Cut-Extrude1, Cut-Extrude2, Mirror1, Cut-Extrude3 and CirPattern1).

The first sketch of a part is called the Base Sketch. The Base sketch is the foundation for the 3D model. In this book, we focus on 2D sketches and 3D features.

There are two modes in the New SOLIDWORKS Document dialog box: *Novice* and *Advanced*. The *Novice* option is the default option with three templates. The *Advanced* mode contains access to additional templates and tabs that you create in system options. Use the *Advanced* mode in this book.

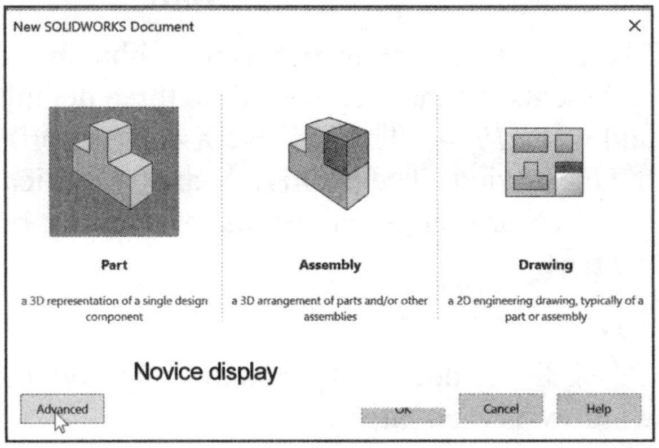

Create a new part.

7) Click **New** from the Menu bar. The New SOLIDWORKS Document dialog box is displayed.

Select the Advanced mode.

8) Click the **Advanced** button as illustrated. The Advanced mode is set. The Templates tab is the default tab. Part is the default template from the New SOLIDWORKS Document dialog box.

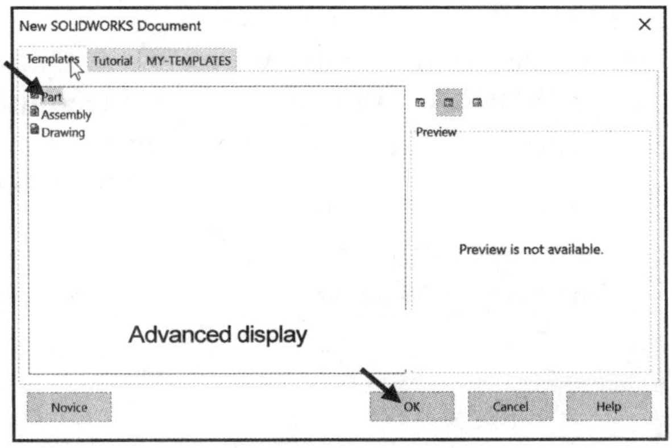

9) Click **OK** from the New SOLIDWORKS Document dialog box.

Illustrations may vary depending on your SOLIDWORKS version and operating system.

View the provided video on the SOLIDWORKS Interface to enhance your experience with this chapter.

The *Advanced* mode remains selected for all new documents in the current SOLIDWORKS session. When you exit SOLIDWORKS, the *Advanced* mode setting is saved.

The default SOLIDWORKS installation contains two tabs in the New SOLIDWORKS Document dialog box: *Templates* and *Tutorial*. The *Templates* tab corresponds to the default SOLIDWORKS templates. The *Tutorial* tab corresponds to the templates utilized in the SOLIDWORKS Tutorials.

Part1 is displayed in the FeatureManager and is the name of the document. Part1 is the default part window name.

The Part Origin is displayed in blue in the center of the Graphics window. The Origin represents the intersection of the three default reference planes: *Front Plane*, *Top Plane* and *Right Plane*. The positive X-axis is horizontal and points to the right of the Origin in the Front view. The positive Y-axis is vertical and points upward in the Front view. The FeatureManager contains a list of features, reference geometry, and settings utilized in the part.

Edit the document units directly from the Graphics window as illustrated.

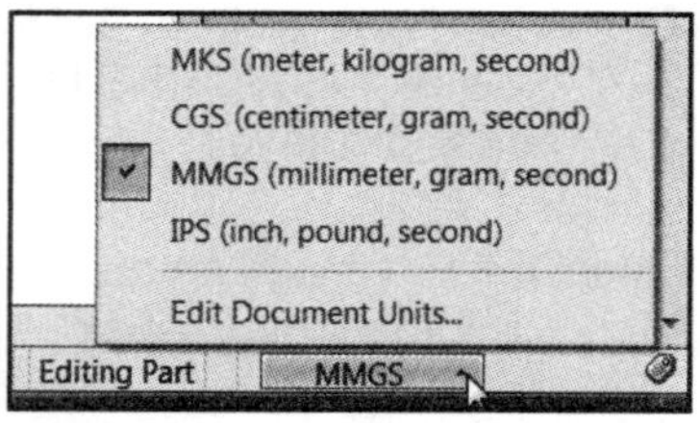

Dynamic Annotation Views : Only available with SOLIDWORKS MBD (Model Based Definition). Provides the ability to control how annotations are displayed when you rotate models.

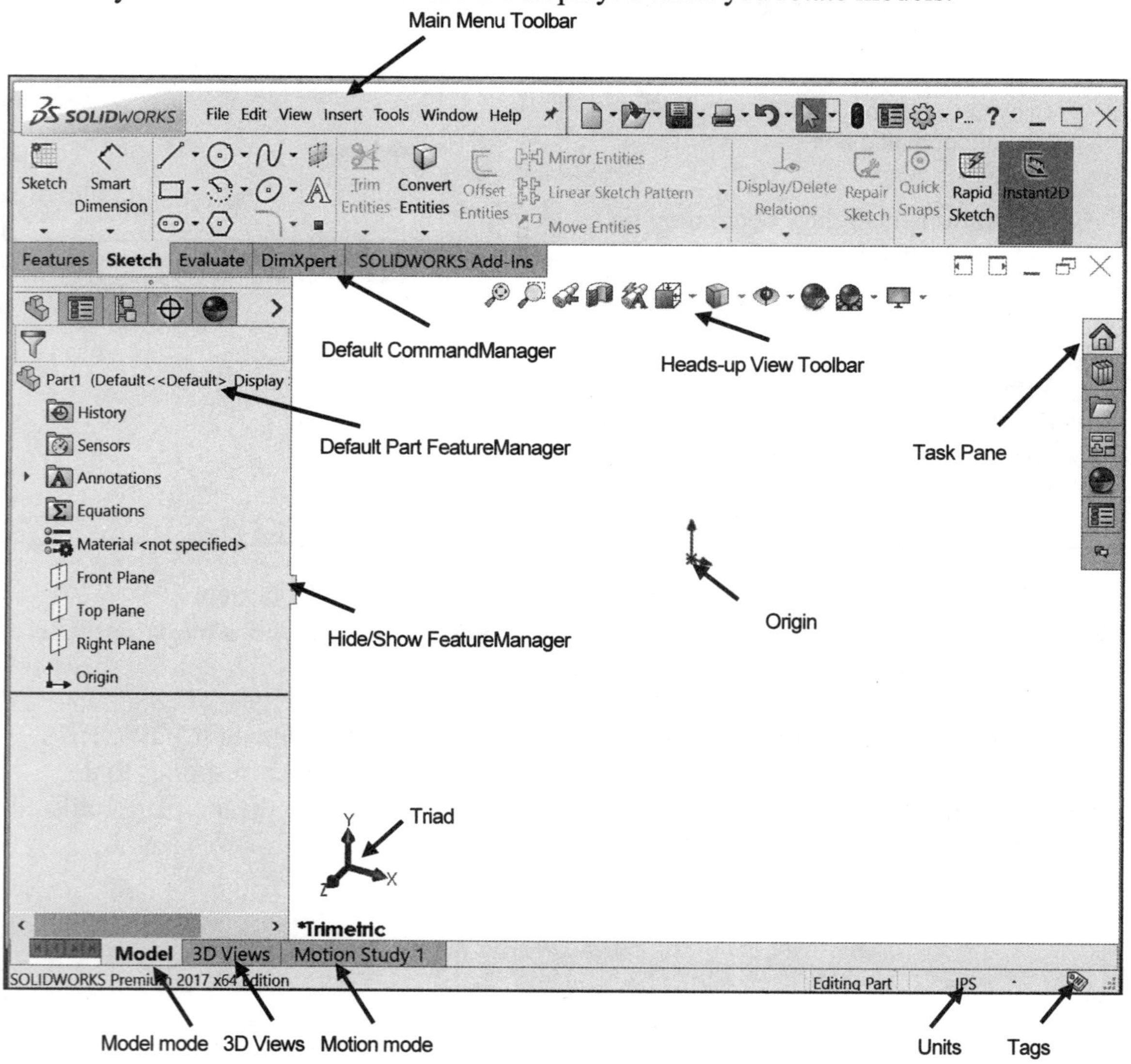

View the Default Sketch Planes.

10) Click the **Front Plane** from the FeatureManager.

11) Click the **Top Plane** from the FeatureManager.

12) Click the **Right Plane** from the FeatureManager.

13) Click the **Origin** from the FeatureManager. The Origin is the intersection of the Front, Top and Right Planes.

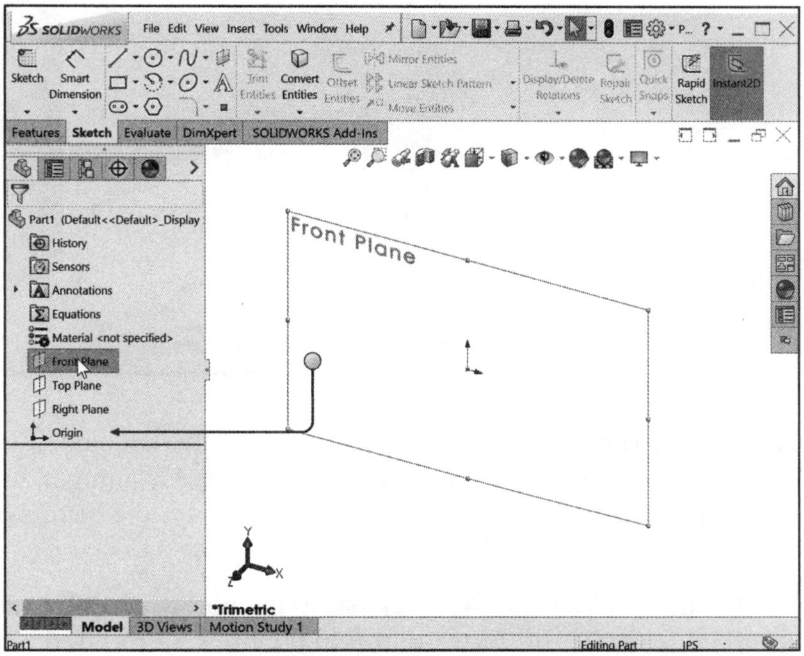

Redeem your code on the inside cover of the book. In the next section, download the SOLIDWORKS in 5 Hours folder to your hard drive. Open the Bracket part. Review the features and sketches in the Bracket FeatureManager. Work directly from your hard drive.

Activity: Download the SOLIDWORKS in 5 Hours folder. Open a Part.

Download the provided SOLIDWORKS in 5 Hours folder. Open an existing SOLIDWORKS part.

14) **Download** the SOLIDWORKS in 5 Hours folder to a local hard drive.

15) Click **Open** from the Menu bar menu.

16) Browse to the **SOLIDWORKS in 5 Hours\Bracket** folder.

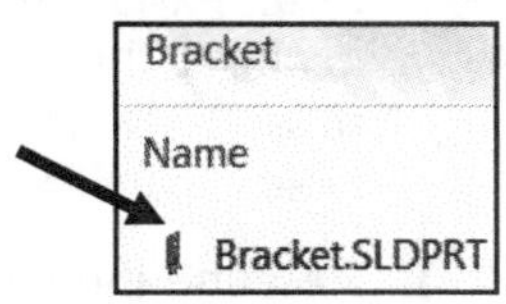

17) Double-click the **Bracket** part. The Bracket part is displayed in the Graphics window.

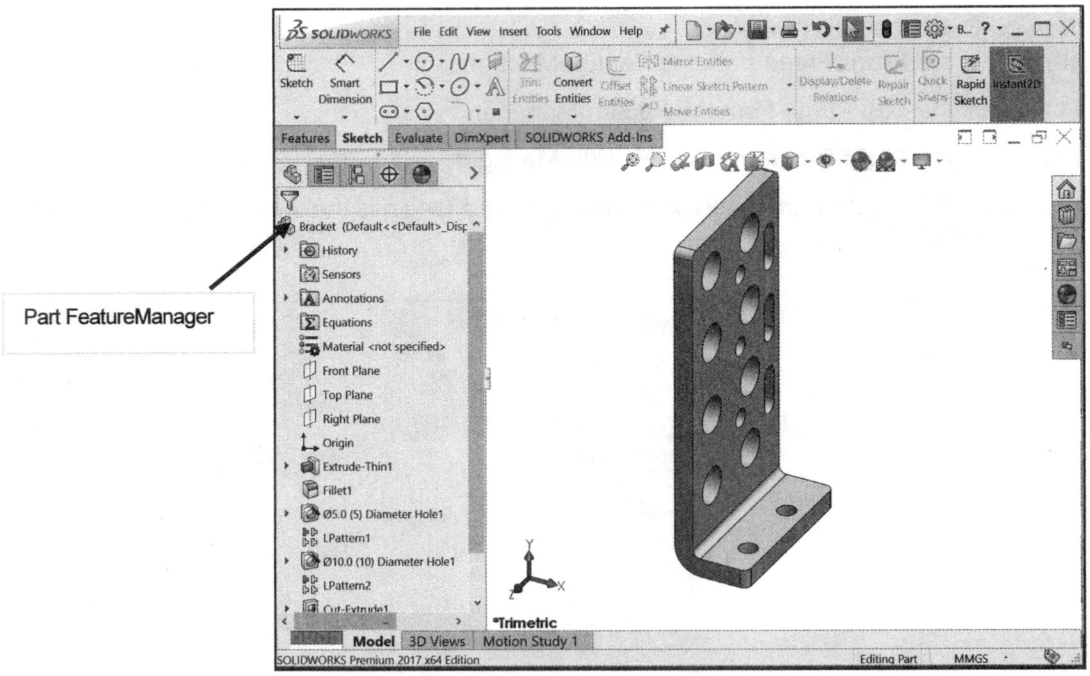

The FeatureManager design tree is located on the left side of the SOLIDWORKS Graphics window. The FeatureManager provides a summarized view of the active part, assembly, or drawing document. The tree displays the details on how the part, assembly or drawing document was created.

Use the FeatureManager rollback bar to temporarily roll back to an earlier state, to absorbed features, roll forward, roll to previous, or roll to the end of the FeatureManager design tree. You can add new features or edit existing features while the model is in the rolled-back state. You can save models with the rollback bar placed anywhere.

In the next section, review the features in the Bracket FeatureManager using the Rollback bar.

Activity: Use the FeatureManager Rollback Bar

Apply the FeatureManager Rollback Bar. Revert to an earlier state in the model.

18) Place the **mouse pointer** over the rollback bar in the FeatureManager design tree as illustrated. The pointer changes to a hand. Note the provided information on the feature. This is called Dynamic Reference Visualization.

19) Drag the **rollback bar** up the FeatureManager design tree until it is above the features you want rolled back. In this case Diameter Hole1.

20) **Release** the mouse button.

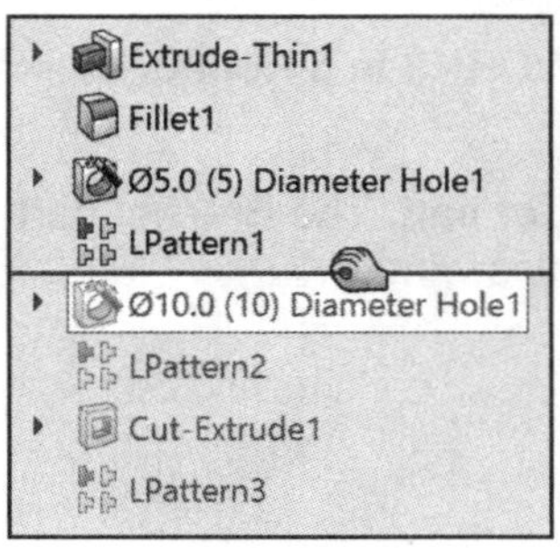

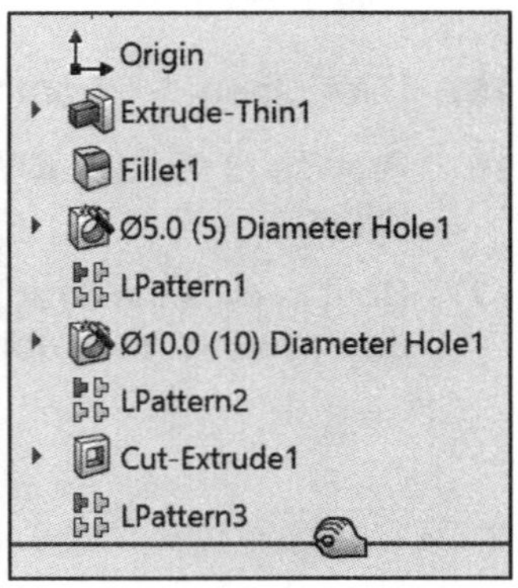

View the first feature in the Bracket Part.

21) Drag the **rollback bar** up the FeatureManager above Fillet1. View the results in the Graphics window.

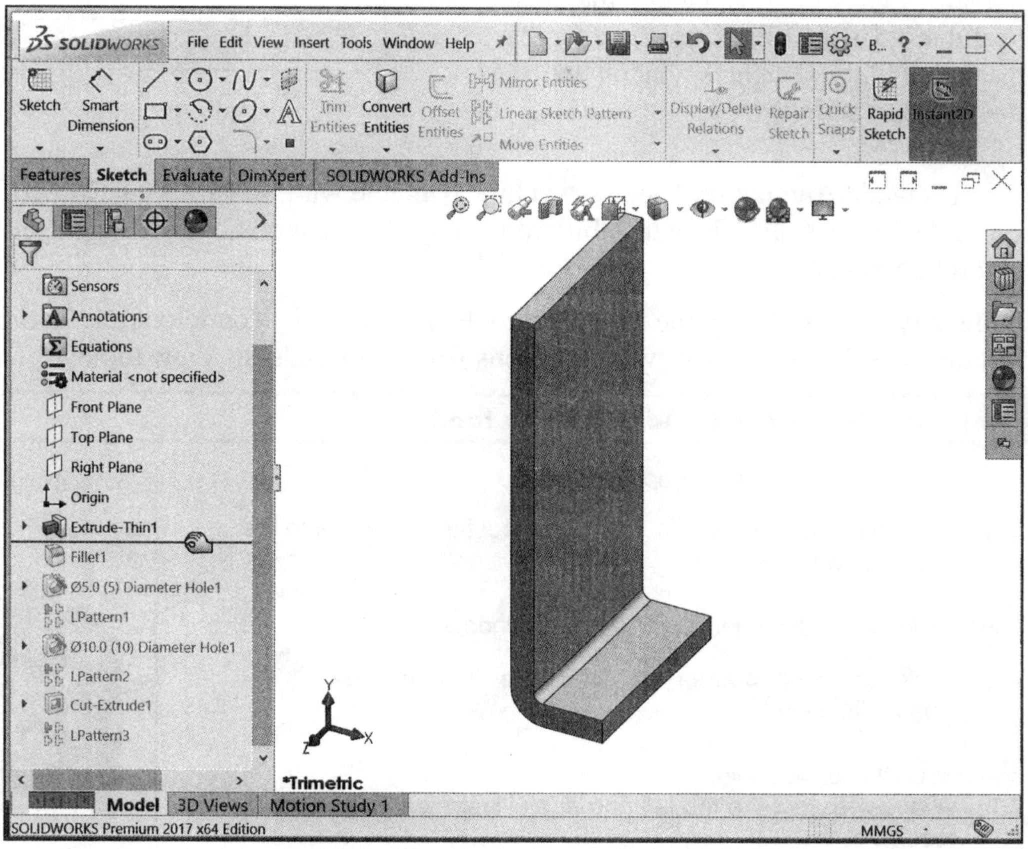

Return to the original Bracket Part FeatureManager.

22) Right-click **Extrude-Thin1** in the FeatureManager. The Pop-up Context toolbar is displayed.

23) Click **Roll to End**. View the results in the Graphics window.

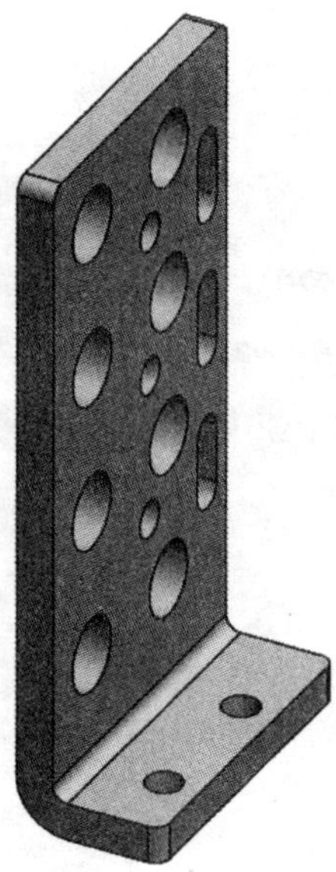

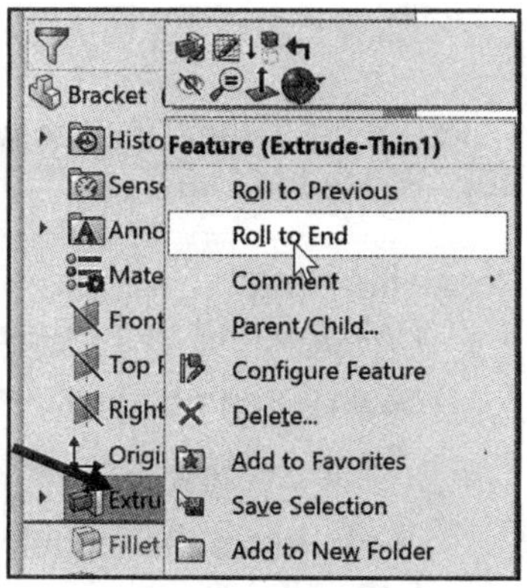

Heads-up View toolbar

SOLIDWORKS provides the user with numerous view options. One of the most useful tools is the Heads-up View toolbar displayed in the Graphics window when a document is active.

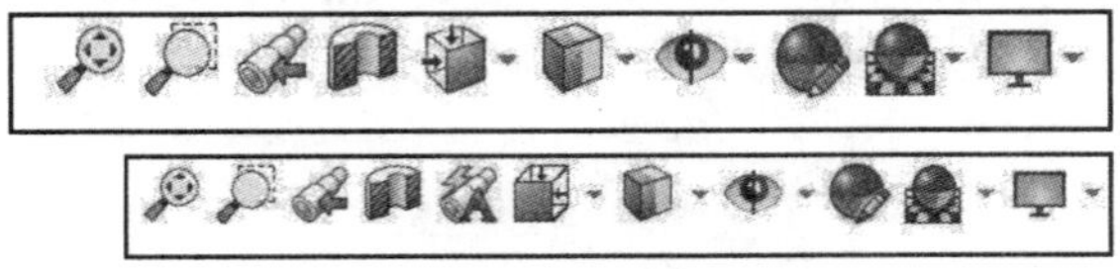

Dynamic Annotation Views : Only available with SOLIDWORKS MBD (Model Based Definition). Provides the ability to control how annotations are displayed when you rotate models.

In the next section, apply the following tools: Zoom to Fit, Zoom to Area, Zoom out, Rotate and select various view orientations from the Heads-up View toolbar.

Activity: Utilize the Heads-up View toolbar

Zoom to Fit the model in the Graphics window.

24) Click the **Zoom to Fit** icon. The tool fits the model to the Graphics window.

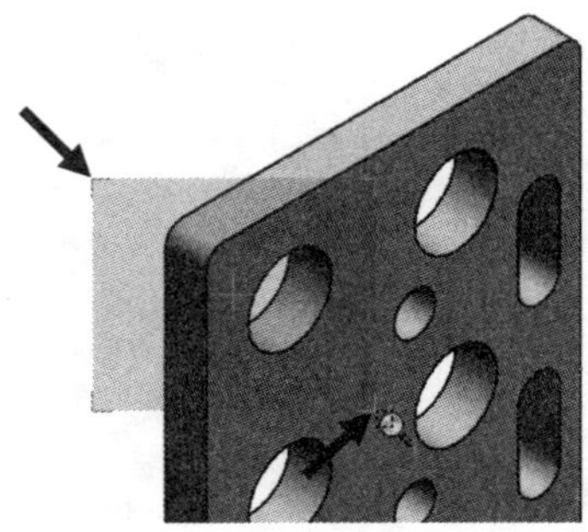

Zoom to Area on the model in the Graphics window.

25) Click the **Zoom to Area** icon. The Zoom to Area icon is displayed.

Zoom in on the top left hole.

26) **Window-select** the top left corner as illustrated. View the results.

De-select the Zoom to Area tool.

27) Click the **Zoom to Area** icon.

Fit the model to the Graphics window.

28) Press the **f** key.

Rotate the model.

29) Hold the **middle mouse button** down. Drag **upward**, **downward**, to the **left** and to the **right** to rotate the model in the Graphics window.

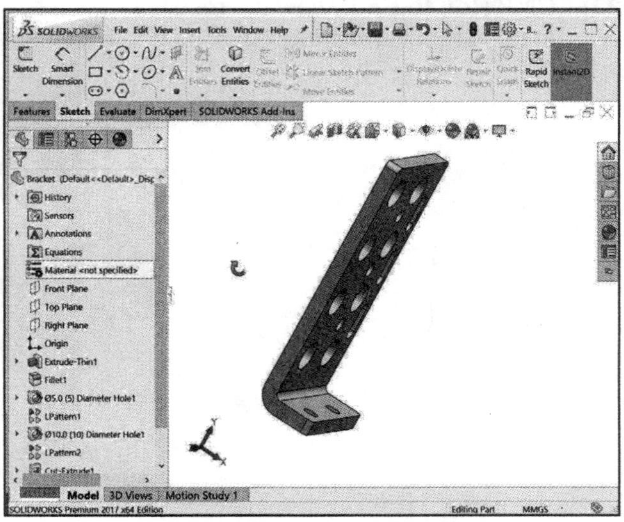

Display a few Standard Views.

30) Click **inside** the Graphics window.

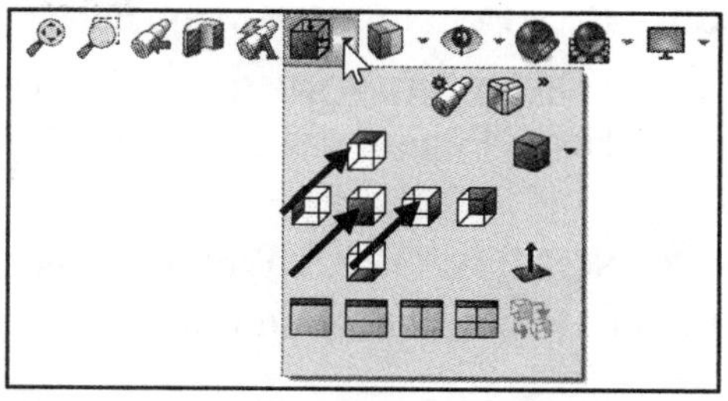

31) Click **Front** from the drop-down Heads-up view toolbar. The model is displayed in the Front view.

32) Click **Right** from the drop-down Heads-up view toolbar. The model is displayed in the Right view.

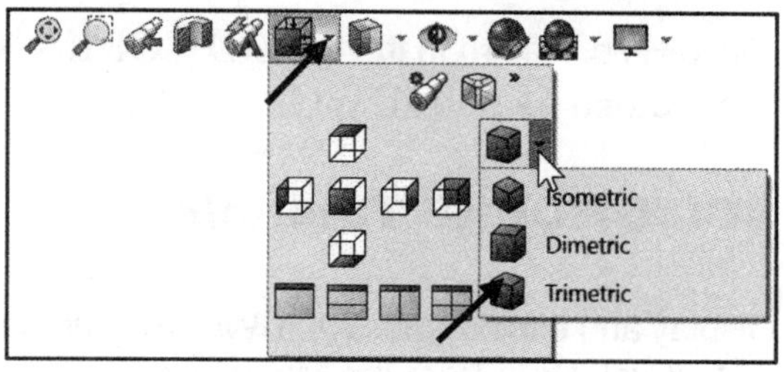

33) Click **Top** from the drop-down Heads-up view toolbar. The model is displayed in the Top view.

Display a Trimetric view of the Bracket model.

34) Click **Trimetric** from the drop-down Heads-up view toolbar as illustrated. Note your options. View the results in the Graphics window.

SOLIDWORKS Help

Help in SOLIDWORKS is context-sensitive and in HTML format. Help is accessed in many ways, including Help buttons in all dialog boxes and PropertyManager (or press F1) and Help tool on the Standard toolbar for SOLIDWORKS Help.

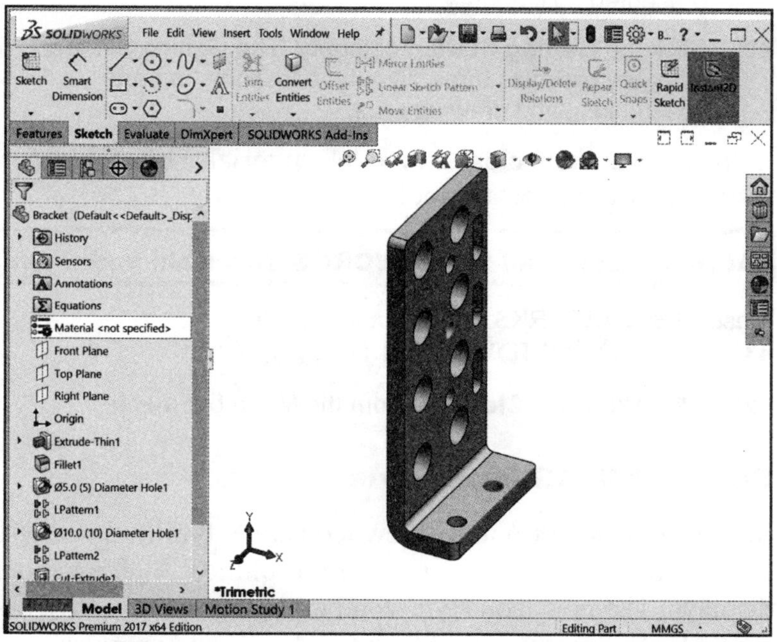

35) Click **Help** from the Menu bar.

36) Click **SOLIDWORKS Help**. The SOLIDWORKS Help Home Page is displayed by default. View your options.

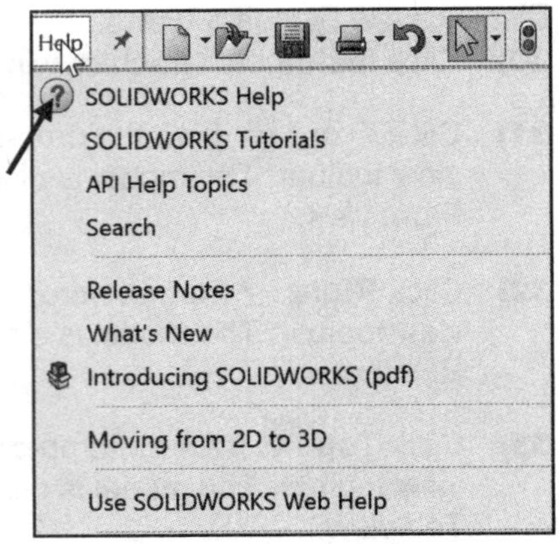

SOLIDWORKS Web Help is active by default under Help in the Main menu.

Close Help. Return to the SOLIDWORKS Graphics window.

37) **Close** SOLIDWORKS Home.

SOLIDWORKS Tutorials

Display and explore the SOLIDWORKS tutorials.

38) Click **Help** from the Menu bar.

39) Click **SOLIDWORKS Tutorials**. The SOLIDWORKS Tutorials are displayed. The SOLIDWORKS Tutorials are presented by category.

40) Click the **Getting Started** category. The Getting Started category provides three 30 minute lessons on parts, assemblies, and drawings.

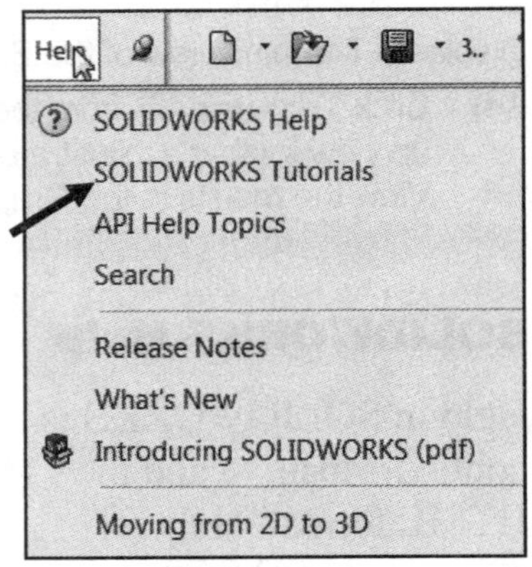

In the next section, close all models, tutorials and view the additional User Interface tools.

Activity: Close all SOLIDWORKS Tutorials and Models

Close all SOLIDWORKS Tutorials and models.

41) **Close** SOLIDWORKS Tutorials.

42) Click **Window**, **Close All** from the Menu bar menu.

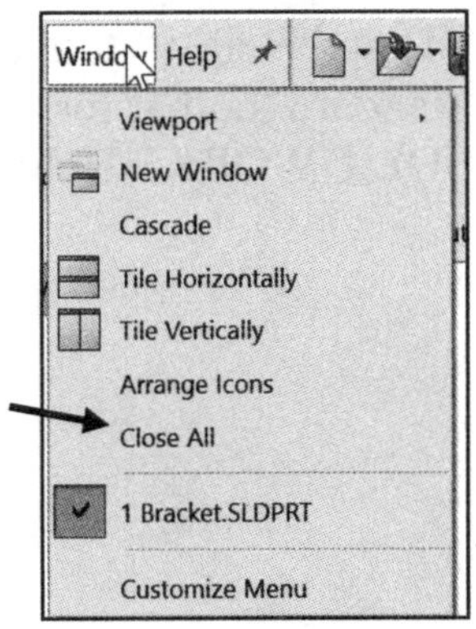

SOLIDWORKS Icon Style

SOLIDWORKS provides a new icon style. It allows vector-based scaling for superior support of high resolution, high pixel density displays. The new icon style standardized the perspective of icons. It also removes non-essential details and emphasizes primary elements. Consistent visual styling applies to all icons.

Additional User Interface Tools

The book utilizes additional areas of the SOLIDWORKS User Interface. Explore an overview of these tools in the next section.

Right-click

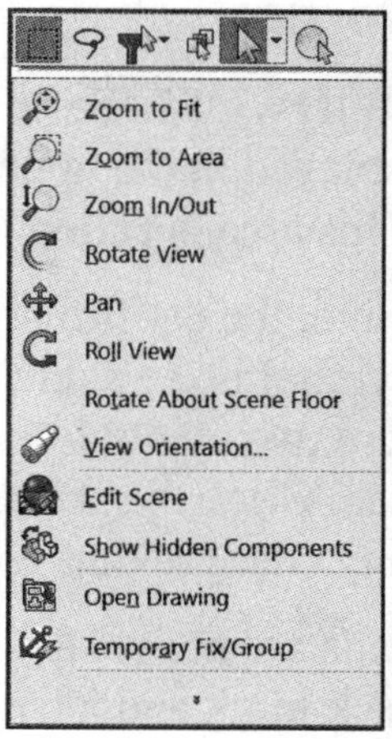

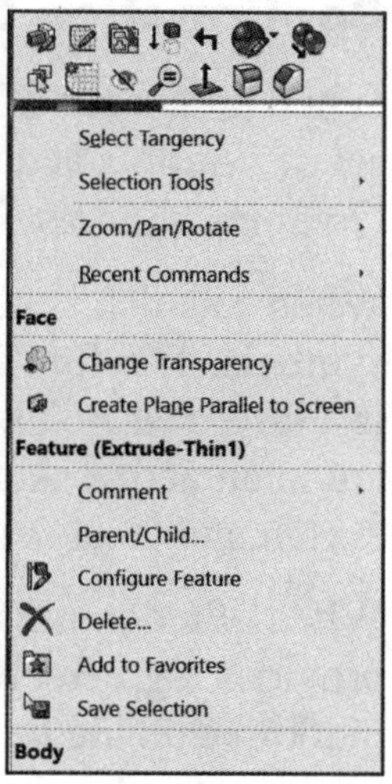

Right-click in the Graphics window on a model, or in the FeatureManager on a feature or sketch to display the Context-sensitive toolbar. If you are in the middle of a command, this toolbar displays a list of options specifically related to that command.

Right-click an empty space in the Graphics window of a part or assembly, and a selection context toolbar above the shortcut menu is displayed. This provides easy access to the most commonly used selection tools.

Consolidated toolbar

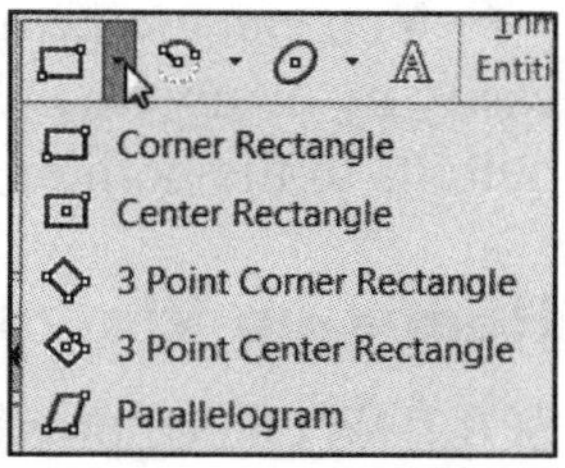

Similar commands are grouped together in the CommandManager. For example, variations of the Rectangle sketch tool are grouped in a single fly-out button as illustrated.

If you select the Consolidated toolbar button without expanding:

For some commands such as Sketch, the most commonly used command is performed. This command is the first listed and the command shown on the button.

For commands such as rectangle, where you may want to repeatedly create the same variant of the rectangle, the last used command is performed. This is the highlighted command when the Consolidated toolbar is expanded.

System feedback icon

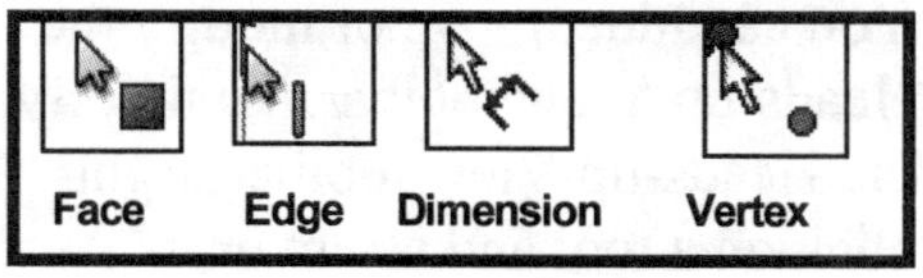

SOLIDWORKS provides system feedback by attaching a symbol to the mouse pointer cursor.

The system feedback symbol indicates what you are selecting or what the system is expecting you to select.

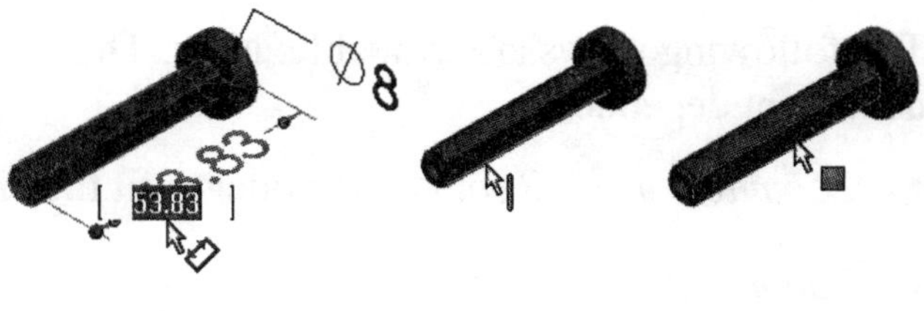

As you move the mouse pointer across your model, system feedback is displayed in the form of a symbol riding next to the cursor as illustrated. This is a valuable feature in SOLIDWORKS.

Confirmation Corner

When numerous SOLIDWORKS commands are active, a symbol or a set of symbols is displayed in the upper right hand corner of the Graphics window. This area is called the Confirmation Corner.

When a sketch is active, the confirmation corner box displays two symbols. The first symbol is the sketch tool icon. The second symbol is a large red X. These two symbols supply a visual reminder that you are in an active sketch. Click the sketch symbol icon to exit the sketch and to save any changes that you made.

When other commands are active, the confirmation corner box provides a green check mark and a large red X. Use the green check mark to execute the current command. Use the large red X to cancel the command.

You can confirm changes you make in sketches and tools more easily by using the D keyboard shortcut to move the OK and Cancel buttons to the pointer location in the Graphics window.

Heads-up View toolbar

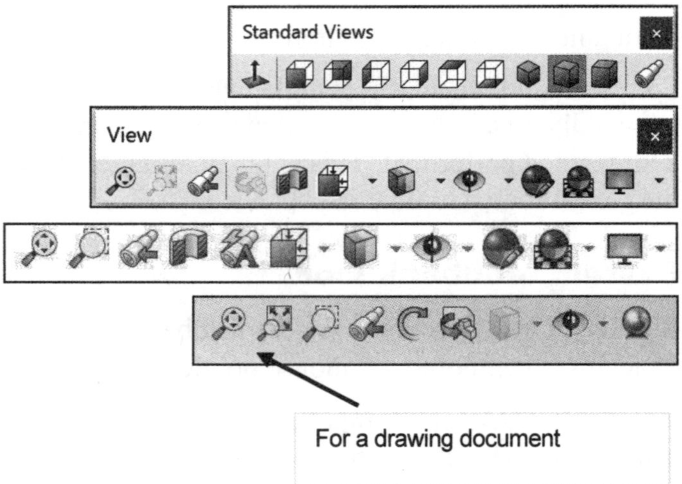

SOLIDWORKS provides the user with numerous view options from the Standard Views, View and Heads-up View toolbar.

The Heads-up View toolbar is a transparent toolbar that is displayed in the Graphics window when a document is active.

You can hide, move or modify the Heads-up View toolbar. To modify the Heads-up View toolbar, right-click on a tool and select or deselect the tools that you want to display.

The following views are available: Note: The available views are document dependent.

- *Zoom to Fit*: Zooms the model to fit the Graphics window.
- *Zoom to Area*: Zooms to the areas you select with a bounding box.
- *Previous View*: Displays the previous view.

- *Section View* : Displays a cutaway of a part or assembly, using one or more cross section planes.

- *Dynamic Annotation Views* : Only available with SOLIDWORKS MBD. Provides the ability to control how annotations are displayed when you rotate models.

The Orientation dialog has an option to display a view cube (in-context View Selector) with a live model preview. This helps the user to understand how each standard view orientates the model. With the view cube, you can access additional standard views. The views are easy to understand and they can be accessed simply by selecting a face on the cube.

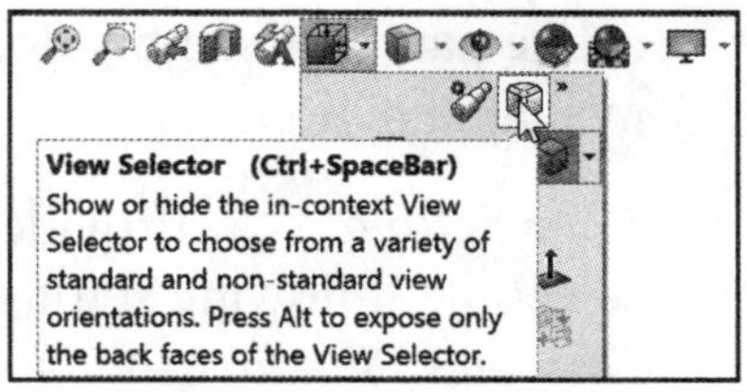

To activate the Orientation dialog box, press (Ctrl + spacebar) or click the View Orientation icon from the Heads up View toolbar. The active model is displayed in the View Selector in an Isometric orientation (default view).

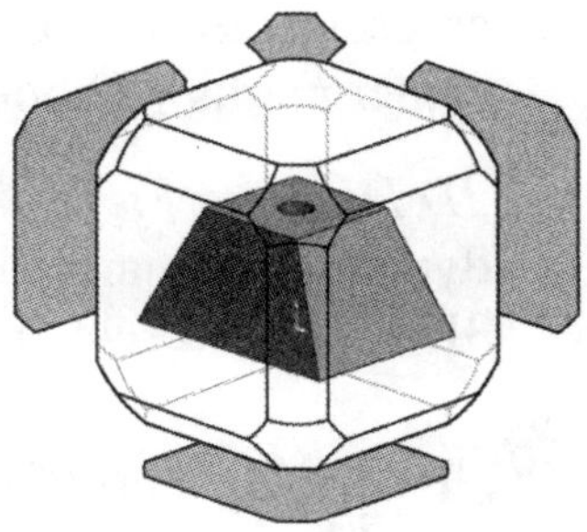

Click the View Selector icon in the Orientation dialog box to show or hide the in-context View Selector.

Press **Ctrl + spacebar** to activate the View Selector.

Press the **spacebar** to activate the Orientation dialog box.

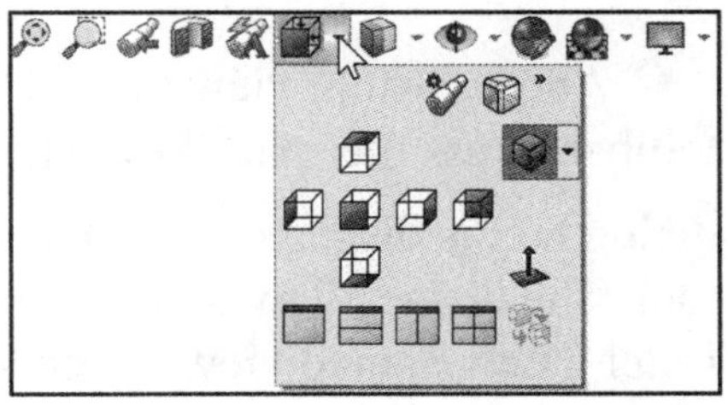

- *View Orientation box* : Provides the ability to select a view orientation or the number of viewports. The available options are *Top, Left, Front, Right, Back, Bottom, Single view, Two view - Horizontal, Two view - Vertical, Four view*. Click the drop-down arrow to access Axonometric views: Isometric, Dimetric and Trimetric.

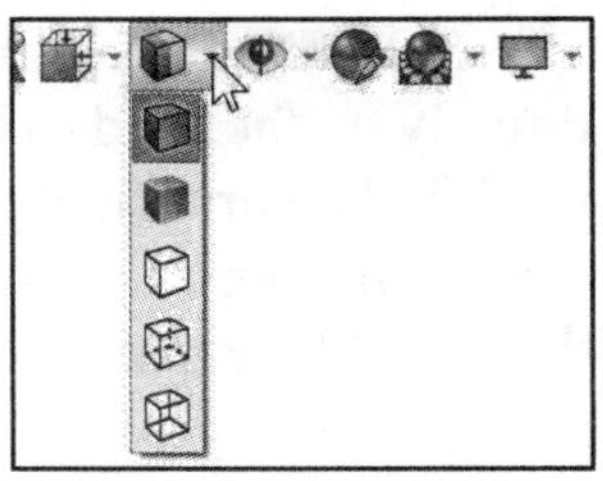

- *Display Style* : Provides the ability to display the style for the active view. The available options are *Wireframe, Hidden Lines Visible, Hidden Lines Removed, Shaded, Shaded With Edges*.

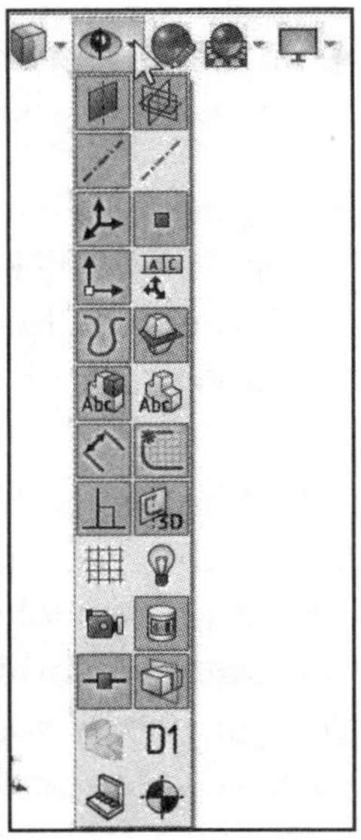

- *Hide/Show Items* : Provides the ability to select items to hide or show in the Graphics window. The available items are document dependent. Note the View Center of Mass icon.
- *Edit Appearance* : Provides the ability to edit the appearance of entities of the model.
- *Apply Scene* : Provides the ability to apply a scene to an active part or assembly document. View the available options.

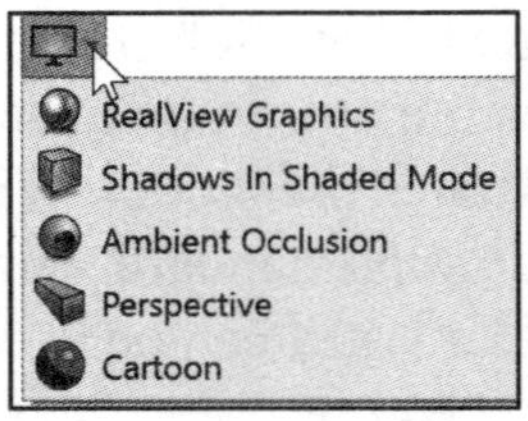

- *View Setting* : Provides the ability to select the following settings: *RealView Graphics*, *Shadows In Shaded Mode*, *Ambient Occlusion*, *Perspective* and *Cartoon*.
- *Rotate view* : Provides the ability to rotate a drawing view. Input Drawing view angle and select the ability to update and rotate center marks with view.

- *3D Drawing View* : Provides the ability to dynamically manipulate the drawing view in 3D to make a selection.

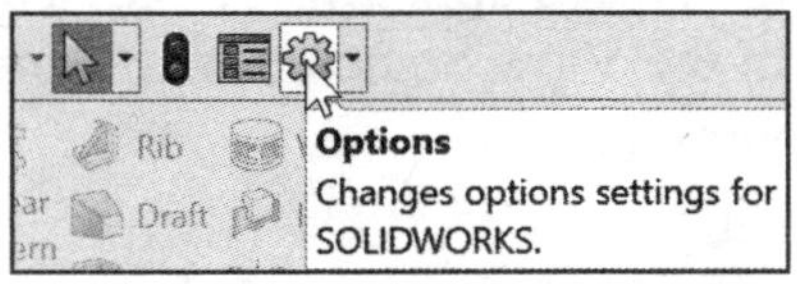

To display a grid for a part, click Options , Document Properties tab. Click Grid/Snaps, check the Display grid box.

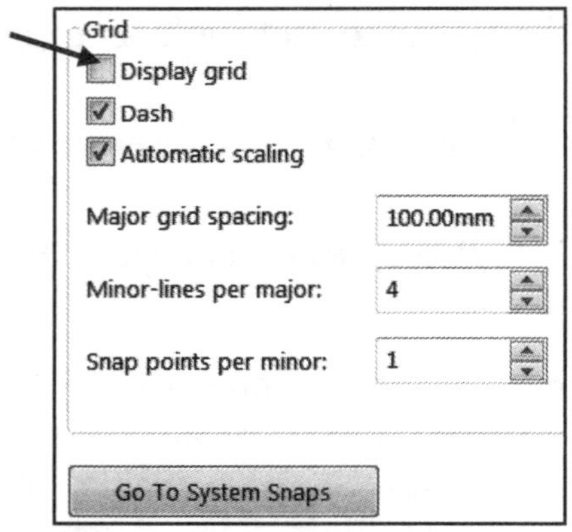

Add a custom view to the Heads-up View toolbar. Press the space key. The Orientation dialog box is displayed. Click the New View tool. The Name View dialog box is displayed. Enter a new named view. Click OK.

SOLIDWORKS provides the ability to click directly on the triad in the Graphic window to modify the part orientation. Hold the Ctrl key down, click an axis of the triad; it rotates about that axis 90 degrees.

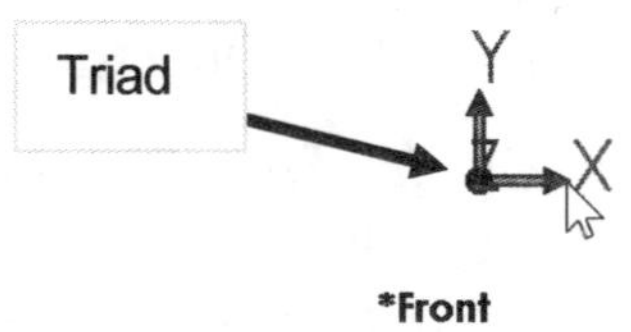

SOLIDWORKS CommandManager

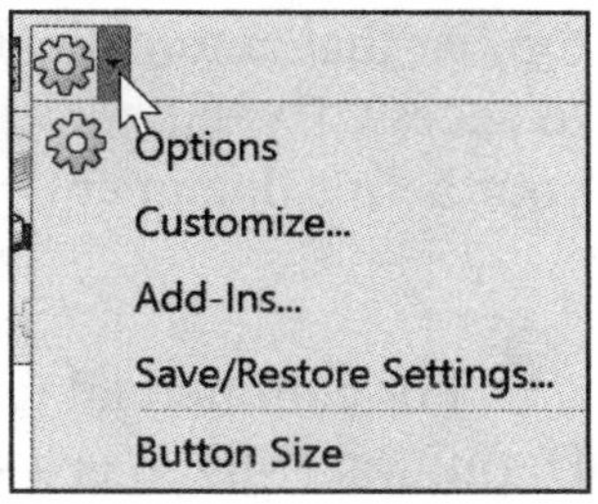

The SOLIDWORKS CommandManager is a Context-sensitive toolbar that automatically updates based on the toolbar you want to access. By default, it has toolbars embedded in it based on your active document type. When you click a tab below the CommandManager, it updates to display that toolbar. For example, if you click the Sketch tab, the Sketch toolbar is displayed.

For commercial users, SOLIDWORKS Model Based Definition (MBD) is a separate application. For education users, SOLIDWORKS MBD is included in the SOLIDWORKS Education Edition as an Add In.

Below is an illustrated CommandManager for a default Part document.

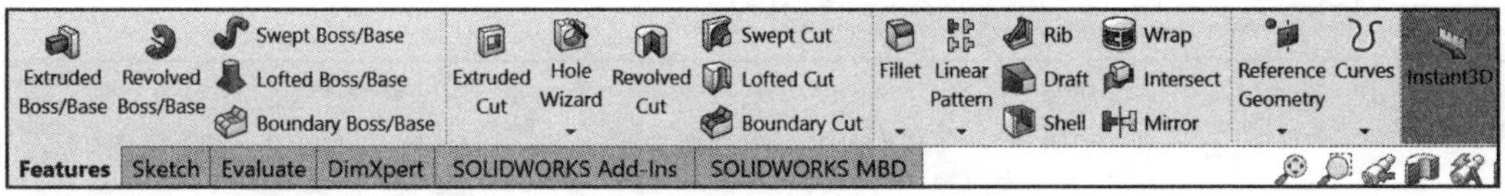

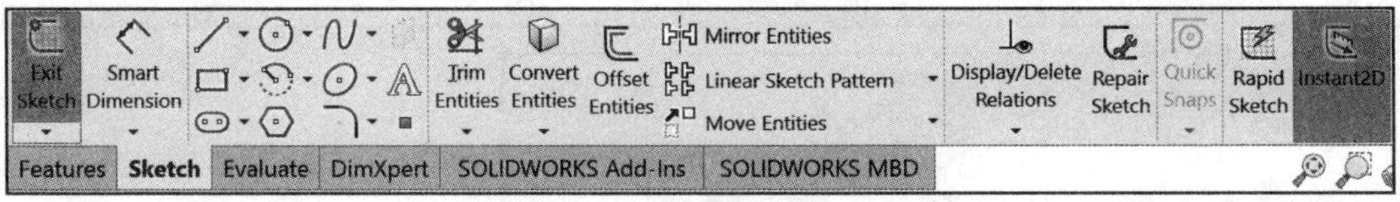

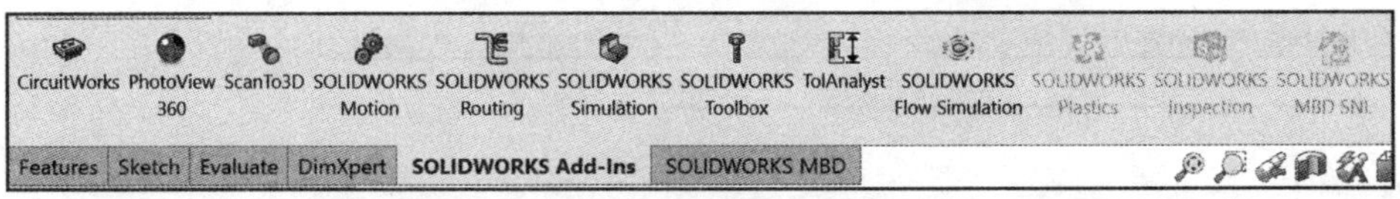

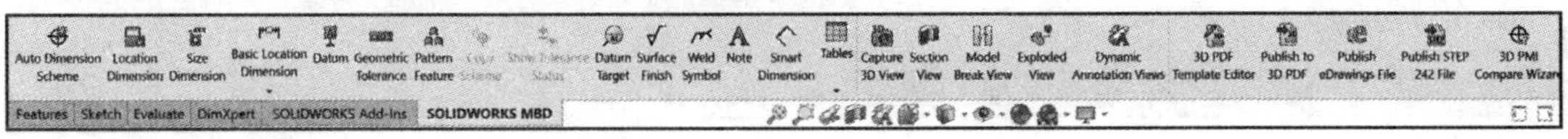

Button sizes. You can set sizes for buttons from the Toolbars tab of the Customize dialog box. To facilitate element selection on touch interfaces such as tablets, you can set up the larger Size buttons and text from the Options menu (Standard toolbar).

The SOLIDWORKS CommandManager is a Context-sensitive toolbar that automatically updates based on the toolbar you want to access. By default, it has toolbars embedded in it based on your active document type.

For commercial users, SOLIDWORKS Model Based Definition (MBD) is a separate application. For education users, SOLIDWORKS MBD is included in the SOLIDWORKS Education Edition as an Add In.

Below is an illustrated CommandManager for a default Drawing document.

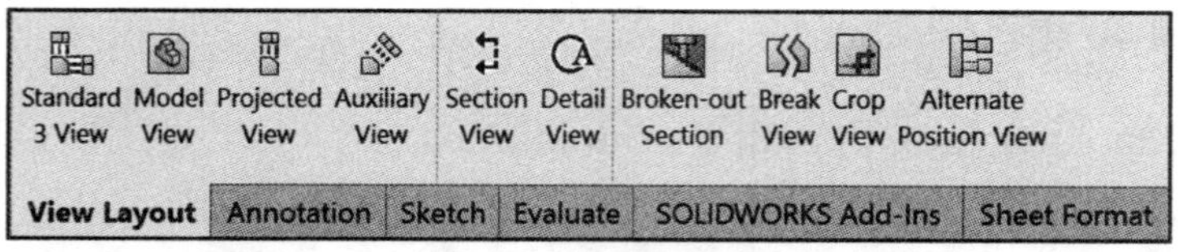

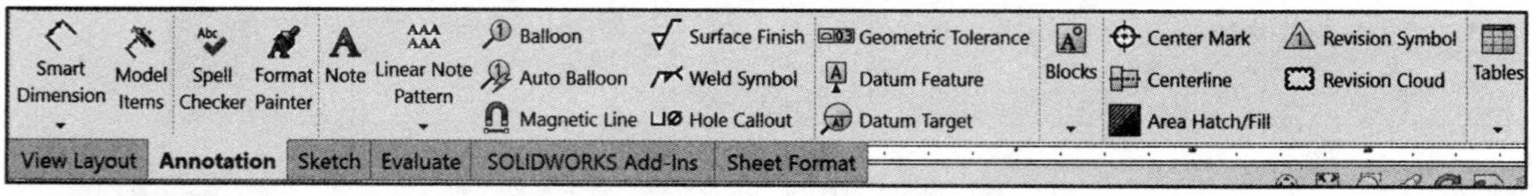

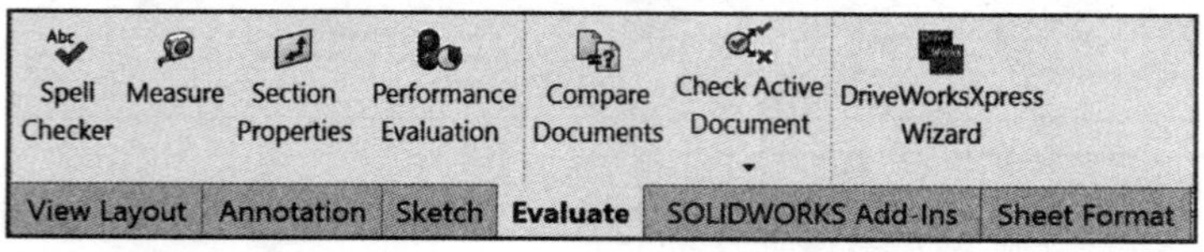

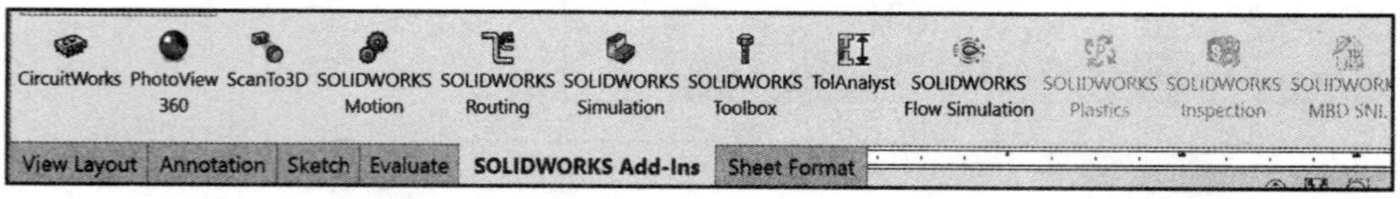

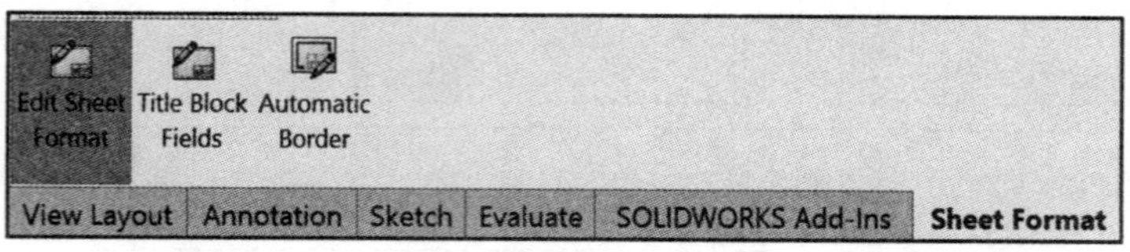

To add a custom tab to your CommandManager, right-click on a tab and click Customize CommandManager from the drop-down menu. The Customize dialog box is displayed. You can also select to add a blank tab as illustrated and populate it with custom tools from the Customize dialog box.

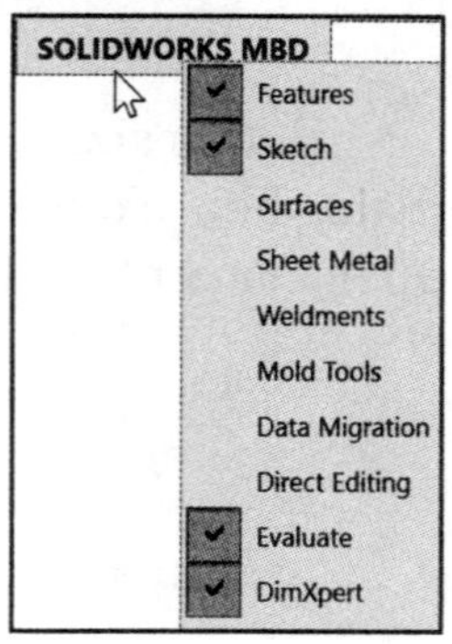

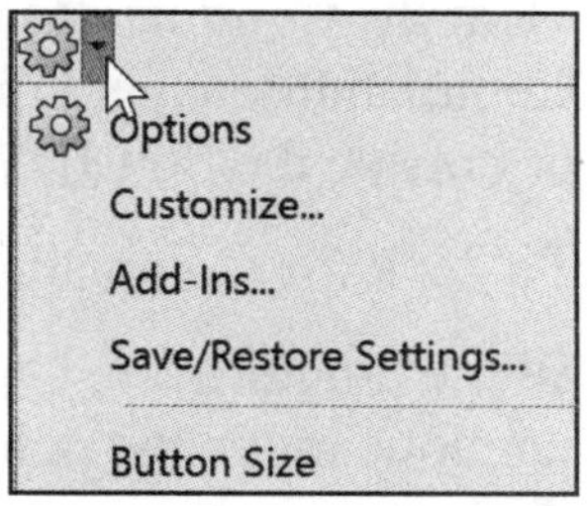

The SOLIDWORKS CommandManager is a Context-sensitive toolbar that automatically updates based on the toolbar you want to access. By default, it has toolbars embedded in it based on your active document type.

For commercial users, SOLIDWORKS Model Based Definition (MBD) is a separate application. For education users, SOLIDWORKS MBD is included in the SOLIDWORKS Education Edition as an Add In.

Below is an illustrated CommandManager for a default Assembly document.

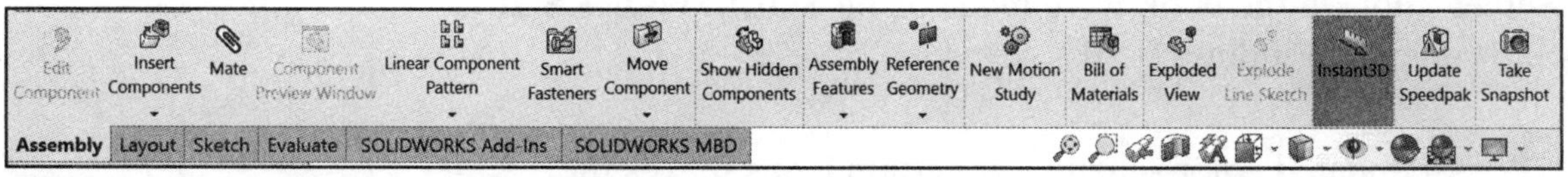

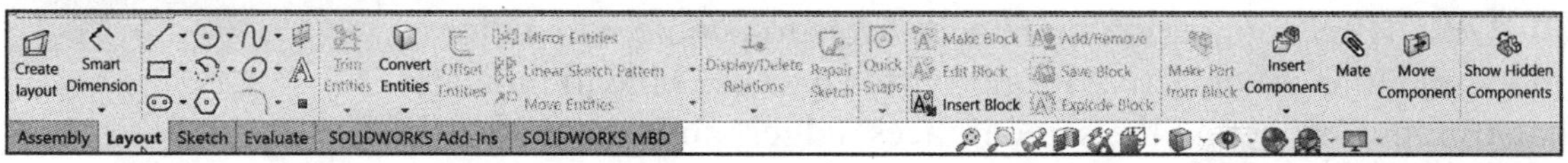

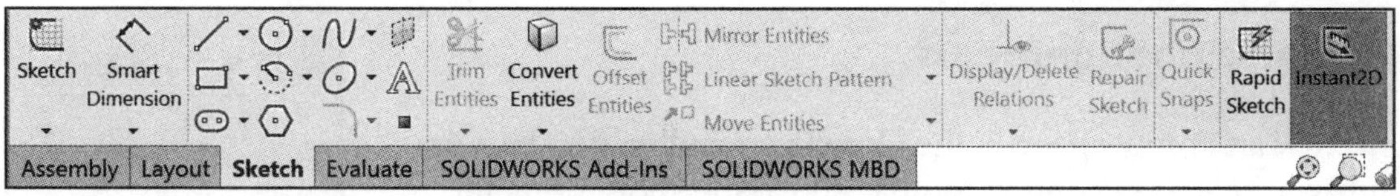

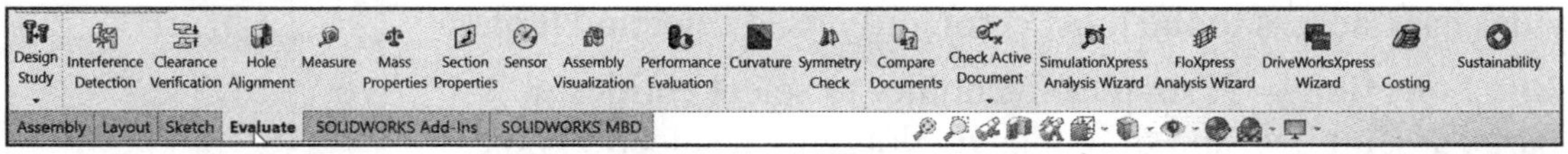

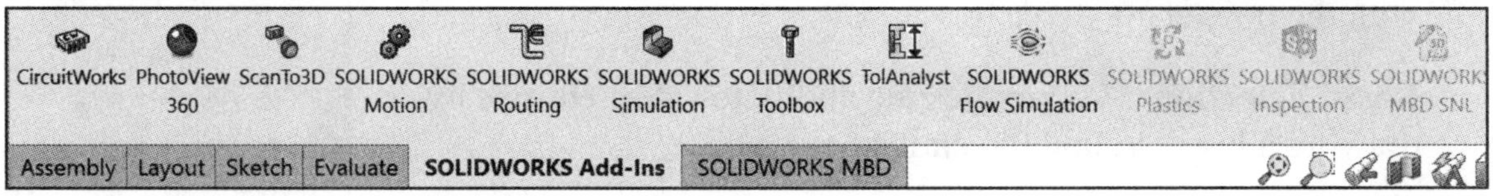

By default, the illustrated options are selected in the Customize box for the CommandManager. Right-click on an existing tab and click Customize CommandManager to view your options.

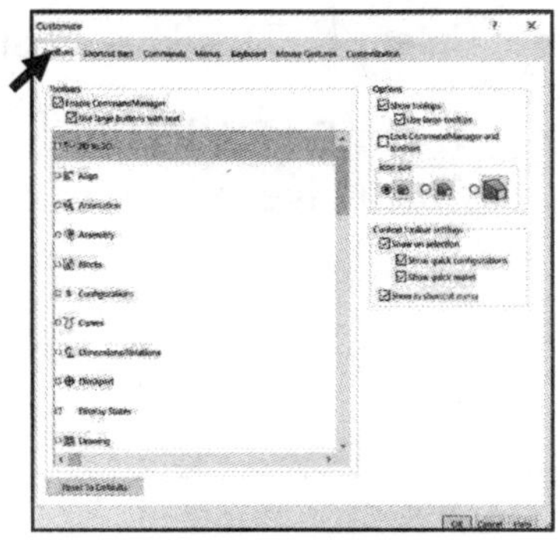

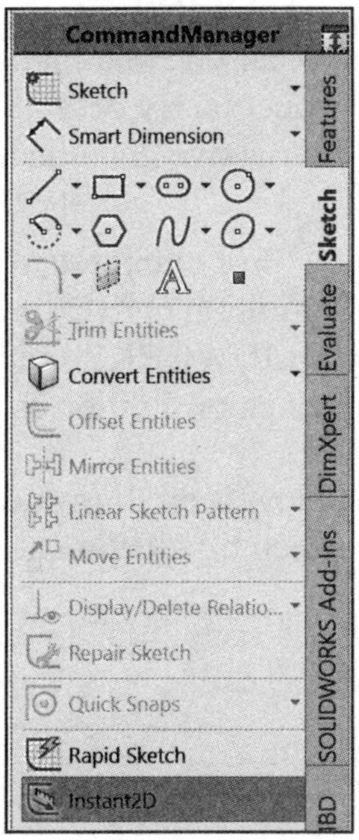

Float the CommandManager. Drag the Features, Sketch or any CommandManager tab. Drag the CommandManager anywhere on or outside the SOLIDWORKS window.

To dock the CommandManager, perform one of the following:

While dragging the CommandManager in the SOLIDWORKS window, move the pointer over a docking icon - Dock above, Dock left, Dock right and click the needed command.

Double-click the floating CommandManager to revert the CommandManager to the last docking position.

Screen shots in the book were made using SOLIDWORKS 2017 SP0 running Windows® 10.

An updated color scheme for certain icons makes the SOLIDWORKS application more accessible to people with color blindness. Icons in the active PropertyManager use blue to indicate what you must select on the screen: faces, edges, and so on.

Selection Enhancements

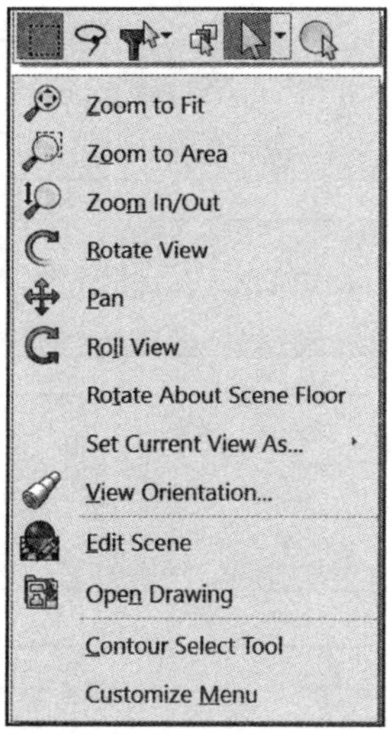

Right-click an empty space in the Graphics window of a part or assembly; a selection context toolbar above the shortcut menu provides easy access to the most commonly used selection tools.

- **Box Selection**. Provides the ability to select entities in parts, assemblies, and drawings by dragging a selection box with the pointer.
- **Lasso Selection**. Provides the ability to select entities by drawing a lasso around the entities.
- **Selection Filters**. Displays a list of selection filter commands.
- **Select Other**. Displays the Select Other dialog box.
- **Select**. Displays a list of selection commands.
- **Magnified Selection**. Displays the magnifying glass, which gives you a magnified view of a section of a model.

Save space in the CommandManager, right-click in the CommandManager and uncheck the Use Large Buttons with Text box. This eliminates the text associated with the tool.

DimXpert provides the ability to graphically check if the model is fully dimensioned and toleranced. DimXpert automatically recognizes manufacturing features. Manufacturing features are not SOLIDWORKS features. Manufacturing features are defined in 1.1.12 of the ASME Y14.5M-1994 Dimensioning and Tolerancing standard. See SOLIDWORKS Help for additional information.

FeatureManager Design Tree

The FeatureManager consists of five default tabs:

- *FeatureManager design tree* tab.
- *PropertyManager* tab.
- *ConfigurationManager* tab.
- *DimXpertManager* tab.
- *DisplayManager* tab.

Select the Hide FeatureManager Tree Area arrows as illustrated to enlarge the Graphics window for modeling.

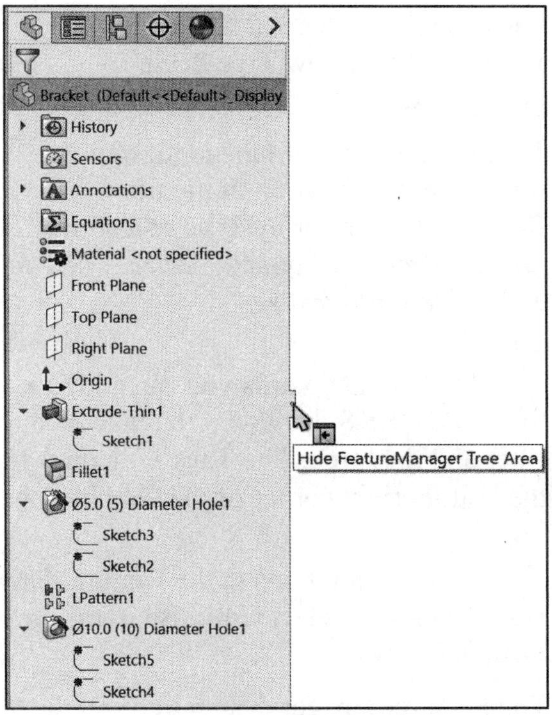

The Sensors tool located in the FeatureManager monitors selected properties in a part or assembly and alerts you when values deviate from the specified limits. There are five sensor types: Simulation Data, Mass properties, Dimensions, Measurement and Costing Data.

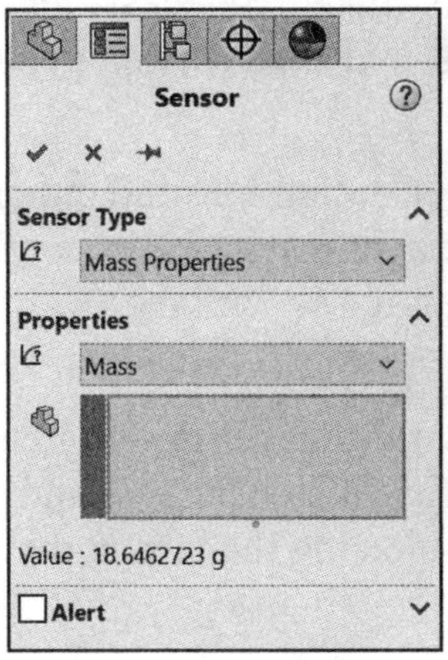

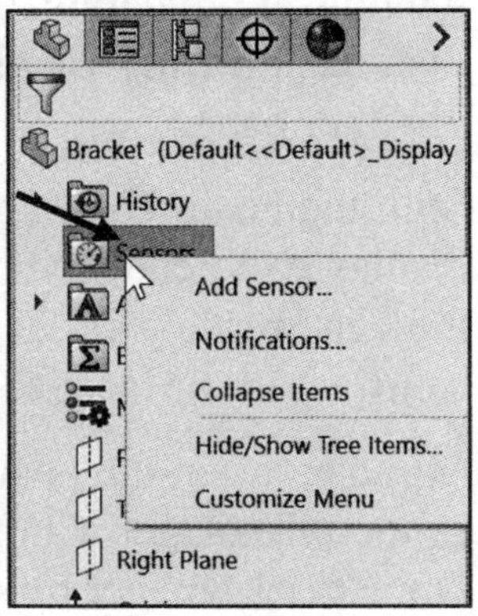

Various commands provide the ability to control what is displayed in the FeatureManager design tree. These are the commands:

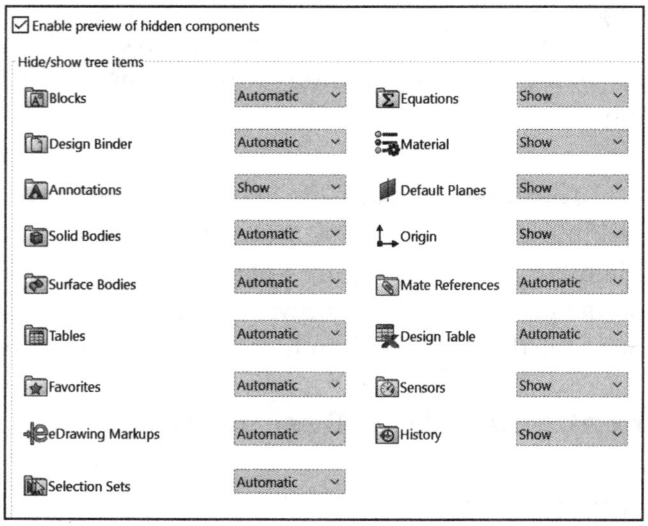

1. Show or Hide FeatureManager items.

Click **Options** from the Menu bar. Click **FeatureManager** from the System Options tab. **Customize** your FeatureManager from the Hide/Show Tree Items dialog box.

2. Filter the FeatureManager design tree. Enter information in the filter field. You can filter by *Type of features, Feature names, Sketches, Folders*, *Mates*, *User-defined tags* and *Custom properties*.

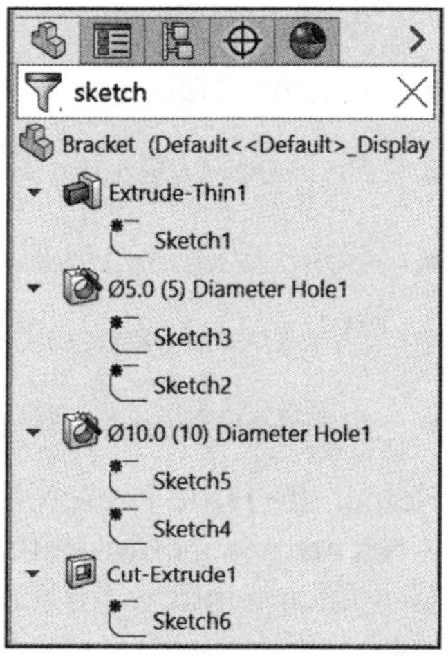

Tags are keywords you can add to a SOLIDWORKS document to make them easier to filter and to search. The Tags icon is located in the bottom right corner of the Graphics window.

Collapse all items in the FeatureManager, **right-click** and select **Collapse items**, or press the **Shift** + **C** keys.

The FeatureManager design tree and the Graphics window are dynamically linked. Select sketches, features, drawing views, and construction geometry in either pane.

Split the FeatureManager design tree and either display two FeatureManager instances, or combine the FeatureManager design tree with the ConfigurationManager or PropertyManager.

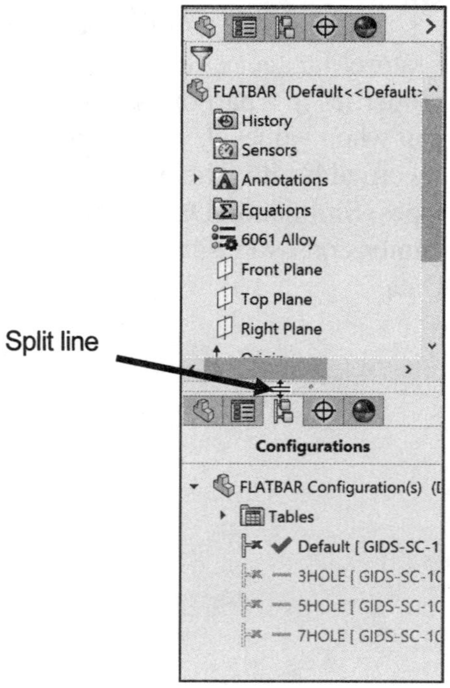

Move between the FeatureManager design tree, PropertyManager, ConfigurationManager and DimXpertManager by selecting the tabs at the top of the menu.

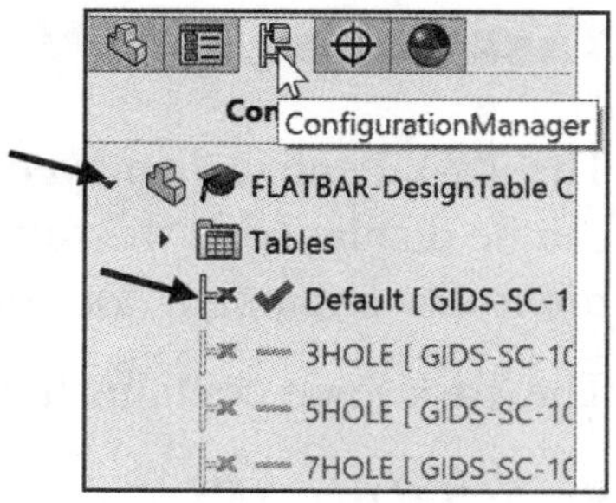

The ConfigurationManager is located to the right of the FeatureManager. Use the ConfigurationManager to create, select and view multiple configurations of parts and assemblies.

The icons in the ConfigurationManager denote whether the configuration was created manually or with a design table.

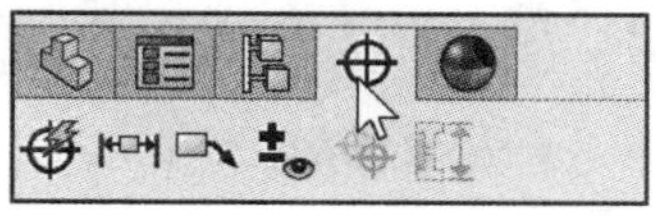

The DimXpertManager tab provides the ability to insert dimensions and tolerances manually or automatically. The DimXpertManager provides the following selections: **Auto Dimension Scheme**, Basic Location Dimension, **Basic Size Dimension** **Show Tolerance Status**, **Copy Scheme** and **TolAnalyst Study**.

Fly-out FeatureManager

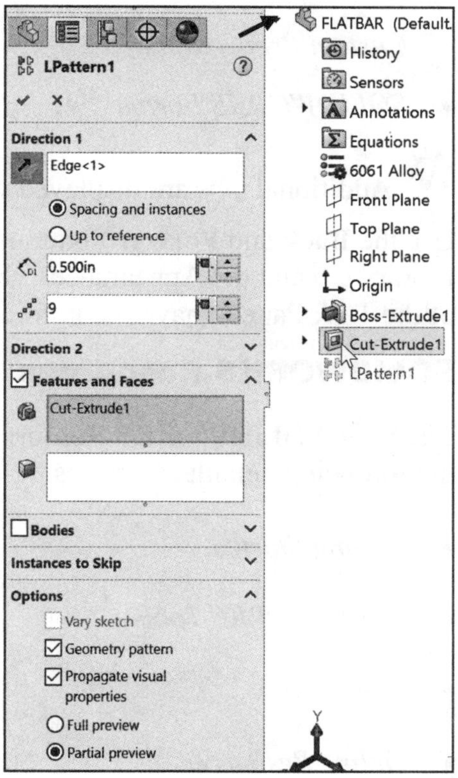

The fly-out FeatureManager design tree provides the ability to view and select items in the PropertyManager and the FeatureManager design tree at the same time.

Throughout the book, you will select commands and command options from the drop-down menu, fly-out FeatureManager, Context toolbar or from a SOLIDWORKS toolbar.

Another method for accessing a command is to use the accelerator key. Accelerator keys are special key strokes, which activate the drop-down menu options. Some commands in the menu bar and items in the drop-down menus have an underlined character.

Press the Alt or Ctrl key followed by the corresponding key to the underlined character activates that command or option.

Illustrations may vary depending on your SOLIDWORKS version and operating system.

Task Pane

The Task Pane is displayed when a SOLIDWORKS session starts. The Task Pane can be displayed in the following states: *visible or hidden, expanded or collapsed, pinned or unpinned, docked or floating*.

The Task Pane contains the following default tabs:

- *SOLIDWORKS Resources* .
- *Design Library* .
- *File Explorer* .
- *View Palette* .
- *Appearances, Scenes and Decals* .
- *Custom Properties* .
- *SOLIDWORKS Forum* .

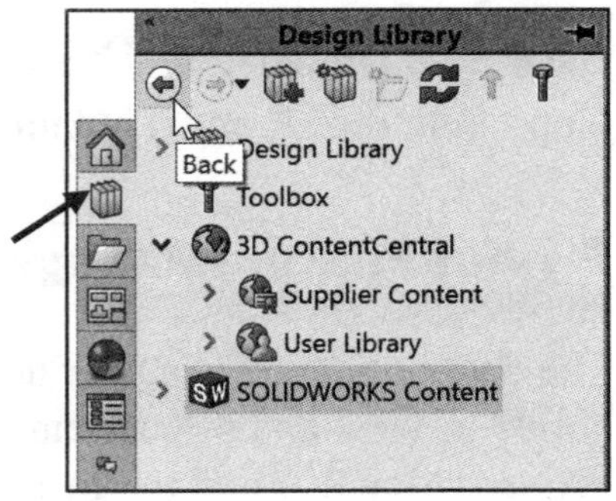

Additional tabs are displayed with Add-Ins.

Use the **Back** and **Forward** buttons in the Design Library tab and the Appearances, Scenes, and Decals tab of the Task Pane to navigate in folders.

SOLIDWORKS Resources

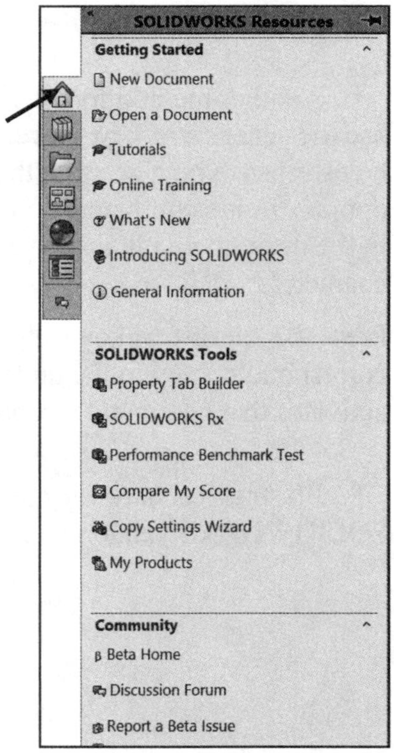

The basic SOLIDWORKS Resources menu displays the following default selections:

- *Getting Started.*
- *SOLIDWORKS Tools.*
- *Community.*
- *Online Resources.*
- *Subscription Services.*
- *Tip of the Day.*

Other user interfaces are available during the initial software installation selection: *Machine Design*, *Mold Design* or *Consumer Products Design*.

Design Library

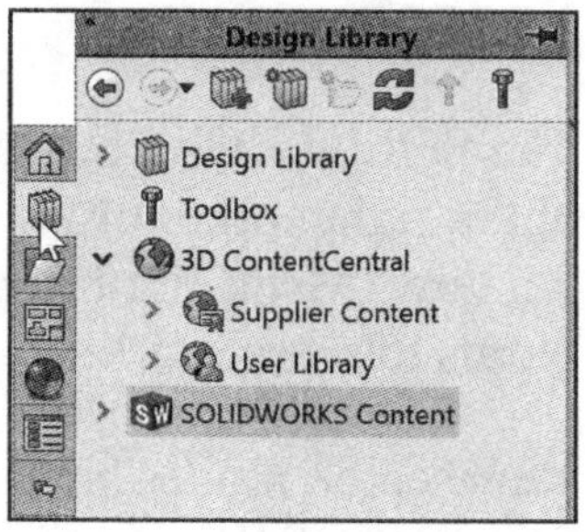

The Design Library contains reusable parts, assemblies, and other elements including library features.

The Design Library tab contains four default selections. Each default selection contains additional sub categories.

These are the default selections:

- *Design Library.*
- *Toolbox.*
- *3D ContentCentral (Internet access required).*
- *SOLIDWORKS Content (Internet access required).*

Activate the SOLIDWORKS Toolbox. Click Tools, Add-Ins.., from the Main menu. Check the SOLIDWORKS Toolbox Library from the Add-ins dialog box or click SOLIDWORKS Toolbox from the SOLIDWORKS Add-Ins tab.

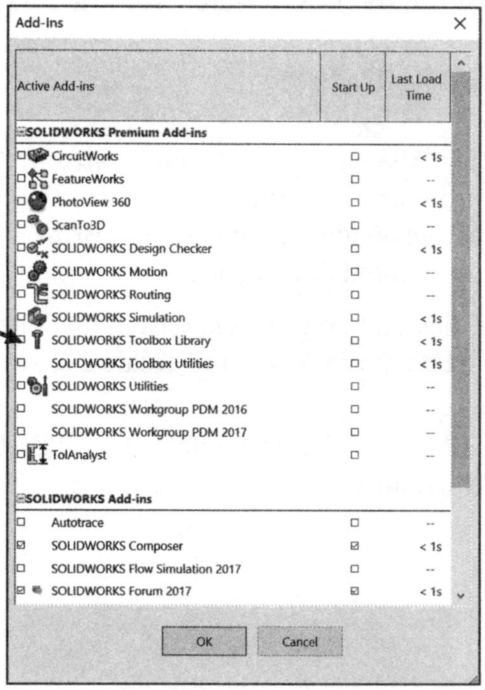

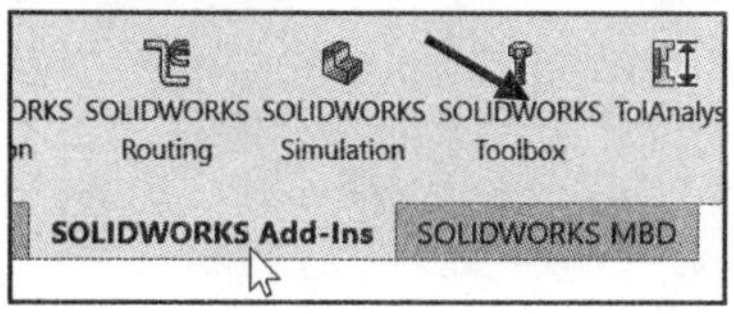

To access the Design Library folders in a non-network environment, click Add File Location and browse to the needed path. Paths may vary depending on your SOLIDWORKS version and window setup. In a network environment, contact your IT department for system details.

File Explorer

File Explorer duplicates Windows Explorer from your local computer and displays:

- *Resent Documents.*
- *Directories.*
- *Open in SOLIDWORKS and Desktop* folders.

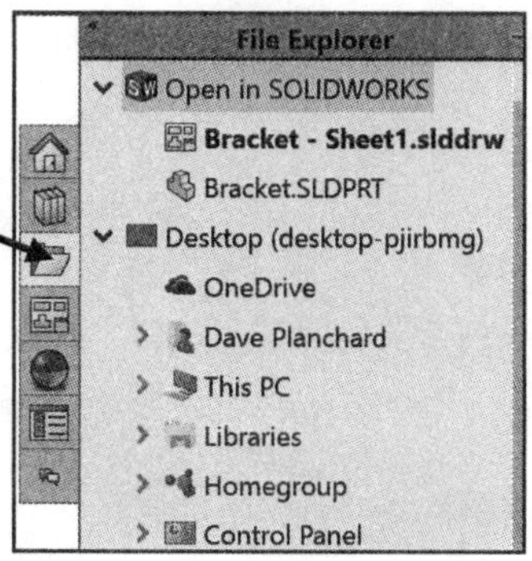

Search

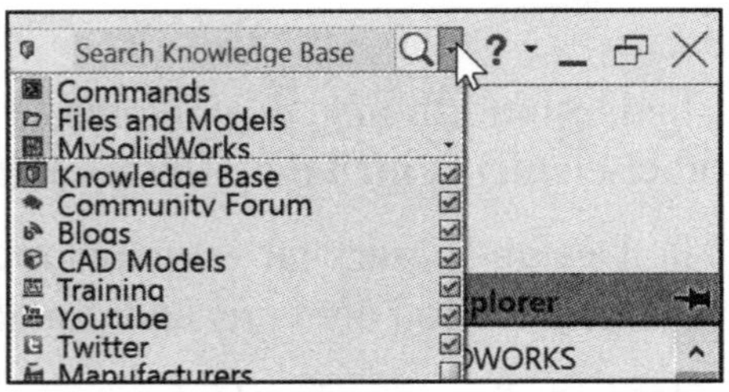

The SOLIDWORKS Search box is displayed in the upper right corner of the SOLIDWORKS Graphics window (Menu Bar toolbar). Enter the text or key words to search.

New search modes have been added to SOLIDWORKS Search as illustrated.

View Palette

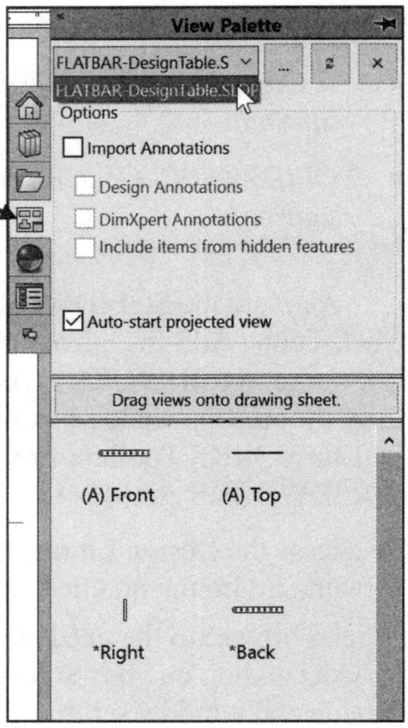

The View Palette  tool located in the Task Pane provides the ability to insert drawing views of an active document, or click the Browse button to locate the desired document.

Click and drag the view from the View Palette into an active drawing sheet to create a drawing view.

The selected model is FLATBAR in the illustration.

Appearances, Scenes and Decals

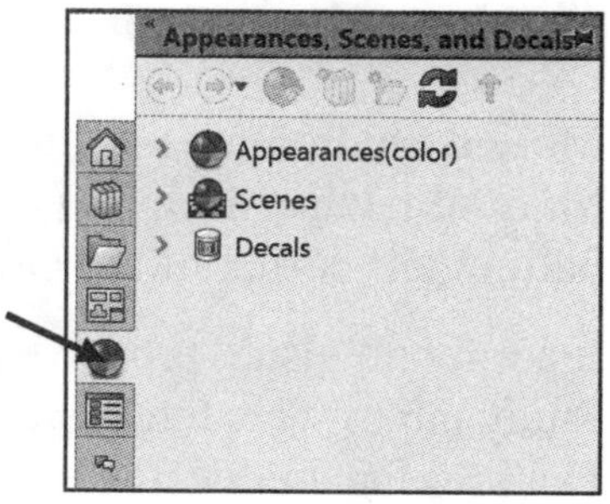

Appearances, Scenes and Decals provide a simplified way to display models in a photo-realistic setting using a library of Appearances, Scenes, and Decals.

An appearance defines the visual properties of a model, including color and texture. Appearances do not affect physical properties, which are defined by materials.

Scenes provide a visual backdrop behind a model. In SOLIDWORKS they provide reflections on the model. PhotoView 360 is an Add-in. Drag and drop a selected appearance, scene or decal on a feature, surface, part or assembly.

Custom Properties

The Custom Properties tool provides the ability to enter custom and configuration specific properties directly into SOLIDWORKS files.

SOLIDWORKS Forum

Click the SOLIDWORKS Forum icon to search directly within the Task Pane. An internet connection is required. You are required to register and to log in for postings and discussions.

User Interface for Scaling High Resolution Screens

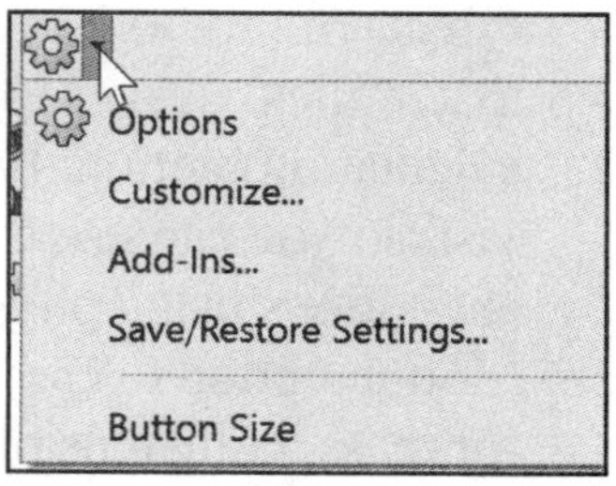

The SOLIDWORKS software supports high-resolution, high-pixel density displays. All aspects of the user interface respond to the Microsoft Windows® display scaling setting. In dialog boxes, PropertyManagers, and the FeatureManager design tree, the SOLIDWORKS software uses your display scaling setting to display buttons and icons at an appropriate size. Icons that are associated with text are scaled to a size appropriate for the text. In addition, for toolbars, you can display Small, Medium, or Large buttons. Click the **Options drop-down arrow** from the Standard Menu bar, and click Button size to size the icons.

Motion Study tab

Motion Studies are graphical simulations of motion for an assembly. Access the MotionManager from the Motion Study tab. The Motion Study tab is located in the bottom left corner of the Graphics window.

Incorporate visual properties such as lighting and camera perspective. Click the Motion Study tab to view the MotionManager. Click the Model tab to return to the FeatureManager design tree.

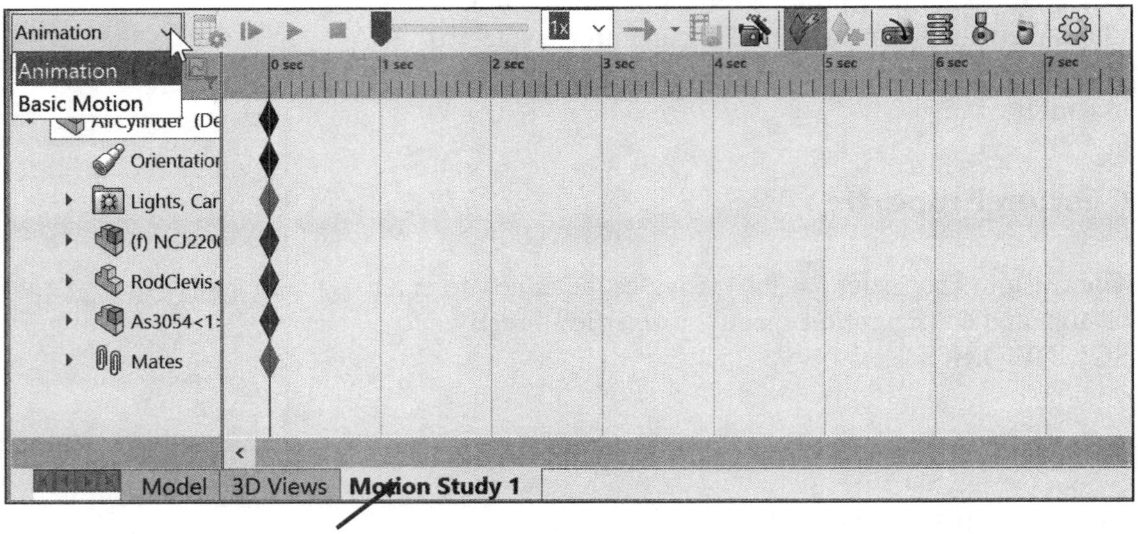

The MotionManager displays a timeline-based interface and provides the following selections from the drop-down menu as illustrated:

- *Animation:* Apply Animation to animate the motion of an assembly. Add a motor and insert positions of assembly components at various times using set key points. Use the Animation option to create animations for motion that do **<u>not</u>** require accounting for mass or gravity.

- *Basic Motion:* Apply Basic Motion for approximating the effects of motors, springs, collisions and gravity on assemblies. Basic Motion takes mass into account in calculating motion. Basic Motion computation is relatively fast, so you can use this for creating presentation animations using physics-based simulations. Use the Basic Motion option to create simulations of motion that account for mass, collisions or gravity.

If the Motion Study tab is not displayed in the Graphics window, click **View**, **MotionManager** from the Menu bar.

3D Views tab

SOLIDWORKS MBD (Model Based Definition) lets you create models without the need for drawings giving you an integrated manufacturing. MBD helps companies define, organize, and publish 3D product and manufacturing information (PMI), including 3D model data in industry standard file formats.

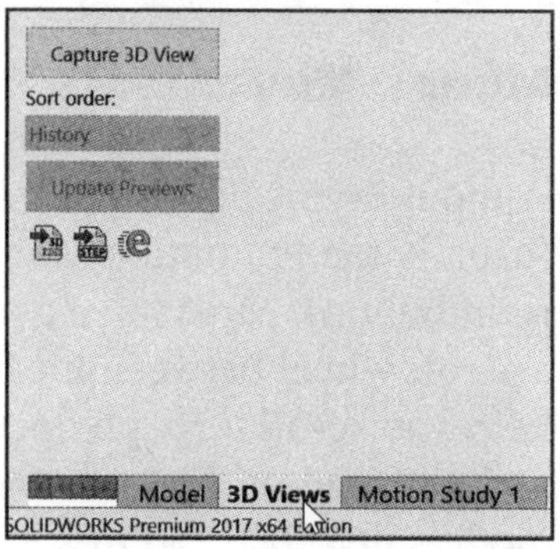

Create 3D drawing views of your parts and assemblies that contain the model settings needed for review and manufacturing. This lets users navigate back to those settings as they evaluate the design.

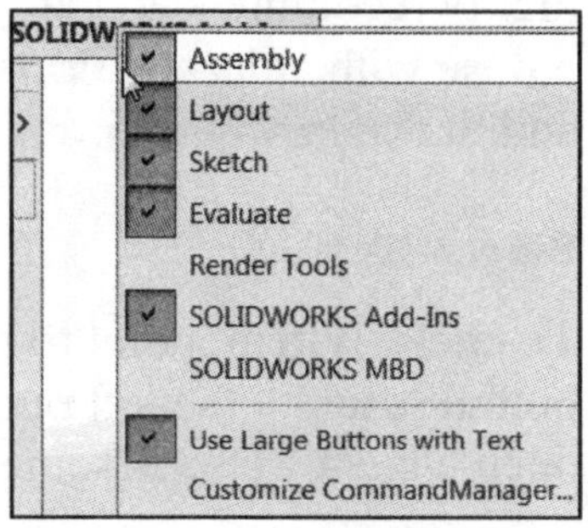

Use the tools in the SOLIDWORKS MBD CommandManager to set up your model with selected configurations, including explodes and abbreviated views, annotations, display states, zoom level, view orientation and section views. Capture those settings so that you and other users can return to them at any time using the 3D view palette.

To access the 3D View palette, click the 3DViews tab at the bottom of the SOLIDWORKS window or the SOLIDWORKS MBD tab in the CommandManager. The Capture 3D View button opens the Capture 3D View PropertyManager, where you specify the 3D view name, and the configuration, display state and annotation view to capture. See SOLIDWORKS help for additional information.

Dynamic Reference Visualization

Dynamic Reference Visualization provides the ability to view the parent relationships between items in the FeatureManager design tree. When you hover over a feature with references in the FeatureManager design tree, arrows display showing the relationships. If a reference cannot be shown because a feature is not expanded, the arrow points to the feature that contains the reference and the actual reference appears in a text box to the right of the arrow. Use Dynamic reference visualization for a part, assembly and ever mates.

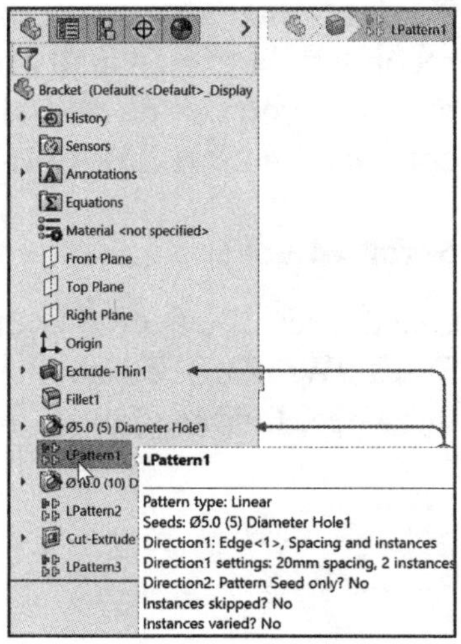

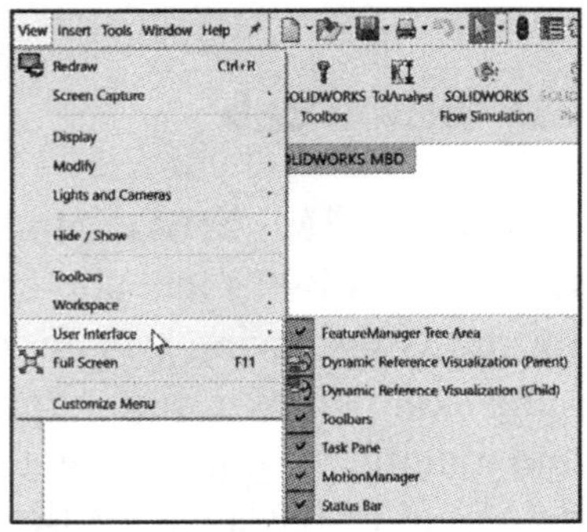

Use Dynamic reference visualization for a part, assembly and ever mates. To display the Dynamic Reference Visualization, click **View ➢ User Interface ➢ Dynamic Reference Visualization** from the Main menu bar.

Mouse Movements

A mouse typically has two buttons: a primary button (usually the left button) and a secondary button (usually the right button). Most mice also include a scroll wheel between the buttons to help you scroll through documents and to Zoom in, Zoom out and rotate models in SOLIDWORKS. It is highly recommended that you use a mouse with at least a Primary, Scroll and Secondary button.

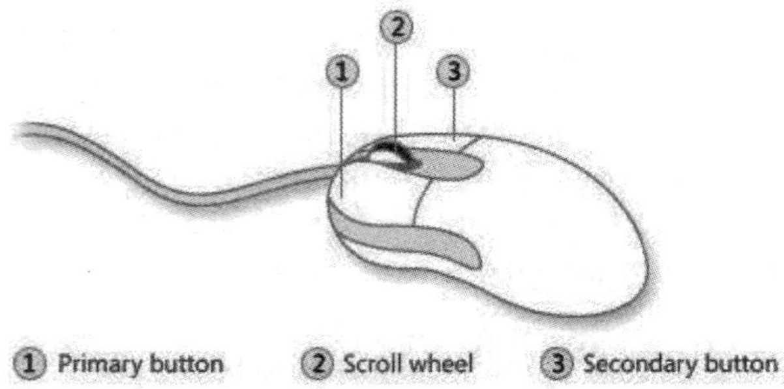

Single-click

To click an item, point to the item on the screen, and then press and release the primary button (usually the left button). Clicking is most often used to select (mark) an item or open a menu. This is sometimes called single-clicking or left-clicking.

Double-click

To double-click an item, point to the item on the screen, and then click twice quickly. If the two clicks are spaced too far apart, they might be interpreted as two individual clicks rather than as one double-click. Double-clicking is most often used to open items on your desktop. For example, you can start a program or open a folder by double-clicking its icon on the desktop.

Right-click

To right-click an item, point to the item on the screen, and then press and release the secondary button (usually the right button). Right-clicking an item usually displays a list of things you can do with the item. Right-click in the open Graphics window or on a command in SOLIDWORKS, and additional pop-up context is displayed.

Scroll wheel

Use the scroll wheel to zoom-in or to zoom-out of the Graphics window in SOLIDWORKS. To zoom-in, roll the wheel backward (toward you). To zoom-out, roll the wheel forward (away from you).

Summary

The SOLIDWORKS User Interface and CommandManager consist of the following options: Menu bar toolbar, Menu bar menu, Drop-down menus, Context toolbars, Consolidated fly-out menus, System feedback icons, Confirmation Corner and Heads-up View toolbar.

The FeatureManager consists of five default tabs: *FeatureManager design tree, PropertyManager, ConfigurationManager, DimXpertManager* and *DisplayManager*.

You learned about SOLIDWORKS Help, SOLIDWORKS Tutorials and basic mouse movements to manipulate your SOLIDWORKS model.

You learned about SOLIDWORKS Help, SOLIDWORKS Tutorials and basic mouse movements to manipulate your SOLIDWORKS model.

Templates are part, drawing and assembly documents which include user-defined parameters. Open a new part, drawing or assembly. Select a template for the new document.

- ***Parts***. The Parts default template is located in the C:\ProgramData\SolidWorks\\SOLIDWORKS 2017\templates\Part.prtdot folder.
- ***Assemblies***. The Assemblies default template is located in the C:\ProgramData\SolidWorks\\SOLIDWORKS 2017\templates\Assembly.asmdot folder.
- ***Drawings***. The Drawings default template is located in the C:\ProgramData\SolidWorks\\SOLIDWORKS 2017\templates\Drawing.drwdot folder.

For commercial users, SOLIDWORKS Model Based Definition (MBD) is a separate application. For education users, SOLIDWORKS MBD is included in the SOLIDWORKS Education Edition as an Add In.

In Chapter 2, you will establish a SOLIDWORKS session. Learn about 2D Sketching and 3D features. Create a new part. Create the Wheel for the Fly Wheel sub-assembly. Utilize the Fly Wheel sub-assembly in the final Stirling Engine assembly.

Apply the following sketch and feature tools: Circle, Line Centerline, Centerpoint Straight Slot, Mirror Entities, Extruded Boss, Extruded Cut, Revolved Boss, Circular Pattern, Hole Wizard and Fillet.

Incorporate design change into a part using proper design intent, along with applying multiple geometric relations: Coincident, Vertical, Horizontal, Tangent and Midpoint and feature and sketch modifications.

Utilize the Material, Mass Properties and Appearance tool on the Wheel.

View the provided videos in the book to enhance the user experience.

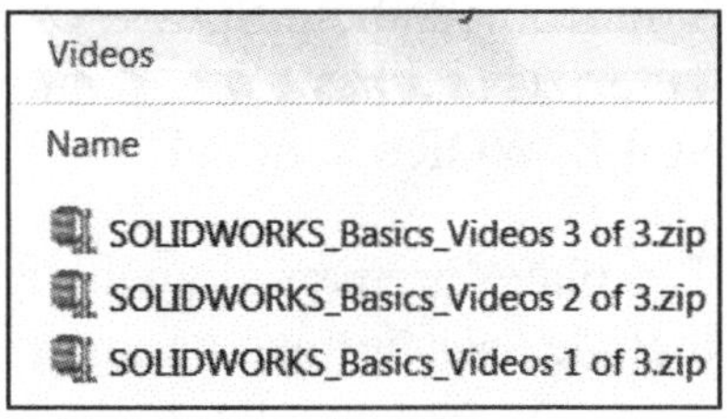

- Start a SOLIDWORKS session.
- Understand the SOLIDWORKS Interface.
- Create 2D Sketches, Sketch Planes and use various Sketch tools.
- Create 3D Features and apply Design Intent.
- Create an Assembly.
- Create fundamental Drawings Part 1 & Part 2.

Chapter 2

2D Sketching, Features and Parts

Below are the desired outcomes and usage competencies based on the completion of Chapter 2.

Desired Outcomes:	Usage Competencies:
• A new part for the Fly Wheel sub-assembly with user defined document properties: o Wheel • Utilize the Fly Wheel sub-assembly in the final Stirling Engine assembly.	• Aptitude to establish a SOLIDWORKS session and set part document properties. • Knowledge of the following sketch and feature tools: Circle, Line, Centerline, Center point Straight Slot, Mirror Entities, Extruded Base, Revolved Boss, Extruded Cut, Circular Pattern, Hole Wizard and Fillet. • Ability to incorporate design change into a part. • Skill to insert multiple Geometric relations. • Comprehend applying Material and using the Mass Properties tool.

Notes:

Chapter 2 - 2D Sketching, Features and Parts

Chapter Objective

Establish a SOLIDWORKS session. Create a new part called Wheel with user defined document properties. The Wheel part is used in the Fly Wheel sub-assembly. The sub-assembly is used in the final Stirling Engine assembly.

On the completion of this chapter, you will be able to:

- Establish a SOLIDWORKS session.
- Set user defined document properties for a part.
- Recognize the default Sketch Planes in the Part FeatureManager.
- Select the correct Sketch plane and orientation for the Wheel.
- Utilize the following Sketch tools: Circle, Line, Centerline, Center point Straight Slot and Mirror Entities.
- Apply and comprehend proper design intent.
- Edit a Sketch and Sketch Plane.
- Insert the following Geometric relations: Coincident, Vertical, Horizontal, Tangent and Midpoint.
- Create and modify the following features: Extruded Base, Revolved Boss, Extruded Cut, Circular Pattern, Hole Wizard and Fillet.
- Apply Material and utilize the Mass Properties tool to verify a design change.
- Utilize and apply the Appearance tool.

Activity: Start a SOLIDWORKS Session. Create a New Part Document.

Start a SOLIDWORKS session.

1) Double-click the **SOLIDWORKS icon** from the Desktop.

2) **Pin** the Menu bar menu as illustrated. Use both the Menu bar menu and the Menu bar toolbar in this book.

Create a New Part Document.

3) Click **New** from the Menu bar or click **File, New** from the Menu bar menu. The New SOLIDWORKS Document dialog box is displayed. Advanced mode is used in this book.

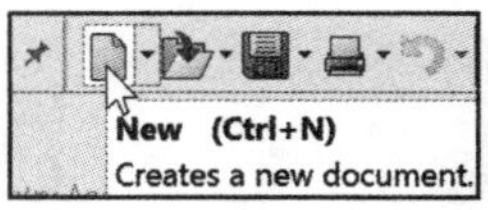

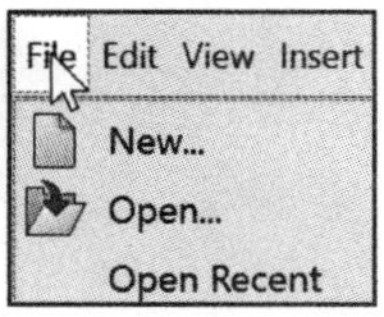

4) Click the **Advanced** tab.

5) Click the **Templates** tab.

6) Double-click **Part** from the New SOLIDWORKS Document dialog box. Part 1 is displayed in the FeatureManager.

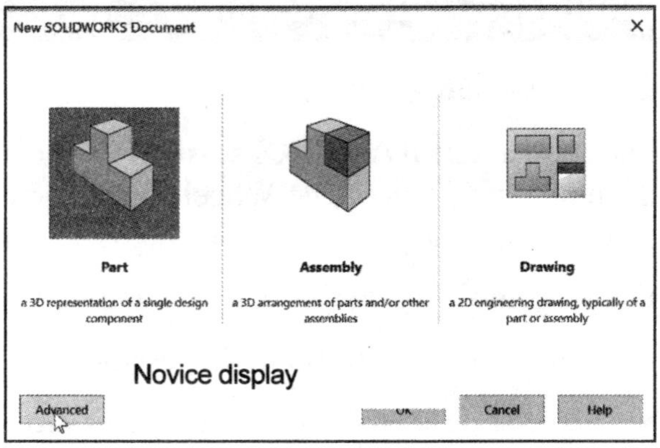

The first system default Part filename is Part1. The system attaches the .sldprt suffix to the created part. The second created part in the same session increments to the filename Part2.

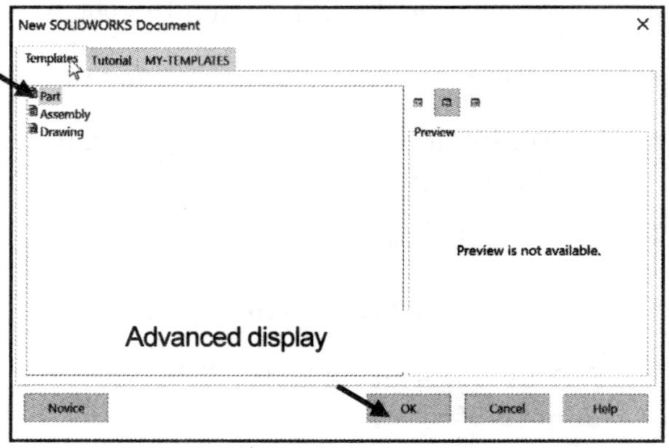

Display the origin.

7) Click **View**, **Hide/Show**, **Origins** from the Main menu. The origin is displayed in the Graphics window.

Directional input refers by default to the global coordinate system (X-, Y- and Z), which is based on Plane1 with its origin located at the origin of the part or assembly. Plane1 (Front) is the first plane that appears in the FeatureManager design tree and can have a different name. The reference triad shows the global X-, Y- and Z-directions.

The three default ⊥ reference planes, displayed in the FeatureManager design tree, represent infinite 2D planes in 3D space.

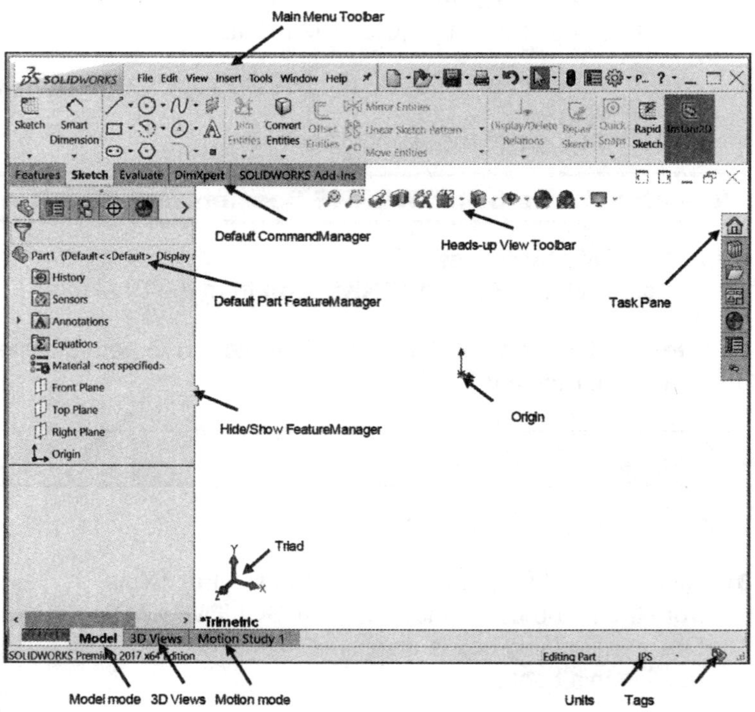

Activity: Set Document Properties for the Wheel

Set Document Properties - Drafting Standard.

8) Click **Options** from the Menu bar toolbar. The System Options General dialog box is displayed.

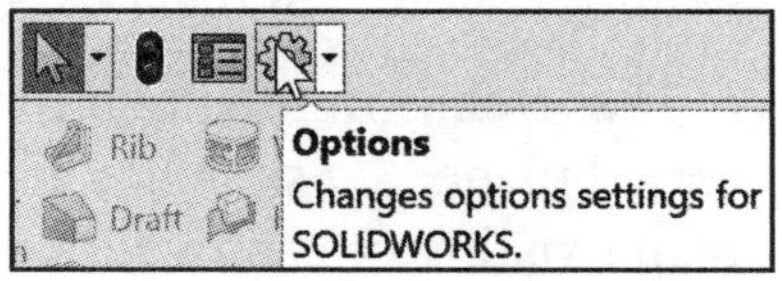

9) Click the **Document Properties** tab.

10) Select **ANSI** from the Overall drafting standard drop-down menu.

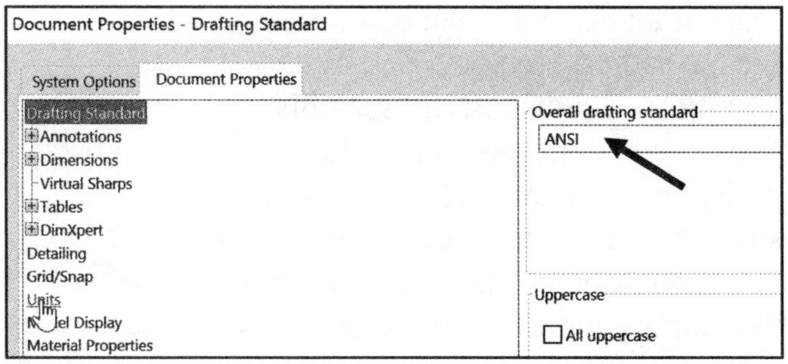

Various detailing options are available depending on the selected standard.

The Overall drafting standard determines the display of dimension text, arrows, symbols, and spacing. Units are the measurement of physical quantities. Millimeter dimensioning and decimal inch dimensioning are the two most common unit types specified for engineering parts and drawings.

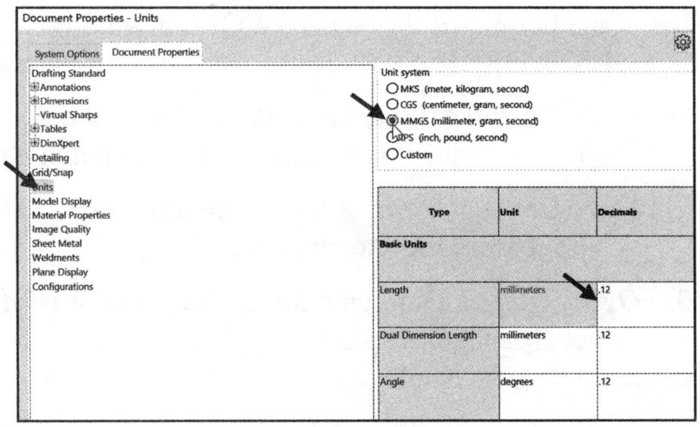

Set Document Properties - Units.

11) Click the **Units** folder.

12) Click **MMGS** (millimeter, gram, second) for Unit system.

13) Select **.12** (two decimal places) for Length basic units.

14) Click **OK** from the Document Properties - Units dialog box. The Part FeatureManager is displayed.

The origin represents the intersection of the Front, Top and Right planes.

View the provided videos on creating 2D Sketches, Sketch Planes, using various Sketch tools along with 3D Features and Design Intent to enhance your user experience.

2D Sketching - Identify the Correct Sketch Plane

Most SOLIDWORKS features start with a 2D sketch. Sketches are the foundation for creating features. SOLIDWORKS provides the ability to create either 2D or 3D sketches.

A 2D sketch is limited to a flat 2D sketch plane located on a reference plane, face or a created plane. 3D sketches are very useful in creating sketch geometry that does not lie on an existing or easily defined plane.

Does it matter what plane you start the base 2D sketch on? Yes. When you create a new part or assembly, the three default planes are aligned with specific views. The plane you select for your first sketch determines the orientation of the part. Selecting the correct plane to start your model is very important.

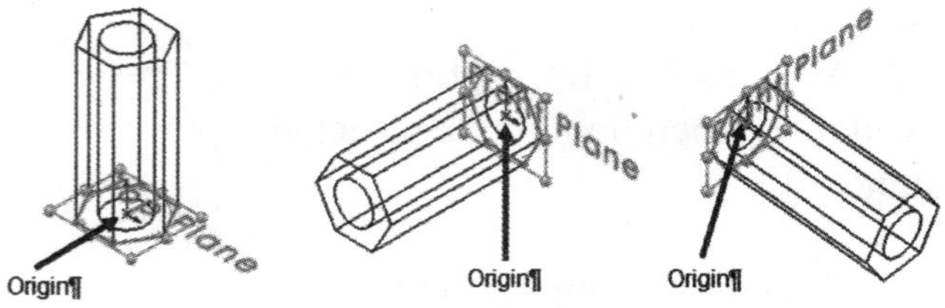

Sketch States

Sketches can exist in any of five states. The state of the sketch is displayed in the status bar at the bottom of the SOLIDWORKS window. The following are the five sketch states in SOLIDWORKS:

1. *Under Defined.* Inadequate definition of the sketch (blue). The FeatureManager displays a minus (-) symbol before the sketch name.
2. *Fully Defined.* Complete information (black). The FeatureManager displays no symbol before the sketch name.
3. *Over Defined.* Duplicate dimensions and or relations (orange - red). The FeatureManager displays a (+) symbol before the sketch name. The What's Wrong dialog box is displayed.
4. *Invalid Solution Found.* Your sketch is solved but results in invalid geometry, for example, a zero length line, zero radius arc or a self-intersecting spline (yellow).
5. *No Solution Found.* Indicates sketch geometry that cannot be resolved (Brown).

Color indicates the state of the individual Sketch entities.

In SOLIDWORKS, it is not necessary to fully dimension or define sketches before you use them to create features. You should fully define sketches before you consider the part finished for manufacturing.

Activity: Create the Base Sketch for the First Feature of the Wheel

In SOLIDWORKS, a 2D profile is called a sketch. The Base sketch is the first sketch in the feature. A sketch requires a sketch plane and a 2D profile. The sketch in this example uses the Front Plane. The 2D profile is a circle. A Geometric relationship and a dimension define the exact size and location of the center point of the circle relative to the origin. The center of the circle is Coincident with the origin. The origin is displayed in red.

Create the Base Sketch.

15) Right-click **Front Plane** from the FeatureManager. The Context toolbar is displayed. This is your Sketch plane. The Sketch toolbar is displayed. Front Plane is your Sketch plane. Note the grid is deactivated for picture clarity.

16) Click **Sketch** from the Context toolbar as illustrated.

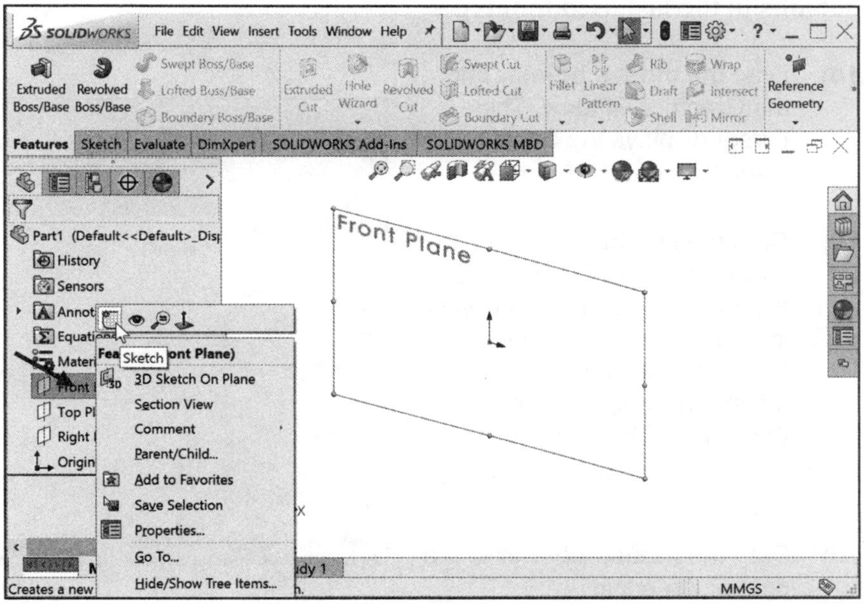

The plane or face you select for the Base sketch determines the orientation of the part.

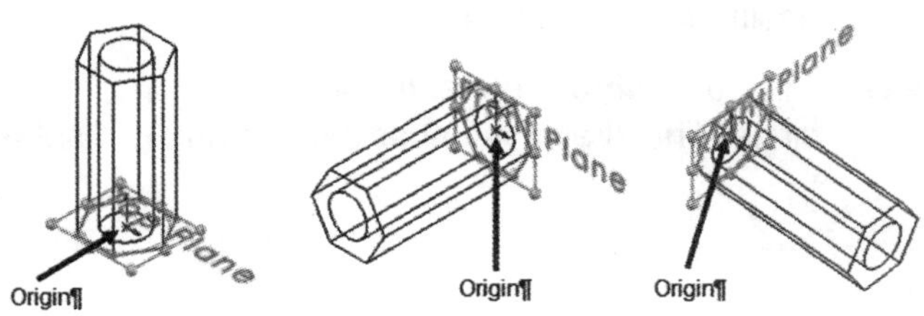

The Front Plane rotates normal to the Sketch Plane.

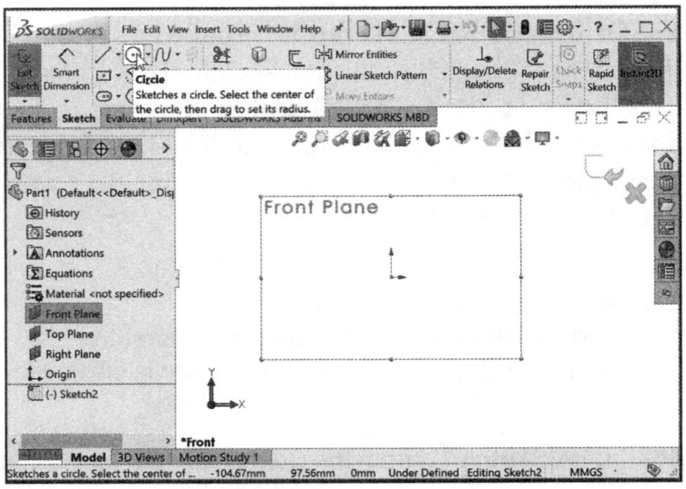

17) Click the **Circle** tool from the Sketch toolbar. The Circle PropertyManager is displayed. The sketch opens in the Front view. The mouse pointer displays the Circle symbol icon. The Front Plane feedback indicates the current Sketch plane.

The Circle-based tool uses a Consolidated Circle PropertyManager. The SOLIDWORKS application defaults to the last used tool type.

18) Drag the **mouse pointer** into the Graphics window. The cursor displays the Circle symbol icon.

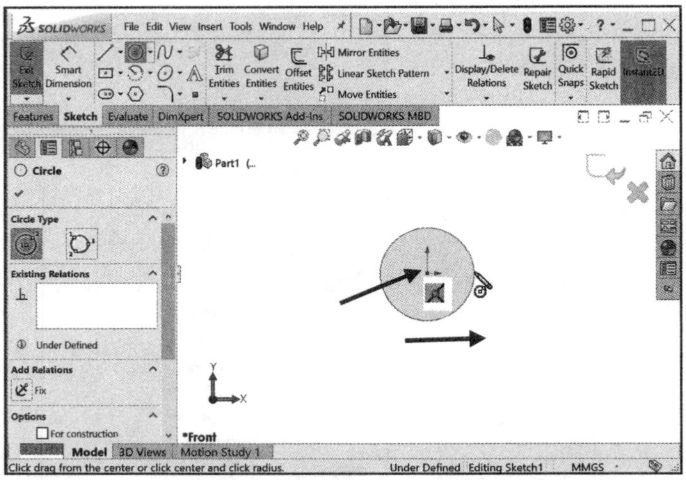

19) Click the **Origin** in the Graphics window. This is the first point of the circle. It is very important that you always reference the sketch to the origin. This helps to fully define the sketch. The cursor displays a Coincident relation to the origin.

20) Drag the **mouse pointer** to the right of the origin (approximately 25mm) to create the circle as illustrated. The center point of the circle is positioned at the origin.

21) Click a **position** to create the circle. The sketch is under defined and is displayed in blue.

View the illustrated sketch relation in the Graphics window.

22) Click **View**, **Hide/Show**, **Sketch Relations** from the Main Menu bar. The sketch relation (Coincident) is displayed in the Graphics window.

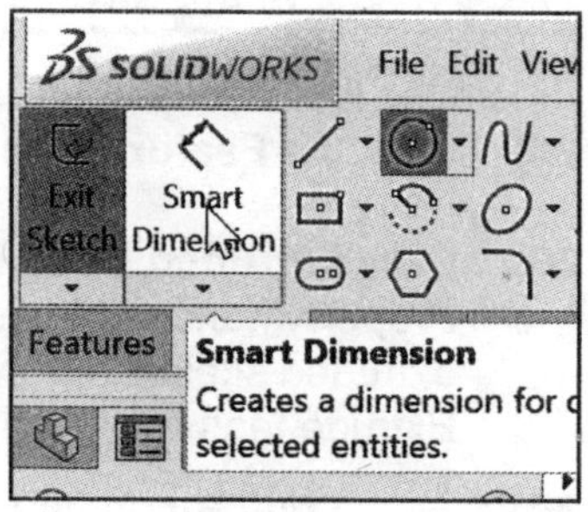

The diameter of the circle is displayed above the mouse pointer as you drag the mouse pointer up and to the right. The diameter displays different values. Define the exact dimension with the Smart dimension tool.

Add a dimension to fully define the sketch.

23) Click the **Smart Dimension** tool from the Sketch toolbar. The cursor displays the Smart Dimension icon.

24) Click the **circumference** of the circle.

25) Click a **position** diagonally above and to the right of the circle in the Graphics window.

26) Enter **20**mm in the Modify dialog box.

27) Click the **Green Check mark** in the Modify dialog box. The diameter of the circle is 20mm. The sketch is fully defined and is displayed in black.

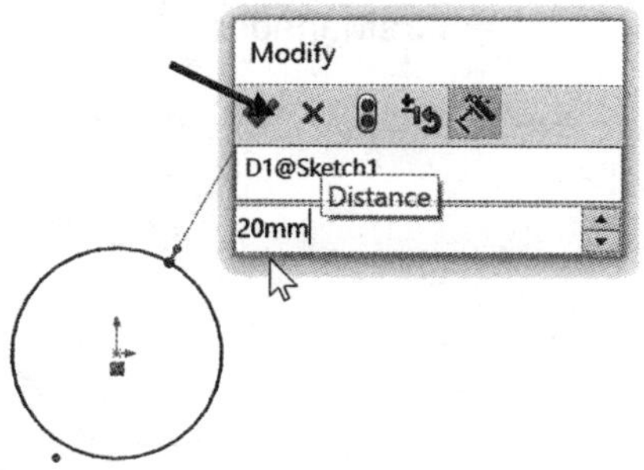

Add relations then dimensions. This keeps the user from having too many unnecessary dimensions. This also helps to show the design intent of the model.

Features

- Features are geometry building blocks.
- Features add or remove material.
- Features are created from sketched profiles or from edges and faces of existing geometry.

What is a Base feature? The Base feature for the Wheel (Extruded Base) is the first feature that is created. The Base feature is the foundation of the part. Keep the Base feature simple.

Activity: Create the First Feature of the Wheel - Extruded Base

Create the first feature of the Wheel. Extrude the sketch.

28) Click the **Features** tab from the CommandManager. The Features toolbar is displayed.

29) Click **Extruded Boss/Base** from the Features toolbar. The Boss-Extrude PropertyManager is displayed. Blind is the default End Condition in Direction 1. The extruded sketch is previewed in a Trimetric view. The preview displays the direction of the Extrude feature.

30) Select **Mid Plane** for End Condition in Direction 1. Note your End Condition options.

31) Enter **20**mm for Depth in Direction 1. Accept the default conditions.

32) Click **OK** from the Boss-Extrude PropertyManager. Boss-Extrude1 is displayed in the FeatureManager.

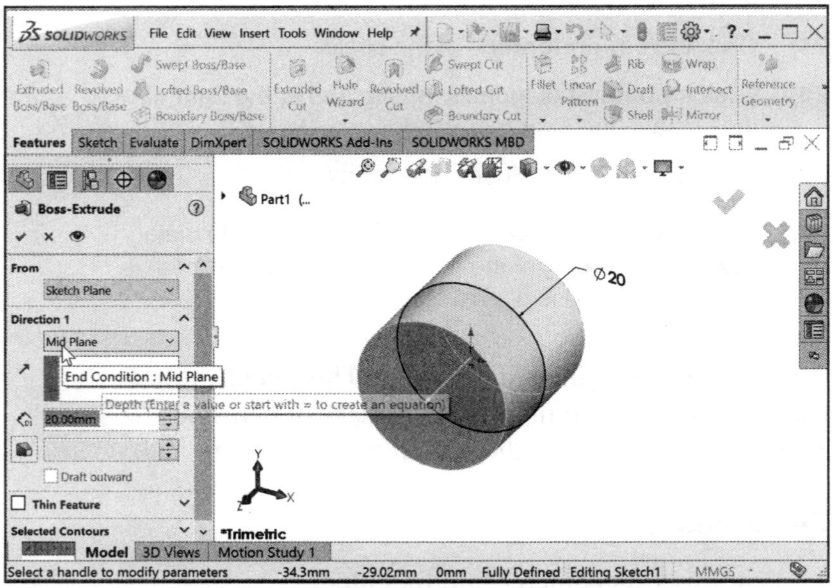

Fit the model to the Graphics window.

33) Press the **f** key.

Design Intent

What is design intent? All designs are created for a purpose. Design intent is the intellectual arrangements of features and dimensions of a design. Design intent governs the relationship between sketches in a feature, features in a part and parts in an assembly.

The SOLIDWORKS definition of design intent is the process in which the model is developed to accept future modifications. Models behave differently when design changes occur.

Design for change. Utilize geometry for symmetry, reuse common features, and reuse common parts. Build change into the following areas that you create: sketch, feature, part, assembly and drawing.

During the sketching process, insert all needed geometric relations and dimensions relative to the origin to fully define the sketch. Reference the origin in the sketch. The origin represents the intersection of the Front, Top and Right Planes.

Start the translation of the initial design functional and geometric requirements into SOLIDWORKS features.

Save the part.

34) Click **Save As** from the Drop-down Menu bar.

35) Click the **DOCUMENTS** file folder. Note: The procedure will be different depending on your operating system.

36) Click **New Folder**.

37) Enter **SOLIDWORKS in 5 Hours** for the folder name.

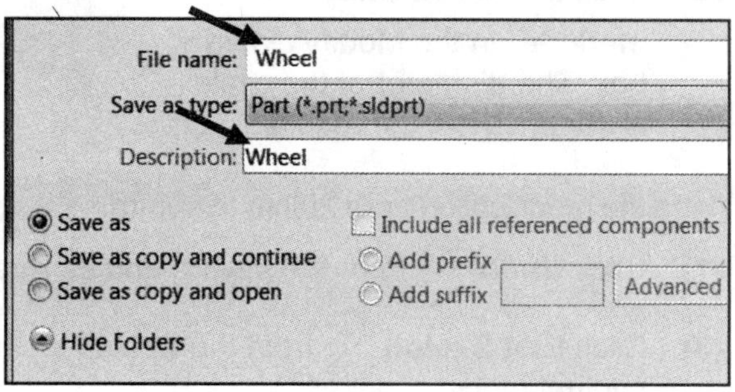

38) Double-click the **SOLIDWORKS in 5 Hours** folder. SOLIDWORKS in 5 Hours is the Save in file folder name.

39) Enter **Wheel** for File name. Enter **Wheel** for Description.

40) Click **Save** from the Save As dialog box. The Wheel FeatureManager is displayed.

41) **Expand** Boss-Extrude1 from the FeatureManager as illustrated. Sketch1 is fully defined. Sketch1 has all needed relations and dimensions relative to the origin.

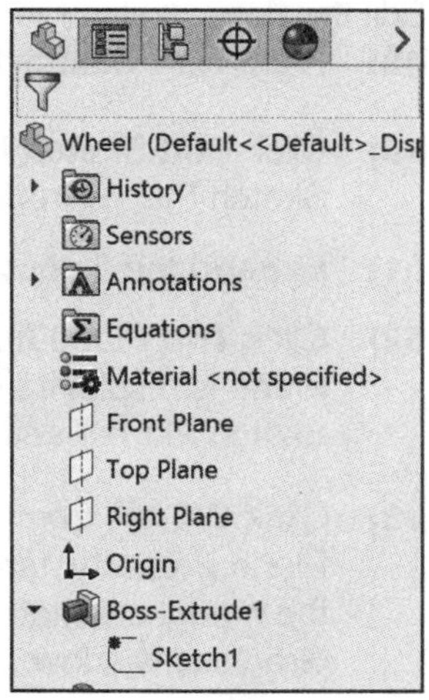

A fully defined sketch has complete information (manufacturing and inspection) and is displayed in black.

Display an Isometric view of the model. Press the **space bar** to display the Orientation dialog box. Click the **Isometric view** icon.

Organize parts into folders. The folder for this chapter is named SOLIDWORKS in 5 Hours. All documents for this book are saved in the SOLIDWORKS in 5 Hours folder.

In the next section, edit the Sketch and Sketch plane.

Activity: Edit the Base Sketch and Sketch Plane

Edit the Base Sketch from 20mm to 40mm.

42) Right-click **Sketch1** in the FeatureMananger.

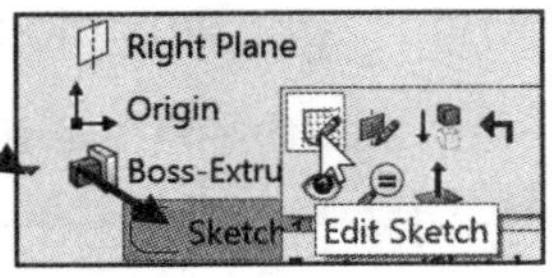

43) Click **Edit Sketch** from the Context toolbar.

44) Double-click **20** in the Graphics window. The Modify dialog box is displayed.

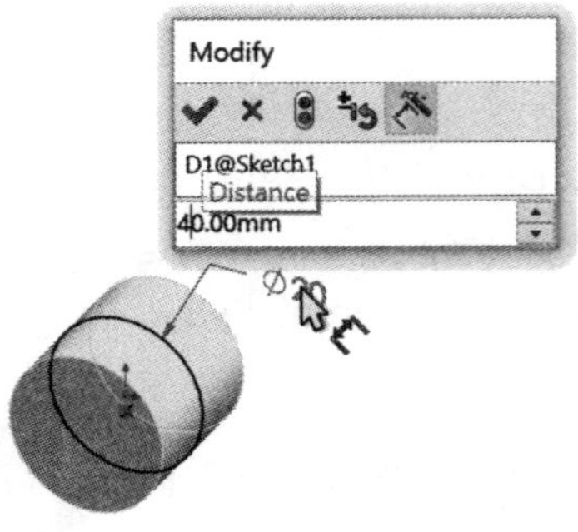

45) Enter **40**mm in the Modify dialog box.

46) Click the **Green Check mark** in the Modify dialog box. The diameter of the circle is 40mm. View the results.

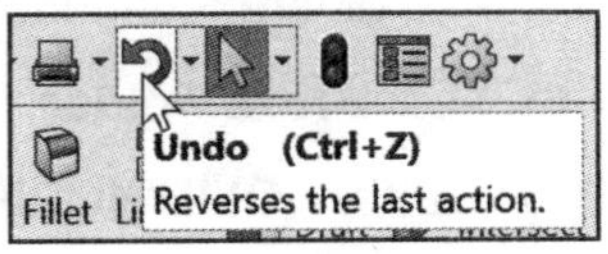

Undo the modification from 20mm to 40mm.

47) Click **Undo** from the Main menu as illustrated.

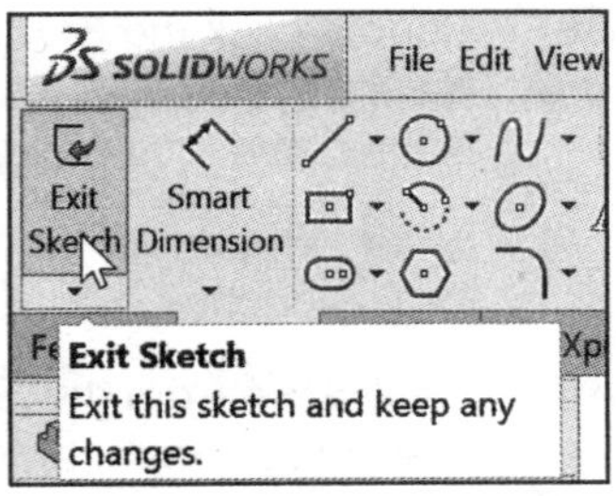

48) Click **Exit Sketch** from the Sketch toolbar to return to the original model.

Edit the Base Sketch Plane.

49) Right-click **Sketch1** in the FeatureMananger.

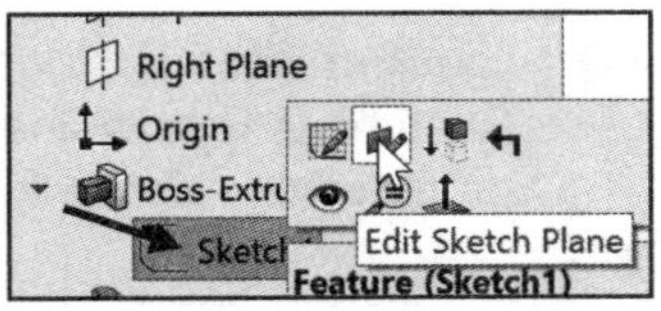

50) Click **Edit Sketch Plane** from the Context toolbar. The Sketch Plane PropertyManager is displayed.

51) **Expand** the fly-out Wheel FeatureManager as illustrated.

52) Click **Top Plane** from the fly-out Wheel FeatureManager. Top Plane is displayed in the Sketch Plane/Face box.

53) Click **OK** from the Sketch Plane PropertyManager. View the model orientation in the Graphics window.

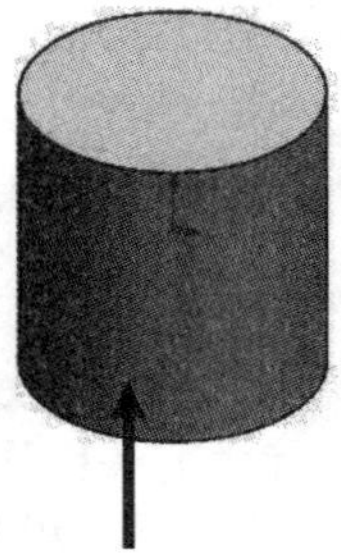

Top Plane

Return to the original orientation.

54) Click **Undo**. The original orientation is displayed (Front Plane).

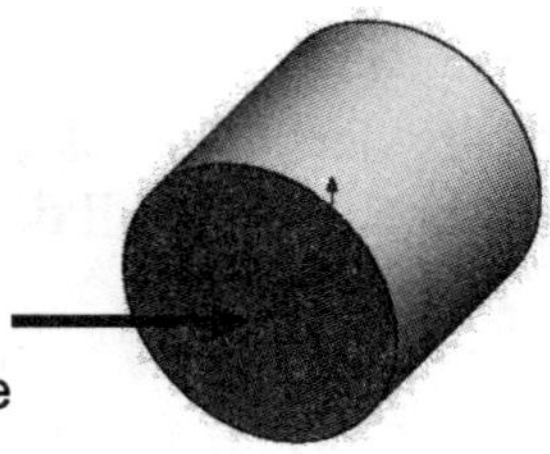

Front Plane

Display Modes, View Modes, View Tools and Appearances

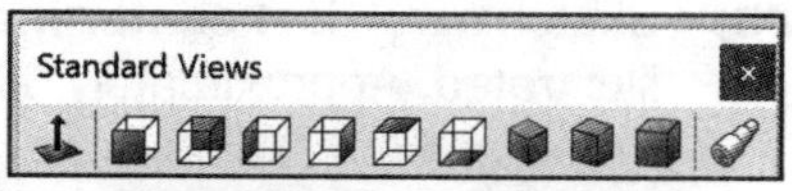

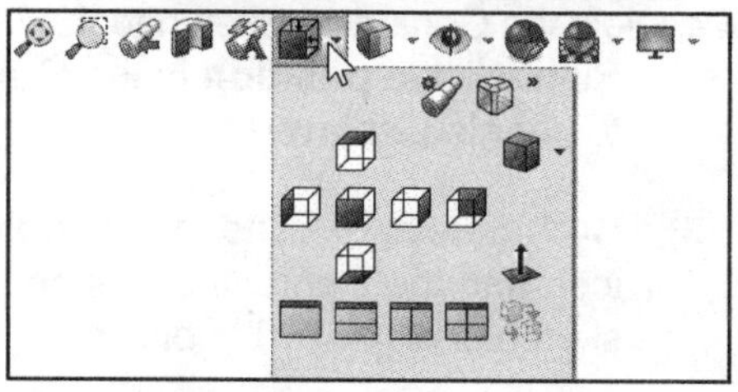

Access the display modes, view modes, view tools and appearances from the Standard Views toolbar and the Heads-up View toolbar. Apply these tools to display the required modes in your document.

The Apply scene tool adds the likeness of a material to a model in the Graphics window without adding the physical properties of the material. Select a scene from the drop-down menu.

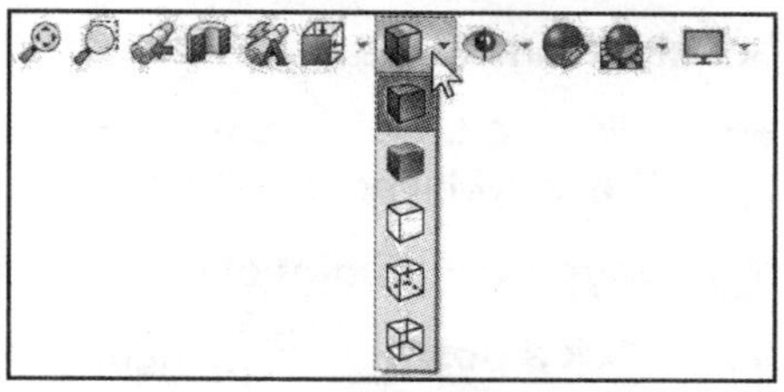

Activity: Create the Second Feature of the Wheel - Revolved Boss

Create the second feature on the Right Plane.

55) Right-click **Right Plane** from the FeatureMananger.

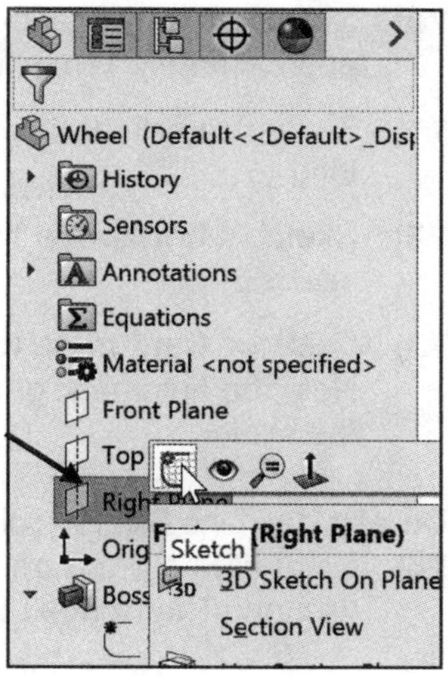

56) Click **Sketch** from the Context toolbar.

Display a Right view and Zoom out.

57) Click **Right view** from the Heads-up View toolbar.

58) Press the **z** key approximately five times to zoom out.

Display the origin.

59) If needed, click **View**, **Hide/Show**, **Origins** from the Main menu. The origin is displayed in the Graphics window.

Create the profile of the Wheel.

60) Click the **Sketch** tab from the CommandManager.

61) Click the **Centerline** Sketch tool from the drop-down menu as illustrated. The Insert Line PropertyManager is displayed.

62) Click the **midpoint** (it is very important that you select the midpoint) of the top edge of Boss-Extrude1 as illustrated. A Midpoint relation is displayed.

63) Sketch a **vertical centerline** from the midpoint as illustrated. Approximately 60mm.

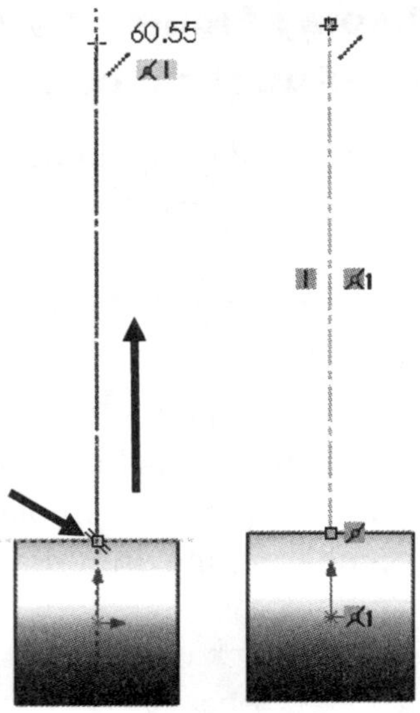

Deselect the Centerline Sketch tool.

64) Right-click a **position** in the Graphics window. The Context toolbar is displayed.

65) Click **Select**. The mouse pointer displays the Select icon and the Centerline Sketch tool is deactivated. The sketch is displayed in black.

Select the Line Sketch tool.

66) Click the **Line** Sketch tool. The Insert Line PropertyManager is displayed.

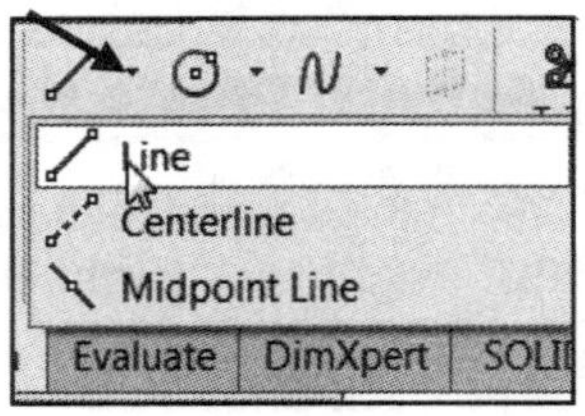

67) Click the **midpoint** of the top edge of Boss-Extrude1.

68) Click a **position** to the right as illustrated. Approximately 4mm long. A horizontal relation is displayed.

69) Click a **position** directly above as illustrated. Approximately 30mm long. A vertical relation is displayed.

70) Sketch an **angle** (approximately 30degrees) **line** approximately 11mm long as illustrated.

71) Sketch a **vertical line** as illustrated. Approximately 16mm long.

72) Sketch a **horizontal line** as illustrated to complete the sketch.

73) Click the **Centerline** to end the sketch. Note the automatic geometric relations in the sketch.

Deselect the Line Sketch tool.

74) Right-click a **position** in the Graphics window. The Context toolbar is displayed.

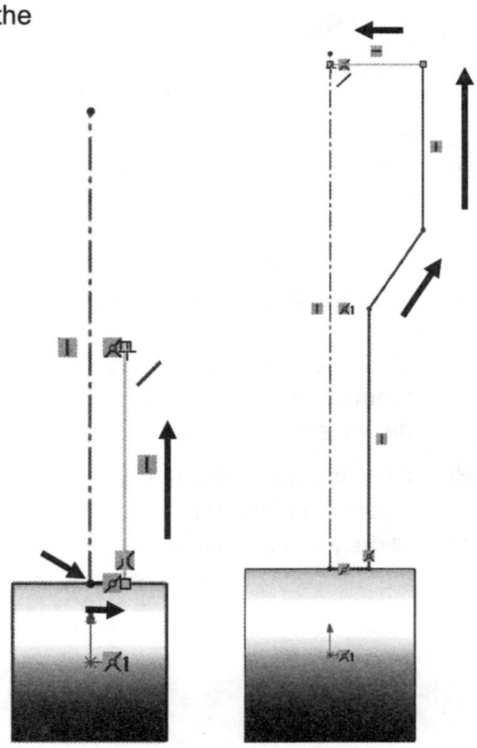

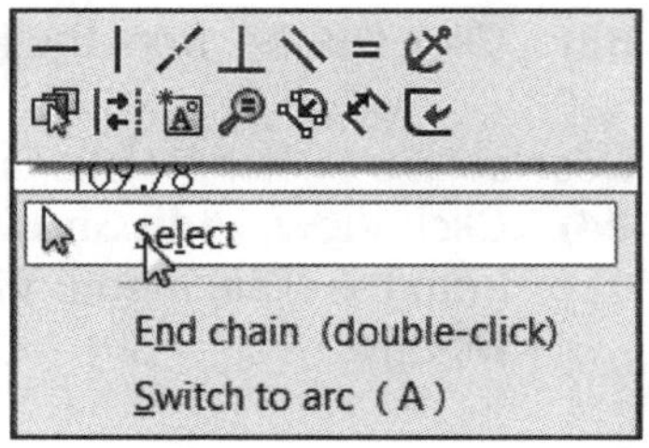

75) Click **Select**. The mouse pointer displays the Select icon and the Centerline Sketch tool is deactivated.

In SOLIDWORKS, relations between sketch entities and model geometry, in either 2D or 3D sketches, are an important means of building in design intent. As you sketch, allow the SOLIDWORKS application to automatically add relations. Automatic relations rely on Inferencing, Pointer display, Sketch Snaps and Quick Snaps. After you sketch, manually add relations if needed and the dimensions to fully define the sketch.

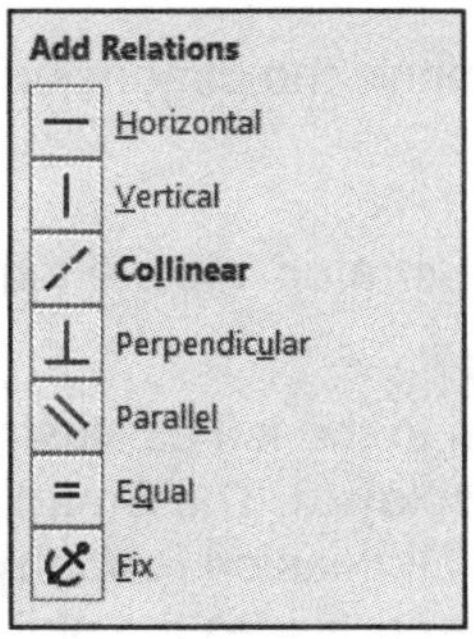

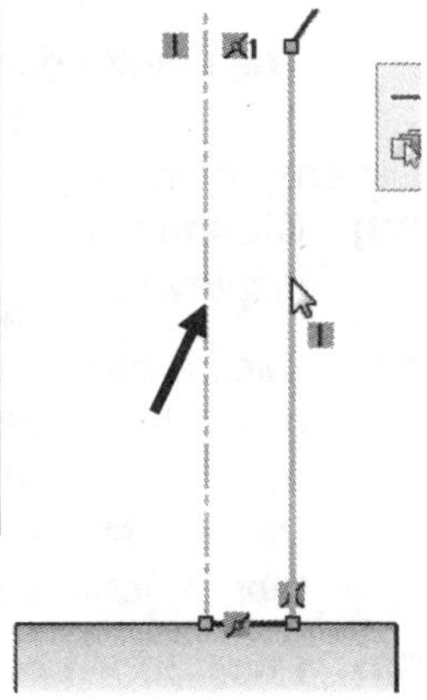

To manually add a geometric relation, click a sketch entity. Hold the Ctrl key down. Click the second sketch entity. The Properties PropertyManager is displayed. Click the needed geometric relation. See SOLIDWORKS Help for additional information.

Add relations, then dimensions. This keeps the user from having too many unnecessary dimensions. This also helps to show the design intent of the model.

Mirror the open sketch profile.

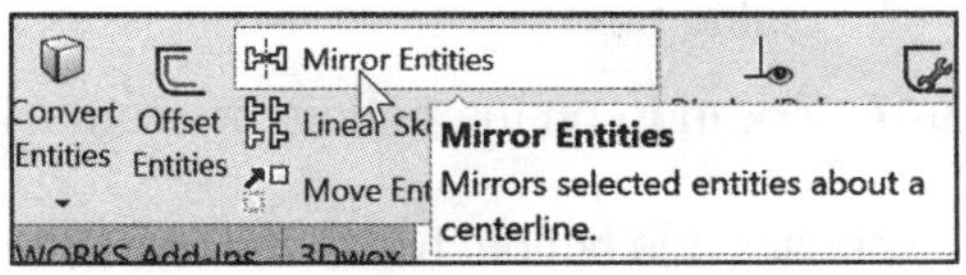

76) Click the **Mirror Entities** Sketch tool. The Mirror PropertyManager is displayed.

77) Click inside the **Mirror about** box.

78) Click the **Centerline** in the Graphics window. Line1 is displayed in the Mirror about box.

79) Click inside the **Entities to mirror** box.

Window-select the sketch entities.

80) Right-click in the **upper left corner** of the Graphics Window as illustrated.

81) **Drag** the mouse pointer to the lower right corner as illustrated.

82) **Release** the mouse button. The 5 sketch entities are displayed in the Entities to mirror box.

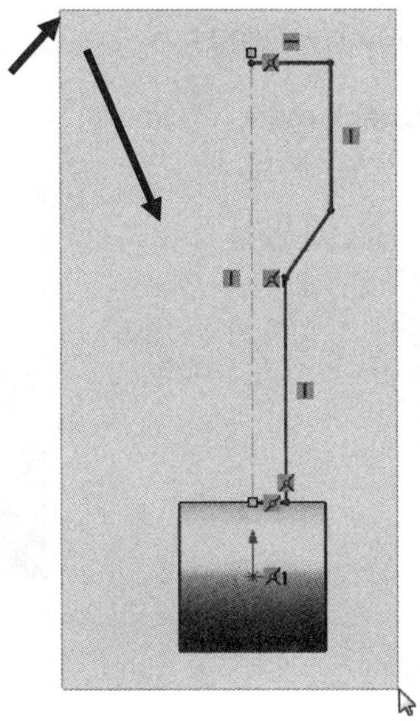

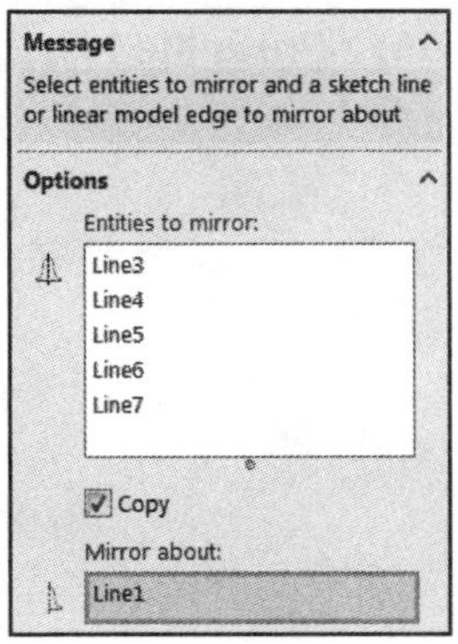

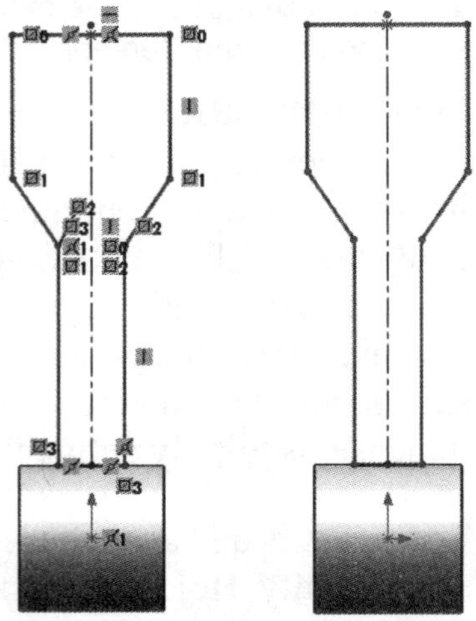

83) Click **OK** from the Mirror PropertyManager.

Deselect the Sketch Relations.

84) Click **View**, **Hide/Show**, uncheck **Sketch Relations** from the Main menu. View the results in the Graphics window.

Dimension the Sketch.

85) Click **Smart Dimension** from the Sketch toolbar.

The pointer displays the dimension symbol icon.

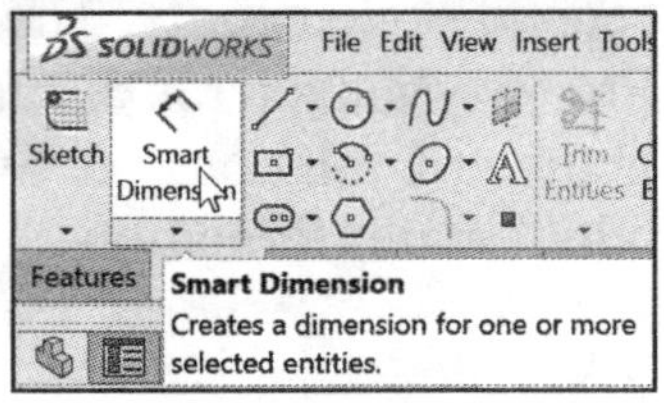

Dimension the angle.

86) Click the **two** illustrated lines. A dimension value is displayed.

87) Click a **position** to the left as illustrated. The Modify dialog box is displayed. The Smart Dimension tool uses the Smart Dimension PropertyManager. The PropertyManager provides the ability to select three tabs. Each tab provides a separate menu.

88) Enter **30**deg in the Modify dialog box. The Dimension Modify dialog box provides the ability to select a unit drop-down menu to modify units in a sketch or feature from the document properties.

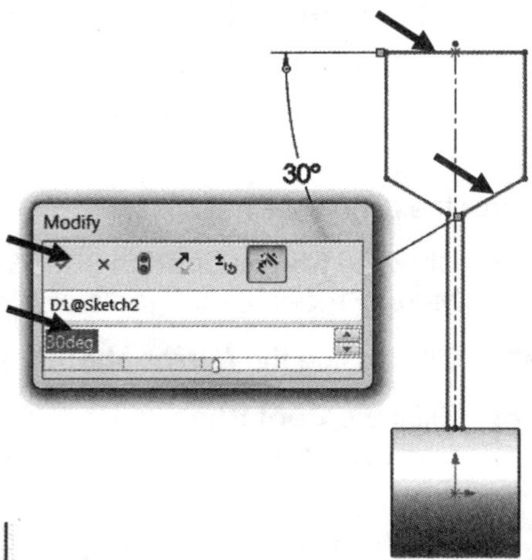

89) Click the **Green Check mark** in the Modify dialog box.

90) **Zoom in** on the bottom horizontal line.

Dimension the bottom horizontal line.

91) Click the **bottom horizontal line** as illustrated.

92) Click a position **below** the model.

93) Enter **4**mm in the Modify dialog box.

94) Click the **Green Check mark** in the Modify dialog box.

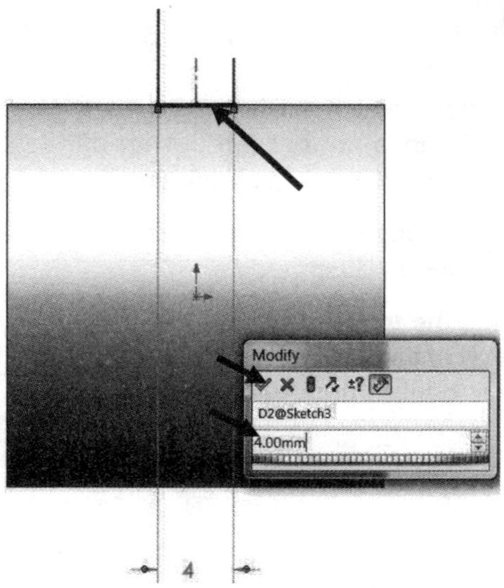

Fit the model to the Graphics window.

95) Press the **f** key.

Dimension the overall width of the top horizontal line.

96) Click the **top horizontal line** as illustrated.

97) Click a position **above** the model.

98) Enter **10**mm in the Modify dialog box.

99) Click the **Green Check mark** in the Modify dialog box.

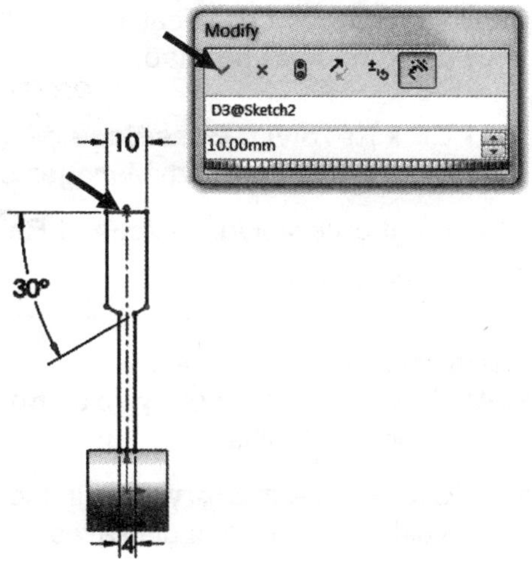

Dimension the first vertical line to the right.

100) Click the **first vertical line** as illustrated.

101) Click a position to the **right** of the line.

102) Enter **30**mm in the Modify dialog box.

103) Click the **Green check mark** in the Modify dialog box.

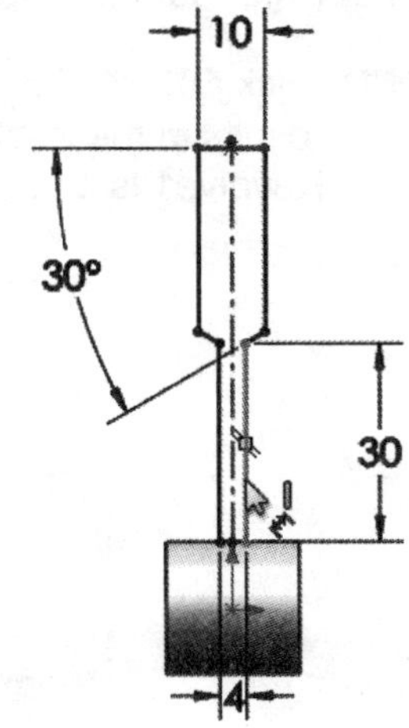

Dimension the overall height.

104) Click the **top horizontal line**.

105) Click the **bottom horizontal line**.

106) Click a position to the **right** of the line as illustrated.

107) Enter **35**mm in the Modify dialog box.

108) Click the **Green check mark** in the Modify dialog box. The sketch is fully defined and is displayed in black.

Display an Isometric view.

109) Click **Isometric view** from the Heads-up View toolbar.

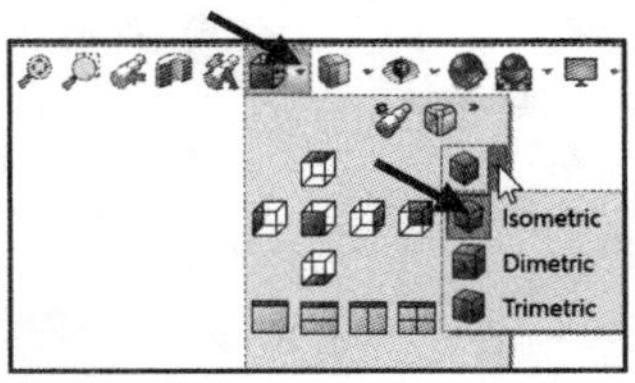

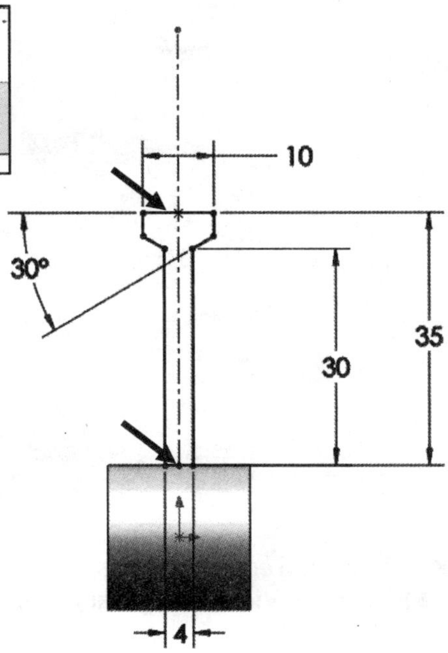

Create a Revolved Boss Feature.

110) Click the **Features** tab.

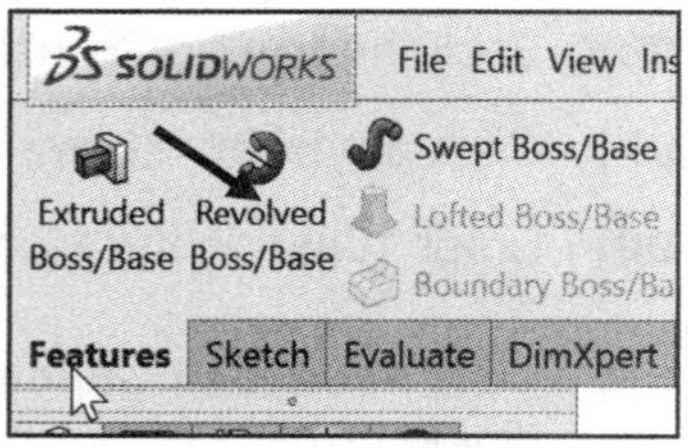

111) Click **Revolved Boss/Base** from the Features toolbar. The Revolve PropertyManager is displayed.

112) Right-click inside the **Axis of Revolution** box.

113) Click **Delete**.

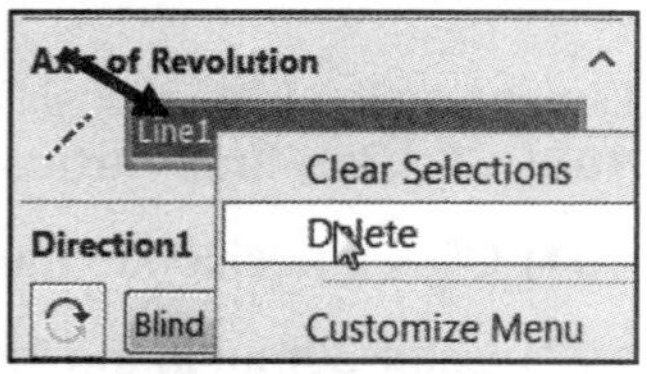

Display the Temporary Axes.

114) Click **View Temporary Axes** from the Hide/Show Items in the Heads-up toolbar.

115) Click the **Temporary Axis** in the Graphics window as illustrated. Axis 1 is displayed in the Axis of Revolution box.

116) Enter **360** for Direction 1 Angle.

117) Click **OK** from the Revolve PropertyManager. View the results in the FeatureManager and in the Graphics window. Revolve1 is created.

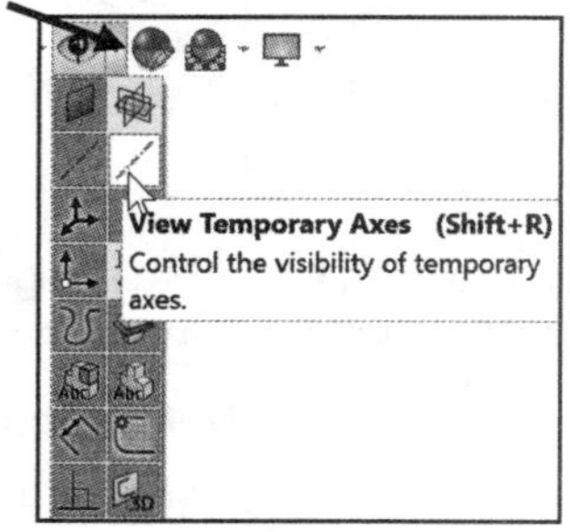

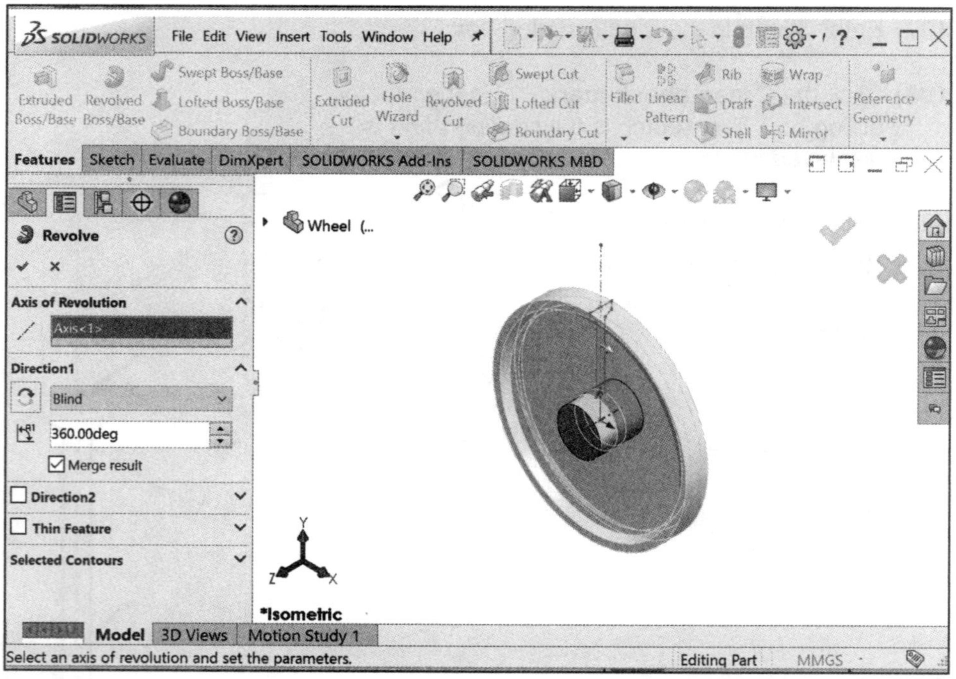

Deactivate the Temporary Axes.

118) Uncheck **View Temporary Axes** from the Hide/Show Items in the Heads-up toolbar.

119) Click **inside** the Graphics window.

120) **Expand** Revolve1 in the FeatureManager. Sketch2 is fully defined.

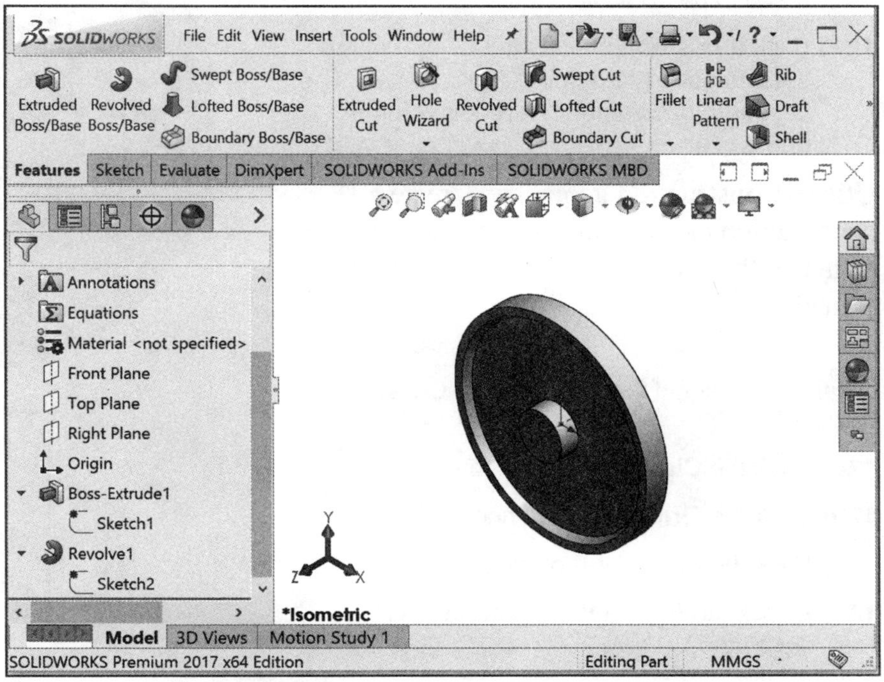

Activity: Create the Third Feature of the Wheel - Extruded Cut (Slot)

Display a Front view.

121) Click **Front view** from the Heads-up View toolbar.

Utilize the Centerpoint Straight Slot Sketch tool on the front face of the Wheel.

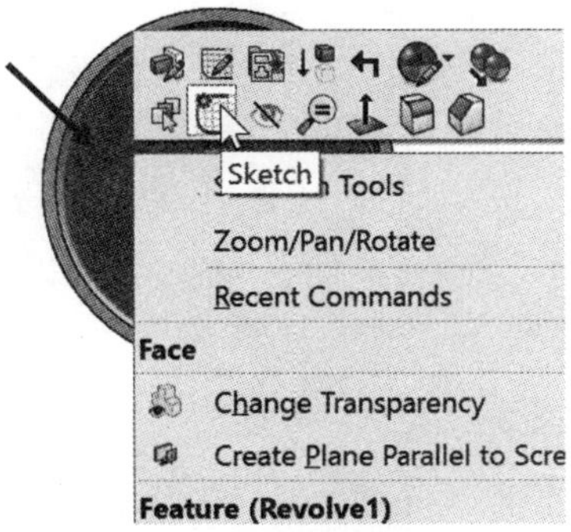

122) Right-click the **front face** of the Wheel as illustrated. The Context toolbar is displayed.

123) Click **Sketch** from the Context toolbar.

124) Click **Centerpoint Straight Slot** from the Consolidated Sketch toolbar. The Slot PropertyManager is displayed.

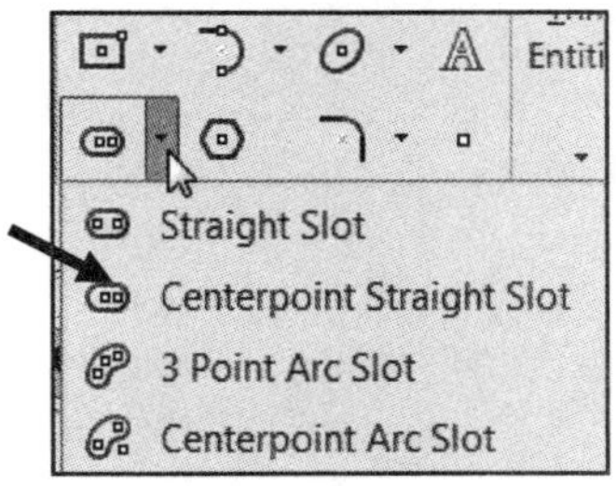

125) Click a **position** directly above the origin (first point).

126) Click a **position** directly above the first point (second point) as illustrated.

127) Click a **position** directly to the right of the second point (third point) as illustrated. The Centerpoint Straight Slot requires three points.

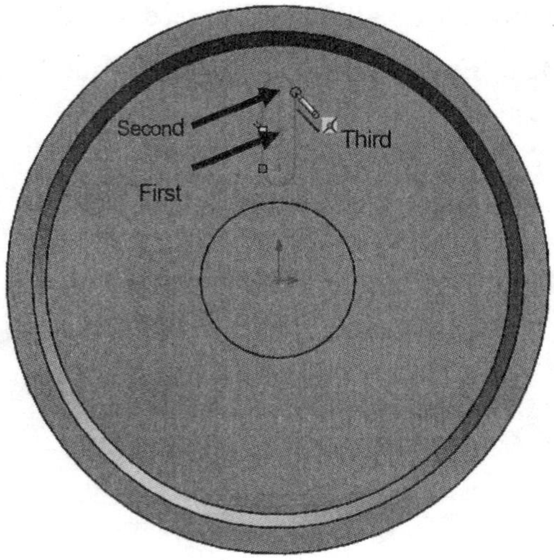

Utilize Construction geometry. Create a construction circle to locate the position of the center of the Slot relative to the Origin of the Wheel.

Locate the center of the slot. Create a Construction Circle.

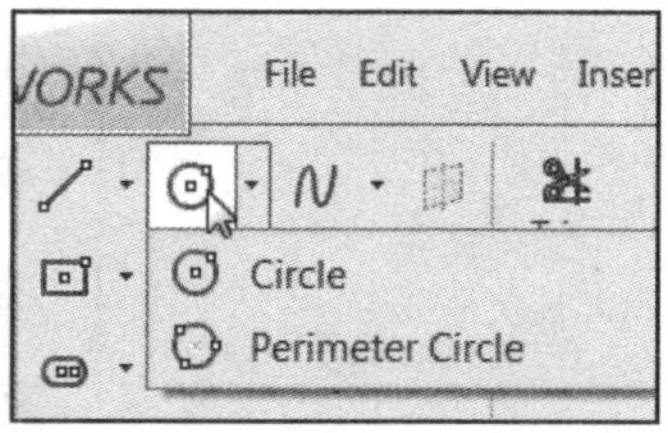

128) Click the **Circle** Sketch tool.

129) Click the **Origin** of the Wheel.

130) Click the **First point** of the slot.

131) Check the **For construction** box as illustrated.

132) Click **OK** from the Circle PropertyManager. A Construction circle is displayed.

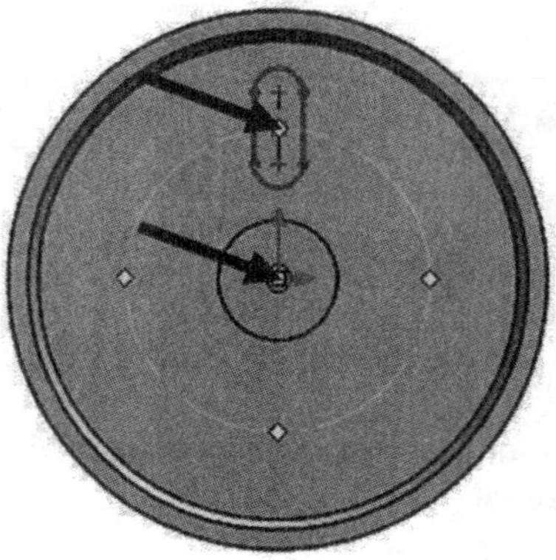

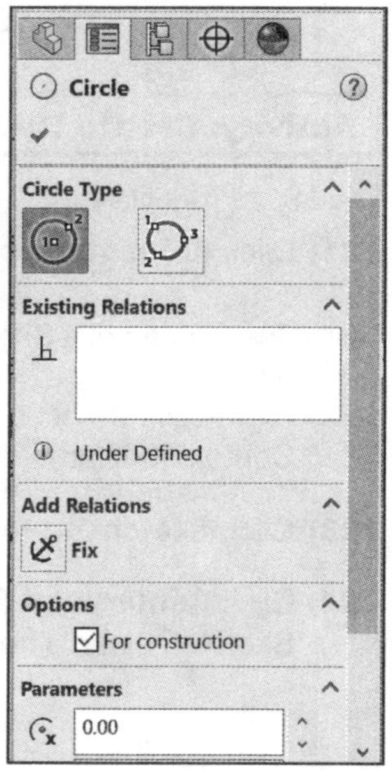

Insert dimensions to fully define the sketch.

133) Click **Smart Dimension** from the Sketch toolbar. The pointer displays the dimension symbol icon.

134) Enter the **dimensions** as illustrated. The sketch is fully defined and is displayed in black.

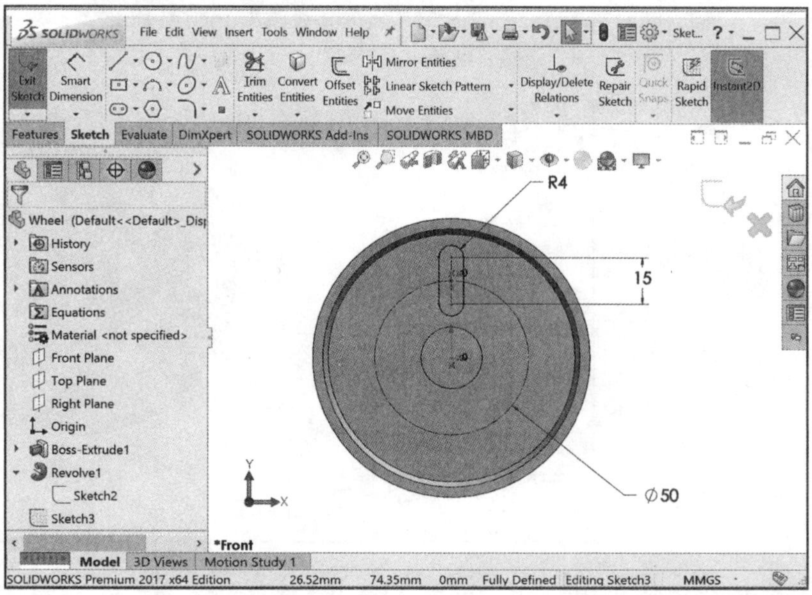

Create the Extruded Cut feature. The Extruded Cut feature is the Seed feature for the Circular Pattern. A Seed feature is the original feature for any type of pattern (linear, circular, sketch driven, curve driven, fill or mirrored pattern).

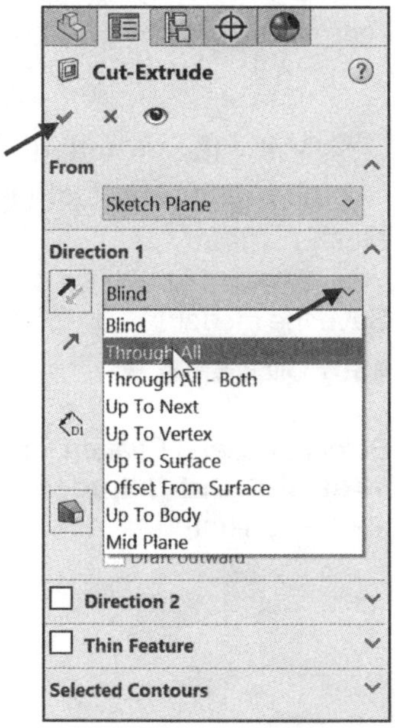

Create the Extruded Cut Feature.

135) Click the **Features** tab. Click **Extruded Cut** from the Features toolbar. The Cut Extrude PropertyManager is displayed.

136) Select **Through All** for End Condition. View your End Condition options.

137) Click **OK** from the Cut-Extrude PropertyManager. View the results in the Graphics window. Cut-Extrude1 is highlighted in the FeatureManager.

Use various end conditions to ensure proper design intent.

View Sketch3.

138) Expand Cut-Extrude1 in the Part FeatureMananger. Sketch3 is fully defined.

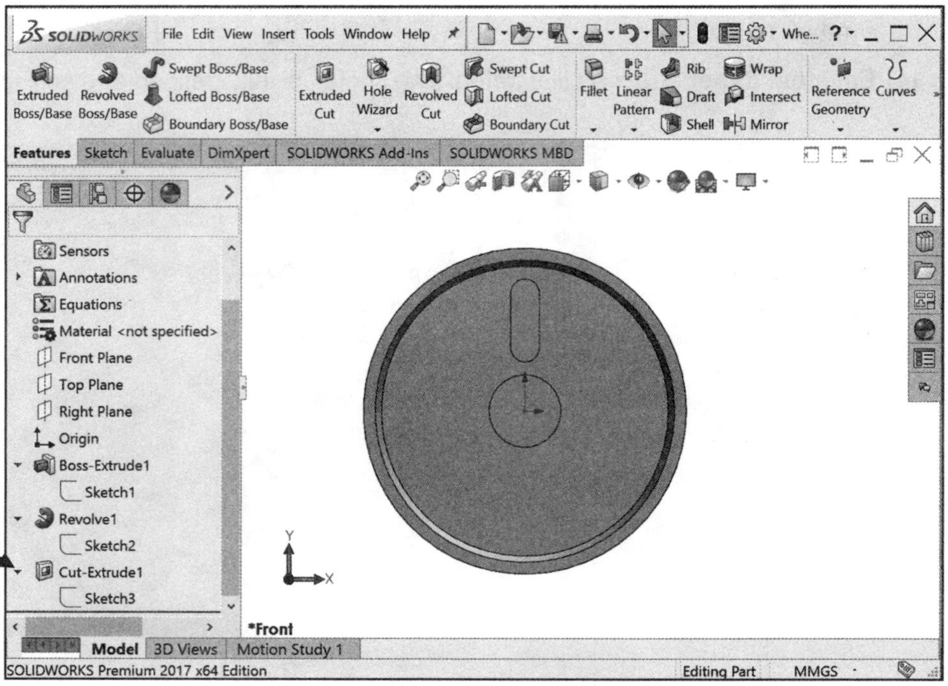

Cut Extrude1 is the seed feature for the Circular Pattern of slots on the Wheel. In the next section, create the Circular Pattern feature.

View the provided videos on creating 2D Sketching, Sketch Planes and Sketch tools along with 3D Features and Design Intent.

Save the model.

139) Click **Save**.

Select the Seed Feature for the Circular Pattern.

140) Click **Cut-Extrude1** in the FeatureManager. Cut-Extrude1 is highlighted.

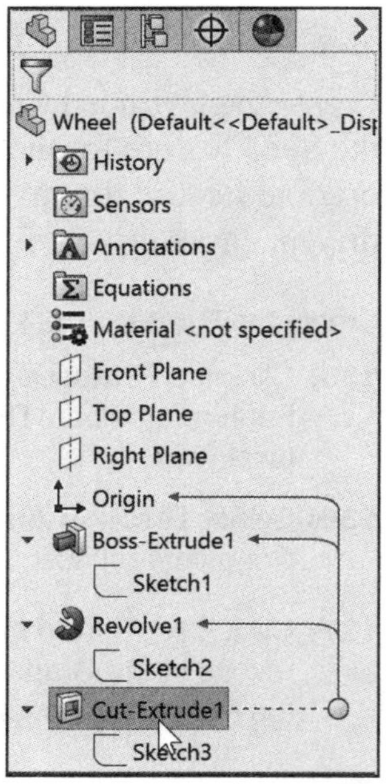

Activity: Create the Fourth Feature of the Wheel - Circular Pattern

Display an Isometric view.

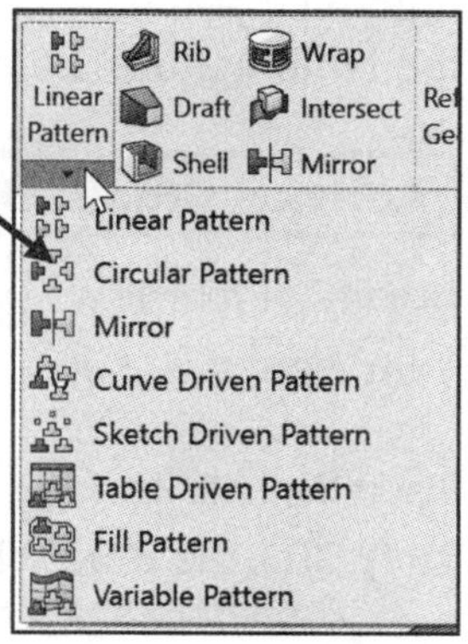

141) Click **Isometric view** from the Heads-up View toolbar.

Create the Circular Pattern feature.

142) Click **Circular Pattern** from the Features toolbar. The Circular Pattern PropertyManager is displayed. Cut-Extrude1 is selected and displayed in the Features to Pattern box.

Display the Temporary Axes.

143) Click **View Temporary Axes** from the Hide/Show Items in the Heads-up toolbar.

144) Click the **Temporary Axis** in the Graphics window. Axis <1> is displayed in the Pattern Axis box.

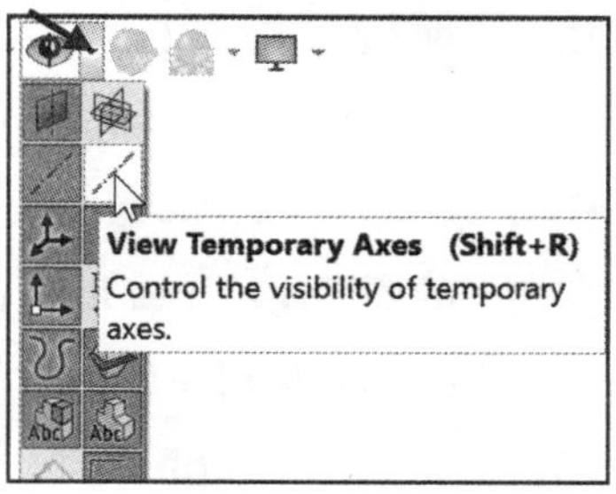

145) Check the **Equal spacing** box.

146) Enter **8** for Number of Instances.

147) Click **OK** from the Circular Pattern PropertyManager. CirPattern1 is displayed in the FeatureManager. View the circular pattern of slots in the model.

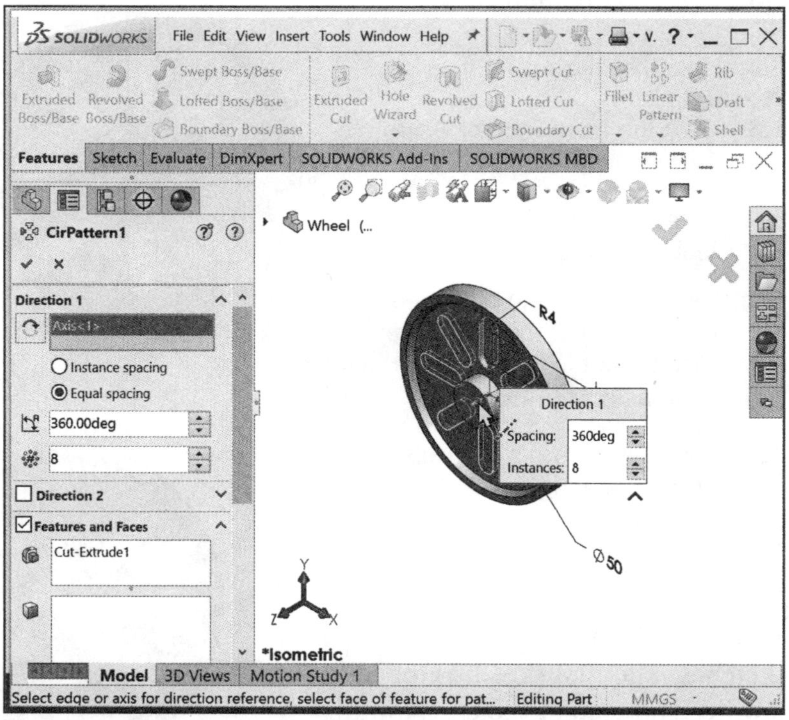

Deactivate the Temporary Axes.

148) Uncheck **View Temporary Axes** from the Hide/Show Items in the Heads-up toolbar.

Save the model.

149) Click **Save**.

The Wheel requires a hole. Apply the Hole Wizard feature. The Hole Wizard creates simple and complex Hole features by stepping through a series of options to define the hole type and hole position. The Hole Wizard requires a face or Sketch plane to position the Hole feature. Select the Front face of the hub.

Activity: Create the Fifth Feature of the Wheel - Hole

Display a Front view.

150) Click **Front view** from the Heads-up View toolbar.

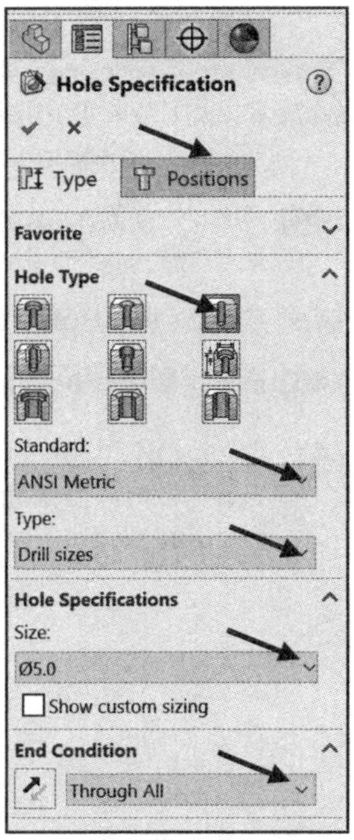

Insert the hole using the Hole Wizard tool.

151) Click the **Hole Wizard** Feature tool. The Hole Specification PropertyManager is displayed.

152) Click the **Type** tab.

153) Click the **Hole** icon for Hole Type.

154) Select **ANSI Metric** for Standard.

155) Select **Drill sizes** for Type.

156) Select **Ø5.0** for Size.

157) Select **Through All** for End Condition. Accept the default settings.

158) Click the **Positions** tab.

Select the Sketch plane for the Hole Wizard.

159) Click the **front face** of Base-Extrude1 as illustrated. Do not click the origin. The Point tool is selected.

160) Click the **origin** to place the center point of the hole. Right-click **Select** in the Graphics window to de-select the Point tool.

161) Click **OK** from the Hole Position PropertyManager. View the results.

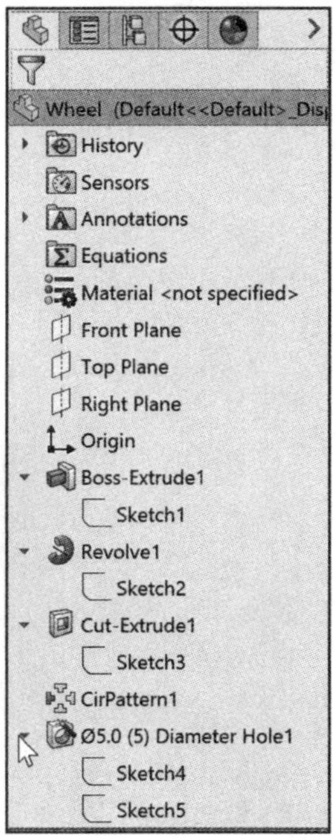

Fit the WHEEL to the Graphics window.

162) Press the **f** key.

The Hole Wizard tool creates two sketches. The first sketch is the hole profile. The second sketch is to fully define the hole location relative to the origin.

Fillet/Round creates a rounded internal or external face on the part. You can fillet all edges of a face, selected sets of faces, selected edges, or edge loops.

In the next section, apply the Fillet feature to the Wheel. Create a Constant Size Fillet feature to 6 edges and 2 faces with a 2mm radius.

Activity: Create the Sixth Feature of the Wheel - Constant Size Fillet Feature

Create a Constant Size Fillet Feature on six edges and two faces.

163) Click the **Fillet** Feature from the Features toolbar. The Fillet PropertyManager is displayed.

164) Click the **Manual** tab.

165) Click **Constant Size Fillet** for Fillet Type.

166) Enter **2**mm for Radius in the Fillet Parameters box.

167) Click the **front narrow face** of Revolve 1 as illustrated. Face1 is displayed in the Items To Fillet box.

168) Click the **front edge** of Boss-Extrude1 in the Graphics window. Edge1 is displayed in the Items To Fillet box.

169) Click the **back edge** of the hub. Edge2 is displayed in the Items To Fillet box.

170) Click the **inside circuluar edge** of Revolve1. Edge3 is displayed in the Items To Fillet box.

171) Rotate the **Wheel** and select the **three edges** and **face** as above. Edge4, Edge5, Edge6 and Face2 are dispayed in the Items To Fillet box.

172) Click **OK** from the Fillet FeatureManager. Fillet1 is displayed in the FeatureManager.

173) **Rotate** the Wheel and view the results in the Graphics window.

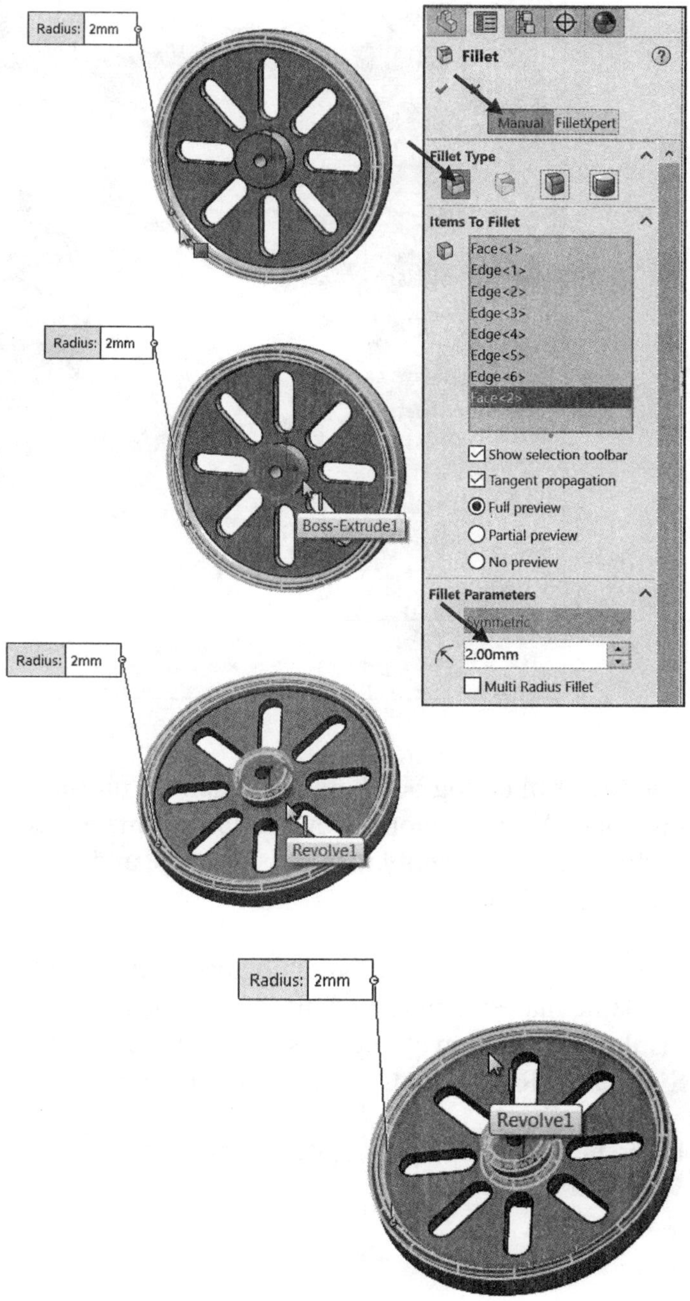

Save the model.

174) Click **Save**.

Display a Trimetric view.

175) Click **Trimetric view** from the Heads-up View toolbar.

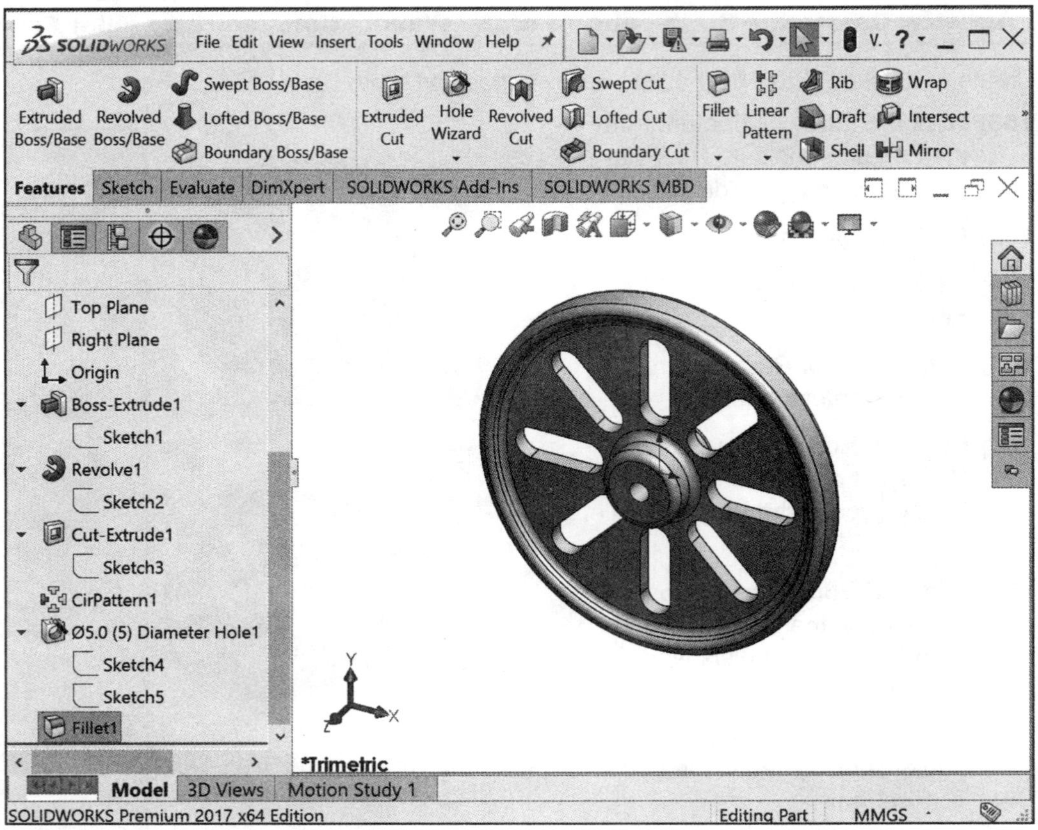

The Material dialog box helps you manage physical materials. You can work with pre-defined materials, create custom materials, apply materials to parts, and manage favorites.

The left side of the Material dialog box contains a tree of available material types and materials. Tabs on the right display information about the selected material. If SOLIDWORKS Simulation is added in, more tabs appear.

In the next section, apply material (6061 Alloy) to the Wheel.

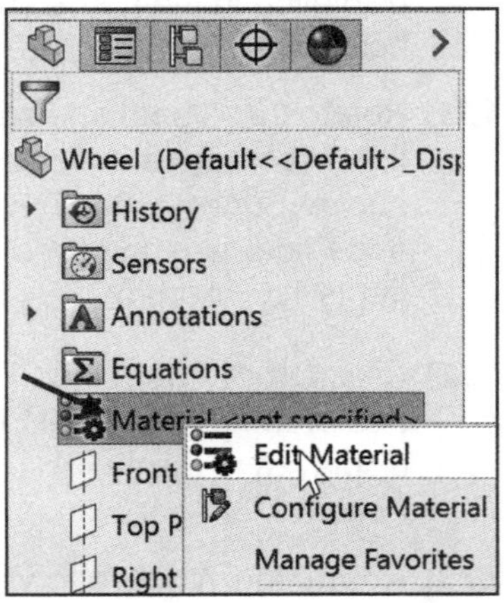

Activity: Apply Material to the Wheel

Apply Material.

176) Right-click **Material** from the FeatureManager.

177) Click **Edit Material**. The Material dialog box is displayed. View your options and material choices.

178) **Expand** the Aluminum Alloy folder.

179) Click **6061 Alloy**.

180) Click **Apply**.

181) Click **Close**. The Material is applied to the model.

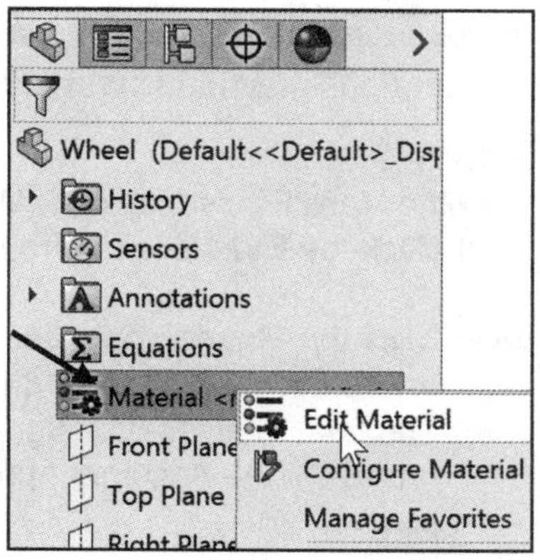

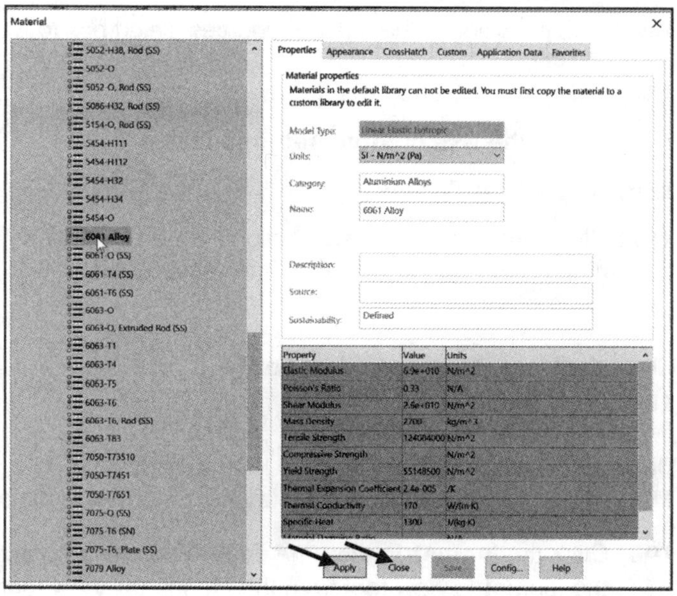

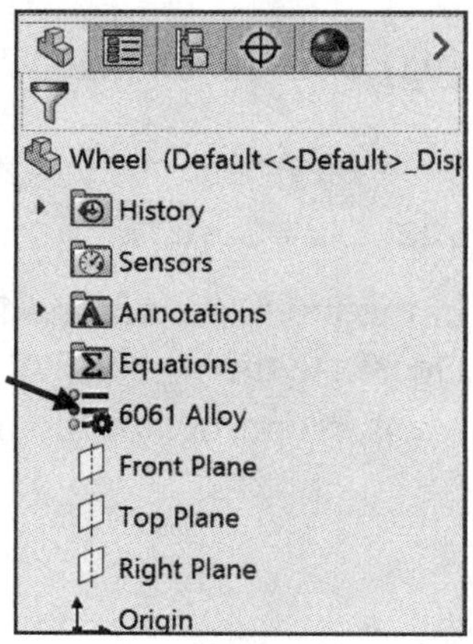

Activity: View the Mass Properties of the Wheel

View the calculated mass properties of the model. You can assign values for mass, center of mass, and moments of inertia to override the calculated values.

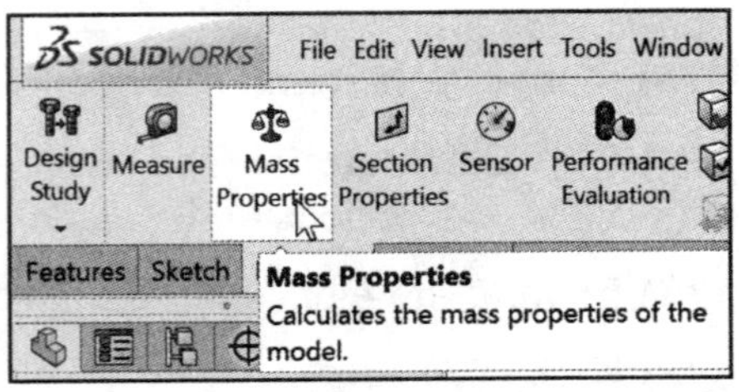

View the Mass Properties of the Wheel.

182) Click the **Evaluate** tab from the CommandManager.

183) Click the **Mass Properties** icon. The Mass Properties dialog box is displayed. View the results. The total mass is 83.27 grams. The numbers represent the document properties (2 decimal places).

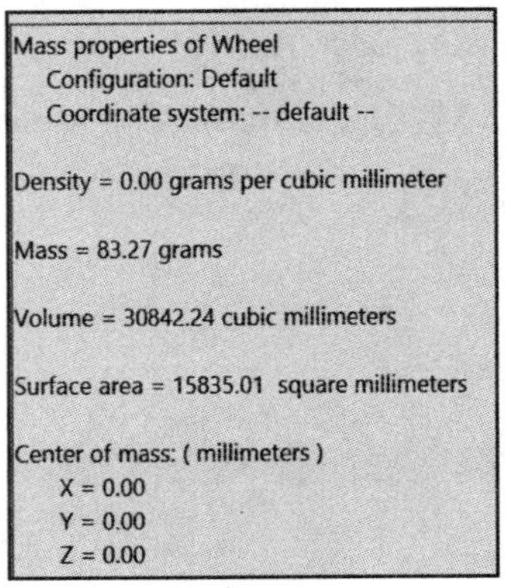

Modify the precision in the Mass Properties dialog box to view Density.

184) Click the **Options** button.

185) Check the **Use custom settings** button.

186) Select **4** for Decimal places.

187) Click **OK** from the Mass/Section Property Options dialog box. Density = .0027 grams per cubic millimeters.

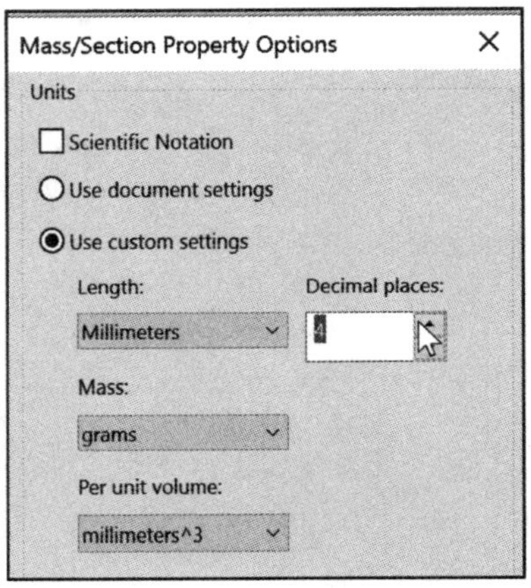

Close the Mass Properties dialog box.

188) Click **Close**.

Display an Isometric view - Shaded With Edges.

189) Press the **space bar** to display the Orientation dialog box.

190) Click the **Isometric view** icon. You can also access the Isometric view tool from the Heads-up View toolbar.

191) Click the **Shaded With Edges** icon.

Save the Wheel.

192) Click **Save**.

In the next section, modify the Circular Pattern feature. Decrease the number of instances from 8 to 4. Compare the Mass Properties of the modified model.

Activity: Modify the Circular Pattern. Decrease the Number of Instances.

Modify the CirPattern1 feature.

193) Right-click **CirPattern1** from the FeatureManager.

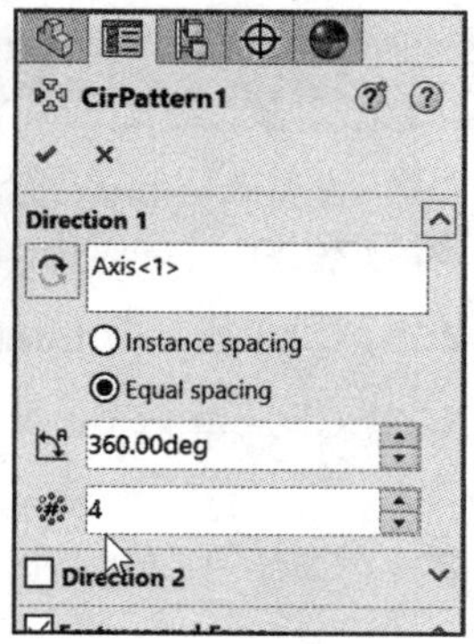

194) Click **Edit Feature** from the Content toolbar. The CirPattern1 PropertyManager is displayed.

195) Enter **4** for Number of Instances.

196) Click **OK** from the CirPattern PropertyManager. View the results in the PropertyManager.

Activity: View the New Mass Properties of the Wheel

197) Click the **Evaluate** tab from the CommandManager.

198) Click the **Mass Properties** icon. The Mass Properties dialog box is displayed. View the results. The total mass is 90.63 grams vs. 83.27 grams. You removed 4 slots (instances) from the model.

Close the Mass Properties dialog box.

199) Click **Close**.

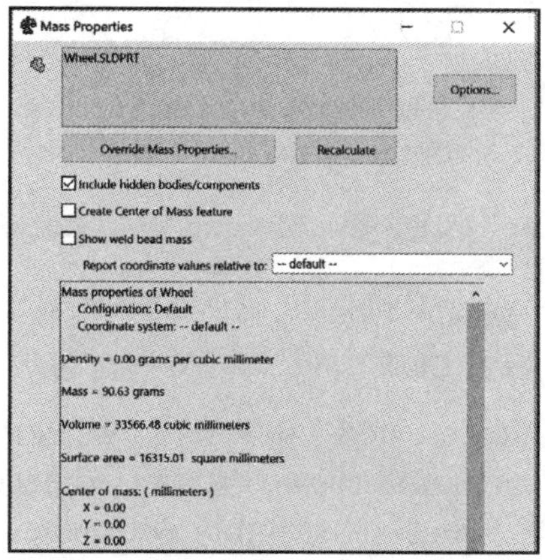

Activity: Modify the Circular Pattern. Return to the Original Instances.

Modify the CirPattern1 feature.

200) Right-click **CirPattern1** from the FeatureManager.

201) Click **Edit Feature** from the Content toolbar. The CirPattern1 PropertyManager is displayed.

202) Enter **8** for Number of Instances.

203) Click **OK** from the CirPattern PropertyManager. View the results in the PropertyManager.

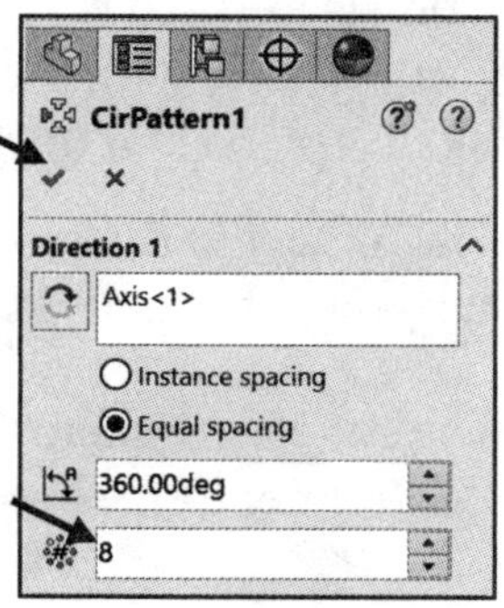

In the next section, add an Appearance to the Wheel. Use the Appearances PropertyManager to apply colors, material appearances, and transparency to parts and assembly components. The Appearance tool does not modify the mass properties.

Activity: Add an Appearance to the Wheel

Add an Appearance to the Wheel.

204) Right-click **Wheel** in the FeatureManager.

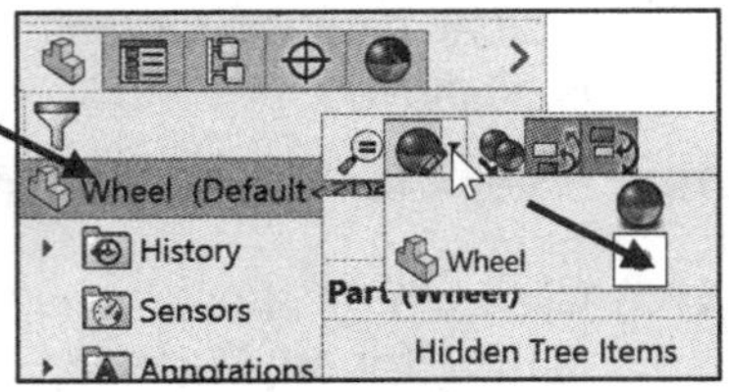

205) Click the **Appearances** drop-down arrow.

206) Click the **Edit color** box. The color PropertyManager is displayed.

207) Click a **color (yellow)** from the Color dialog box.

208) Click **OK** from the color PropertyManager. View the results in the Graphics window.

Display an Isometric view - Shaded With Edges.

209) Press the **space bar** to display the Orientation dialog box.

210) Click the **Isometric view** icon. You can also access the Isometric view tool from the Heads-up View toolbar.

211) Click the **Shaded With Edges** icon.

Save the Wheel.

212) Click **Save**. You are finished with the part.

You created a new part (Wheel) that is used in the next chapter to create the Fly Wheel sub-assembly. The Fly Wheel sub-assembly with other provided components is used to create the final Stirling Engine assembly.

Summary

You established a SOLIDWORKS session and created a new part (Wheel) with user defined document properties. The correct Sketch plane and orientation for the Wheel was selected.

The Wheel part is used in the Fly Wheel sub-assembly. The sub-assembly is used in the final Stirling Engine assembly.

The following sketch tools were utilized: Circle, Line, Centerline, Center point Straight Slot and Mirror Entities.

The following features were utilized: Extruded Boss/Base, Extruded Cut, Revolved Boss/Boss, Hole Wizard, Circular Pattern and Fillet.

Material and Appearance were applied with the proper design intent.

During the creation of the Wheel you learned about various Sketch states, editing Sketches and Features along with applying the following geometric relations: Coincident, Vertical, Horizontal, Tangent and Midpoint.

View the provided videos on creating 2D Sketching, Sketch Planes and Sketch tools along with 3D Features and Design Intent to enhance your user experience.

In Chapter 3, establish a SOLIDWORKS session and create two new assemblies with user defined document properties:

- Fly Wheel
- Stirling Engine

Insert the following Standard and Quick mate types: Coincident, Concentric, Distance and Tangent.

Utilize the following assembly tools: Insert Component, Suppress, Un-suppress, Mate, Move Component, Rotate Component, Interference Detection, Hide, Show, Flexible, Ridge and Multiple mate mode.

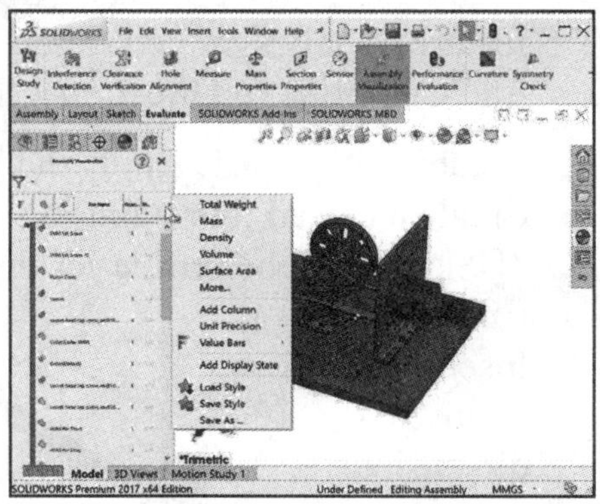

Create an Exploded View with animation.

Apply the Measure and Mass Properties tool to modify a component in the Stirling Engine assembly.

Exercises - Build Additional Parts

Tutorial: Mass-Volume 2-1

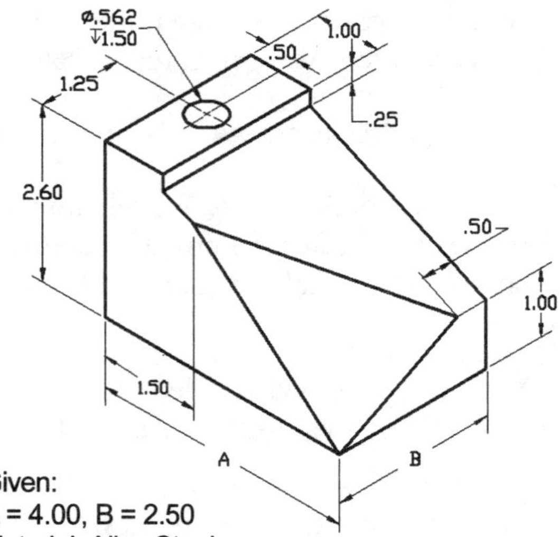

Given:
A = 4.00, B = 2.50
Material: Alloy Steel
Density = .278 lb/in^3
Units: IPS
Decimal places = 2

Build this model. Calculate the overall mass of the part and locate the Center of mass with the provided information.

1. **Create** a New part in SOLIDWORKS.
2. **Build** the illustrated model. Note the Depth/Deep ↧ symbol with a 1.50 dimension associated with the hole. The hole Ø.562 has a three decimal place precision. Insert three features: Extruded Base (Boss-Extrude1) and two Extruded Cuts. Insert a 3D sketch for the first Extruded Cut feature.

There are numerous ways to build the models in this chapter. A goal is to display different design intents and techniques.

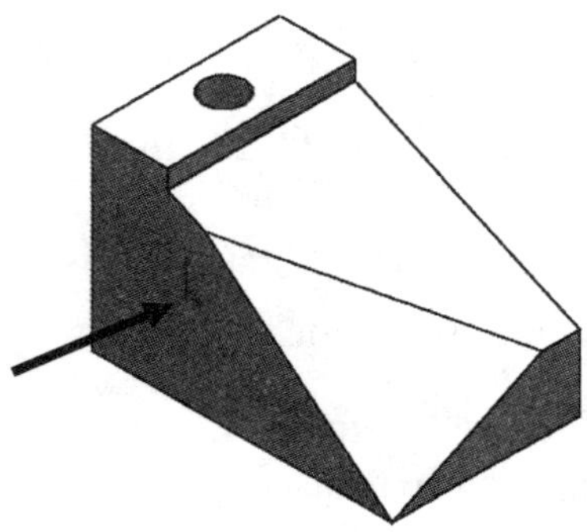

3. **Set** the document properties for the model.
4. Create **Sketch1**. Select the Front Plane as the Sketch plane. The part Origin is located in the lower left corner of the sketch. Insert the required geometric relations and dimensions.
5. Create the **Extruded Base (Boss-Extrude1)** feature. Apply symmetry. Select the Mid Plane End Condition in Direction 1. Depth = 2.50in.

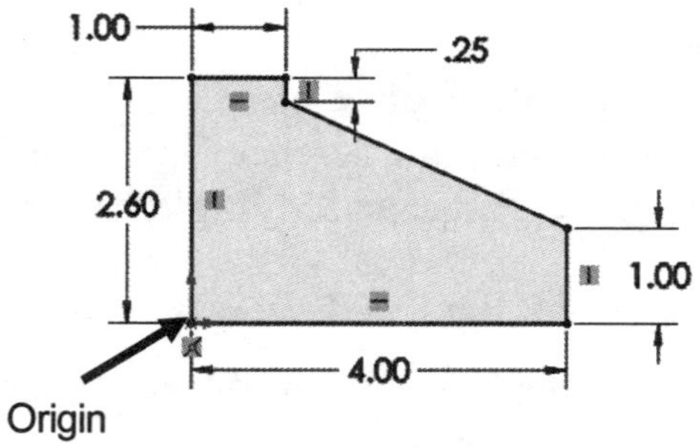

6. Create **3DSketch1**. Apply the Line Sketch tool. Create a closed four point 3D sketch. 3DSketch1 is the profile for the first Extruded Cut feature. Insert the required dimensions.

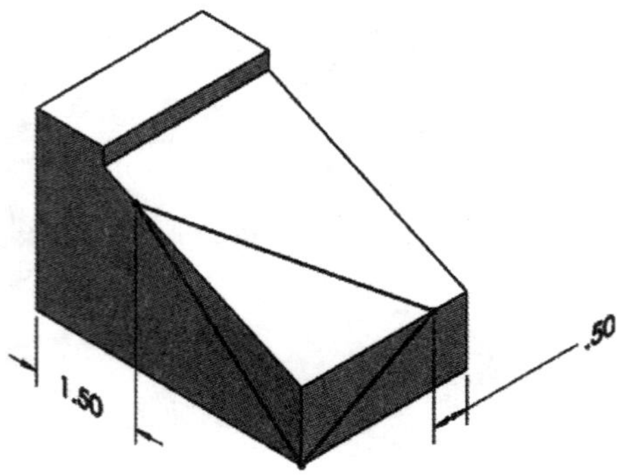

7. Create the first **Extruded Cut** feature. Blind is the default End Condition. Select the top face as illustrated to be removed. Note the direction of the extrude feature.

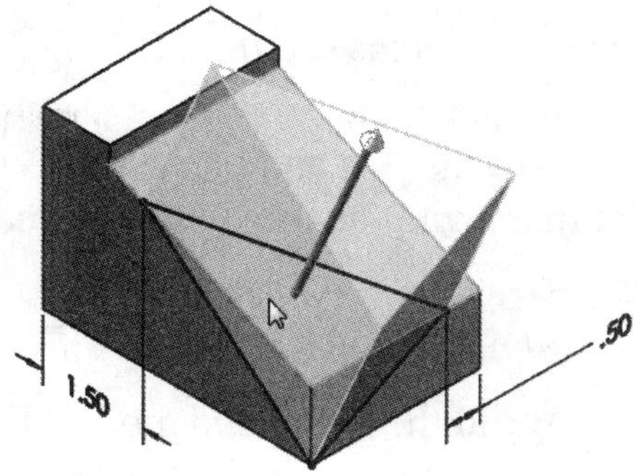

8. Create **Sketch2**. Select the top flat face of Boss-Extrude1. Sketch a circle. Insert the required geometric relations and dimensions. The hole diameter Ø.562 has a three decimal place precision.

9. Create the second **Extruded Cut** feature. Blind is the default End Condition. Depth = 1.50in. Note: For the exam, you do not need to insert the Depth/Deep ↧ symbol or note.

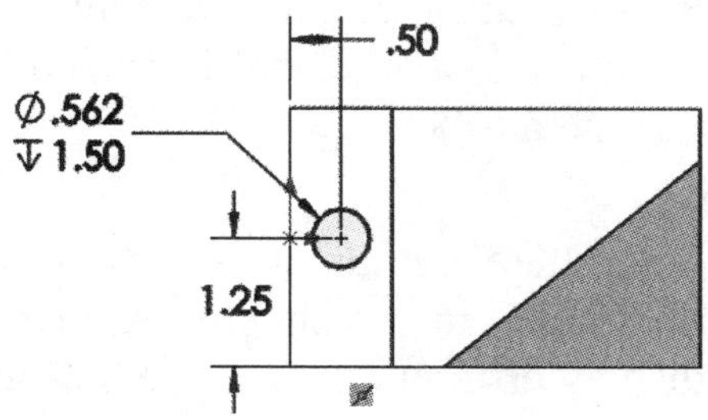

10. **Assign** Alloy Steel material to the part.

11. **Calculate** the overall mass. The overall mass = 4.97 pounds.

12. **Locate** the Center of mass. The location of the Center of mass is derived from the part Origin.

- X: 1.63 inches
- Y: 1.01 inches
- Z: -0.04 inches

View the triad location of the Center of mass for the part.

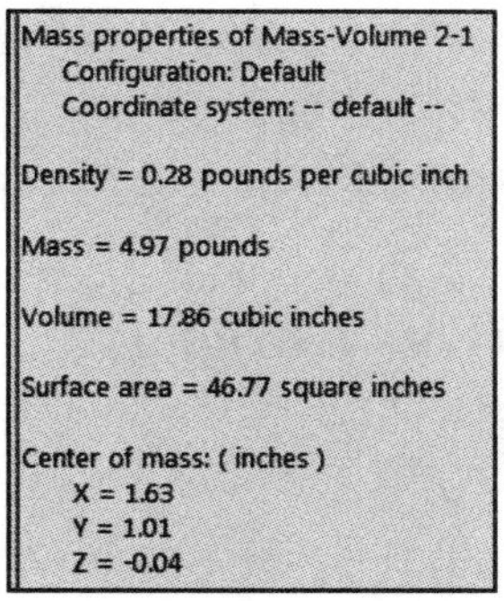
Mass properties of Mass-Volume 2-1
Configuration: Default
Coordinate system: -- default --

Density = 0.28 pounds per cubic inch

Mass = 4.97 pounds

Volume = 17.86 cubic inches

Surface area = 46.77 square inches

Center of mass: (inches)
X = 1.63
Y = 1.01
Z = -0.04

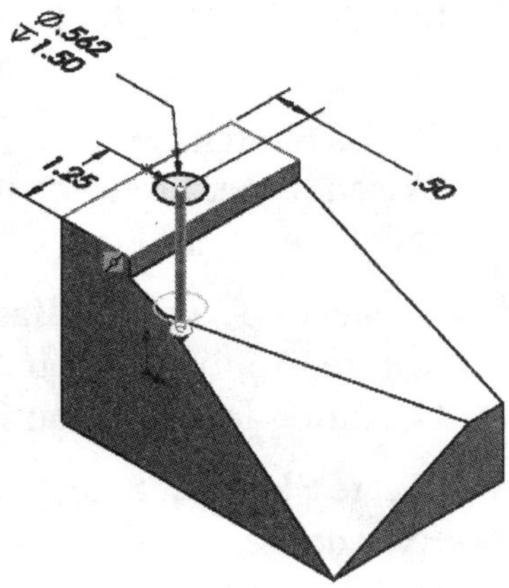

13. **Save** the part and name it Mass-Volume 2-1.

14. **Close** the model.

As an exercise, calculate the overall mass of the part using 6061 Alloy.

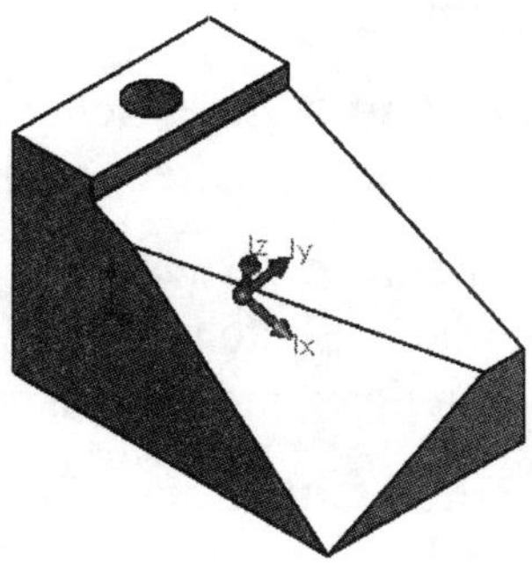

Modify the "A" dimension from 4.00 to 4.50. Modify the hole dimension from Ø.562 to Ø.575. The overall mass of the part = 1.93 pounds.

Save the part and name it Mass-Volume 2-1A.

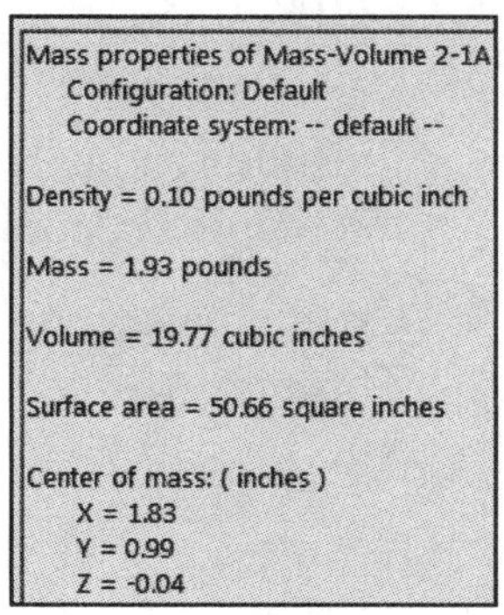
Mass properties of Mass-Volume 2-1A
Configuration: Default
Coordinate system: -- default --

Density = 0.10 pounds per cubic inch

Mass = 1.93 pounds

Volume = 19.77 cubic inches

Surface area = 50.66 square inches

Center of mass: (inches)
X = 1.83
Y = 0.99
Z = -0.04

Tutorial: Mass-Volume 2-2

Build this model. Calculate the overall mass of the part and locate the Center of mass with the provided information.

1. **Create** a New part in SOLIDWORKS.
2. **Build** the illustrated model. Think about the required steps to build this part. Insert four features: Extruded Base, two Extruded Cuts and a Fillet.

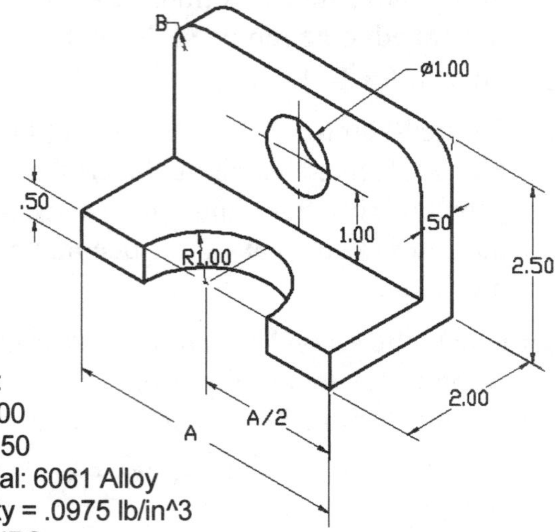

Given:
A = 4.00
B = R.50
Material: 6061 Alloy
Density = .0975 lb/in^3
Units: IPS
Decimal places = 2

There are numerous ways to build the models in this chapter. A goal is to display different design intents and techniques.

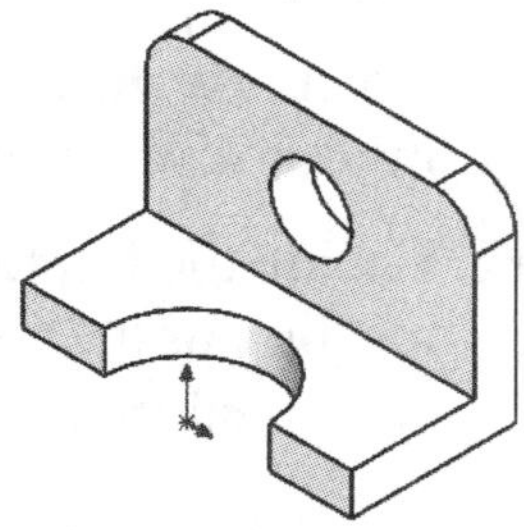

3. **Set** the document properties for the model.
4. Create **Sketch1**. Select the Right Plane as the Sketch plane. Insert the required geometric relations and dimensions.

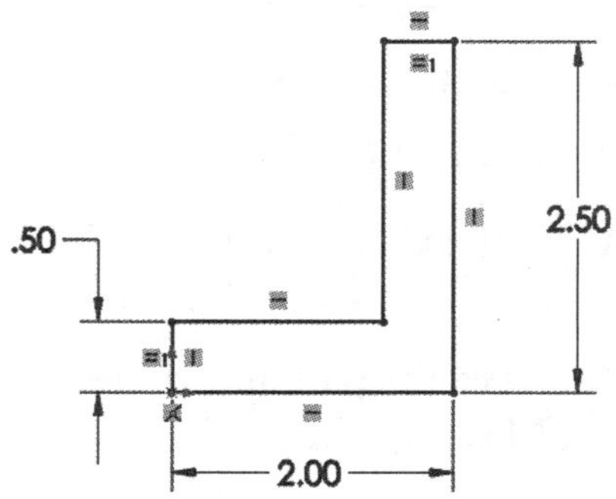

5. Create the **Extruded Base (Boss-Extrude1)** feature. Apply symmetry. Select the Mid Plane End Condition for Direction 1. Depth = 4.00in.
6. Create **Sketch2**. Select the top flat face of Boss-Extrude1 as the Sketch plane. Sketch a circle. The center of the circle is located at the part Origin. Insert the required dimension.
7. Create the first **Extruded Cut** feature. Select Through All for End Condition in Direction 1.
8. Create **Sketch3**. Select the front vertical face of Extrude1 as the Sketch plane. Sketch a circle. Insert the required geometric relations and dimensions.

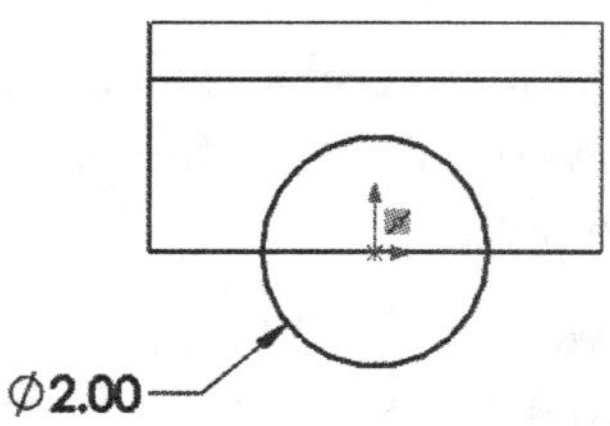

9. Create the second **Extruded Cut** feature. Select Through All for End Condition in Direction 1.

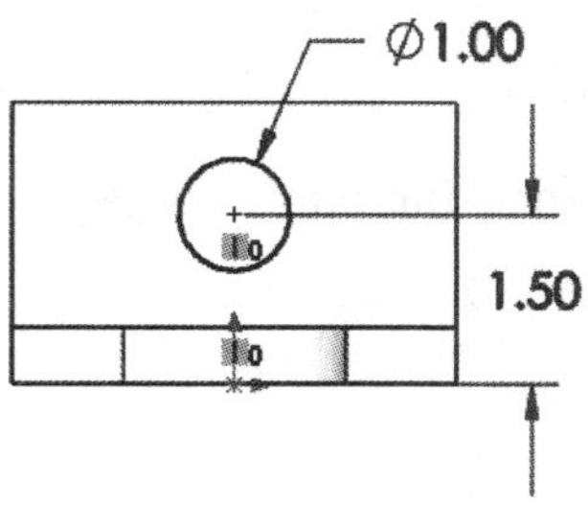

10. Create the **Fillet** feature. Constant radius is selected by default. Fillet the top two edges as illustrated. Radius = .50in.

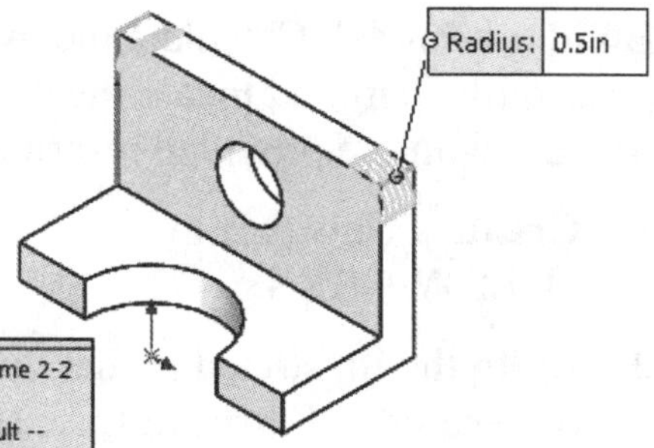

A Fillet feature removes material. Selecting the correct radius value is important to obtain the correct mass and volume answer in the exam.

11. **Assign** the defined material to the part.

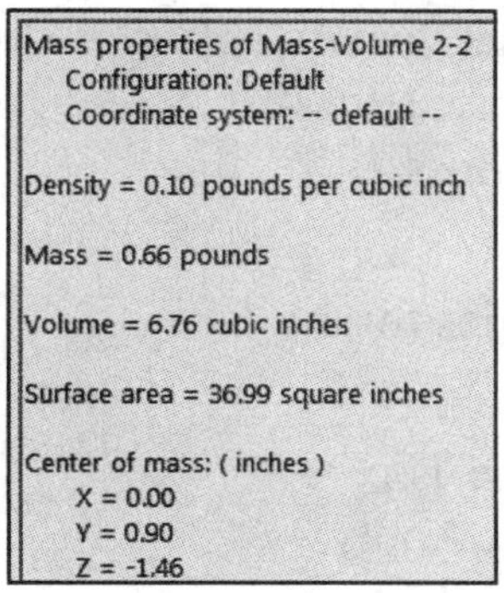
Mass properties of Mass-Volume 2-2
Configuration: Default
Coordinate system: -- default --

Density = 0.10 pounds per cubic inch

Mass = 0.66 pounds

Volume = 6.76 cubic inches

Surface area = 36.99 square inches

Center of mass: (inches)
X = 0.00
Y = 0.90
Z = -1.46

12. **Calculate** the overall mass. The overall mass = 0.66 pounds.

13. **Locate** the Center of mass. The location of the Center of mass is derived from the part Origin.

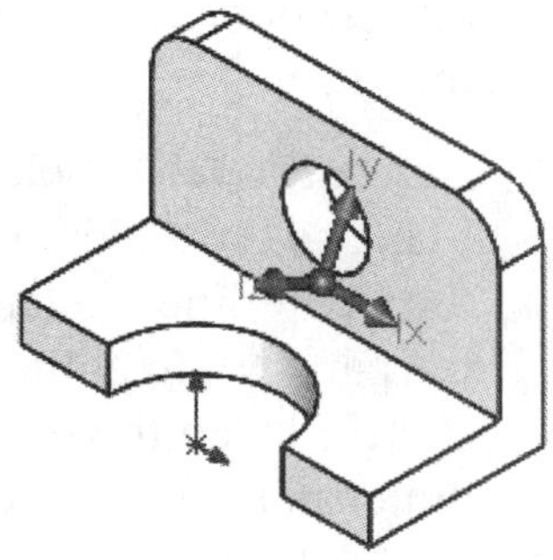

- X: 0.00 inches
- Y: 0.90 inches
- Z: -1.46 inches

Note: Tangent edges and Origin is displayed for educational purposes.

14. **Save** the part and name it Mass-Volume 2-2.

15. **Close** the model.

As an exercise, calculate the overall mass of the part using the MMGS unit system, and assign 2014 Alloy material to the part.

The overall mass of the part = 310.17 grams.

Save the part and name it Mass-Volume 2-2-MMGS.

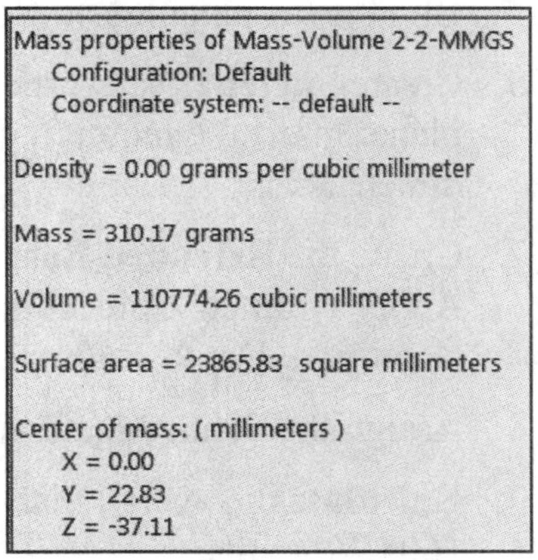
Mass properties of Mass-Volume 2-2-MMGS
Configuration: Default
Coordinate system: -- default --

Density = 0.00 grams per cubic millimeter

Mass = 310.17 grams

Volume = 110774.26 cubic millimeters

Surface area = 23865.83 square millimeters

Center of mass: (millimeters)
X = 0.00
Y = 22.83
Z = -37.11

Tutorial: Mass-Volume 2-3

Build this model. Calculate the overall mass of the part and locate the Center of mass with the provided information.

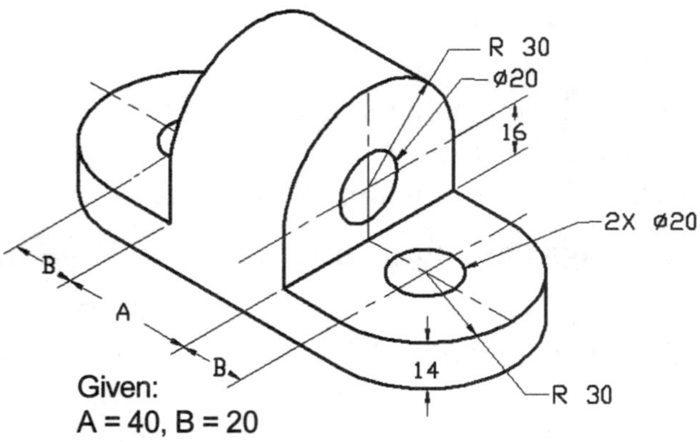

Given:
A = 40, B = 20
All Thru Holes
Material: Copper
Density = .0089 g/mm^3
Units: MMGS

1. **Create** a New part in SOLIDWORKS.
2. **Build** the illustrated model. Insert two features: Extruded Base (Boss-Extrude1) and Extruded Boss (Boss-Extrude2).
3. **Set** the document properties for the model.
4. Create **Sketch1**. Select the Top Plane as the Sketch plane. Apply the Centerline Sketch tool. Locate the part Origin at the center of the sketch. Insert the required geometric relations and dimensions. Note: This is a good case to use the Slot Sketch tool.

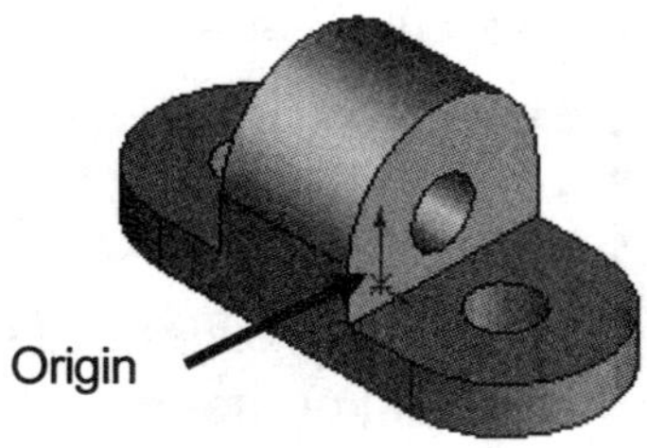

5. Create the **Extruded Base (Boss-Extrude1)** feature. Blind is the default End Condition. Depth = 14mm.
6. Create **Sketch2**. Select the Right Plane as the Sketch plane. Insert the required geometric relations and dimensions.

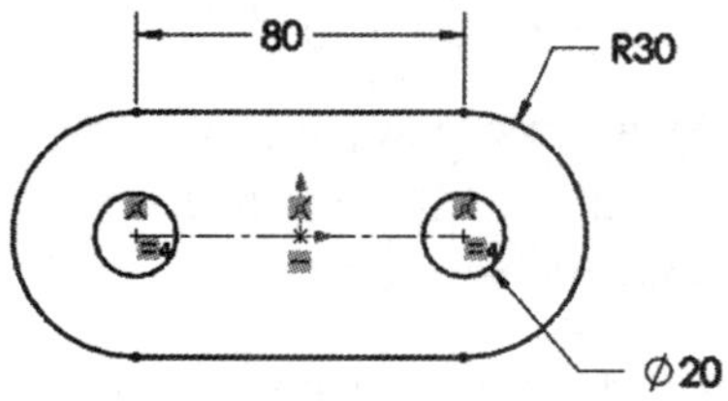

7. Create the **Extruded Boss (Boss-Extrude2)** feature. Apply symmetry. Select the Mid Plane End Condition. Depth = 40mm.
8. **Assign** the defined material to the part.
9. **Calculate** the overall mass. The overall mass = 1605.29 grams.

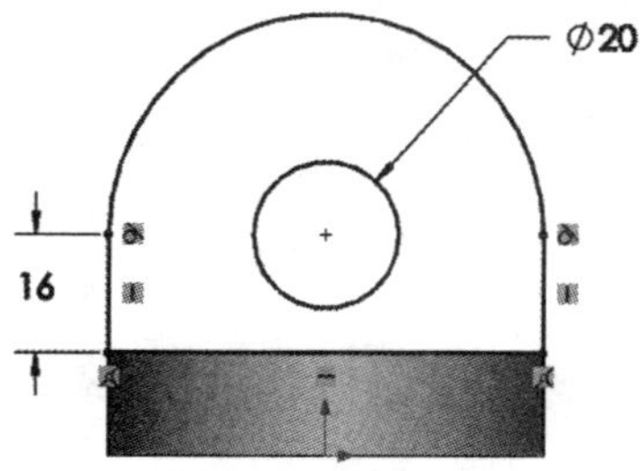

10. **Locate** the Center of mass. The location of the Center of mass is derived from the part Origin.

Density = 0.01 grams per cubic millimeter
Mass = 1605.29 grams
Volume = 180369.91 cubic millimeters
Surface area = 29918.76 square millimeters
Center of mass: (millimeters)
X = 0.00
Y = 19.79
Z = 0.00

- X: 0.00 millimeters
- Y: 19.79 millimeters
- Z: 0.00 millimeters

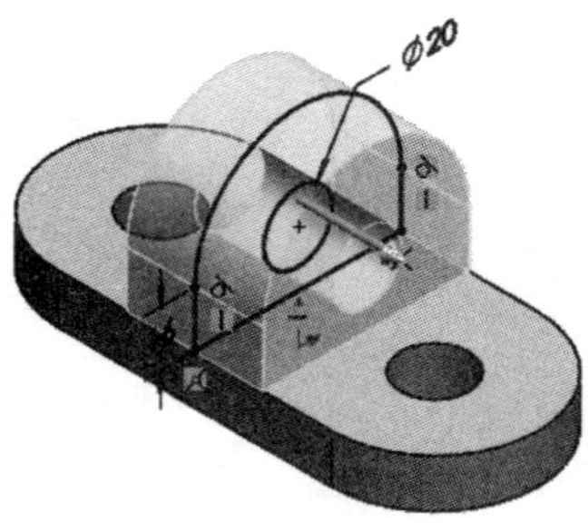

11. **Save** the part and name it Mass-Volume 2-3.
12. **Close** the model.

There are numerous ways to build the models in this chapter.

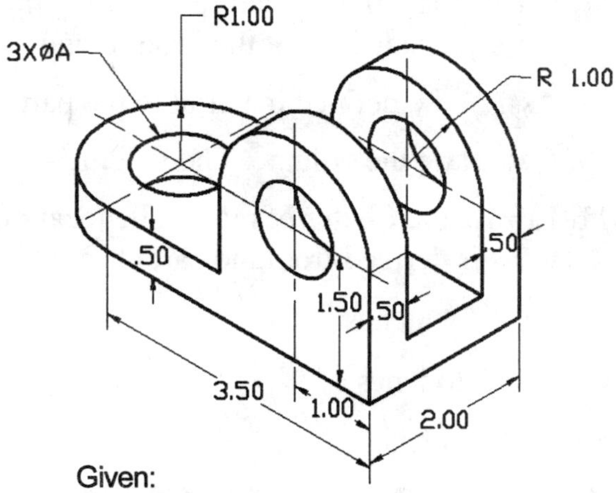

Given:
A = Ø1.00
All Thru Holes
Material: Brass
Density = .307 lb/in^3
Units: IPS
Decimal places = 2

Tutorial: Mass-Volume 2-4

Build this model. Calculate the volume of the part and locate the Center of mass with the provided information.

1. **Create** a New part in SOLIDWORKS.
2. **Build** the illustrated model. Insert three features: Extruded Base (Boss-Extrude1), Extruded Boss (Boss-Extrude2) and Mirror. Three holes are displayed with an Ø1.00in.
3. **Set** the document properties for the model.
4. Create **Sketch1**. Select the Top Plane as the Sketch plane. Apply the Tangent Arc and Line Sketch tool. Insert the required geometric relations and dimensions. Note the location of the Origin.
5. Create the **Extruded Base (Boss-Extrude1)** feature. Blind is the default End Condition. Depth = .50in.
6. Create **Sketch2**. Select the front vertical face of Extrude1 as the Sketch plane. Insert the required geometric relations and dimensions.

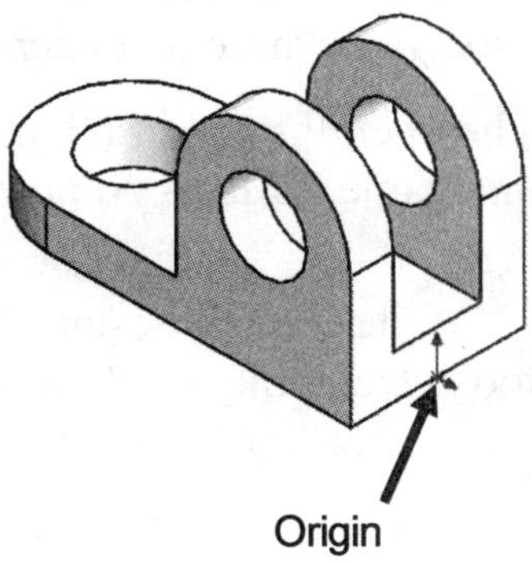

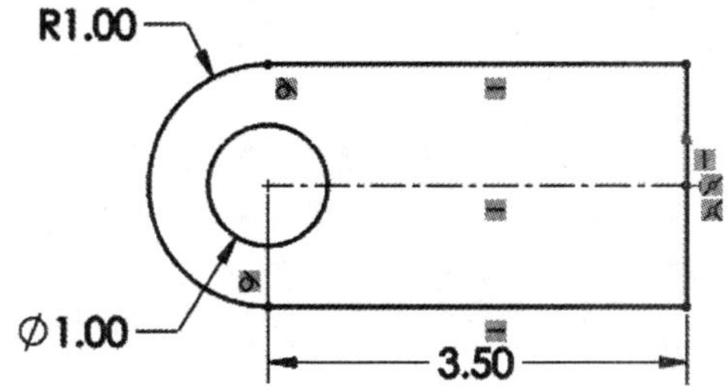

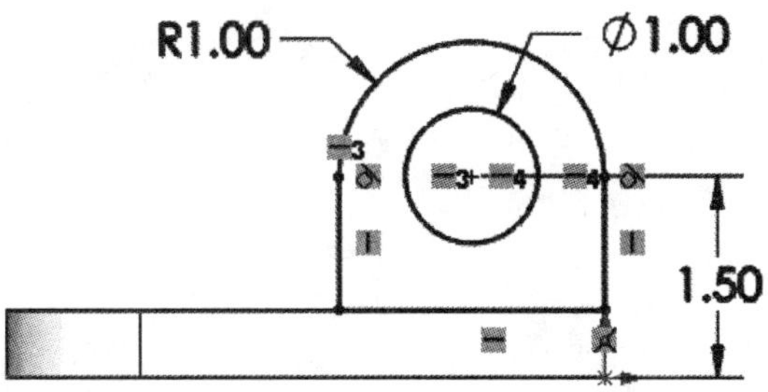

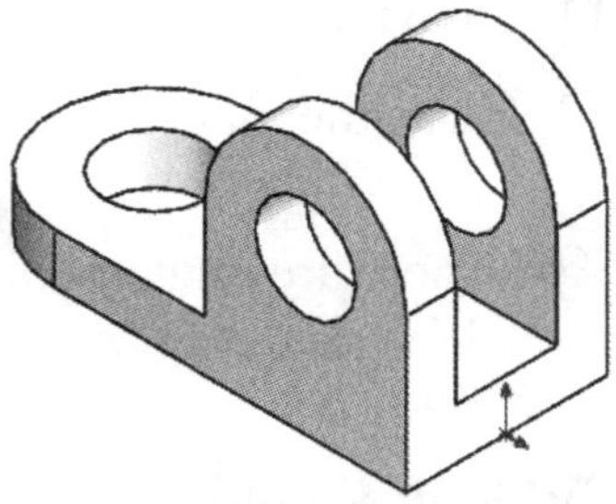

7. Create the **Extruded Boss (Boss-Extrude2)** feature. Blind is the default End Condition in Direction 1. Depth = .50in. Note the direction of the extrude.
8. Create the **Mirror** feature. Apply Symmetry. Mirror Boss-Extrude2 about the Front Plane.
9. **Assign** the defined material to the part.
10. **Calculate** the volume. The volume = 6.68 cubic inches.
11. **Locate** the Center of mass. The location of the Center of mass is derived from the part Origin.

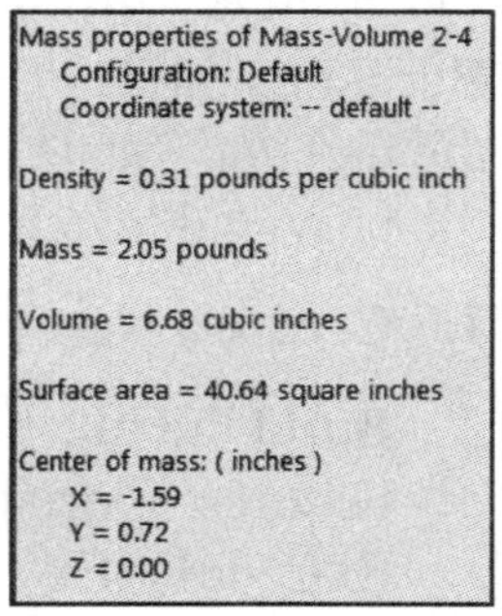

Mass properties of Mass-Volume 2-4
Configuration: Default
Coordinate system: -- default --

Density = 0.31 pounds per cubic inch

Mass = 2.05 pounds

Volume = 6.68 cubic inches

Surface area = 40.64 square inches

Center of mass: (inches)
X = -1.59
Y = 0.72
Z = 0.00

- X: -1.59 inches
- Y: 0.72 inches
- Z: 0.00 inches

View the triad location of the Center of mass for the part.

12. **Save** the part and name it Mass-Volume 2-4.
13. **Close** the model.

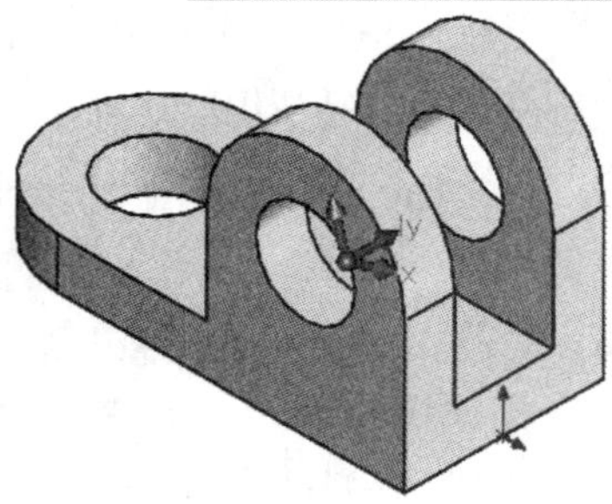

As an exercise, calculate the overall mass of the part using the IPS unit system, and assign Copper material to the part. Modify the hole diameters from 1.00in to 1.125in.

The overall mass of the part = 2.05 pounds. Save the part and name it Mass-Volume 2-4A.

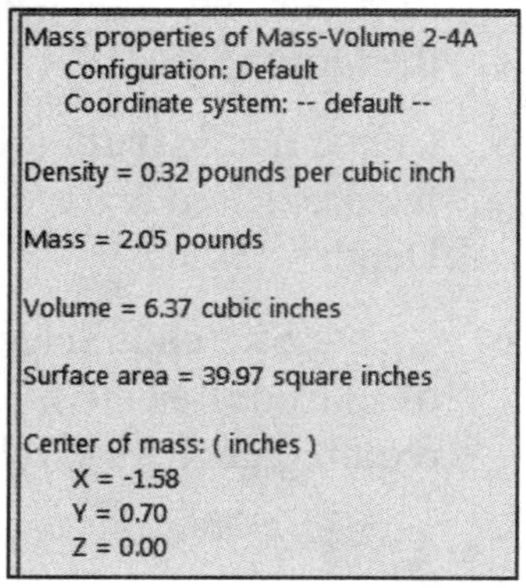

Mass properties of Mass-Volume 2-4A
Configuration: Default
Coordinate system: -- default --

Density = 0.32 pounds per cubic inch

Mass = 2.05 pounds

Volume = 6.37 cubic inches

Surface area = 39.97 square inches

Center of mass: (inches)
X = -1.58
Y = 0.70
Z = 0.00

The book is designed to expose the new user to many tools, techniques and procedures. It may not always use the most direct tool or process.

Tutorial: Mass-Volume 2-5

Build this model. Calculate the overall mass of the part and locate the Center of mass with the provided information.

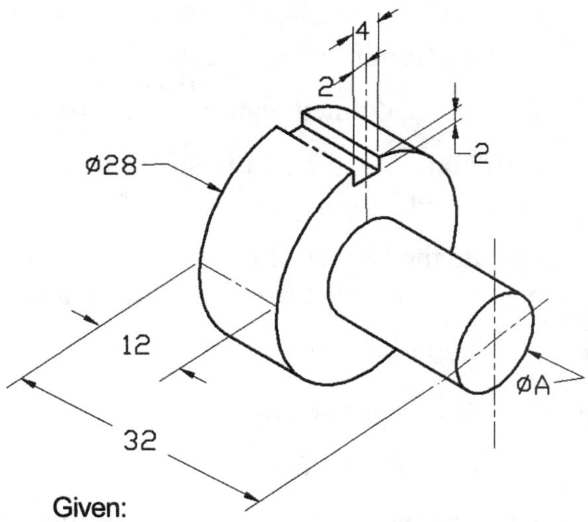

Given:
A = Ø12
Material: Cast Alloy Steel
Density = .0073 g/mm^3
Units: MMGS

1. **Create** a New part in SOLIDWORKS.
2. **Build** the illustrated model. Insert a Revolved Base feature and Extruded Cut feature to build this part.
3. **Set** the document properties for the model.
4. Create **Sketch1**. Select the Front Plane as the Sketch plane. Apply the Centerline Sketch tool for the Revolve1 feature. Insert the required geometric relations and dimensions. Sketch1 is the profile for the Revolve1 feature.
5. Create the **Revolved Base** feature. The default angle is 360deg. Select the centerline for the Axis of Revolution.

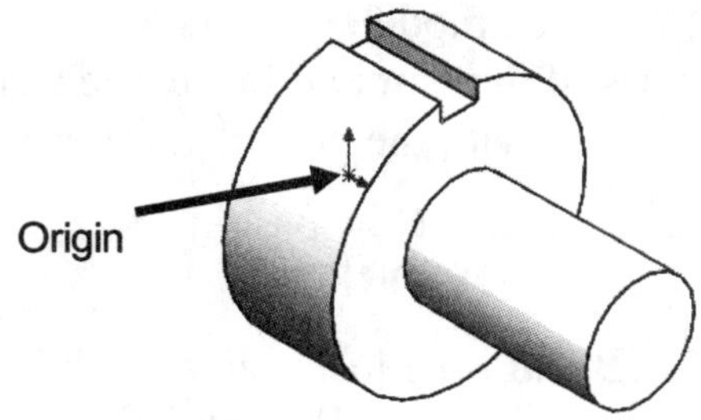

A Revolve feature adds or removes material by revolving one or more profiles around a centerline.

6. Create **Sketch2**. Select the right large circular face of Revolve1 as the Sketch plane. Apply reference construction geometry. Use the Convert Entities and Trim Sketch tools. Insert the required geometric relations and dimensions.

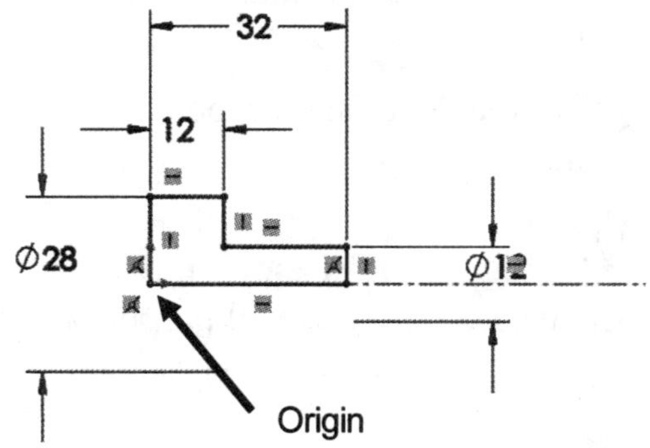

You could also use the 3 Point Arc Sketch tool instead of the Convert Entities and Trim Sketch tools to create Sketch2.

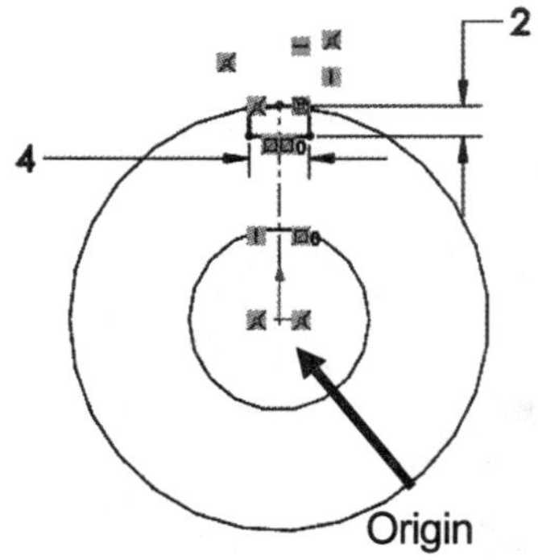

7. Create the **Extruded Cut** feature. Select Through All for End Condition in Direction 1.
8. **Assign** the defined material to the part.
9. **Calculate** the overall mass. The overall mass = 69.77 grams.
10. **Locate** the Center of mass. The location of the Center of mass is derived from the part Origin.

- X = 9.79 millimeters
- Y = -0.13 millimeters
- Z = 0.00 millimeters

11. **Save** the part and name it Mass-Volume 2-5.
12. **Close** the model.

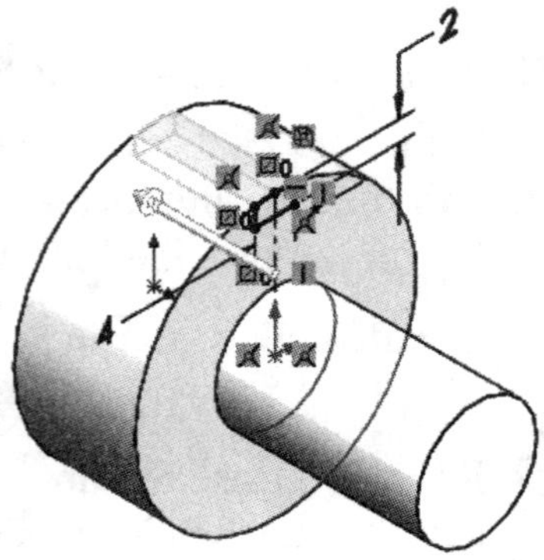

Mass properties of Mass-Volume 2-5
Configuration: Default
Coordinate system: -- default --

Density = 0.01 grams per cubic millimeter

Mass = 69.77 grams

Volume = 9557.27 cubic millimeters

Surface area = 3069.83 square millimeters

Center of mass: (millimeters)
X = 9.79
Y = -0.13
Z = 0.00

Tutorial: Mass-Volume 2-6

Build this model. Calculate the overall mass of the part and locate the Center of mass with the provided information.

1. **Create** a New part in SOLIDWORKS.
2. **Build** the illustrated model. Insert two features: Extruded Base (Boss-Extrude1) and Revolved Boss.
3. **Set** the document properties for the model.

Tangent edges and Origin are displayed for educational purposes.

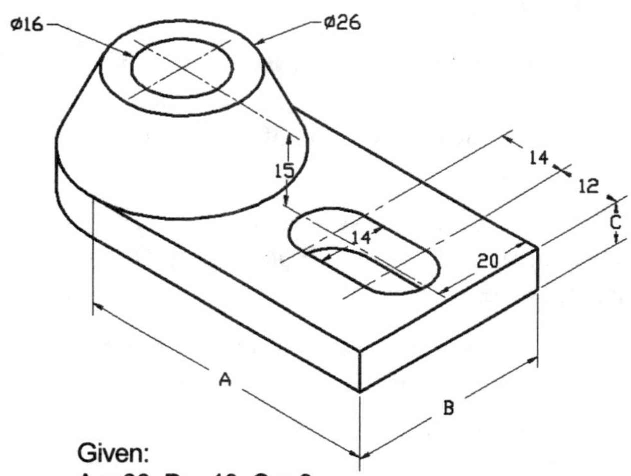

Given:
A = 60, B = 40, C = 8
Material: Cast Alloy Steel
Density = .0073 g/mm^3
Units: MMGS

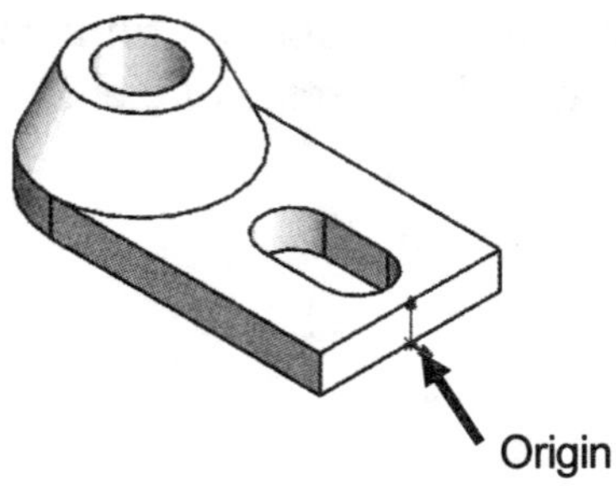

4. Create **Sketch1**. Select the Top Plane as the Sketch plane. Apply construction geometry. Apply the Tangent Arc and Line Sketch tool. Insert the required geometric relations and dimensions.

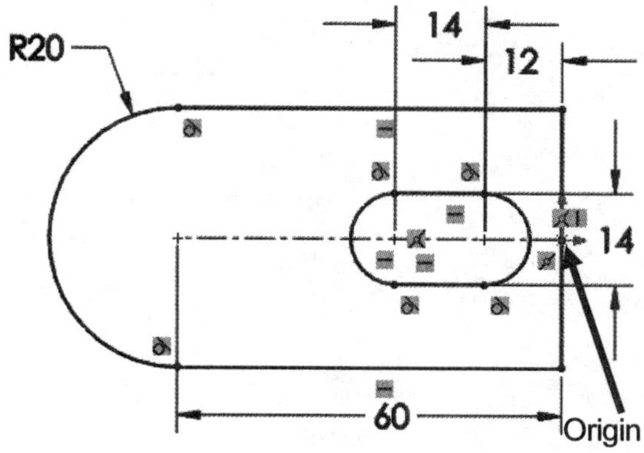

5. Create the **Extruded Base** feature. Blind is the default End Condition. Depth = 8mm.

6. Create **Sketch2**. Select the Front Plane as the Sketch plane. Apply construction geometry for the Revolved Boss feature. Insert the required geometric relations and dimension.

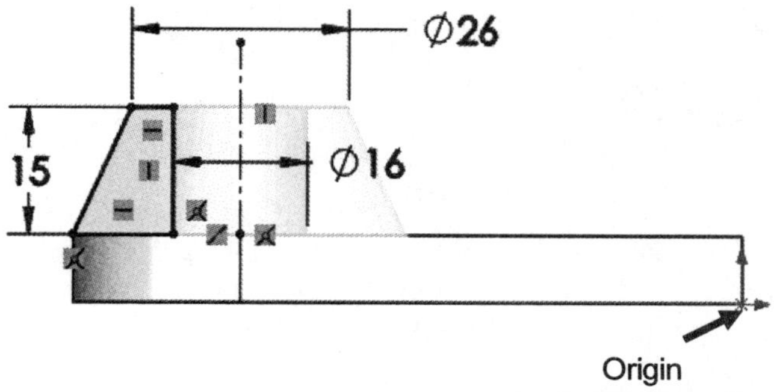

7. Create the **Revolved Boss** feature. The default angle is 360deg. Select the centerline for Axis of Revolution.

8. **Assign** the defined material to the part.

9. **Calculate** the overall mass. The overall mass = 229.46 grams.

10. **Locate** the Center of mass. The location of the Center of mass is derived from the part Origin.

- X = -46.68 millimeters
- Y = 7.23 millimeters
- Z = 0.00 millimeters

11. **Save** the part and name it Mass-Volume 2-6.

12. **Close** the model.

Mass properties of Mass-Volume 2-6
Configuration: Default
Coordinate system: -- default --

Density = 0.01 grams per cubic millimeter

Mass = 229.46 grams

Volume = 31433.02 cubic millimeters

Surface area = 9459.63 square millimeters

Center of mass: (millimeters)
X = -46.68
Y = 7.23
Z = 0.00

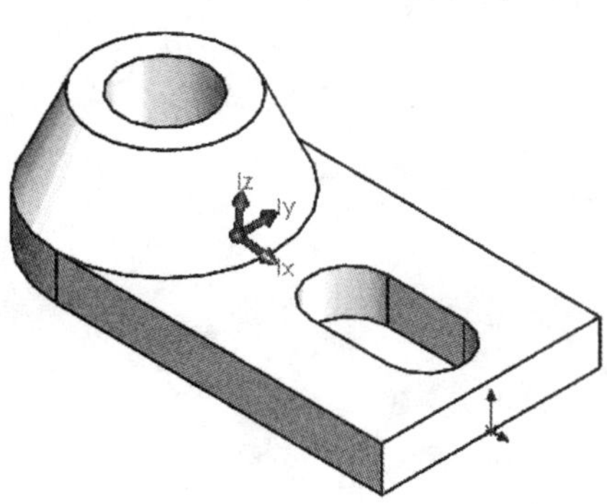

Notes:

Chapter 3

Assembly Modeling - Bottom up method

Below are the desired outcomes and usage competencies based on the completion of Chapter 3.

Desired Outcomes:	Usage Competencies:

• Two new assemblies with user defined document properties:
  • Fly Wheel.
  • Stirling Engine.
• An Exploded view with animation of the Fly Wheel assembly.
	• Set Document Properties as they relate to an Assembly.
	• Comprehend the assembly process. Insert parts/sub-components into an assembly.
	• Ability to apply Standard mates and Quick mates (Coincident, Concentric, Distance and Tangent) in an assembly using the Bottom-up design approach.
	• Utilize the following assembly tools: Insert Component, Mate, Hide, Show, Move, Rotate, Modify, Flexible, Ridge and Multiple mate mode.
	• Apply the Measure and Mass Properties tool.
	• Incorporate design changes into an assembly.

Notes:

Chapter 3 - Assembly Modeling - Bottom up method

Chapter Objective

Create two new assemblies. The first assembly is the Fly Wheel. The second assembly is the Stirling Engine. The Fly Wheel is a sub-assembly of the final Stirling Engine assembly.

On the completion of this chapter, you will be able to:

- Create a new assembly document.
- Set user defined document properties for an assembly.
- Understand assembly modeling approach.
- Comprehend linear and rotational motion.
- Insert parts and sub-assemblies in an assembly.
- Insert and edit the following Standard mates:
  - Coincident, Concentric, Distance and Tangent.
- Incorporate design changes in an assembly.
- Edit and Modify features and components in an assembly.
- Utilize the following assembly tools: Insert Component, Mate, Hide, Show, Move, Rotate, Modify, Flexible, Ridge and Multiple mate mode.
- Create an Exploded View with animation.
- Apply the Measure and Mass Properties tool.
- Apply the Pack and Go tool.

Activity: Start a SOLIDWORKS Session. Create a New Assembly.

Start a SOLIDWORKS session.

1) Double-click the **SOLIDWORKS icon** from the desktop.

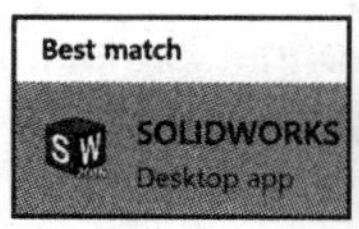

2) **Pin** the Menu bar as illustrated. Use both the Menu bar menu and the Menu bar toolbar in this book.

Create a New Assembly Document.

3) Click **New** from the Menu bar or click **File, New** from the Menu bar menu. The New SOLIDWORKS Document dialog box is displayed. Note: Advanced mode is used in this book.

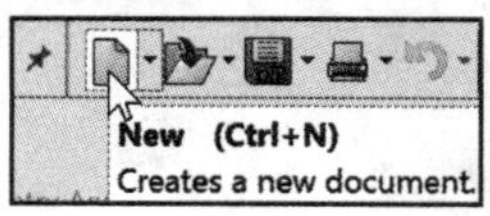

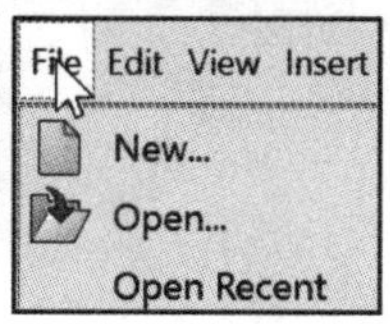

4) Click the **Templates** tab.

5) Double-click **Assembly** from the New SOLIDWORKS Document dialog box. The Begin Assembly PropertyManager is displayed.

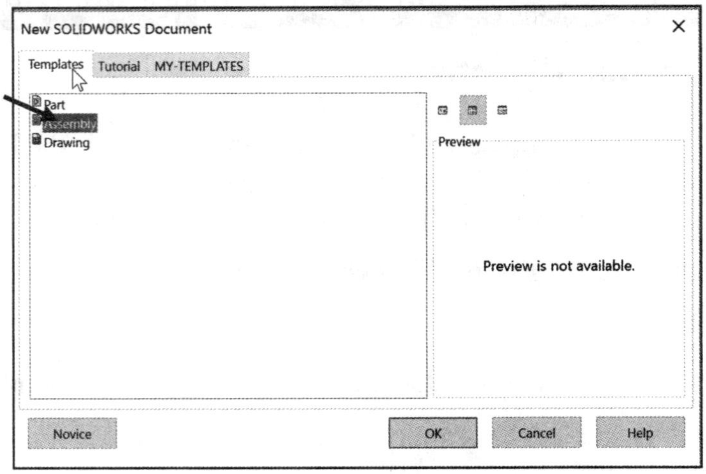

6) Click **Cancel** from the Open dialog box.

7) Click **Cancel** ✖ from the Assebmly FeatureManager. Assem1 is displayed in the FeatureManager.

The first system default Assembly filename is Assem1. The system attaches the .sldasm to the created assembly. The second created assembly in the same session increments to the filename Assem2.

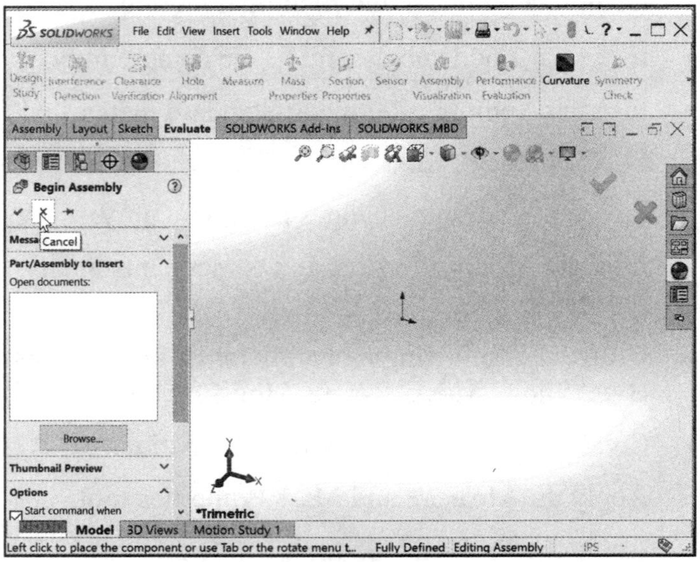

The Begin Assembly PropertyManager and the Insert Component PropertyManager is displayed when a new or existing assembly is opened, if the Start command when creating new assembly box is checked.

Display the origin.

8) Click **View**, **Hide/Show**, **Origins** from the Main menu. The origin is displayed in the Graphics window.

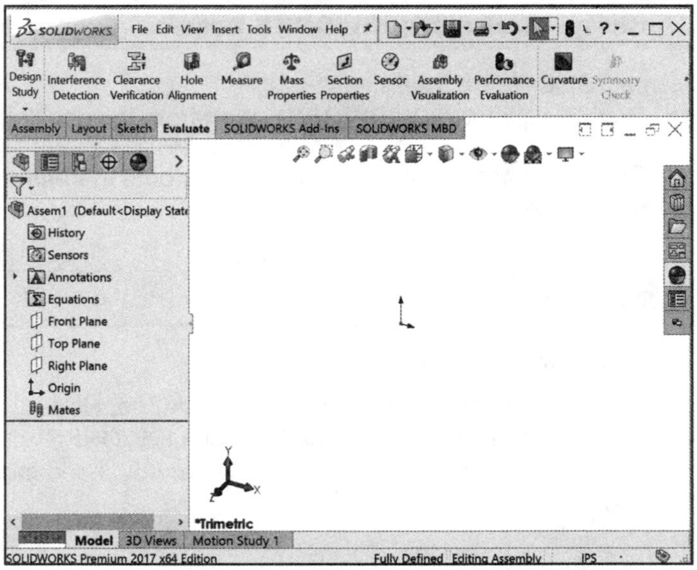

View the provided video on Creating an Assembly to enhance your user experience in this chapter.

Directional input refers by default to the global coordinate system (X, Y and Z), which is based on Plane1 with its origin located at the origin of the part or assembly. Plane1 (Front) is the first plane that appears in the FeatureManager design tree and can have a different name. The reference triad shows the global X-, Y- and Z-directions.

Activity: Set Document Properties for the Fly Wheel Assembly

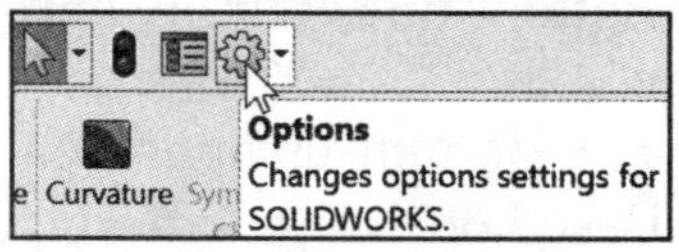

9) Click **Options** from the Menu bar. The System Options General dialog box is displayed.

10) Click the **Document Properties** tab.

11) Select **ANSI** from the Overall drafting standard drop-down menu. Various Detailing options are available depending on the selected standard.

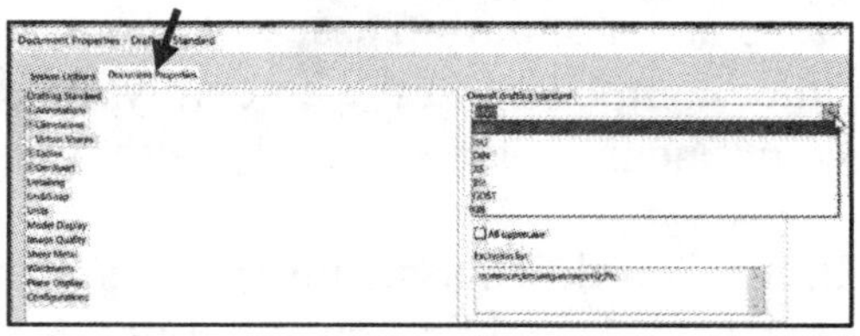

Various detailing options are available depending on the selected standard.

The Overall drafting standard determines the display of dimension text, arrows, symbols, and spacing. Units are the measurement of physical quantities. Millimeter dimensioning and decimal inch dimensioning are the two most common unit types specified for engineering parts and drawings.

Set Document Properties - Units.

12) Click the **Units** folder.

13) Click **MMGS** (millimeter, gram, second) for Unit system.

14) Select **.12,** (two decimal places) for Length basic units.

15) Click **OK** from the Document Properties - Units dialog box. The Assembly FeatureManager is displayed.

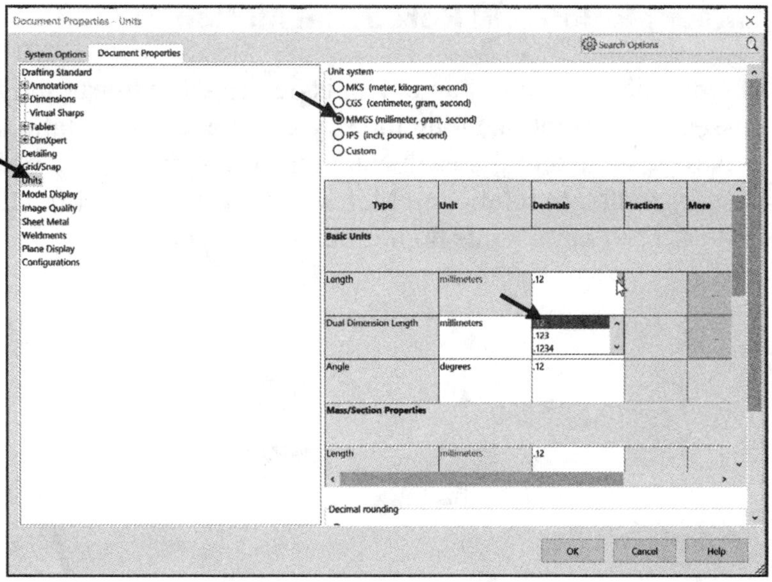

The Origin represents the intersection of the Front, Top and Right Planes.

Assembly Modeling Approach

In SOLIDWORKS, components and their assemblies are directly related through a common file structure. Changes in the components directly affect the assembly and vice versa. You can create assemblies using the Bottom-up assembly approach, Top-down assembly approach or a combination of both methods. This chapter focuses on the Bottom-up assembly approach.

The Bottom-up approach is the traditional method that combines individual components. Based on design criteria, the components are developed independently. The three major steps in a Bottom-up assembly approach are create each component independent of any other component in the assembly, insert the components into the assembly, and mate the components in the assembly as they relate to the physical constraints of your design.

In the Top-down assembly approach, major design requirements are translated into layout sketches, assemblies, sub-assemblies and components.

In the Top-down approach, you do not need all of the required component design details. Individual relationships are required.

Example: A computer. The inside of a computer can be divided into individual key sub-assemblies such as a motherboard, disk drive, power supply, etc. Relationships between these sub-assemblies must be maintained for proper fit.

Linear Motion and Rotational Motion

In dynamics, motion of an object is described in linear and rotational terms. Components possess linear motion along the x, y and z-axes and rotational motion around the x, y and z-axes. In an assembly, each component has *six degrees* of freedom: three translational (linear) and three rotational. Mates remove degrees of freedom. All components are rigid bodies. The components do not flex or deform.

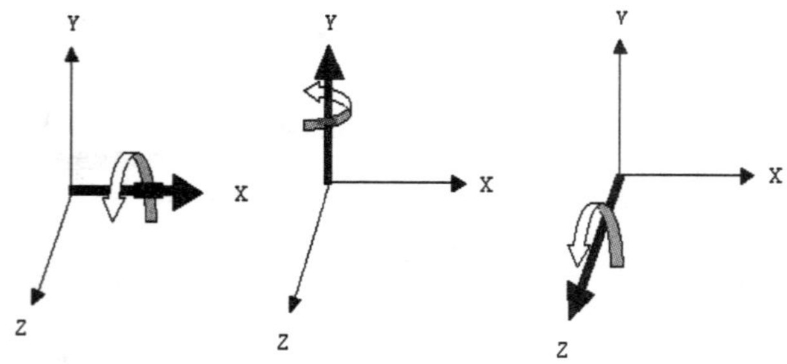

Activity: Insert the First Component into the Fly Wheel Assembly

The first component is the foundation of the assembly. The Bracket is the first component in the Fly Wheel assembly. The Bushing is the second component in the Fly Wheel assembly. All needed components for this chapter including the Wheel are located in the SOLIDWORKS in 5 Hours\FLY WHEEL folder.

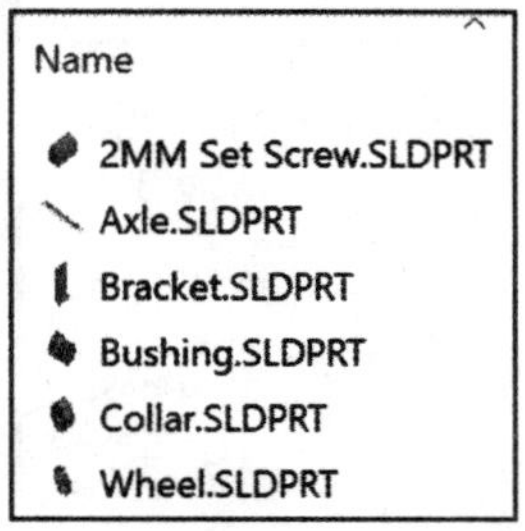

Add components to assemblies utilizing the following techniques:

- Utilize the Insert Components Assembly tool.
- Utilize Insert, Component from the Menu bar.
- Drag a component from Windows Explorer (3D ContentCentral) into the Assembly.
- Drag a component from the SOLIDWORKS Design Library into the Assembly.
- Drag a component from an Open part file into the Assembly.

Insert the Bracket component.

16) Click **Insert Component** from the Assembly toolbar. The Insert Component PropertyManager is displayed.

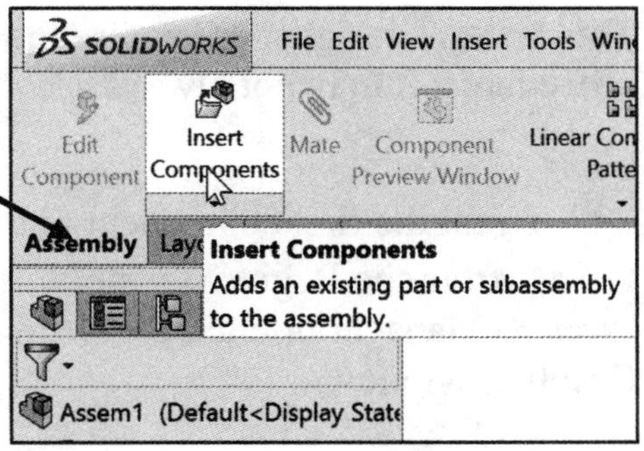

17) Click the **Browse** button.

18) Browse to the **SOLIDWORKS in 5 Hours\FLY WHEEL** folder.

19) Click the **Filter Parts (*.pt;*sldprt)** icon to view all parts in the folder.

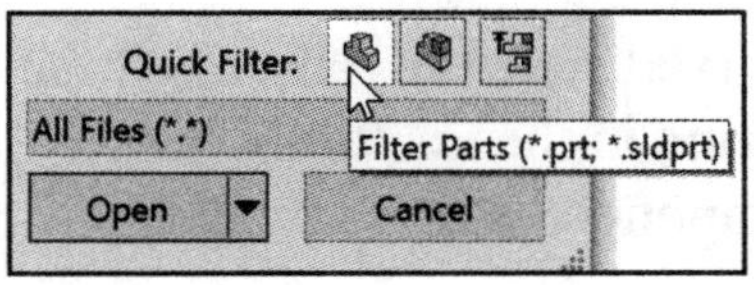

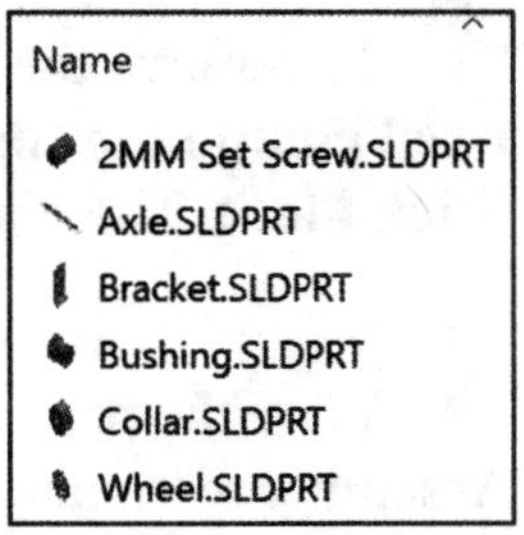

20) Double-click the **Bracket** part.

21) Click **OK** from the Insert Component PropertyManager. The Bracket is fixed to the origin. It cannot translate or rotate.

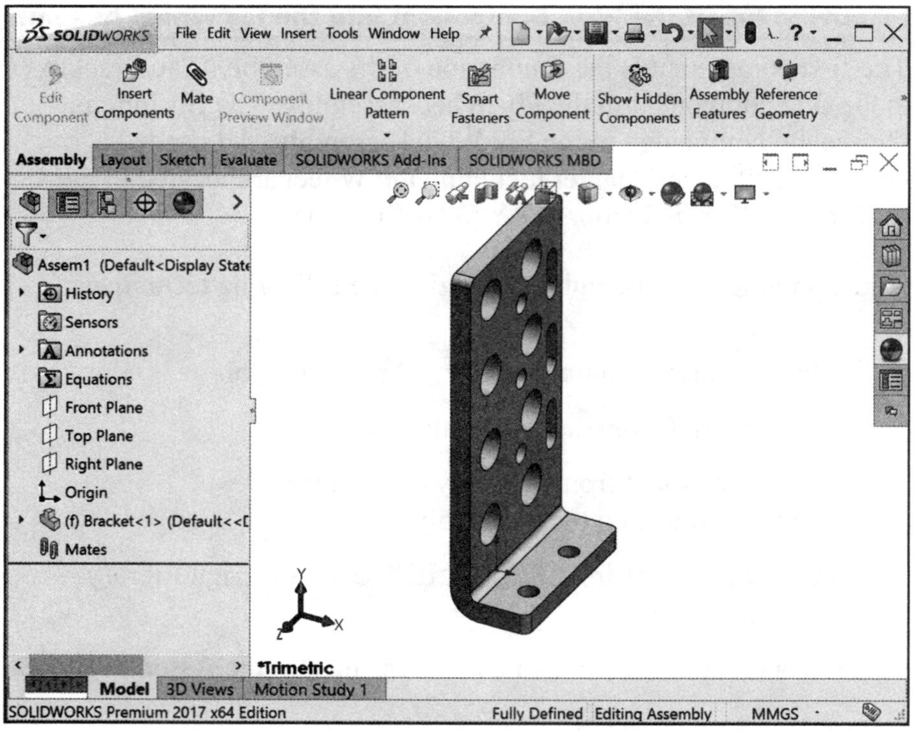

This book is designed to expose the SOLIDWORKS user to numerous tools and procedures. It may not always use the simplest and most direct process.

To fix the first component to the Origin, click OK from the Begin Assembly PropertyManager or click the Origin in the Graphics window.

To remove the fixed state (f), right-click the **fixed component name** in the FeatureManager. Click **Float**. The component is free to move.

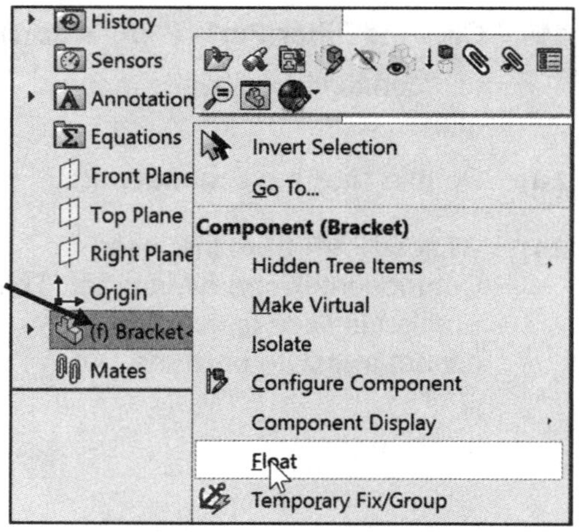

View the provided video on Creating an Assembly to enhance your user experience in the chapter.

Display an Isometric view of the model. Press the **space bar** to display the Orientation dialog box. Click the **Isometric view** icon.

Save the Assembly.

22) Click **Save As** from the Drop-down Menu bar.

23) Browse to the **SOLIDWORKS in 5 Hours** folder.

24) Enter **Fly Wheel** for the File name.

25) Enter **Fly Wheel** for the Description.

26) Click **Save** from the Save As dialog box. The Fly Wheel Assembly FeatureManager is displayed.

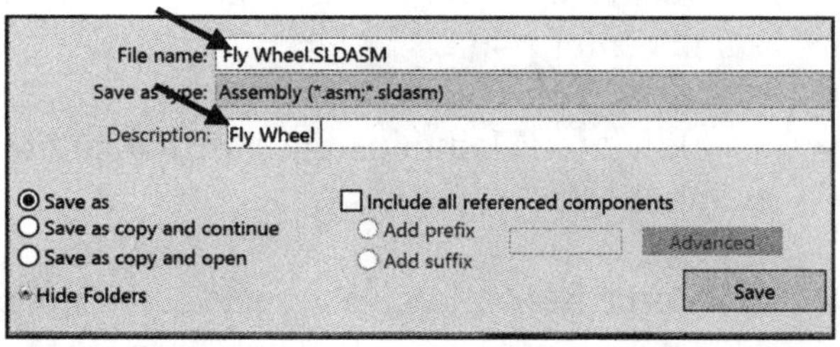

Organize parts, assemblies and drawings into folders. All documents for this book are saved in the SOLIDWORKS in 5 Hours folder.

Mate Types

Mates provide the ability to create geometric relationships between assembly components. Mates define the allowable directions of rotational or linear motion of the components in the assembly. Move a component within its degrees of freedom in the Graphics window to view the behavior of an assembly.

Mates are solved together as a system. The order in which you add mates does not matter. All mates are solved at the same time. You can suppress mates just as you can suppress features.

The Mate PropertyManager provides the ability to select either the **Mates** or **Analysis** tab. Each tab has a separate menu. The **Analysis** tab requires the ability to run SOLIDWORKS Motion. The Analysis tab is not covered in this book. The Mate PropertyManager displays the appropriate selections based on the type of mate you create. The components in the Fly Wheel assembly utilize Standard Mate types.

Review **Standard**, **Advanced** and **Mechanical** Mates types.

Standard Mates:

Components are assembled with various mate types. These are the Standard Mate types:

- **Coincident Mate**: Locates the selected faces, edges, or planes so they use the same infinite line. A Coincident mate positions two vertices for contact.

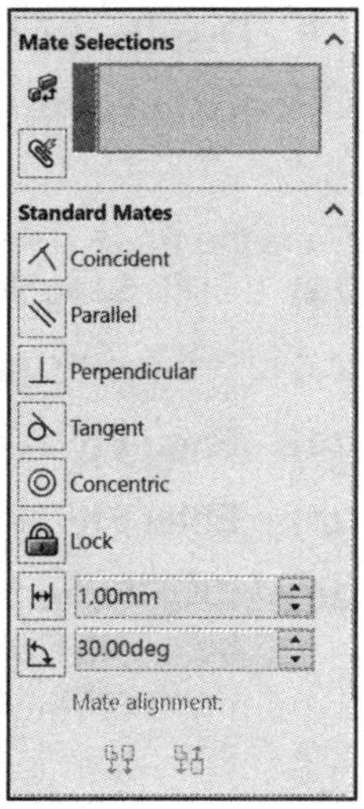

- **Parallel Mate**: Locates the selected items to lie in the same direction and to remain a constant distance apart.

- **Perpendicular Mate**: Locates the selected items at a 90° angle to each other.

- **Tangent Mate**: Locates the selected items in a tangent mate. At least one selected item must be either a conical, cylindrical, or spherical face.

- **Concentric Mate**: Locates the selected items so they can share the same center point.

- **Lock Mate**: Maintains the position and orientation between two components.

- **Distance Mate**: Locates the selected items with a specified distance between them. Use the drop-down arrow box or enter the distance value directly.

- **Angle Mate**: Locates the selected items at the specified angle to each other. Use the drop-down arrow box or enter the angle value directly.

There are two Mate Alignment options. The Aligned option positions the components so that the normal vectors from the selected faces point in the same direction. The Anti-Aligned option positions the components so that the normal vectors from the selected faces point in opposite directions.

Use for positioning only. When selected, components move to the position defined by the mate, but a mate is not added to the FeatureManager design tree. A mate appears in the Mates box so you can edit and position the components, but nothing appears in the FeatureManager design tree when you close the Mate PropertyManager.

Advanced Mates:

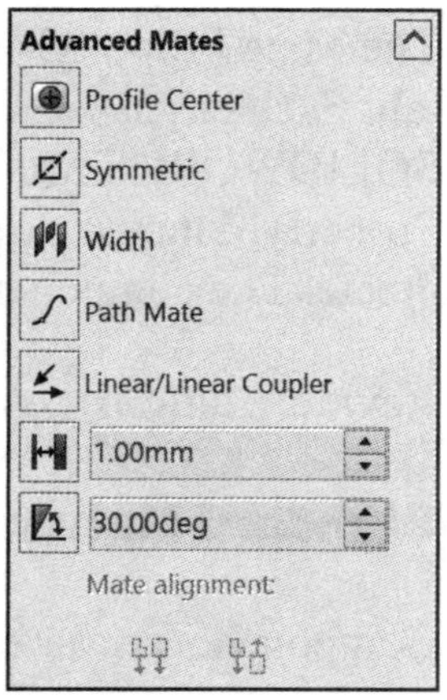

These are the Advanced Mate types:

- **Profile Center**: Mate to Center automatically center-aligns common component types such as rectangular and circular profiles to each other and fully defines the components.

- **Symmetric Mate**: Positions two selected entities to be symmetric about a plane or planar face. A Symmetric Mate does not create a Mirrored Component.

- **Width Mate**: Centers a tab within the width of a groove.

- **Path Mate**: Constrains a selected point on a component to a path.

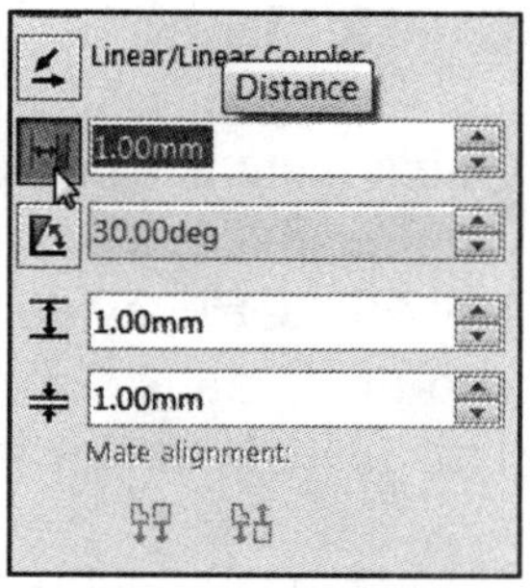

- **Linear/LinearCoupler Mate**: Establishes a relationship between the translation of one component and the translation of another component.

- **Distance (Limit) Mate**: Locates the selected items with a specified distance between them. Use the drop-down arrow box or enter the distance value directly.

- **Angle Mate**: Locates the selected items at the specified angle to each other. Use the drop-down arrow box or enter the angle value directly.

Mechanical Mates:

These are the Mechanical Mate types:

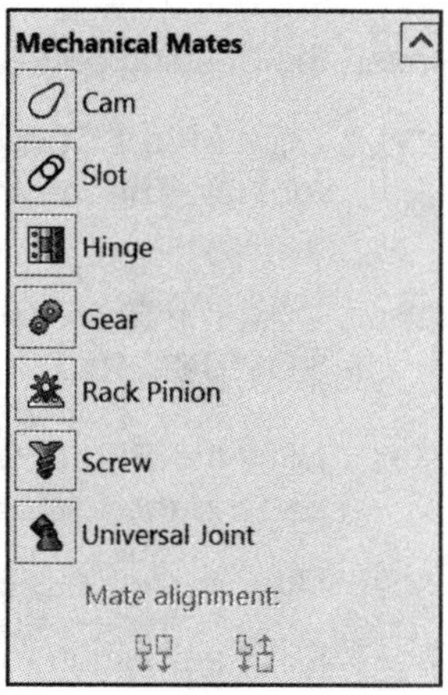

- **Cam Mate**: Forces a plane, cylinder, or point to be tangent or coincident to a series of tangent extruded faces.

- **Slot Mate**: Mate bolts to straight or arced slots and you can mate slots to slots. Select an axis, cylindrical face, or a slot to create slot mates.

- **Hinge**: Limits the movement between two components to one rotational degree of freedom. It has the same effect as adding a Concentric mate plus a Coincident mate.

- **Gear Mate**: Forces two components to rotate relative to one another around selected axes.

- **Rack Pinion Mate**: Provides the ability to have Linear translation of a part; rack causes circular rotation in another part, pinion, and vice versa.

- **Screw Mate**: Constrains two components to be concentric, and also adds a pitch relationship between the rotation of one component and the translation of the other.

- **Universal Joint Mate**: The rotation of one component (the output shaft) about its axis is driven by the rotation of another component (the input shaft) about its axis.

Mates reflect the physical behavior of a component in an assembly. In this project, the two most common Mate types are Concentric and Coincident.

Quick Mate:

Quick mate is a procedure to mate components together in SOLIDWORKS. No command (click Mate from the Assembly CommandManager) needs to be executed. Hold the Ctrl key down, make your selections, release the Ctrl key and a Quick Mate pop-up menu is displayed below the context toolbar. Select the mate and you are finished. This mate behavior is similar to the way you add sketch relations.

Utilize the Quick mate procedure on Standard mates, Cam mate, Profile Center mate, Slot mate, Symmetric mate and Width mate. Use the Quick mate procedure for reference geometry (such as planes, axes, and points) along with model geometry (such as faces, edges and vertices).

Activity: Insert and Mate the Second Component - Bushing

Insert the Bushing part into the Fly Wheel Assembly.

27) Click **Insert Component** from the Assembly toolbar. The Insert Component PropertyManager is displayed.

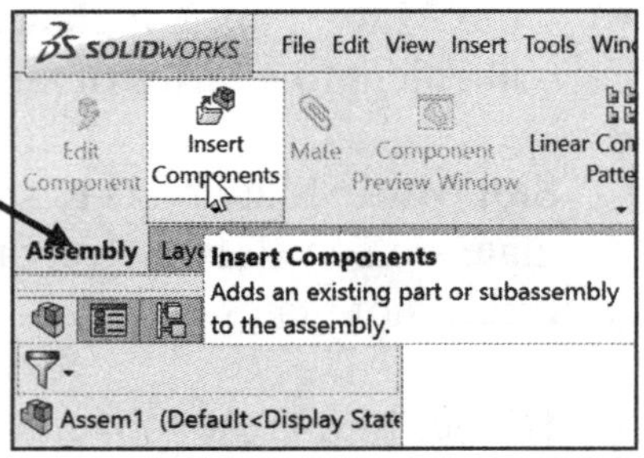

28) Click the **Browse** button. Browse to the **SOLIDWORKS in 5 Hours\FLY WHEEL** folder.

29) Click the **Filter Parts (*.pt;*sldprt)** icon to view all parts in the folder.

30) Double-click the **Bushing** part.

31) Click a position to the **left** of the Bracket as illustrated.

32) Click **OK** from the Insert Component PropertyManager. The Bushing is displayed.

Insert a Concentric Mate between the outside cylindrical face of the Bushing and the cylindrical face of the top right hole.

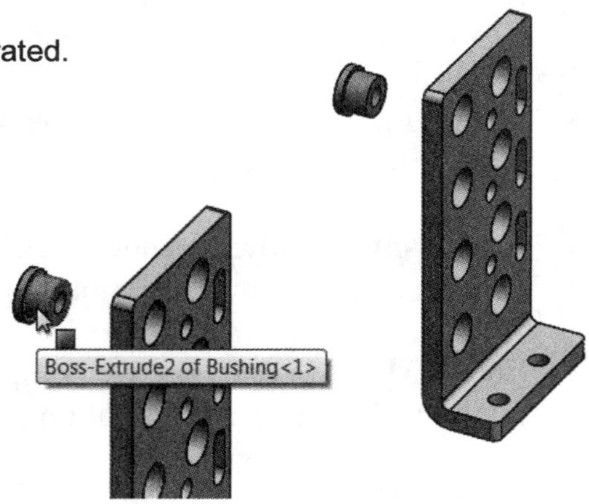

33) Hold the **Ctrl** key down.

34) Click the **outside cylindrical face** of the Bushing.

35) Click **cylindrical face** of the top right hole as illustrated.

36) Release the **Ctrl** key. The Mate Pop-up menu is displayed.

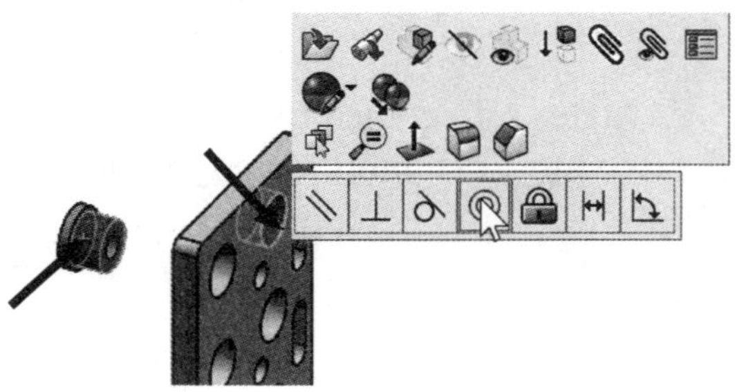

37) Click **Concentric** from The Mate Pop-up menu. A Concentric mate locates the selected items so they can share the same center point.

Insert a Coincident Mate between the flat circular face of the Bushing and the back face of the Bracket.

38) **Rotate** the model to view the back face of the Bracket.

39) Click the **back face** of the Bracket.

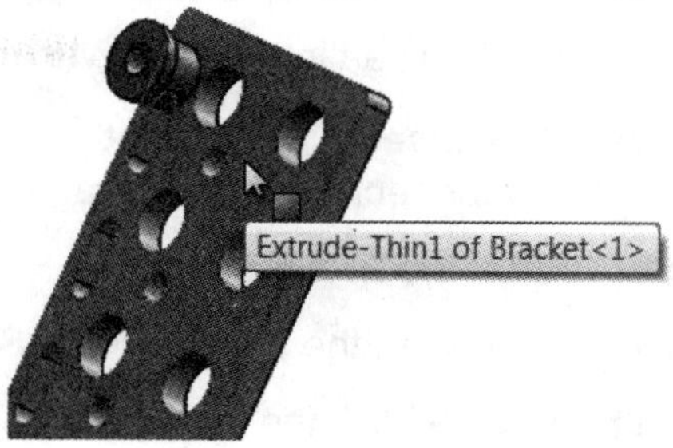

40) **Rotate** the model to view the flat circular face of the Bushing.

41) Hold the **Ctrl** key down.

42) Click the **flat circular face** of the Bushing.

43) Release the **Ctrl** key. The Mate Pop-up menu is displayed.

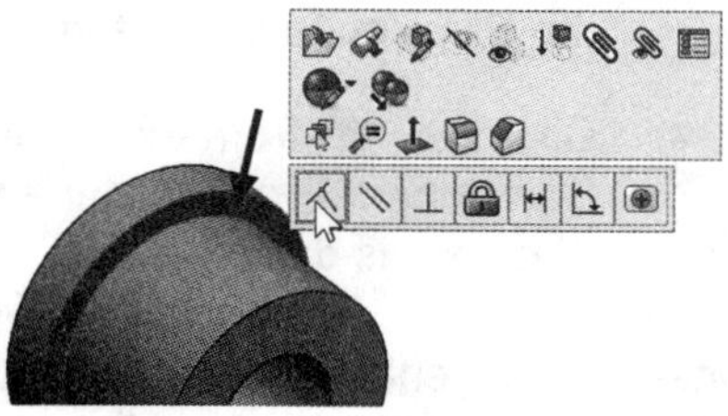

44) Click **Coincident** from The Mate Pop-up menu. A Coincident mate locates the selected faces, edges or planes so they use the same infinite lines.

If needed, deselect the Origins.

45) Uncheck **View Origins** from the Hide/Show Items in the Heads-up toolbar.

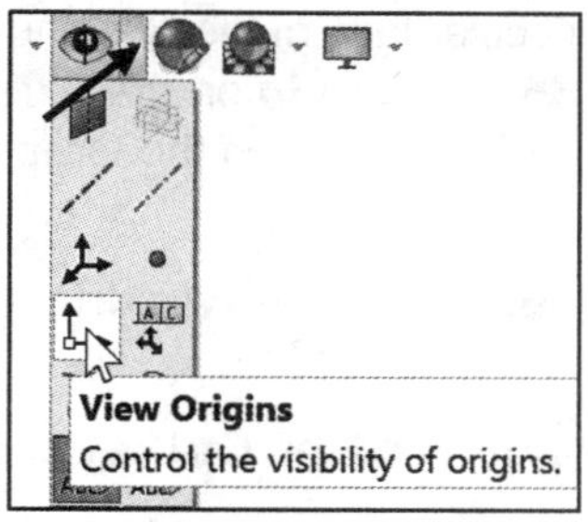

Display a Trimetric view.

46) Click **Trimetric view** from the Heads-up toolbar.

Expand the Mates folder.

47) **Expand** the Mates folder as illustrated. View the results.

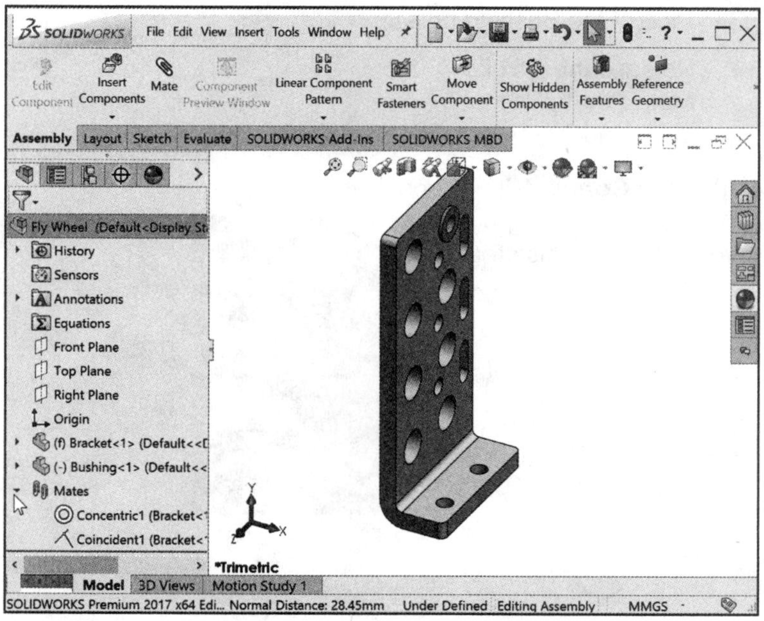

Save the model.

48) Click **Save**.

If you delete a Mate and then recreate it, the Mate numbers will be different (increase).

Determine the static and dynamic behavior of mates in each sub-assembly before creating the top level assembly.

Activity: Insert and Mate the Third Component - Axle

Insert the Axle part into the Fly Wheel Assembly.

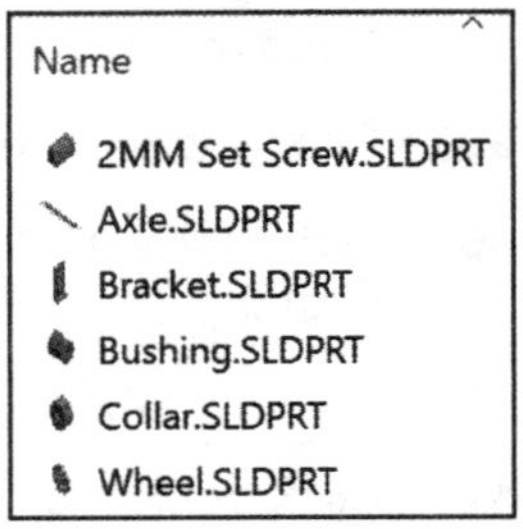

49) Click **Insert Component** from the Assembly toolbar. The Insert Component PropertyManager is displayed.

50) Click the **Browse** button.

51) Browse to the **SOLIDWORKS in 5 Hours\FLY WHEEL** folder.

52) Double-click the **Axle** part.

53) Click a position to the **right** of the Bracket as illustrated.

54) Click **OK** from the Insert Component PropertyManager. The Axle is displayed.

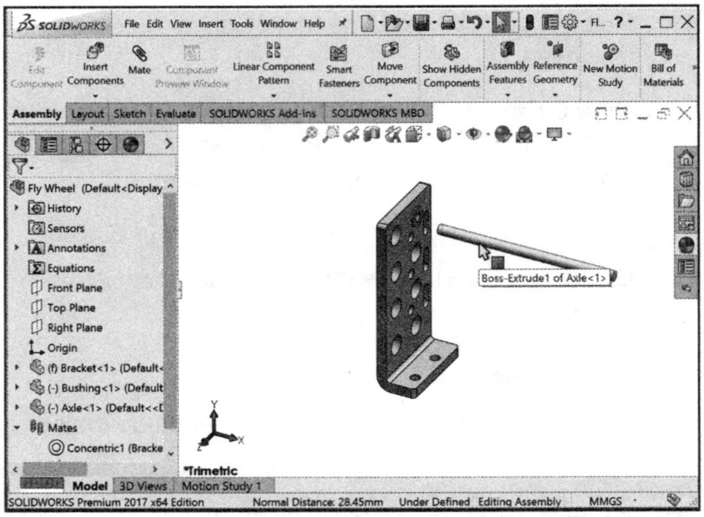

Insert a Concentric Mate between the circular face of the Axle and the circular face of the Bushing hole.

55) **Zoom-in** on the Axle and Bushing in the Graphics window.

56) Click the **cylindrical face of the Axle**.

57) Hold the **Ctrl** key down.

58) Click the inside **cylindrical face** of the Bushing hole.

59) Release the **Ctrl** key. The Mate Pop-up menu is displayed.

60) Click **Concentric** from The Mate Pop-up menu. Concentric2 is created.

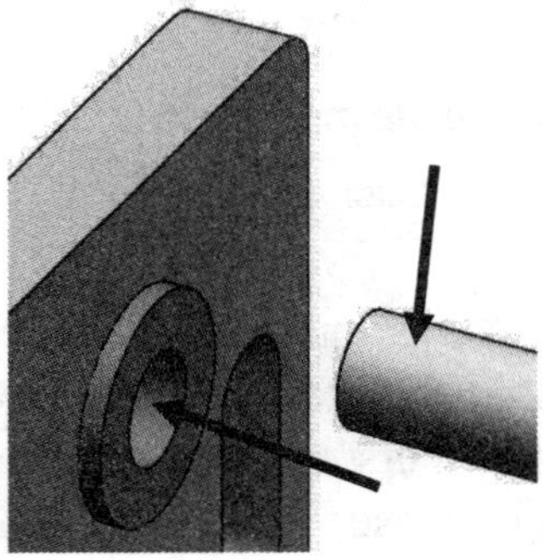

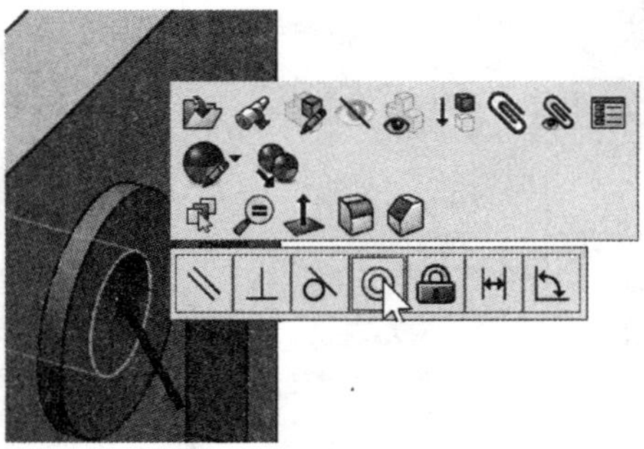

Create a Distance Mate between the back face of the Bushing and the front face of the Axle.

61) **Rotate** the model to view the back face of the Bracket.

62) Click the **back face** of the Bushing.

63) Hold the **Ctrl** key down.

64) Click the **flat face** of the Axle as illustrated.

65) Release the **Ctrl** key. The Mate pop-up menu is displayed.

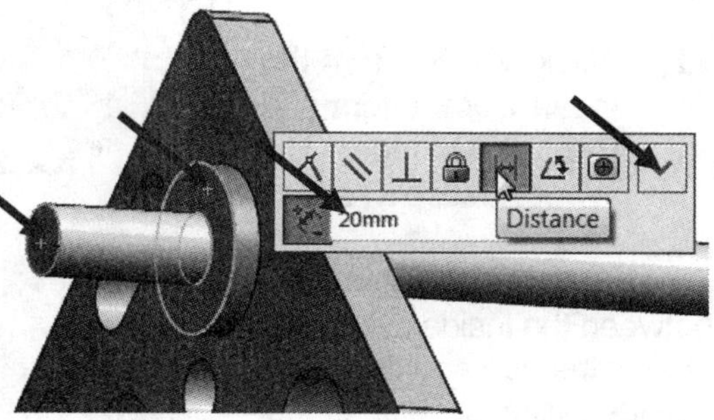

66) Click **Distance** mate from the Mate pop-up menu.

67) Enter **20**mm for Distance.

68) Click the **Green Check mark** from the Mate pop-up menu. Distance1 is created. A Distance mate locates the selected items with a specified distance between them.

Display a Trimetric view.

69) Click **Trimetric view** from the Heads-up View toolbar.

Save the model.

70) Click **Save**.

Activity: Insert and Mate the Fourth Component - Wheel

Insert the Wheel part into the Fly Wheel Assembly. The Wheel part was created in Chapter 2. If you did not create the part, insert the Wheel part from the SOLIDWORKS in 5 Hours\FLY WHEEL folder.

71) Click **Insert Component** . from the Assembly toolbar. The Insert Component PropertyManager is displayed.

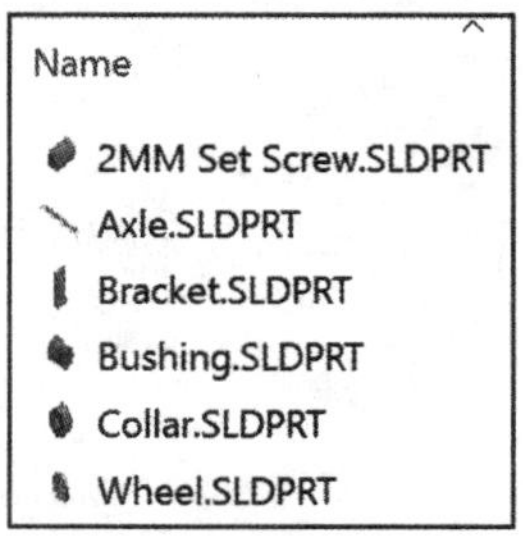

72) Click the **Browse** button.

73) Browse to the **SOLIDWORKS in 5 Hours\FLY WHEEL** folder.

74) Click the **Filter Parts (*.pt;*sldprt)** icon to view all parts in the folder.

75) Double-click the **Wheel** part.

76) Click a position to the **right** of the Bracket as illustrated.

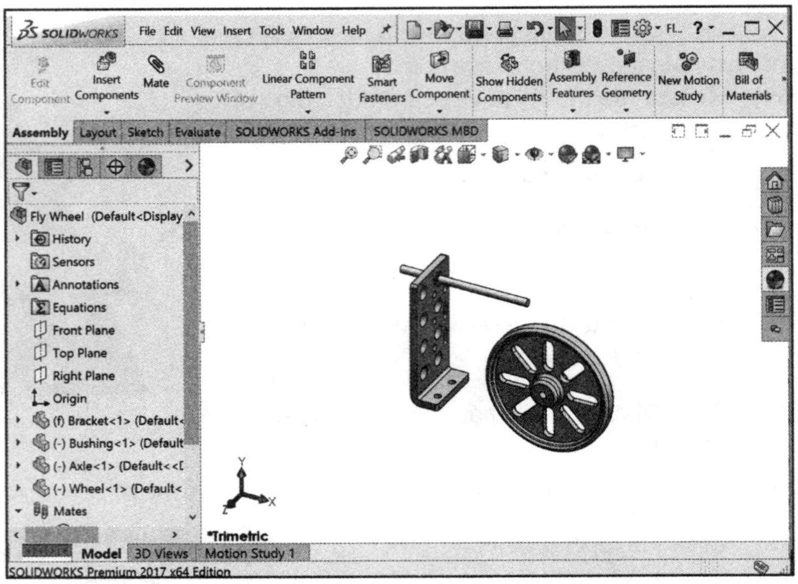

77) Click **OK** ✔ from the Insert Component PropertyManager. The Wheel is displayed.

Insert a Concentric Mate between the inside cylindrical face of the hub and the outside cylindrical face of the Axle.

78) **Zoom-in** on the Wheel and Axle in the Graphics window.

79) Click the **inside cylindrical face** of the Wheel hole (Hub).

80) Hold the **Ctrl** key down.

81) Click the **cylindrical face** of the Axle.

82) Release the **Ctrl** key. The Mate Pop-up menu is displayed.

83) Click **Concentric** ◎ from the Mate Pop-up menu.

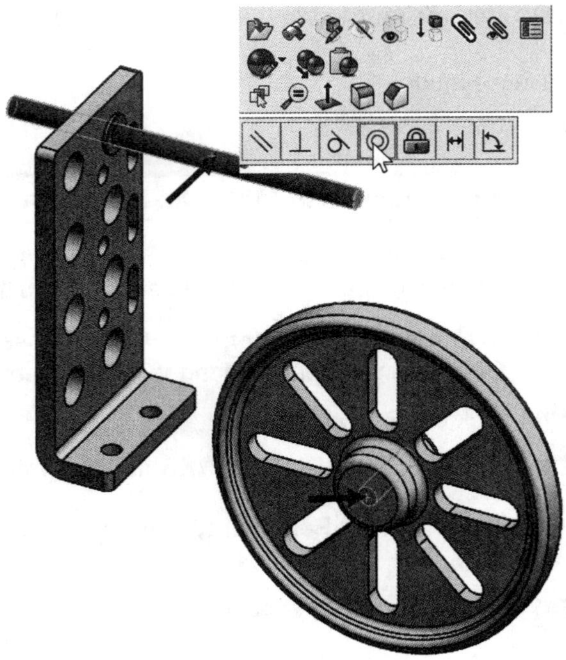

Insert a Distance Mate between the back face of the hub and the front face of the Bushing.

84) **Rotate** the assembly to view the back face of the hub.

85) Click the **back face** of the hub as illustrated.

86) **Rotate** and **Zoom in** on the front face of the Bushing.

87) Hold the **Ctrl** key down.

88) Click the **front face** of the Bushing as illustrated.

89) Release the **Ctrl** key. The Mate Pop-up menu is displayed.

90) Click **Distance** mate from the Mate pop-up menu.

91) Enter **.1**mm for Distance.

92) Click the **Green Check mark** from the Mate pop-up menu. Distance2 is created. A Distance mate locates the selected items with a specified distance between them.

Fit the model to the Graphics window.

93) Press the **f** key.

Display a Trimetric view.

94) Click **Trimetric view** from the Heads-up View toolbar.

Save the model.

95) Click **Save**.

Rotate the Wheel in the Assembly.

96) Click on the **Wheel** and drag to view the Wheel rotate.

View the Created Mates.

97) **Expand** the Mates folder. View the created mates.

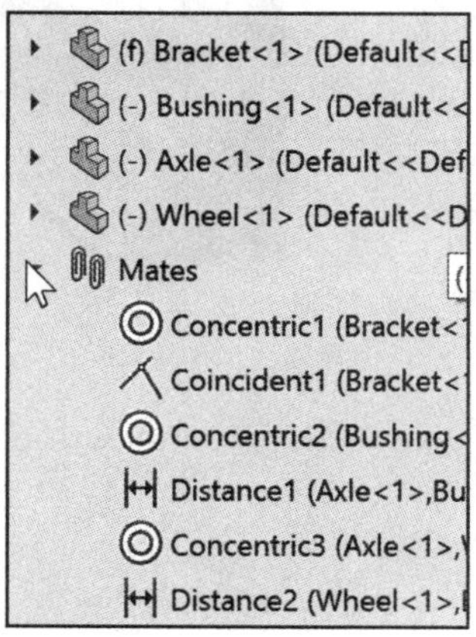

Activity: Insert and Mate the Fifth Component - Collar

Insert the Collar part into the Fly Wheel Assembly.

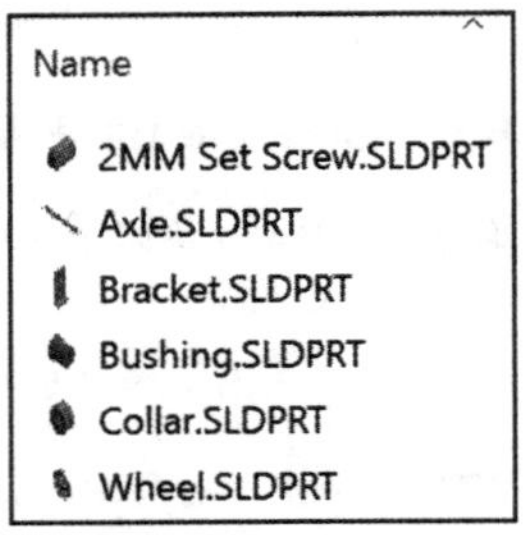

98) Click **Insert Component** from the Assembly toolbar. The Insert Component PropertyManager is displayed.

99) Click the **Browse** button.

100) Browse to the **SOLIDWORKS in 5 Hours\FLY WHEEL** folder.

101) Double-click the **Collar** part.

102) Click a position to the **right** of the assembly as illustrated.

103) Click **OK** from the Insert Component PropertyManager. The Collar is displayed.

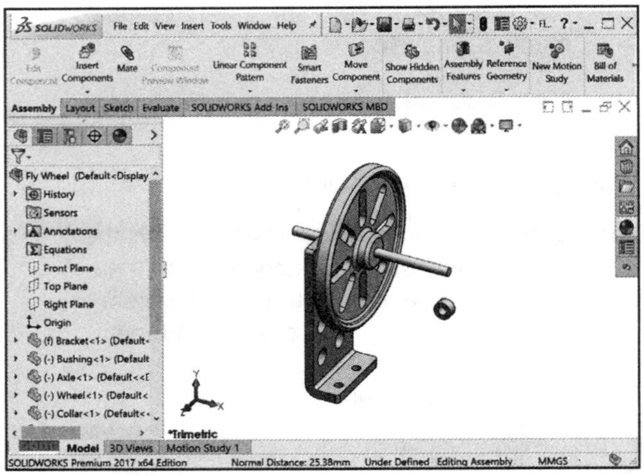

Insert a Concentric Mate between the inside cylindrical face of the Collar and the outside cylindrical face of the Axle.

104) **Zoom-in** on the Fly Wheel assembly in the Graphics window.

105) Click the **inside cylindrical face** of the Collar.

106) Hold the **Ctrl** key down.

107) Click the **outside cylindrical face** of the Axle.

108) Release the **Ctrl** key. The Mate Pop-up menu is displayed.

109) Click **Concentric** from the Mate Pop-up menu.

Insert Coincident Mate between the back face of the Collar and the front face of the hub.

110) Rotate the assembly to view the back face of the Collar.

111) Click the **back face** of the Collar as illustrated.

112) Rotate and **Zoom in** on the front face of the hub.

113) Hold the **Ctrl** key down.

114) Click the **front face** of the hub as illustrated.

115) Release the **Ctrl** key. The Mate Pop-up menu is displayed.

116) Click **Coincident** from the Mate Pop-up menu.

Fit the model to the Graphics window.

117) Press the **f** key.

Display a Trimetric view.

118) Click **Trimetric view** from the Heads-up View toolbar.

Rotate the Collar in the Assembly.

119) Click on the **Collar** and drag. The Collar is free to rotate.

120) Position the **2MM hole** towards the top as illustrated.

View the Created Mates.

121) Expand the Mates folder. View the created mates.

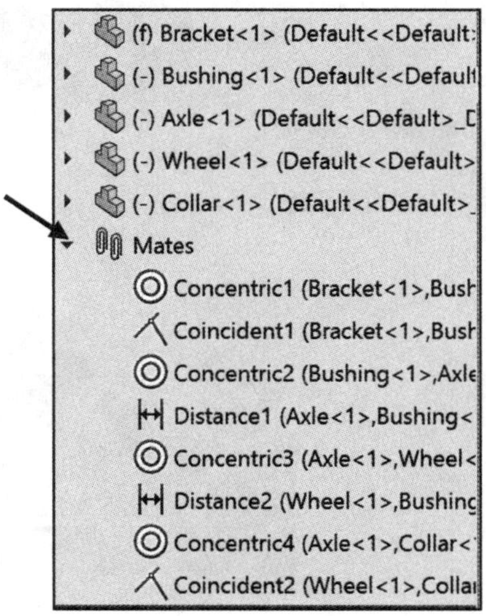

Activity: Insert and Mate the Sixth Component - 2MM Set Screw

Insert the 2MM Set Screw into the Collar.

122) Click **Insert Component** from the Assembly toolbar. The Insert Component PropertyManager is displayed.

123) Click the **Browse** button.

124) Browse to the **SOLIDWORKS in 5 Hours\FLY WHEEL** folder.

125) Double-click the **2MM Set Screw** part.

126) Click a position at the **top of the Collar** as illustrated.

127) Click **OK** from the Insert Component PropertyManager. The 2MM Set Screw is displayed.

Insert a Concentric Mate between the inside cylindrical face of the Collar and the outside face of the 2MM Set Screw using the Anti-Aligned option.

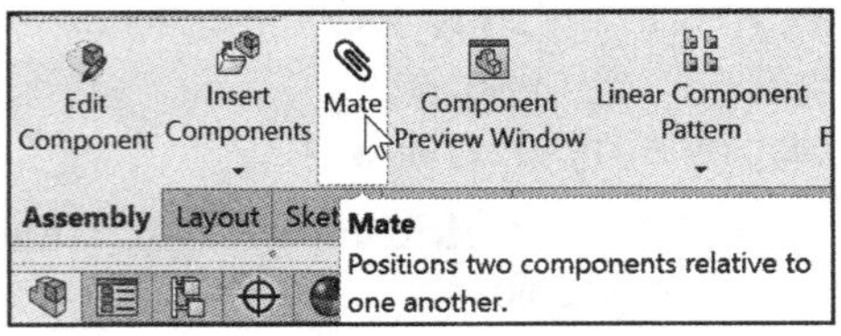

128) **Zoom-in** on the Collar and the 2MM Set Screw part.

129) Click the **Mate** tool from the Assembly toolbar. The Mate PropertyManager is displayed.

130) Pin the Mate PropertyManager. Click the Keep Visible icon.

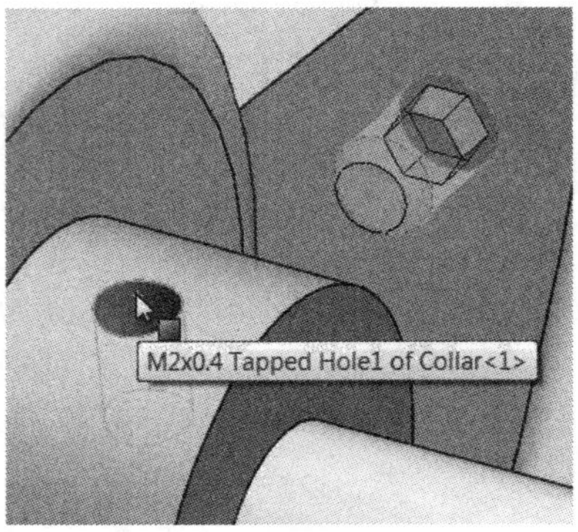

131) Click the **inside cylindrical face** of the Collar.

132) Click the **outside cylindrical face** of the **2MM Set Screw** part.

133) Click **Flip Mate Alignment (Anti-Aligned)**. Concentric mate is selected by default.

134) Click **OK** from the Concentric Mate PropertyManager.

Insert a Tangent Mate between the flat face of the 2MM Set Screw and the cylindrical face of the Axle.

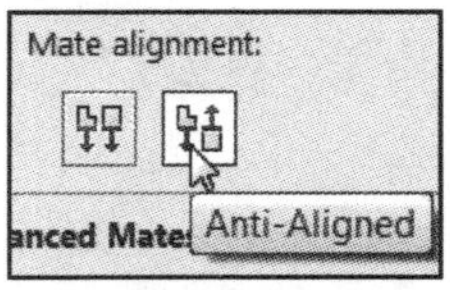

135) **Rotate** and **Zoom-in** on the flat face of the 2MM Set Screw part as illustrated.

136) Click the **flat face** of the 2MM Set Screw as illustrated.

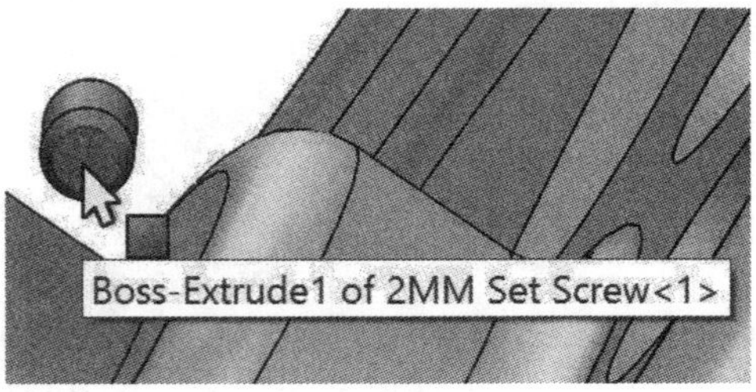

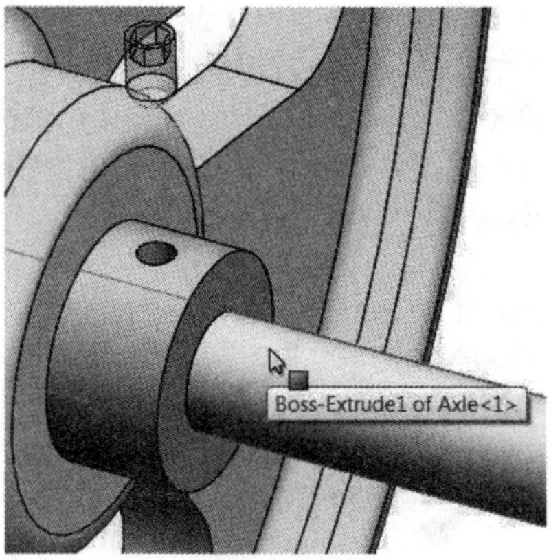

137) Click the **cylindrical face** of the Axle. Tangent mate is selected by default.

138) Click **OK** from the Tangent Mate PropertyManager.

139) Un-Pin the Mate PropertyManager. Click the **Keep Visible** icon as illustrated.

140) Click **OK** from the Mate PropertyManager. View the created mates in the Mates folder.

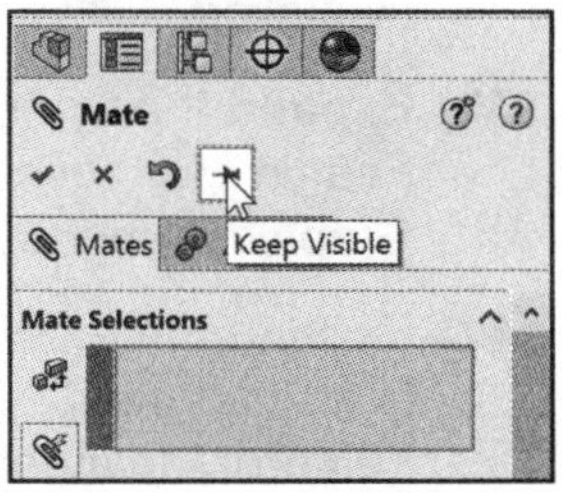

Fit the Assembly to the Graphics window.
141) Press the **f** key.

Display a Trimetric view.

142) Click **Trimetric view** from the Heads-up View toolbar.

Save the model.

143) Click **Save** .

144) Click **Rebuild** and **save**. View the results.

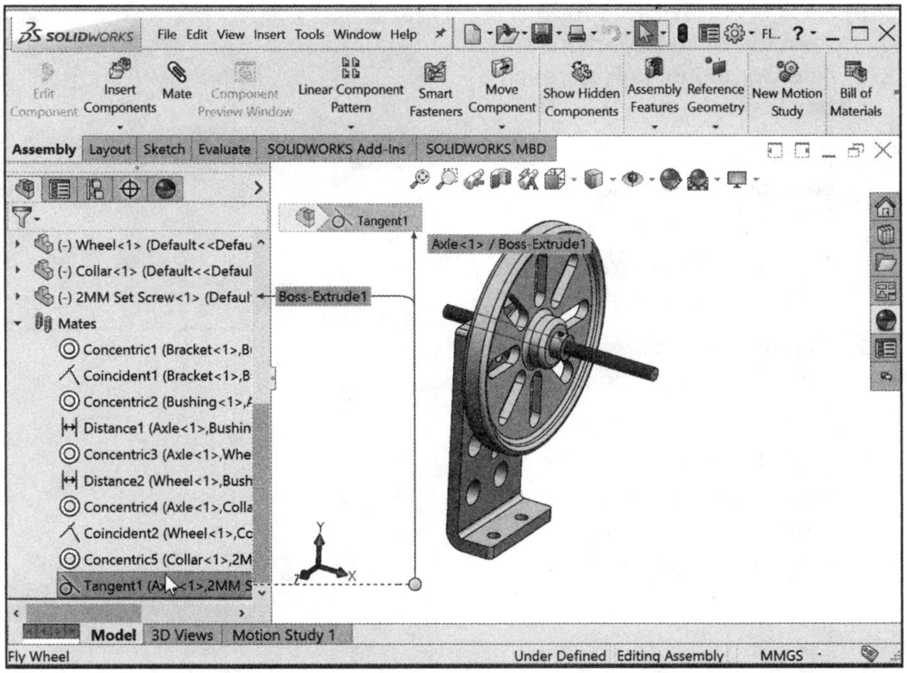

Rotate the Axle. The Collar moves separately about the Axle. The Wheel moves separately about the Axle. Align the Wheel and Collar so they rotate with respect to the Axle. Insert a Coincident mate between the three planes (Top Plane) for proper assembly movement.

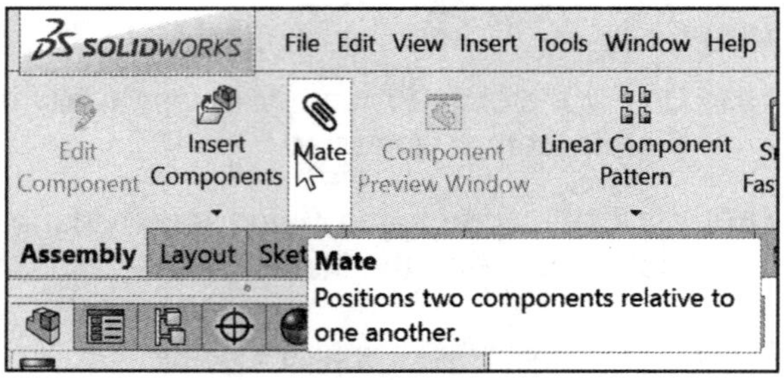

Insert a Coincident mate using the multiple mate mode between the Top Plane of the Axle, Wheel and Collar.

145) Click the **Mate** tool from the Assembly toolbar. The Mate PropertyManager is displayed.

146) **Expand** the fly-out FeatureManager from the Graphics window.

147) **Expand** the Axle component from the fly-out FeatureMananger.

148) Click **Top Plane** from the fly-out FeatureMananger.

149) Click **Multiple mate mode** from the Mate Selections box. The Components Reference box is displayed.

150) **Expand** the Wheel component from the fly-out FeatureManager.

151) Click **Top Plane** from the fly-out FeatureManager.

152) **Expand** the Collar component from the fly-out FeatureManager.

153) Click **Top Plane** from the fly-out FeatureManager. Coincident mate is selected by default.

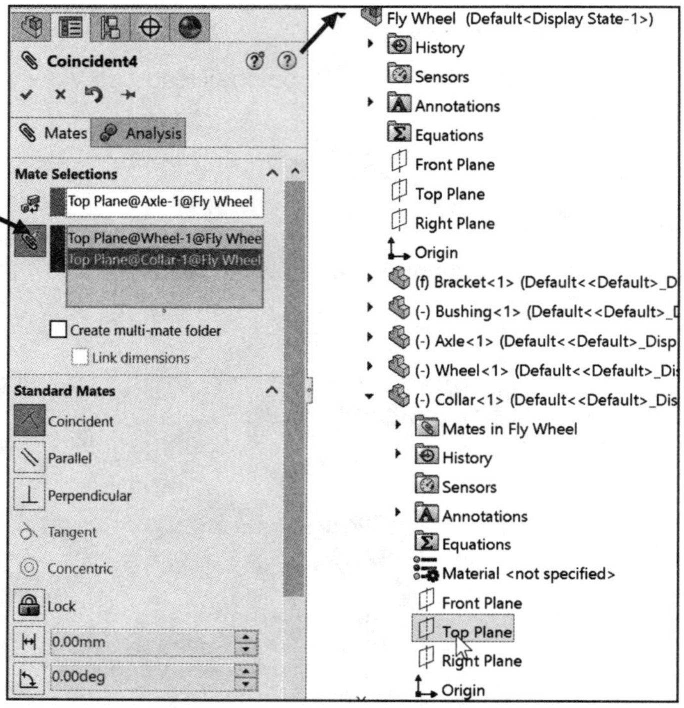

154) Click **OK** from the Coincident Mate PropertyManager.

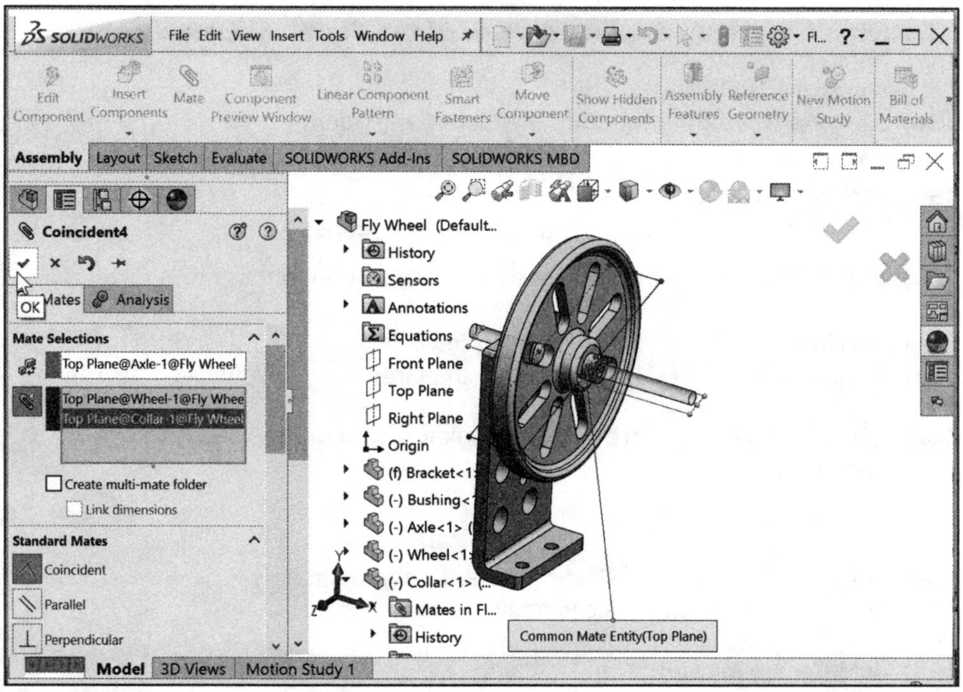

155) **Rotate** the Wheel and view the results. Rotate the Wheel back to the original orientation where the **2MM Set Screw** part is on top.

Display a Trimetric view.

156) Click **Trimetric view** from the Heads-up View toolbar.

Save the model.

157) Click **Save**.

Exploded View

An Exploded view shows an assembly's components spread out but positioned to show how they fit together when assembled. You create exploded views by selecting and dragging parts in the graphics area, and creating one or more explode steps. In exploded views you can:

- Evenly space exploded stacks of components (hardware, washers and so on).
- Attach a new component to the existing explode steps of another component. This is useful if you add a new part to an assembly that already has an exploded view.
- If a subassembly has an exploded view, reuse that view in a higher-level assembly.
- Add explode lines to indicate component relationships.

In the next section, create an Exploded view of the Fly Wheel assembly.

Activity: Create an Exploded View of the Fly Wheel Assembly

Create an Exploded View.

158) Click the **Assembly** tab from the CommandManager.

159) Click the **Exploded View** icon. The Explode PropertyManager is displayed. View your options.

160) Click the **Regular step (translate and rotate)** button.

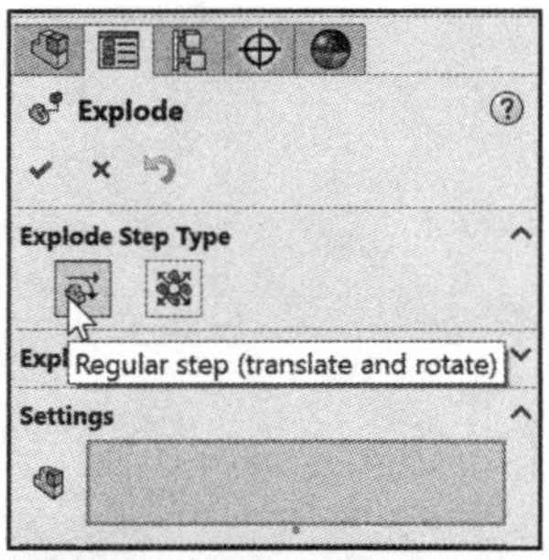

Create Explode Step 1 with the 2MM Set Screw.

161) **Zoom-in** on the 2MM Set Screw in the Graphics window.

162) Click the **2MM Set Screw**. A Manipulator icon is displayed.

163) **Zoom-out** to view the assembly.

164) Drag the Manipulator icon upward - approximately 30mm using the Graphics window ruler.

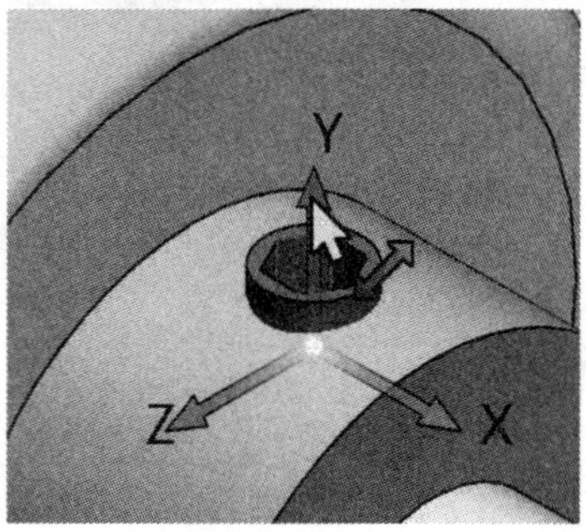

165) Release the **Manipulator** icon.

166) Click **inside** the Graphics window. Explode Step1 is created.

Create Explode Step 2. Select the 2MM Set Screw and the Collar.

167) Click the **2MM Set Screw**. A Manipulator icon is displayed.

168) Hold the **Ctrl** key down.

169) Click the **Collar**. A Manipulator icon is displayed.

170) Release the **Ctrl** key.

171) **Zoom-out** to view the Fly Wheel assembly.

172) Drag the Manipulator icon to the right of the assembly - approximately 140mm using the Graphics window ruler.

173) Release the **Manipulator** icon.

174) Click **inside** the Graphics window. Explode Step2 is created.

Create Explode Step3.

175) Click the **Wheel** from the Graphics window. A Manipulator icon is displayed.

176) Drag the Manipulator icon to the right of the assembly - approximately 120mm using the Graphics window ruler.

177) Release the **Manipulator** icon.

178) Click **inside** the Graphics window. Explode Step3 is created.

Create Explode Step4.

179) Click the **Axle** from the Graphics window. A Manipulator icon is displayed.

180) Drag the Manipulator icon to the right of the assembly - approximately 40mm using the Graphics window ruler.

181) Release the **Manipulator** icon.

182) Click **inside** the Graphics window. Explode Step4 is created.

Create Explode Step5.

183) Click the **Bushing** from the Graphics window. A Manipulator icon is displayed.

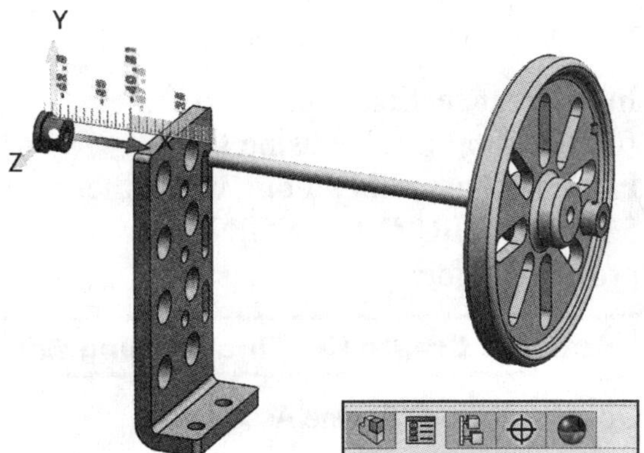

184) Drag the Manipulator icon to the left of the assembly - approximately 40mm - using the Graphics window ruler.

185) Click **inside** the Graphics window. Explode Step5 is created.

186) Click **OK** from the Explode PropertyManager.

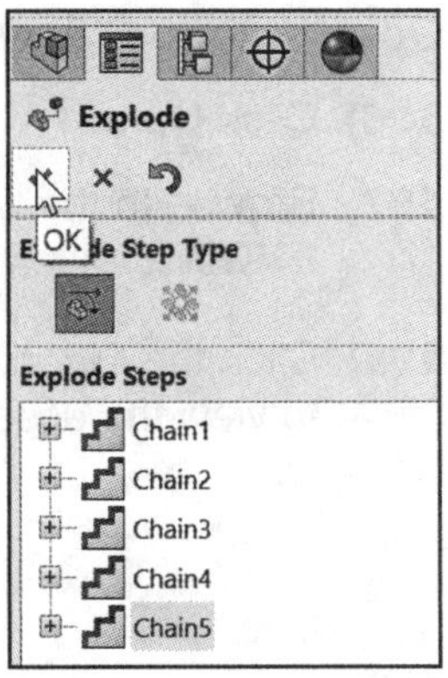

View the Animate collapse of the Exploded Fly Wheel Assembly.

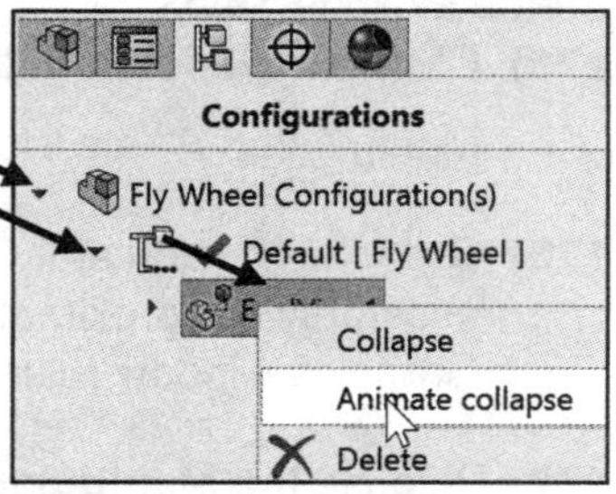

187) Click the **ConfigurationManager** tab as illustrated.

188) **Expand** the Default folder in the ConfigurationManager as illustrated.

189) Right-click **ExpView1**.

190) Click **Animate collapse**. The Animation Controller is displayed.

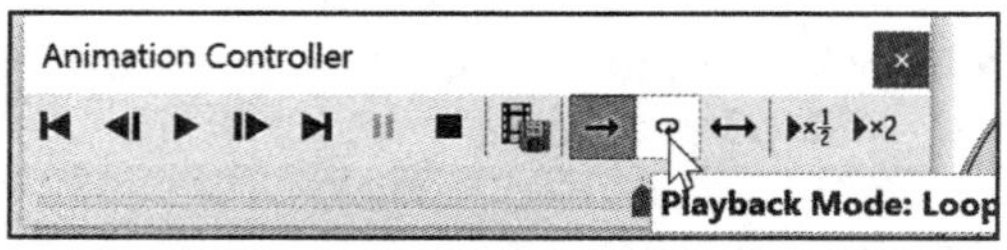

191) Click **Playback Mode: Loop**. View the results in the Graphics window.

192) Click **End**.

193) **Close** the Animation Controller.

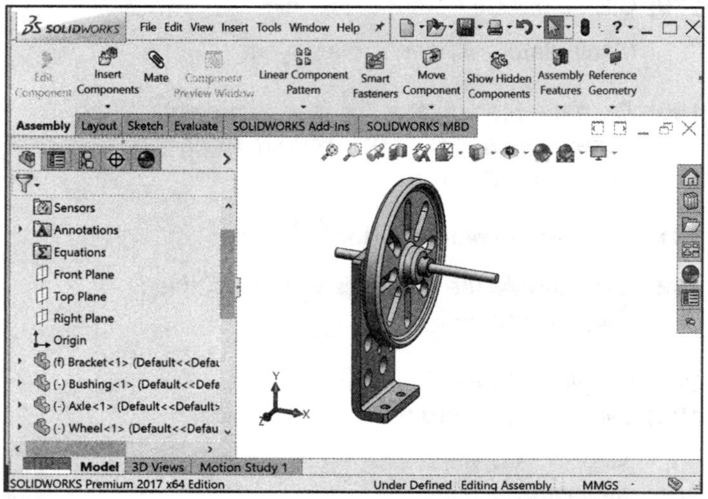

Return to the Assembly FeatureManager.

194) Click the **FeatureManager Design Tree** icon.

Close all documents.

195) Click **Window**, **Close All** from the Main menu. Are you finished with the assembly? The Fly Wheel assembly is a sub-assembly to the final Stirling Engine assembly.

In the next section, create the final Stirling Engine using the Fly Wheel assembly along with other provided components from the SOLIDWORKS in 5 Hours\STIRLING ENGINE folder. Use the components and sub-assemblies in the provided folder.

Activity: Create the Final Stirling Engine Assembly

Open the Sterling Engine Assembly.

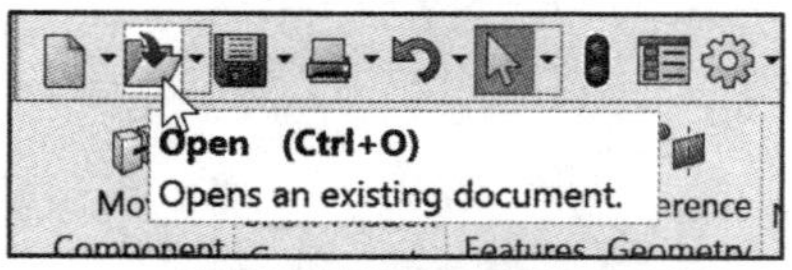

196) Click **Open** from the Main menu.

197) Browse to the **SOLIDWORKS in 5 Hours\STIRLING ENGINE** folder.

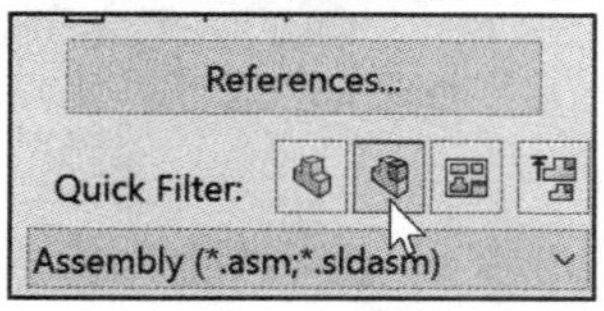

198) Click the **Filter Assemblies (*asm; *sldasm)** icon to view the assemblies in the folder.

199) Double-click the **Stirling Engine** assembly. The Stirling Engine is displayed in the Graphics window.

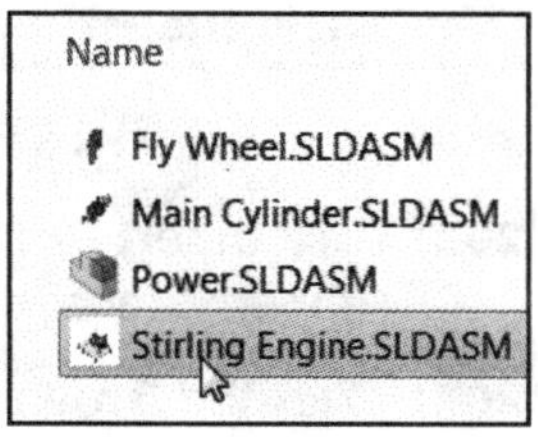

200) **Review** the Feature Manager. The Feature Manager is made up of components. Components are sub-assemblies and parts. There are two sub-assemblies: Main Cylinder and Power. Both are displayed in a Flexible state.

The Plate and Bracket are designed for flexibility to support other components in the future.

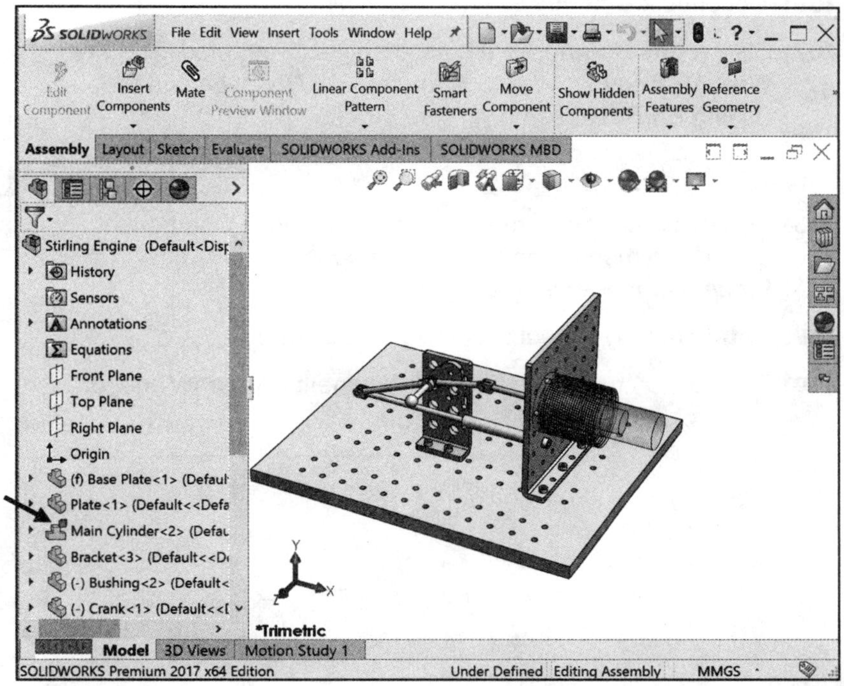

Activity: Hide the Plate Component

Hide the Plate component.

201) Right-Click **Plate** from the Assembly FeatureManager.

202) Click **Hide Components** from the Context toolbar.

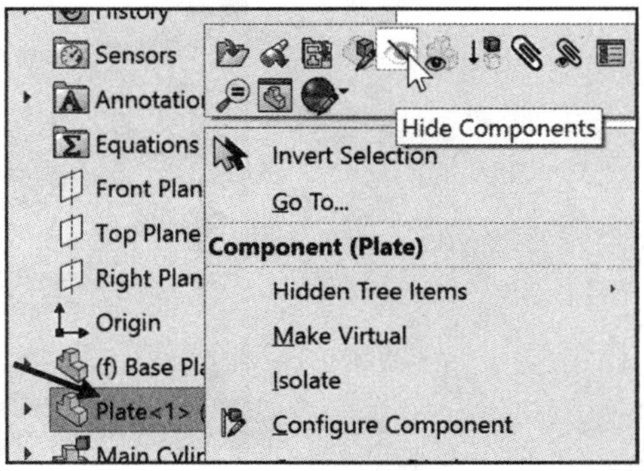

Activity: Insert and Rotate the Fly Wheel Assembly

Insert the Fly Wheel assembly.

203) Click **Insert Component** from the Assembly toolbar. The Insert Component PropertyManager is displayed.

204) Click the **Browse** button.

205) Browse to the **SOLIDWORKS in 5 Hours\STIRLING ENGINE** folder.

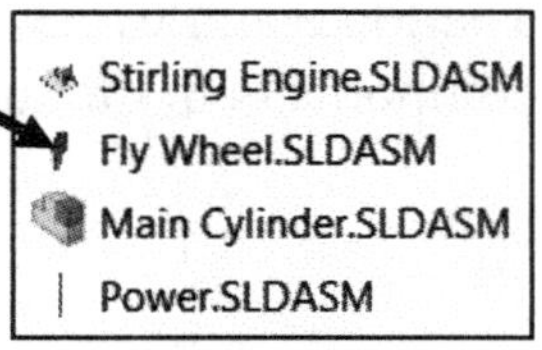

206) Double-click the **Fly Wheel** assembly.

207) Click a **position** above the assembly as illustrated. The Fly Wheel is free to translate. Drag the Fly Wheel behind the Stirling Engine assembly.

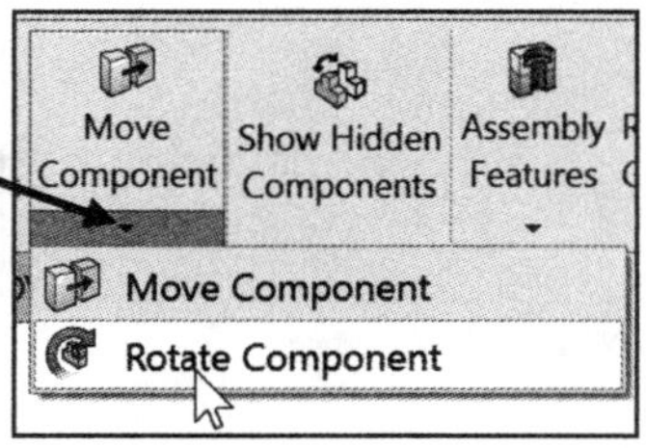

Rotate the Fly Wheel assembly.

208) Click **Rotate Component** from the Move Component drop-down menu. The Rotate Component PropertyManager is displayed.

209) **Rotate** the Fly Wheel assembly as illustrated.

210) Click **OK** ✔ from the Rotate Component PropertyManager.

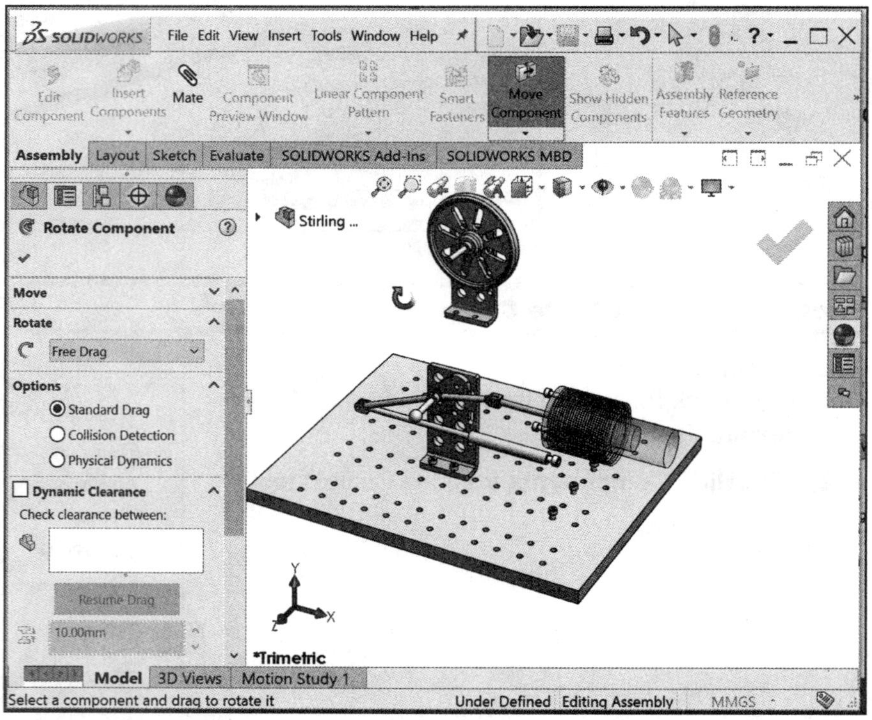

Activity: Mate the Fly Wheel Assembly

Insert a Concentric mate between the cylindrical face of the Axle and the cylindrical face of the Crank hole.

211) Click the **cylindrical face** of the Axle.

212) Click **Front view**.

213) **Rotate** and **Zoom in** on the Crank hole.

214) Hold the **Ctrl** key down.

215) Click the **inside cylindrical face** of the Crank hole as illustrated.

216) Release the **Ctrl** key. The Mate Pop-up menu is displayed.

217) Click **Concentric** from The Mate Pop-up menu. A Concentric mate locates the selected items so they can share the same center point.

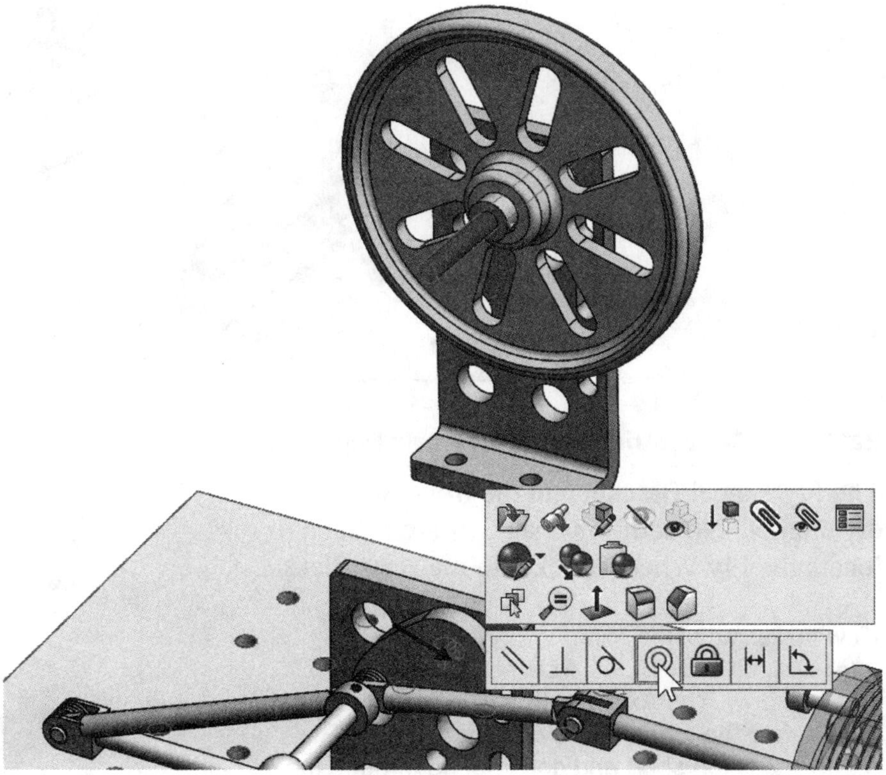

Insert a Concentric mate between the cylindrical face of the Bracket hole and the cylindrical face of the Base Plate hole directly aligned above with the Axle.

218) Rotate and **Zoom** in as illustrated. If needed move the Fly Wheel assembly.

219) Hold the **Ctrl** key down.

220) Click the inside **cylindrical face** of Bracket hole as illustrated.

221) Click the **cylindrical face** of the Base Plate hole as illustrated.

222) Release the **Ctrl** key. The Mate Pop-up menu is displayed.

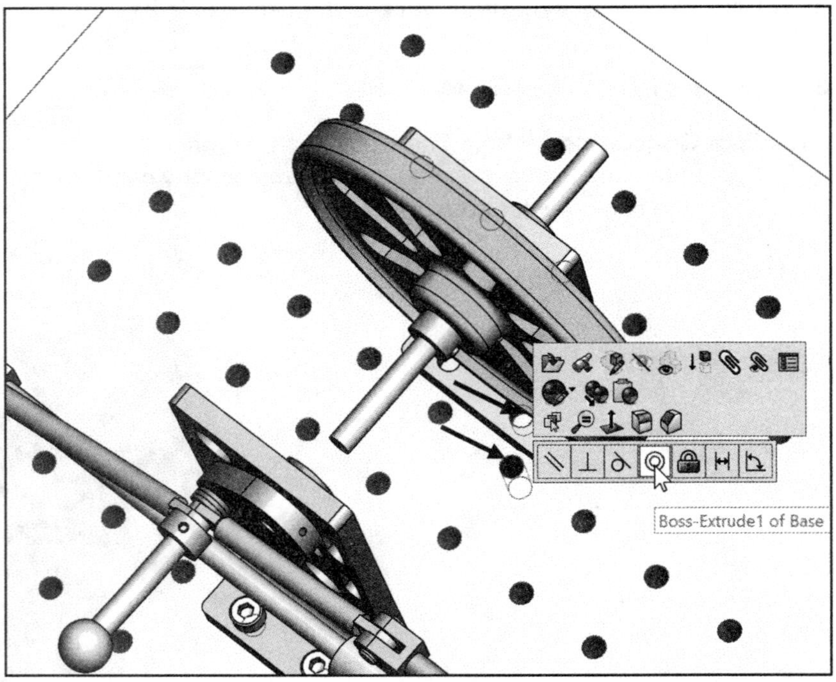

223) Click **Concentric** from The Mate Pop-up menu.

The Fly Wheel Bracket and the front Bracket are aligned. No additional spacers are needed to locate the Fly Wheel Bracket to the Base Plate.

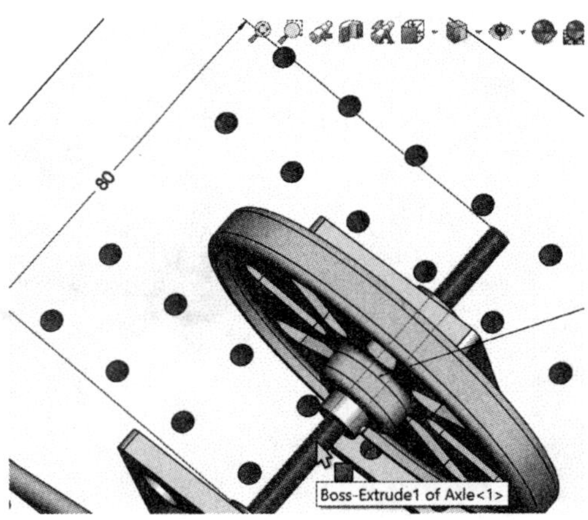

View the length of the Axle.

224) Double-click on the **Axle** in the Graphics window. The Axle length is 80mm. If needed, rotate the model to view the dimension. The Axle is too short and does not go through the Crank. The Axle ends at the back face of the Bushing.

In the next section, apply the Measure tool to locate the needed length of the Axle.

Apply the Measure tool.

225) Press the **f** key to fit the model to the Graphics window.

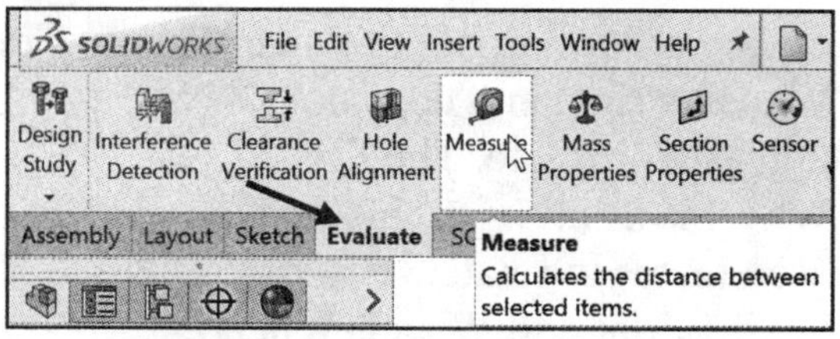

226) Click the **Evaluate** tab from the CommandManager.

227) Click the **Measure** tool. The Measure dialog box is displayed.

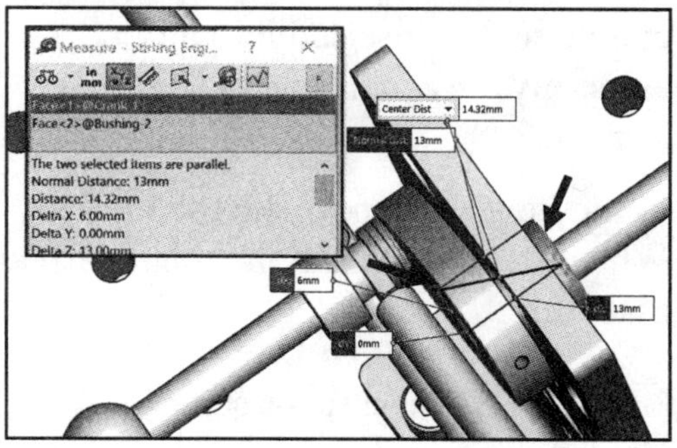

228) **Zoom in** and **Rotate** on the Bushing and Crank components as illustrated.

229) Click the **back face** of the Bushing.

230) Click the **front face** of the Crank. The Normal Distance between the two faces is 13mm.

231) **Close** the Measure dialog box.

You can Right-click on the Axle and apply the Select-other tool to view the end of the Axle and to select the face for the Measure tool. See SOLIDWORKS Help for additional information.

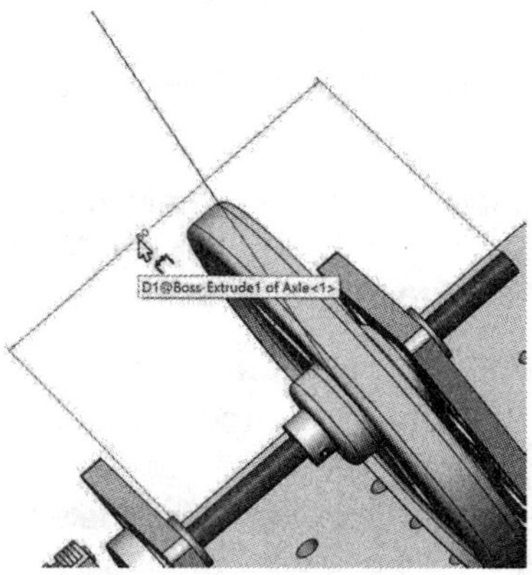

Fit the model to the Graphics window.

232) Press the **f** key.

Modify the Axle length.

233) Double click on the **Axle** in the Graphics window. View the dimensions.

234) Click the **80** dimension. If needed open the Axle part in the assembly.

235) Modify the overall length to **93**mm.

236) Click the **Rebuild** icon from the Main menu. The Axle is the correct length.

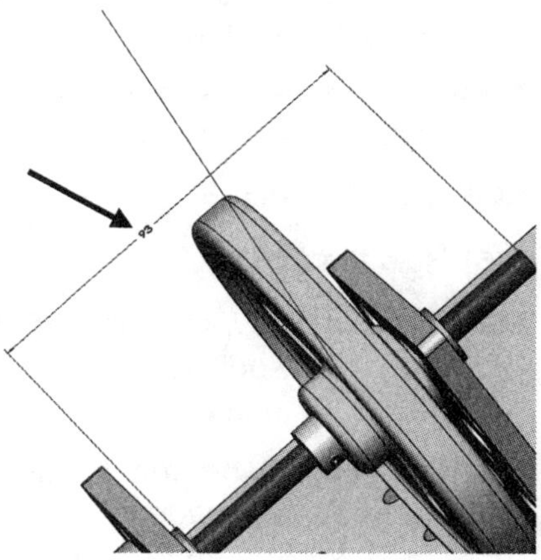

Display a Trimetric view.

237) Click **Trimetric view** from the Heads-up View toolbar.

Save the model.

238) Click **Save**.

239) Click **Save All**.

Click and drag the Handle to rotate the Crank. The Crank rotates. The linkage controls the linear motion of the Power Piston. The Main Cylinder Piston translates. The Fly Wheel is rigid and does not translate or rotate. The Fly Wheel is a sub-assembly and used mates to rotate the Axle, Shaft Collar and Wheel. When a component is inserted into an assembly, any mates are solved as rigid.

In the next section, make the Fly Wheel flexible within the main assembly.

Make the Fly Wheel sub-assembly Flexible.

240) Right-click **Fly Wheel** from the Assembly FeatureMananger.

241) Click **Make Subassembly Flexible** from the Pop-up Content toolbar.

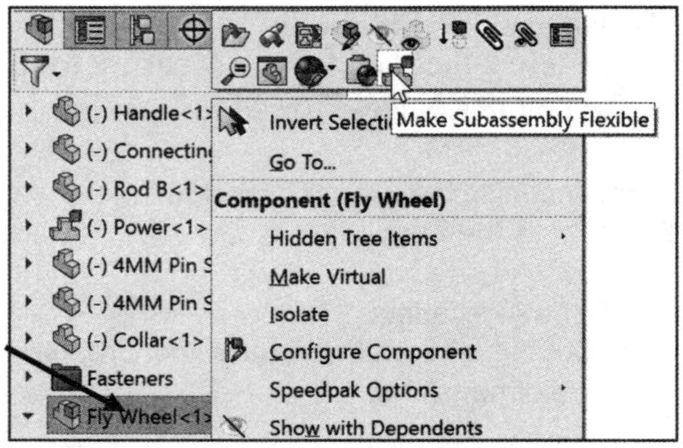

242) **Rotate** the Wheel in the Graphics window. The Axle of the Fly Wheel assembly is free to rotate. The Crank is free to rotate.

In the next section, apply mates to control the rotation of the Crank and Axle.

Insert a Coincident Mate between the Top Plane of the Axle and the Top Plane of the Crank.

243) **Expand** the Fly Wheel component from the FeatureManager.

244) **Expand** the Axle component from the FeatureManager.

245) Click **Top Plane**.

246) Hold the **Ctrl** key down.

247) **Expand** the Crank component from the fly-out FeatureMananger.

248) Click **Top Plane** from the fly-out FeatureManager.

249) Release the **Ctrl** key. The Mate Pop-up menu is displayed.

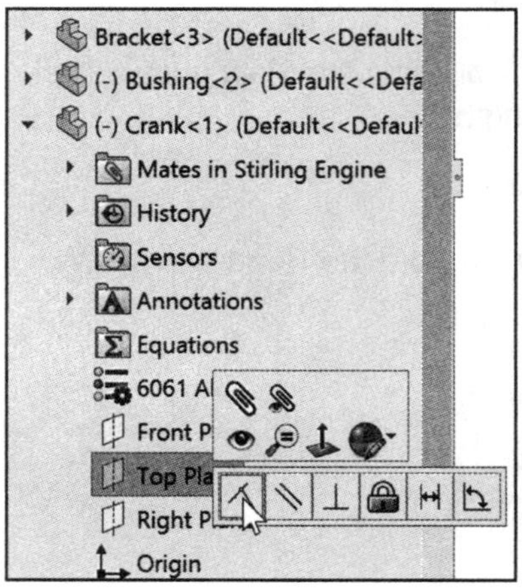

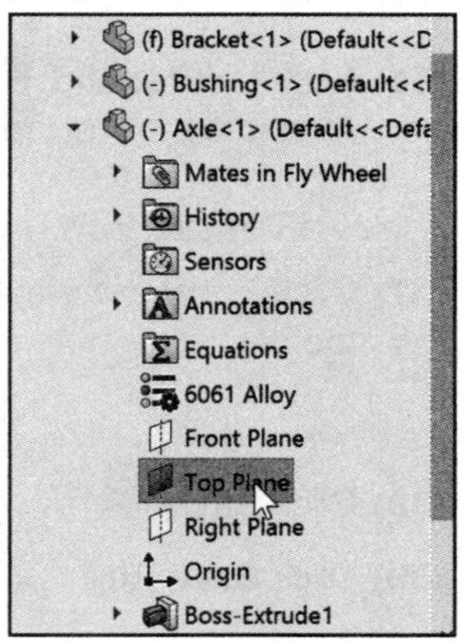

250) Click **Coincident** mate from the Mate pop-up menu. Note if these two planes were not coincident, a parallel plane could be used to control rotation.

251) **Rotate** the Crank. The Fly Wheel, Crank and Axle all rotate together.

Display the Plate.

252) Right-click **Plate** from the Assembly FeatureManager.

253) Click **Show Components** for the Content toolbar. View the final assembly in the Graphics window.

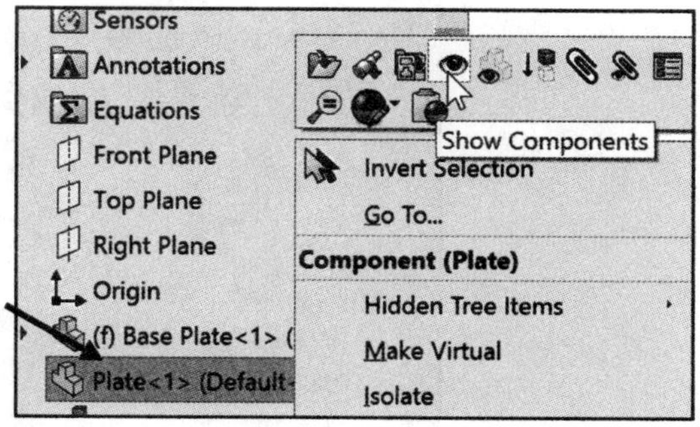

Display a Trimetric view.

254) Click **Trimetric view** from the Heads-up View toolbar.

Save the model.

255) Click **Save**.

256) Click **Rebuilt and Save**.

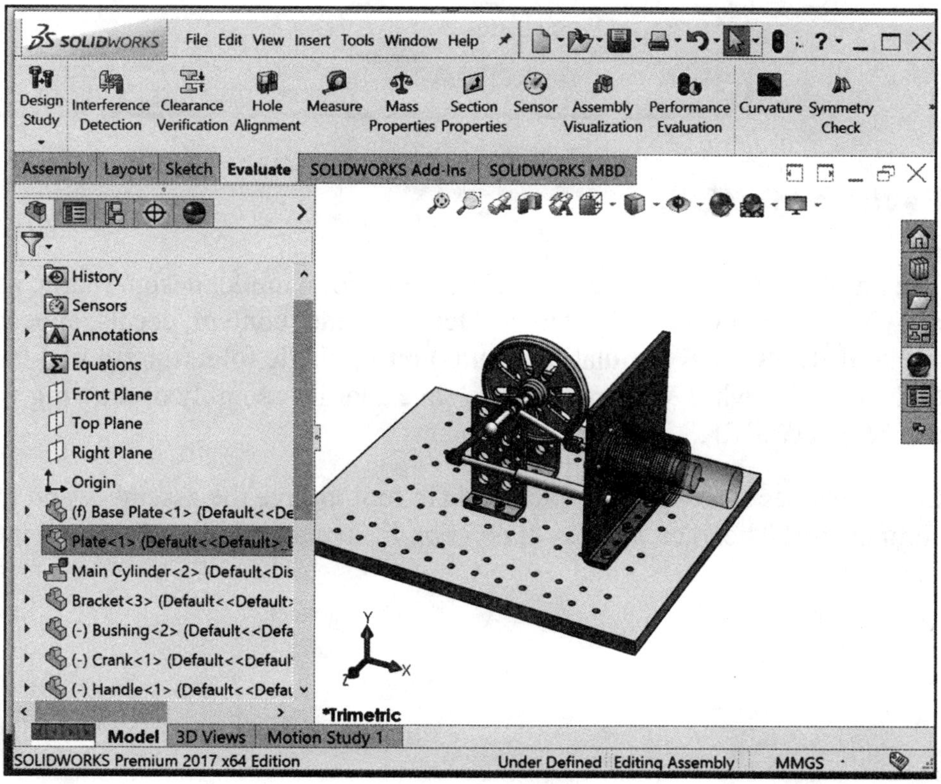

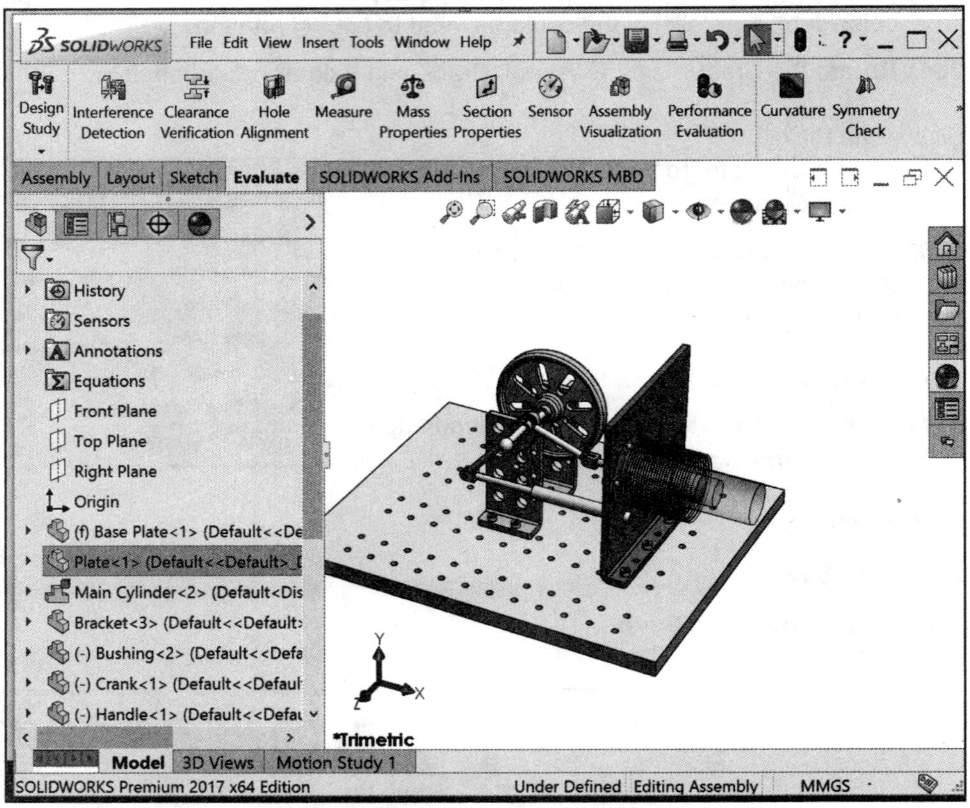

Pack and Go

The Pack and Go tool gathers all related files for a model design (parts, assemblies, drawings, references, design tables, Design Binder content, decals, appearances, scenes and SOLIDWORKS Simulation results) into a single folder or zip file. It's one of the best tools to utilize when you are trying to save a large assembly or drawing with references and SOLIDWORKS Toolbox components.

In the next section apply the Pack and Go tool to save the assembly and all toolbox components. The Pack and Go dialog box lists related files to be saved into a folder or zip file.

Activity: Pack and Go the Stirling Engine Assembly

Save the Assembly using Pack and Go to a Zip file.

257) Click **File**, **Pack and Go** from the Main menu bar. The Pack and Go dialog box is displayed. The dialog box lists related files to be saved into a folder or zip file. For additional information see SOLIDWORKS Help.

258) Check the **Include Toolbox components** box.

259) Check **Save to Zip file** as illustrated.

260) **Browse** to the SOLIDWORKS in 5 Hours folder.

261) Enter the **File name**. Click **Save** from the Save As dialog box.

262) Click **Save** from the Pack and Go dialog box. A Zip file is created of the assembly and all reference components.

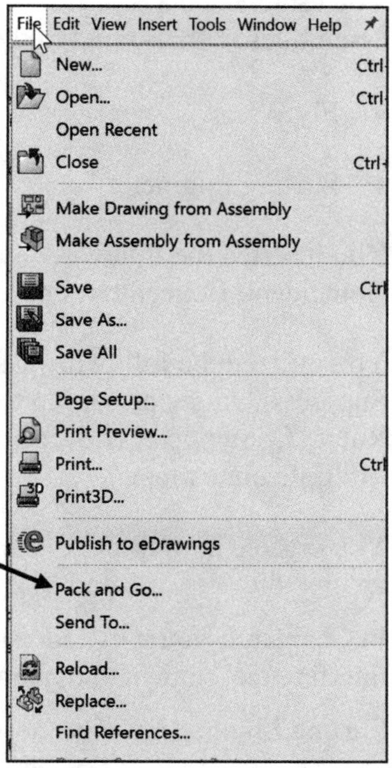

Close all models.

263) Click **Window, Close All** from the Main menu. You are finished with this chapter.

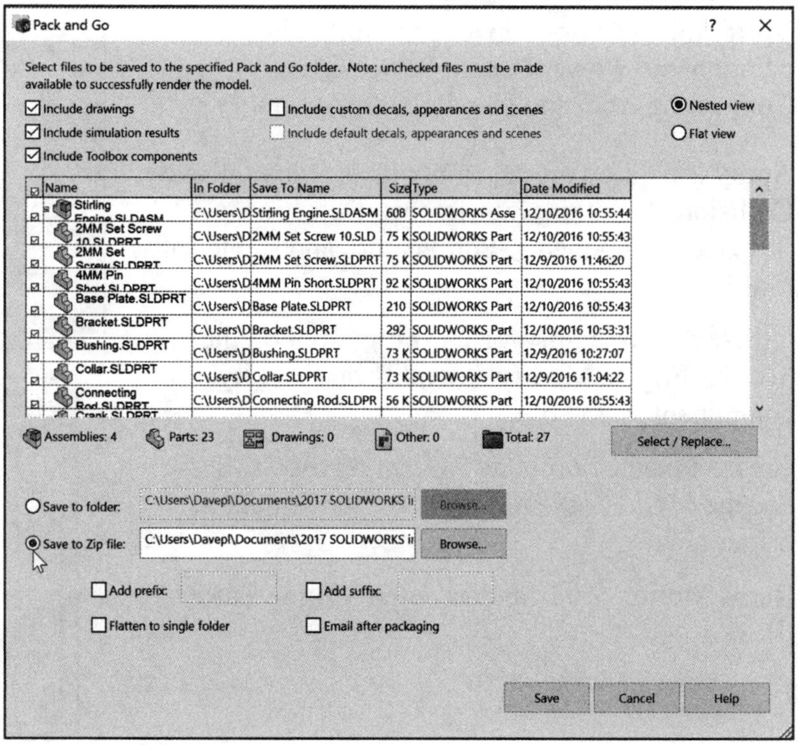

Summary

You established a SOLIDWORKS session and created two new assemblies with user defined document properties:

- Fly Wheel.
- Stirling Engine.

You inserted the following Standard and Quick mate types: Coincident, Concentric, Distance and Tangent.

You utilized the following assembly tools: Insert Component, Suppress, Un-suppress, Mate, Move Component, Rotate Component, Hide, Show, Flexible, Ridge and Multiple mate mode.

You created an Exploded View with animation and applied the Measure and Mass Properties tool.

In Chapter 4, you will address clearance, interference, static and dynamic behavior of the Stirling Engine Modified Assembly.

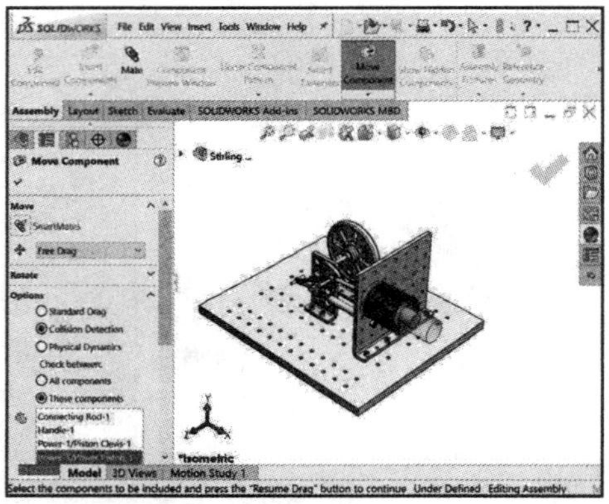

Verify the behavior between the following components: Power Piston, Power Clevis, Connecting Rod, and Handle in the assembly.

Apply the following assembly tools: Move, Rotate, Collision Detection, Interference Detection, Selected Components, Edit Feature and Center of Mass.

Utilize the Assembly Visualization tool on the Stirling Engine Modify assembly and sort by component mass.

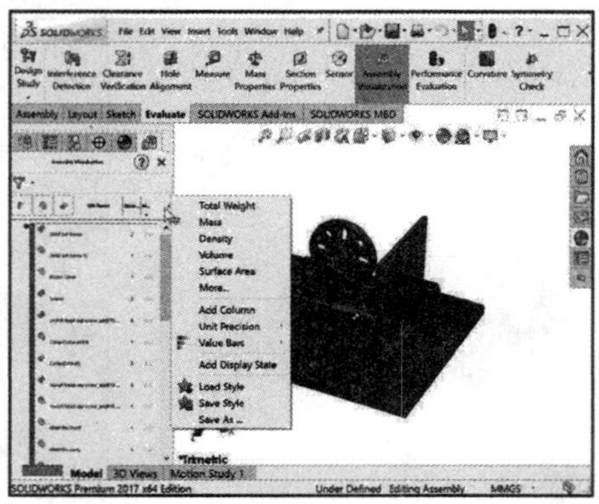

Create a new Coordinate System on the Stirling Engine Modify assembly relative to the default origin.

Run a Motion Study and save the Motion Study AVI file.

Build an Assembly from a Detailed Dimensioned Illustration

Tutorial 3-1

Build this assembly. Locate the Center of mass of the model with respect to the illustrated coordinate system.

The assembly contains the following: (1) Clevis component, (3) Axle components, (2) 5 Hole Link components, (2) 3 Hole Link components, and (6) Collar components. All holes Ø.190 THRU unless otherwise noted. Angle A = 150deg. Angle B = 120deg. Unit system: IPS.

Note: The location of the illustrated coordinate system: (+X, +Y, +Z).

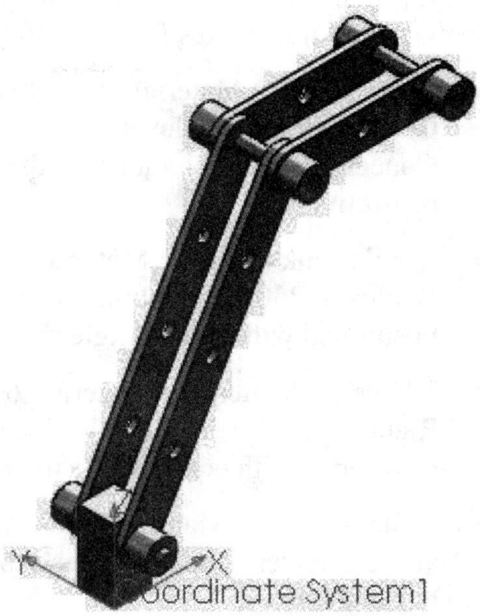

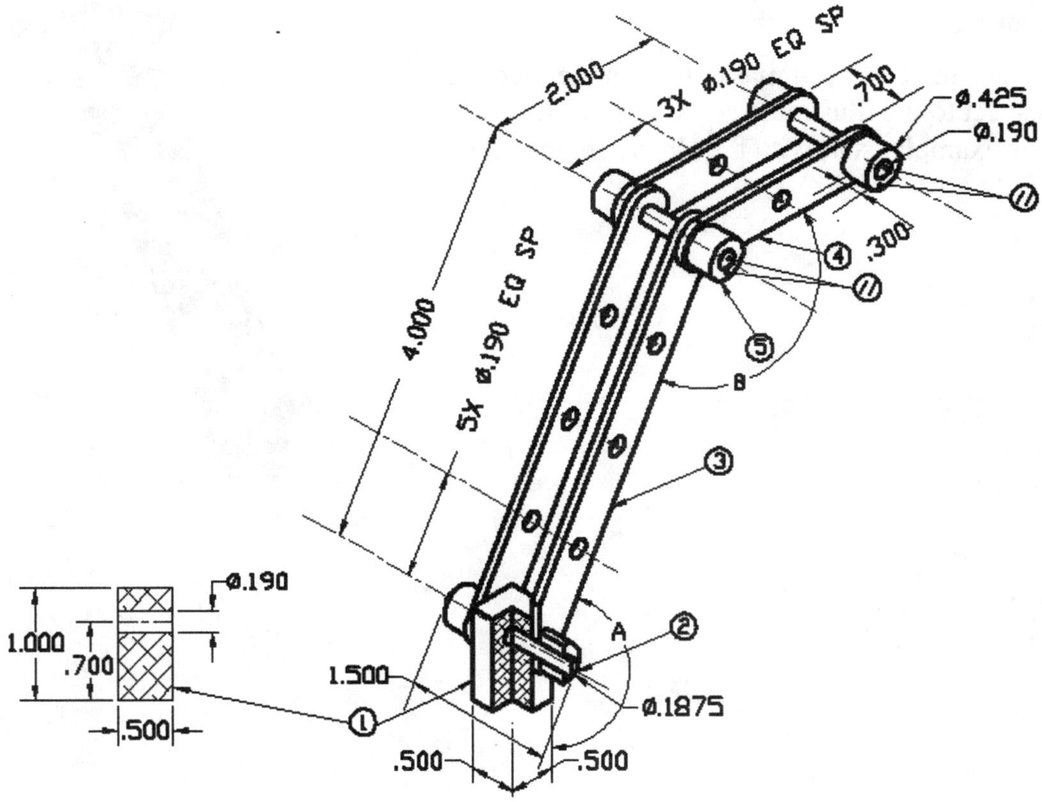

Clevis (Item 1): Material: 6061 Alloy. The two (5) Hole Link components are positioned with equal Angle mates (150deg) to the Clevis component.

- Axle (Item 2): Material: AISI 304. The first Axle component is mated Concentric and Coincident to the Clevis. The second and third Axle components are mated Concentric and Coincident to the 5 Hole Link and the 3 Hole Link components respectively.
- 5 Hole Link (Item 3): Material: 6061 Alloy. Material thickness = .100in. Radius = .250in. Five holes located 1in. on center. The 5 Hole Link components are positioned with equal Angle mates, (120deg) to the 3 Hole Link components.
- 3 Hole Link (Item 4): Material: 6061 Alloy. Material thickness = .100in. Radius = .250in. Three holes located 1in. on center. The 3 Hole Link components are positioned with equal Angle mates, (120deg) to the 5 Hole Link components.
- Collar (Item 5): Material: 6061 Alloy. The Collar components are mated Concentric and Coincident to the Axle and the 5 Hole Link and 3 Hole Link components respectively.

Think about the steps that you would take to build the illustrated assembly. Identify the first fixed component. Insert the required Standard mates.

Locate the Center of mass of the model with respect to the illustrated coordinate system. In this example, start with the Clevis component.

Tutorial Assembly Model 3-1

Create the assembly. The illustrated assembly contains the following components: (1) Clevis component, (3) Axle components, (2) 5 Hole Link components, (2) 3 Hole Link components, and (6) Collar components. All holes Ø.190 THRU unless otherwise noted. Angle A = 150deg, Angle B = 120deg. Set decimal place to 2. Unit system: IPS.

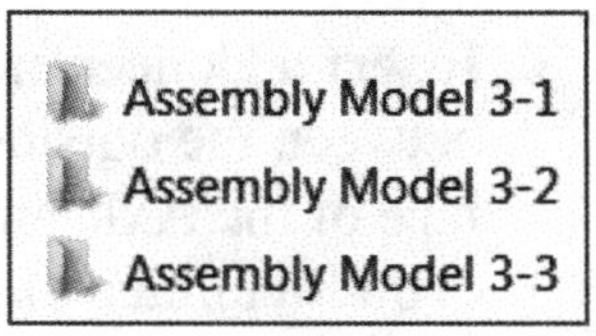

1. **Download** the needed components from the SOLIDWORKS in 5 Hours\Chapter 3 Homework folder.
2. **Create** a new IPS assembly in SOLIDWORKS. The created models are displayed in the Open documents box.

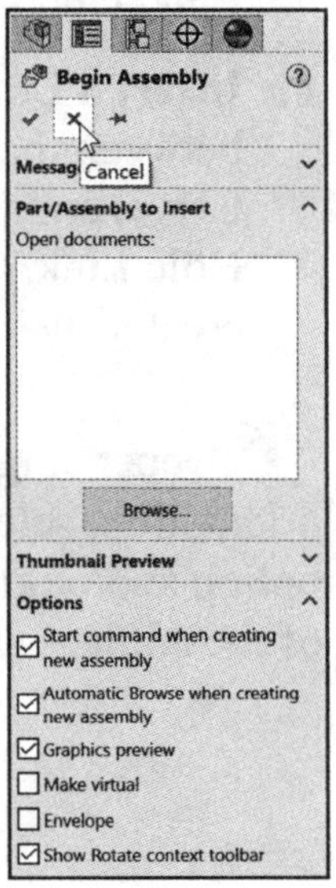

3. Click **Cancel** ✖ from the Begin Assembly PropertyManager. Assem1 is the default document name. Assembly documents end with the extension .sldasm.
4. **Set** the document properties for the model. **Insert** the Clevis part.
5. **Fix** the component to the assembly Origin. Click OK from the Insert Component PropertyManager. The Clevis is displayed in the Assembly FeatureManager and in the Graphics window.

Fix the position of a component so that it cannot move with respect to the assembly Origin. By default, the first part in an assembly is fixed; however, you can float it at any time.

6. **Insert** the Axle part above the Clevis component as illustrated. Note the location of the Origin. **Clear** the origin view from the Graphics window.
7. **Insert** a Concentric mate between the inside cylindrical face of the Clevis and the outside cylindrical face of the Axle. The selected face entities are displayed in the Mate Selections box. Concentric1 is created.

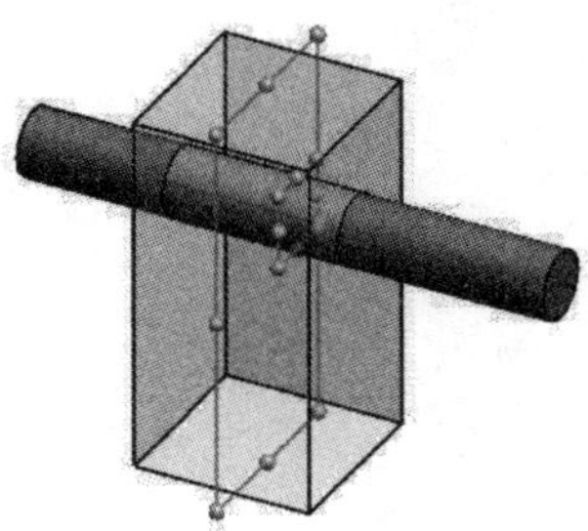

8. **Insert** a Coincident mate between the Right Plane of the Clevis and the Right Plane of the Axle. Coincident1 mate is created.

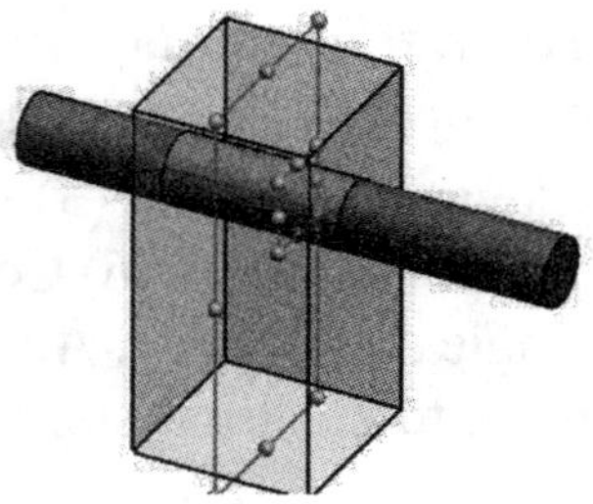

9. **Insert** the 5 Hole Link part. Locate and rotate the component as illustrated.

10. **Insert** a Concentric mate between the outside cylindrical face of the Axle and the inside cylindrical face of the 5 Hole Link. Concentric2 is created.

11. **Insert** a Coincident mate between the right face of the Clevis and the left face of the 5 Hole Link. Coincident2 is created.

Depending on the component orientation, select the Flip direction option and/or enter the supplement of the angle.

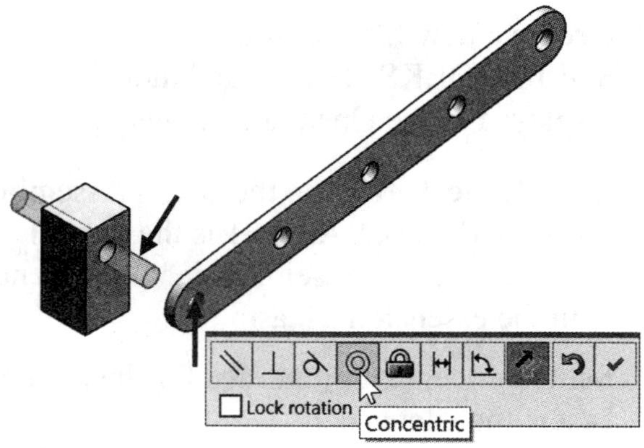

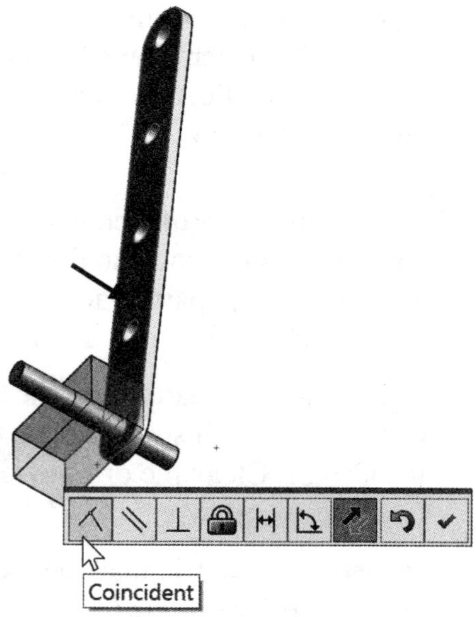

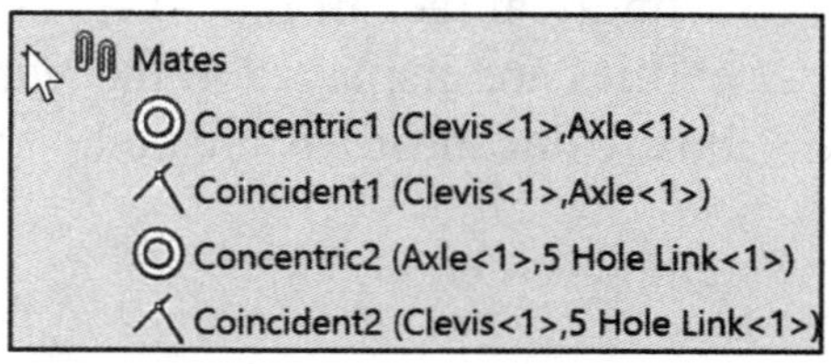

12. **Insert** an Angle mate between the bottom face of the 5 Hole Link and the back face of the Clevis. Angle = 30deg. The selected faces are displayed in the Mate Selections box. Angle1 is created. Flip direction if needed.

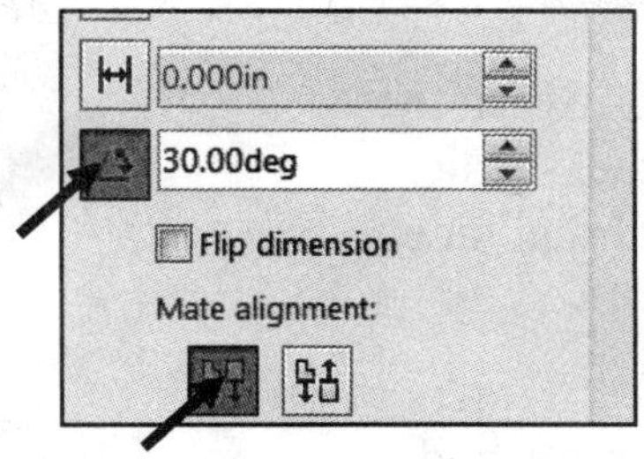

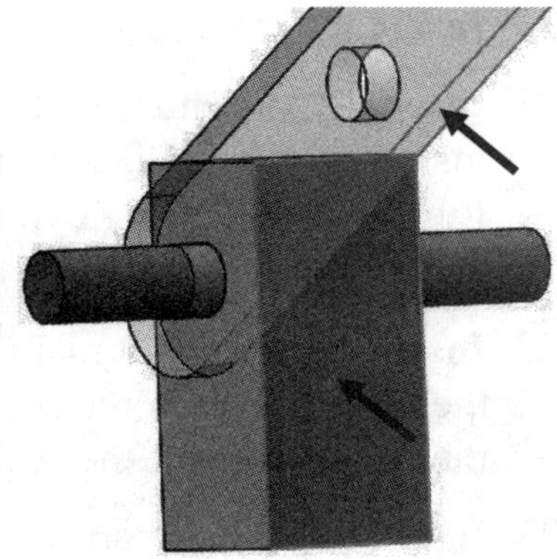

13. **Insert** the second Axle part. Locate the second Axle component near the end of the 5 Hole Link as illustrated.

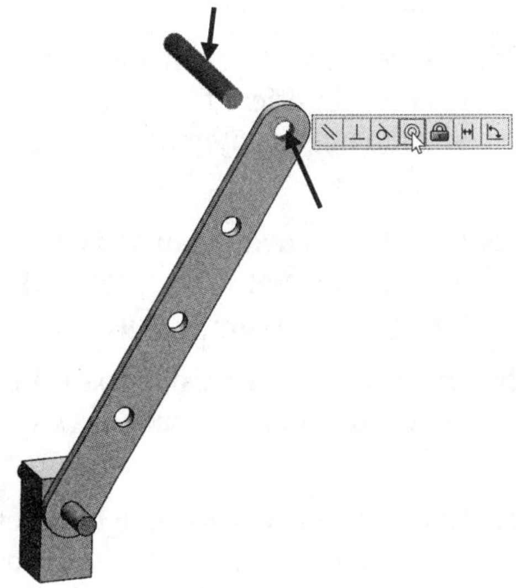

14. **Insert** a Concentric mate between the inside cylindrical face of the 5 Hole Link and the outside cylindrical face of the Axle. Concentric3 is created.

15. **Insert** a Coincident mate between the Right Plane of the assembly and the Right Plane of the Axle. Coincident3 is created.

16. **Insert** the 3 Hole Link part. Locate and rotate the component as illustrated.

17. **Insert** a Concentric mate between the outside cylindrical face of the Axle and the inside cylindrical face of the 3 Hole Link. Concentric4 is created.

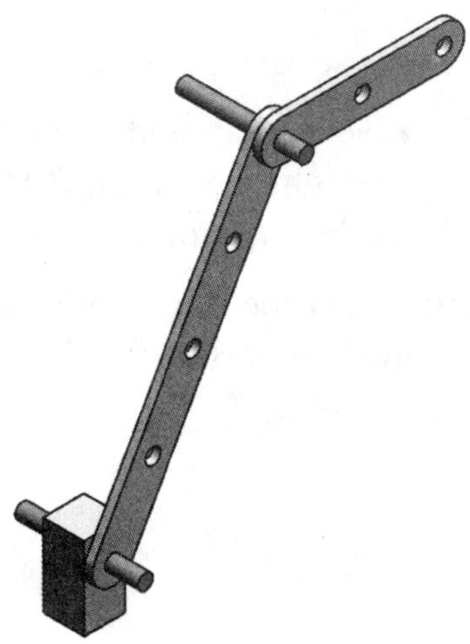

18. **Insert** a Coincident mate between the right face of the 5 Hole Link and the left face of the 3 Hole Link.

19. **Insert** an Angle mate between the bottom face of the 5 Hole Link and the bottom face of the 3 Hole Link. Angle = 60deg. Angle2 is created.

Depending on the component orientation, select the Flip direction option and/or enter the supplement of the angle when needed.

Apply the Measure tool to check the angle.

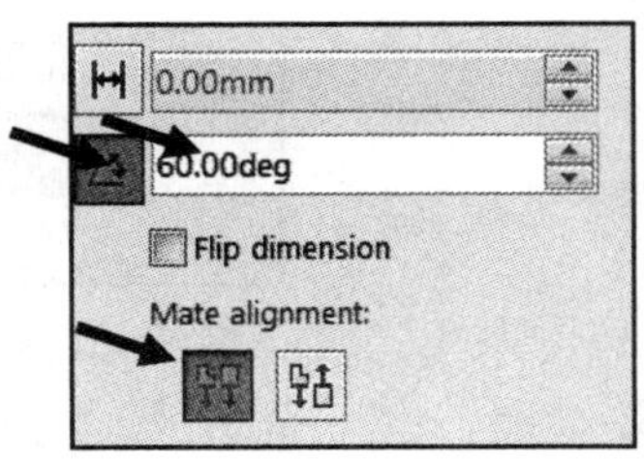

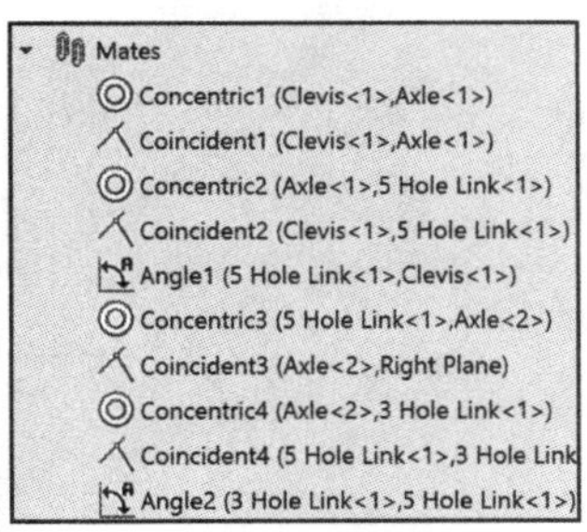

20. **Insert** the third Axle part.
21. **Insert** a Concentric mate between the inside cylindrical face of the 3 Hole Link and the outside cylindrical face of the Axle.
22. **Insert** a Coincident mate between the Right Plane of the assembly and the Right Plane of the Axle.
23. **Insert** the Collar part. Locate the Collar near the first Axle component.
24. **Insert** a Concentric mate between the inside cylindrical face of the Collar and the outside cylindrical face of the first Axle.
25. **Insert** a Coincident mate between the right face of the 5 Hole Link and the left face of the Collar.
26. **Insert** the second Collar part. Locate the Collar near the second Axle component.
27. **Insert** a Concentric mate between the inside circular face of the second Collar and the outside circular face of the second Axle.
28. **Insert** a Coincident mate between the right face of the 3 Hole Link and the left face of the second Collar.
29. **Insert** the third Collar part. Locate the Collar near the third Axle component.

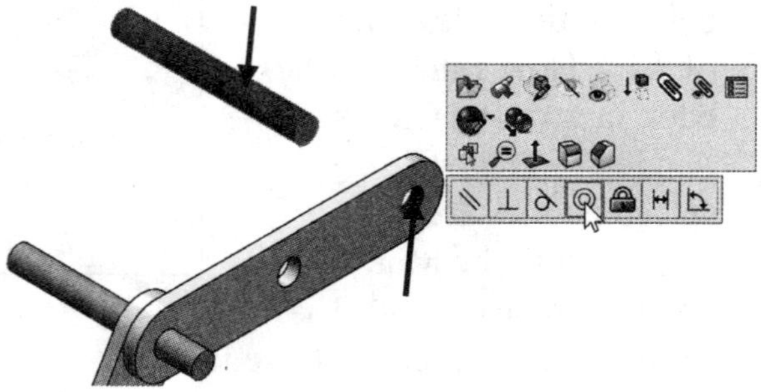

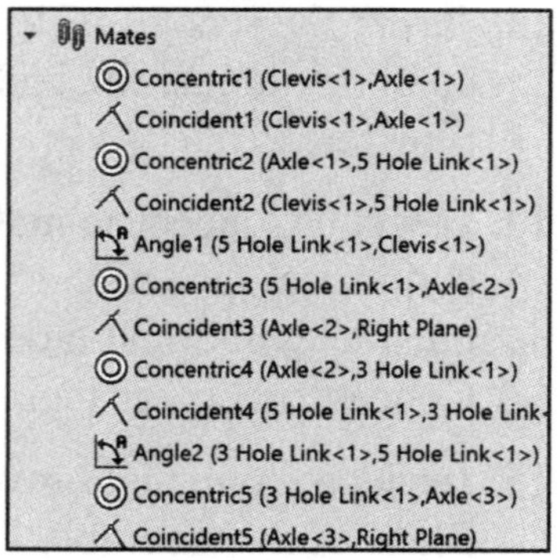

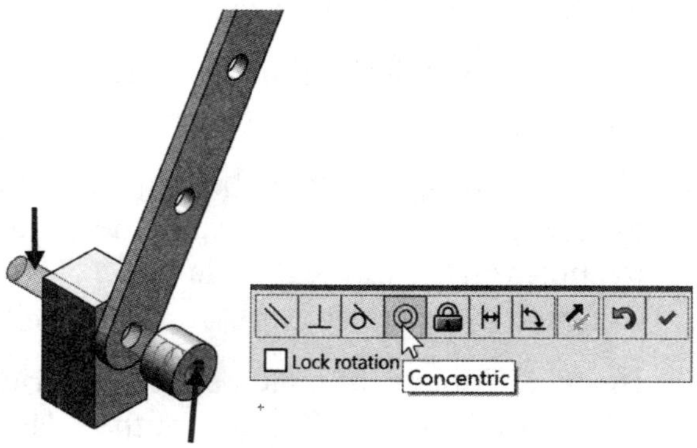

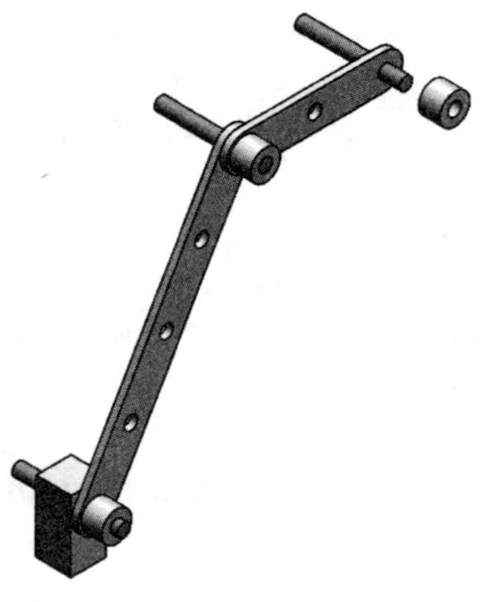

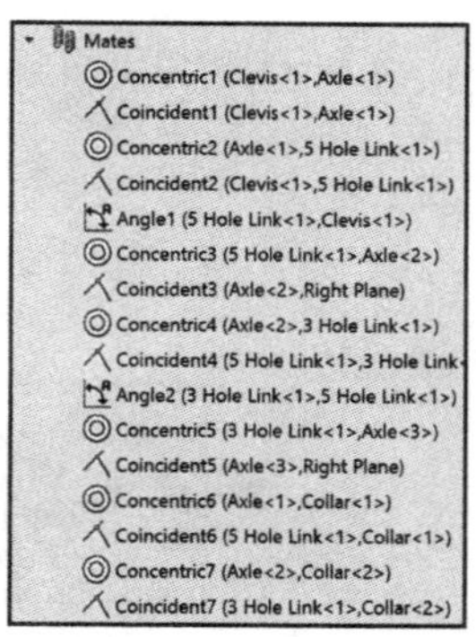

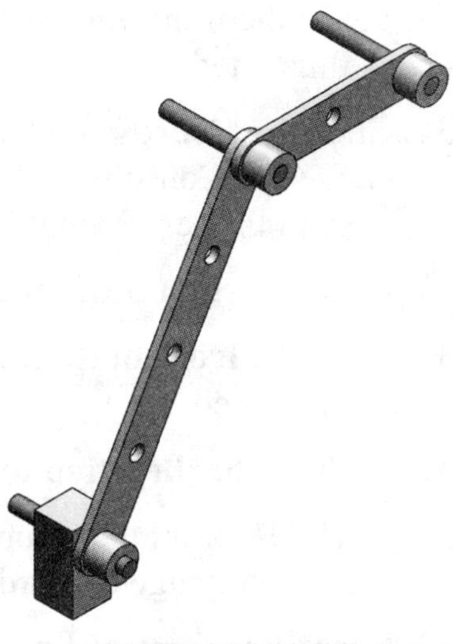

30. **Insert** a Concentric mate between the inside cylindrical face of the Collar and the outside cylindrical face of the third Axle.
31. **Insert** a Coincident mate between the right face of the 3 Hole Link and the left face of the third Collar.
32. **Mirror** the components. Mirror the three Collars, 5 Hole Link and 3 Hole Link about the Right Plane. If using an older version of SOLIDWORKS, check the Recreate mates to new components box. Click Next in the Mirror Components PropertyManager. Check the Preview instanced components box.

Click **Insert, Mirror Components** from the Menu bar menu or click the **Mirror Components** tool from the Linear Component Pattern Consolidated toolbar.

If using an older release of SOLIDWORKS, no check mark in the Components to Mirror box indicates that the components are copied. The geometry of a copied component is unchanged from the original, only the orientation of the component is different.

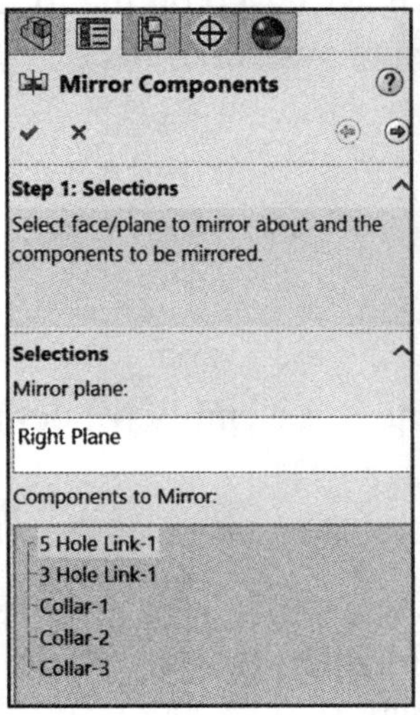

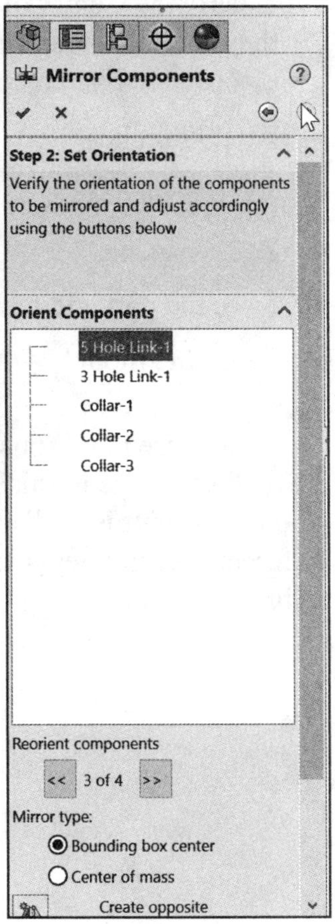

Create the coordinate system location for the assembly.

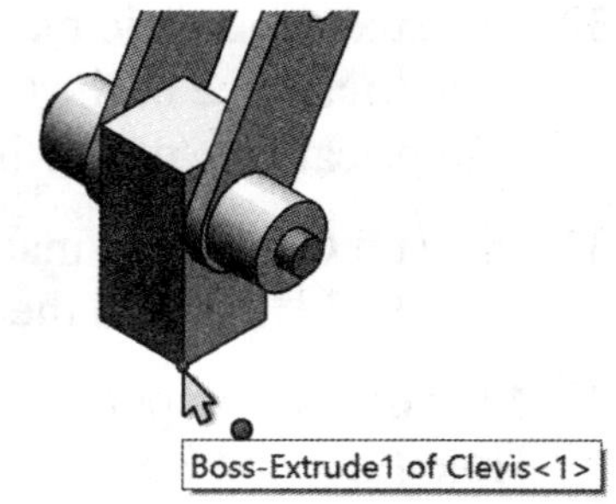

33. Select the front right **vertex** of the Clevis component as illustrated.
34. Click the **Coordinate System** tool from the Reference Geometry Consolidated toolbar. The Coordinate System PropertyManager is displayed.
35. Click the **right bottom edge** of the Clevis component.
36. Click the **front bottom edge** of the Clevis component as illustrated.

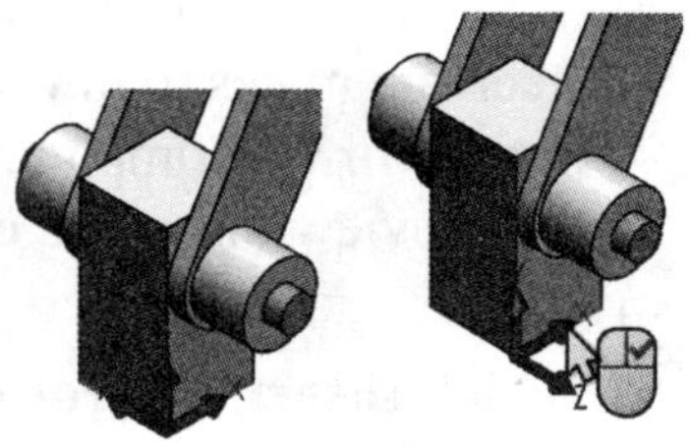

37. Address the **direction** for X, Y, Z as illustrated.
38. Click **OK** from the Coordinate System PropertyManager. Coordinate System1 is displayed.
39. **Locate** the Center of mass based on the location of the illustrated coordinate system. Select Coordinate System1.

- X: 1.79 inches
- Y: 0.25 inches
- Z: 2.61 inches

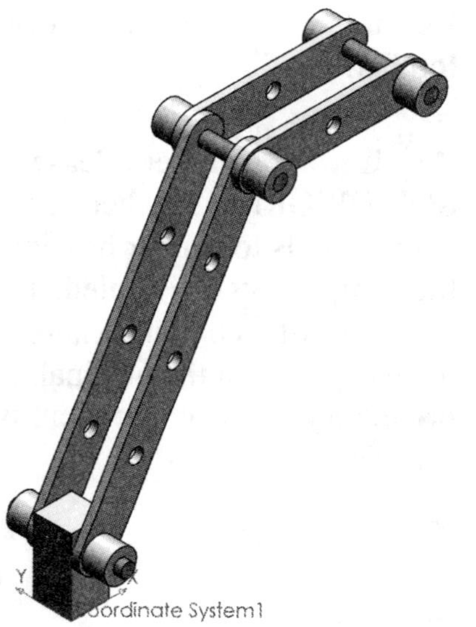

40. **Save** the part and name it Assembly Modeling 3-1.
41. **Close** the model.

There are numerous ways to create the models in this chapter. A goal of this text is to display different design intents and techniques.

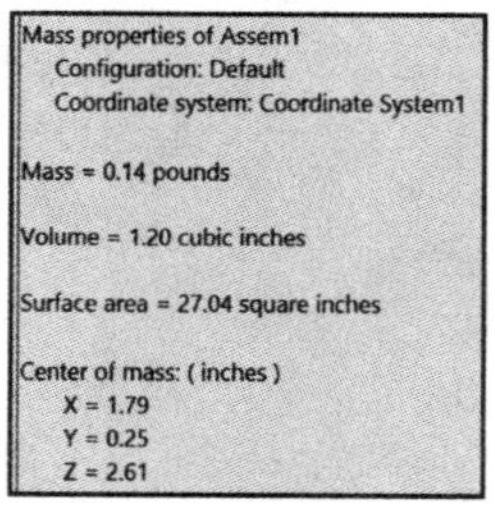
Mass properties of Assem1
Configuration: Default
Coordinate system: Coordinate System1

Mass = 0.14 pounds

Volume = 1.20 cubic inches

Surface area = 27.04 square inches

Center of mass: (inches)
X = 1.79
Y = 0.25
Z = 2.61

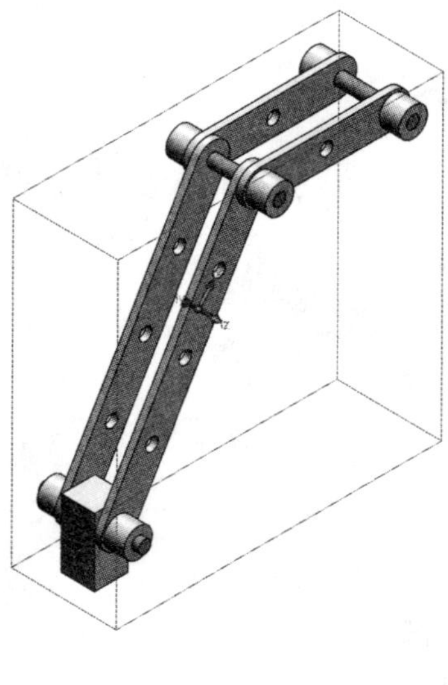

Tutorial: Assembly Model 3-2

Build this assembly. Locate the Center of mass of the model with the illustrated coordinate system. Set decimal place to 2. Unit system: MMGS.

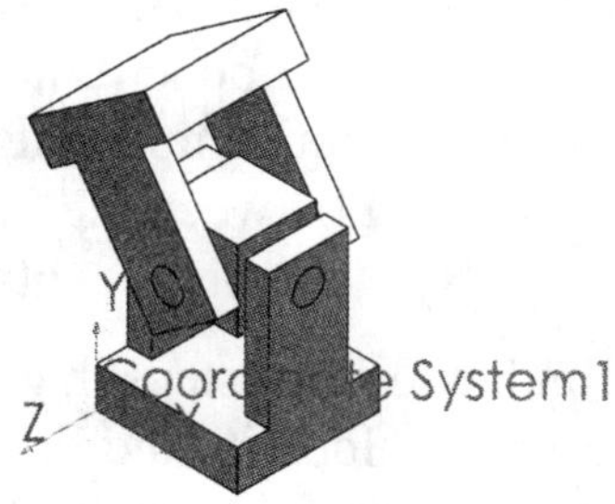

The assembly contains the following: (2) U-Bracket components, (4) Pin components and (1) Square block component.

- U-Bracket (Item 1): Material: AISI 304. Two U-Bracket components are combined together Concentric to opposite holes of the Square block component. The second U-Bracket component is positioned with an Angle mate, to the right face of the first U-Bracket and a Parallel mate between the top face of the first U-Bracket and the top face of the Square block component. Angle A = 125deg.

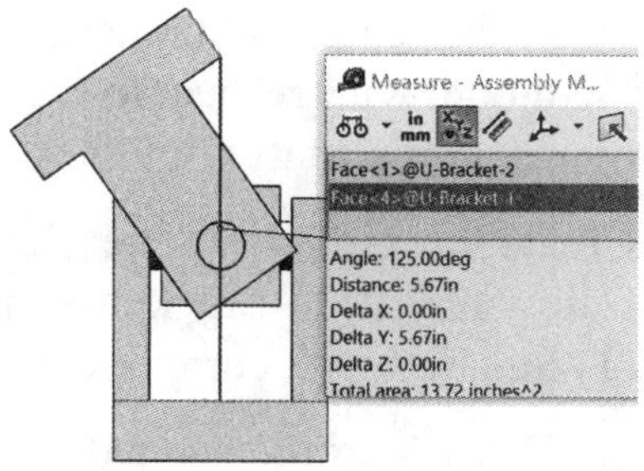

- Square block (Item 2): Material: AISI 304. The Pin components are mated Concentric and Coincident to the 4 holes in the Square block (no clearance). The depth of each hole = 10mm.

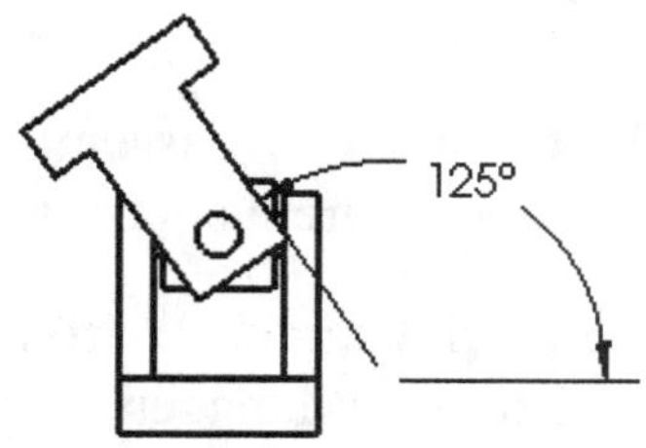

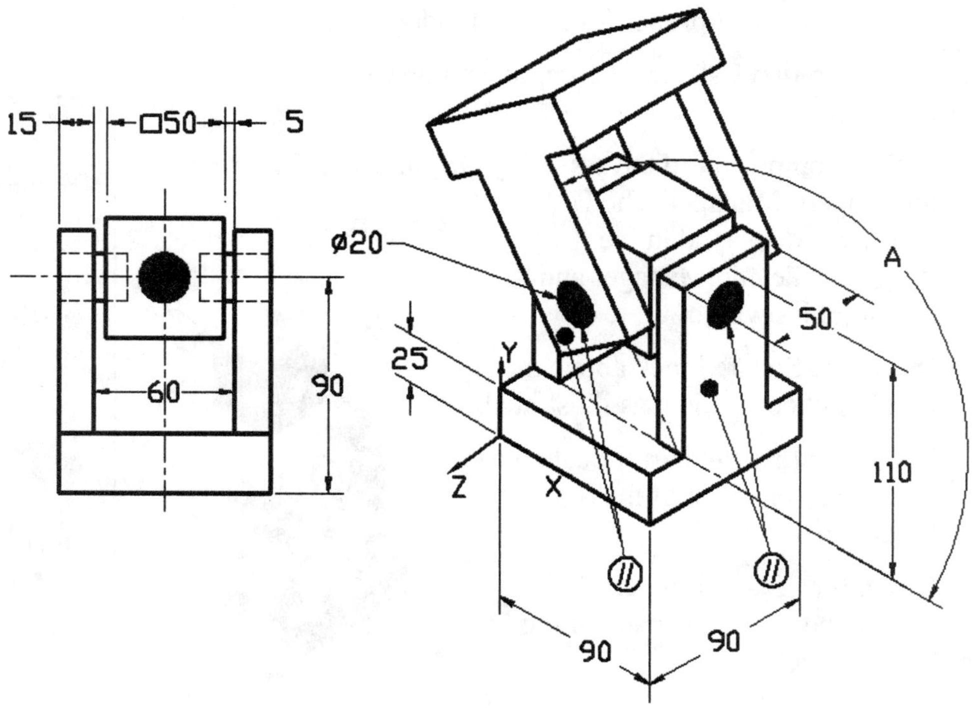

- Pin (Item 3): Material: AISI 304. The Pin components are mated Concentric to the hole (no clearance). The end face of the Pin components are Coincident to the outer face of the U-Bracket components. The Pin component has a 5mm spacing between the Square block component and the two U-Bracket components.

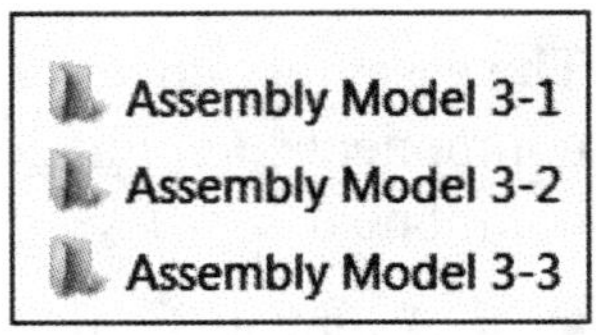

Think about the steps that you would take to build the illustrated assembly. Identify the first fixed component. This is the Base component of the assembly.

Insert the required Standard mates. Locate the Center of mass of the model with respect to the illustrated coordinate system. In this example, start with the U-Bracket part.

Create the assembly. The illustrated assembly contains the following: (2) U-Bracket components, (4) Pin components and (1) Square block component. Unit system: MMGS.

1. **Download** the needed components from the SOLIDWORKS in 5 Hours\Chapter 3 Homework folder to create the assembly.

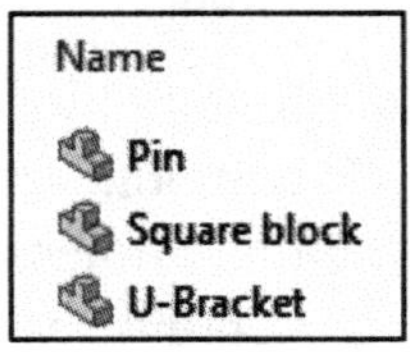

2. **Create** a new assembly in SOLIDWORKS. The created models are displayed in the Open documents box.
3. Click **Cancel** from the Begin Assembly PropertyManager.
4. **Set** the document properties for the model.
5. **Insert** the first U-Bracket component into the assembly document.
6. **Fix** the component to the assembly Origin. Click OK from the PropertyManager. The U-Bracket is displayed in the Assembly FeatureManager and in the Graphics window.

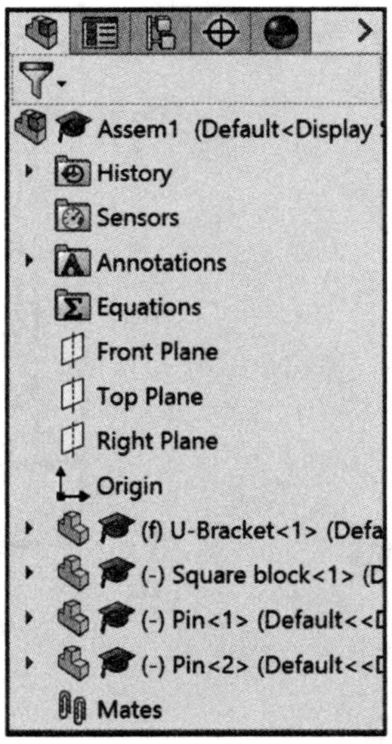

7. **Insert** the Square block above the U-Bracket component as illustrated.
8. **Insert** the first Pin part. Locate the first Pin to the front of the Square block.
9. **Insert** the second Pin part. Locate the second Pin to the back of the Square block.

10. **Insert** the third Pin part. Locate the third Pin to the left side of the Square block. Rotate the Pin.
11. **Insert** the fourth Pin part. Locate the fourth Pin to the right side of the Square block. Rotate the Pin.

12. **Insert** a Concentric mate between the inside cylindrical face of the Square block and the outside cylindrical face of the first Pin. The selected face entities are displayed in the Mate Selections box. Concentric1 is created.
13. **Insert** a Coincident mate between the inside back circular face of the Square block and the flat back face of the first Pin. Coincident1 mate is created.
14. **Insert** a Concentric mate between the inside cylindrical face of the Square block and the outside cylindrical face of the second Pin. The selected face sketch entities are displayed in the Mate Selections box. Concentric2 is created.
15. **Insert** a Coincident mate between the inside back circular face of the Square block and the front flat face of the second Pin. Coincident2 mate is created.

16. **Insert** a Concentric mate between the inside cylindrical face of the Square block and the outside cylindrical face of the third Pin. The selected face sketch entities are displayed in the Mate Selections box. Concentric3 is created.
17. **Insert** a Coincident mate between the inside back circular face of the Square block and the right flat face of the third Pin. Coincident3 mate is created.
18. **Insert** a Concentric mate between the inside circular face of the Square block and the outside cylindrical face of the fourth Pin. The selected face entities are displayed in the Mate Selections box. Concentric4 is created.
19. **Insert** a Coincident mate between the inside back circular face of the Square block and the left flat face of the fourth Pin. Coincident4 mate is created.

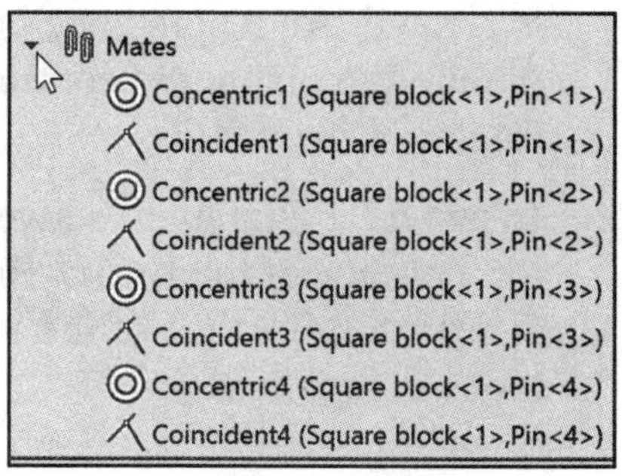

20. **Insert** a Concentric mate between the inside right cylindrical face of the Cut-Extrude feature on the U-Bracket and the outside cylindrical face of the right Pin. Concentric5 is created.

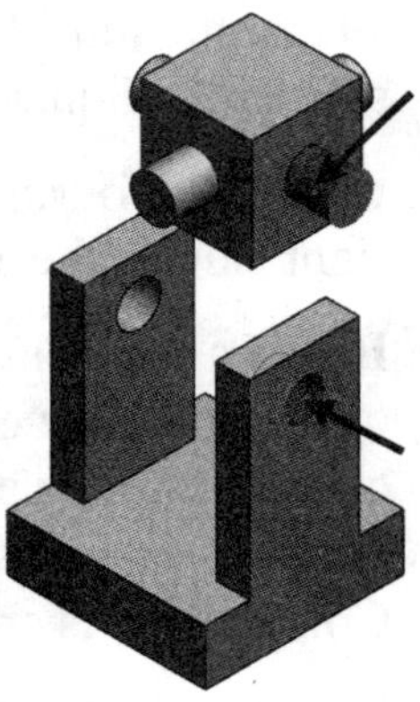

21. **Insert** a Coincident mate between the Right Plane of the Square block and the Right Plane of the assembly. Coincident5 is created.

22. **Insert** the second U-Bracket part above the assembly. Position the U-Bracket as illustrated.

23. **Insert** a Concentric mate between the inside cylindrical face of the second U-Bracket component and the outside cylindrical face of the second Pin. The mate is created.

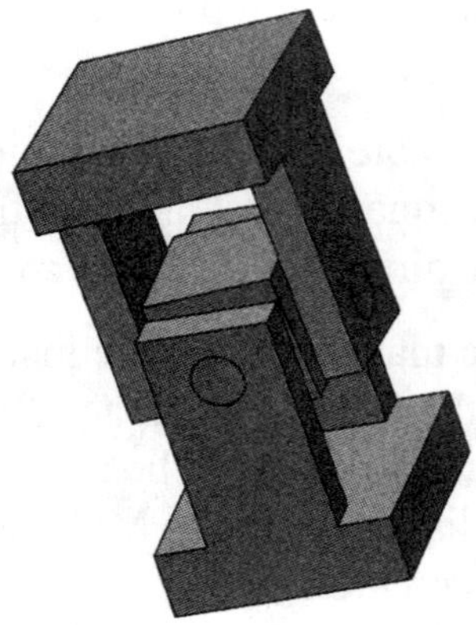

24. **Insert** a Coincident mate between the outside circular edge of the second U-Bracket and the back flat face of the second Pin. The mate is created.

There are numerous ways to mate the models in this chapter. A goal is to display different design intents and techniques.

25. **Insert** an Angle mate between the top flat face of the first U-Bracket component and the front narrow face of the second U-Bracket component as illustrated. Angle1 is created. An Angle mate is required to obtain the correct Center of mass.

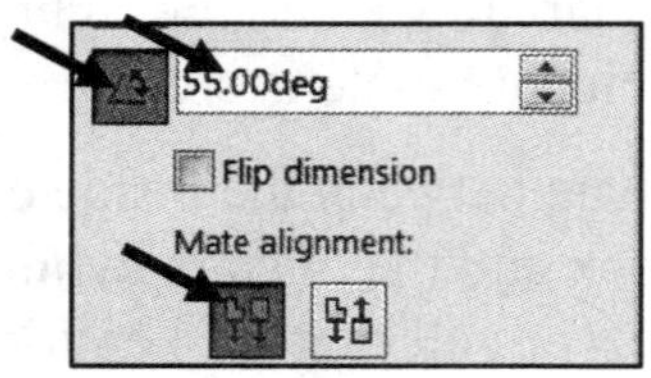

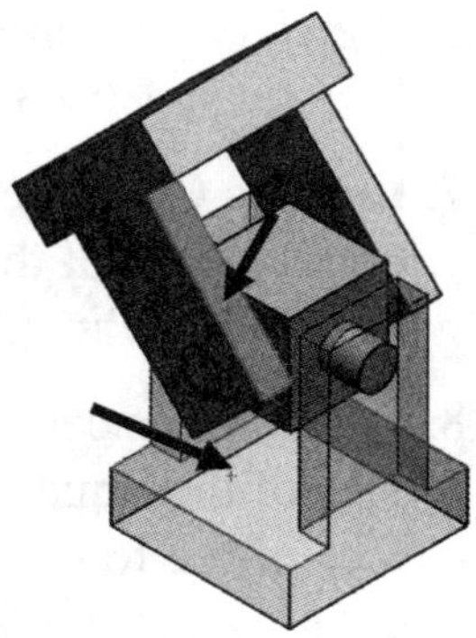

26. **Insert** a Parallel mate between the top flat face of the first U-Bracket and the top flat face of the Square block component.

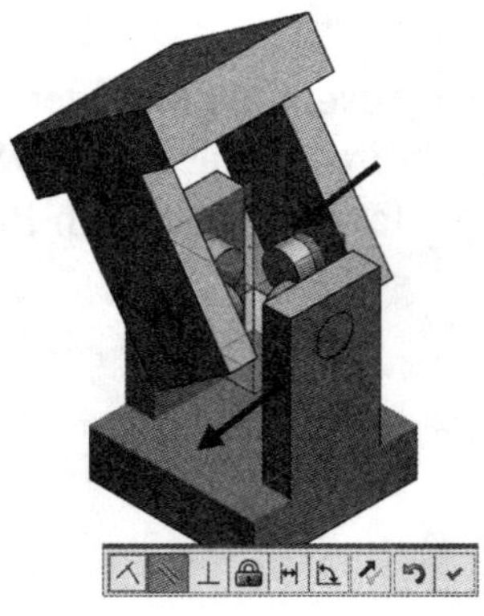

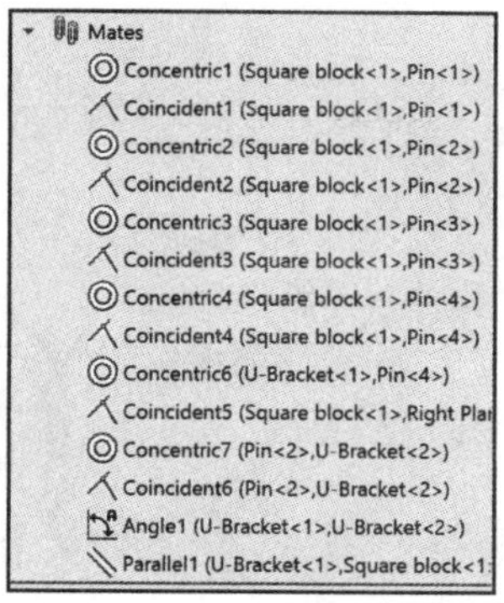

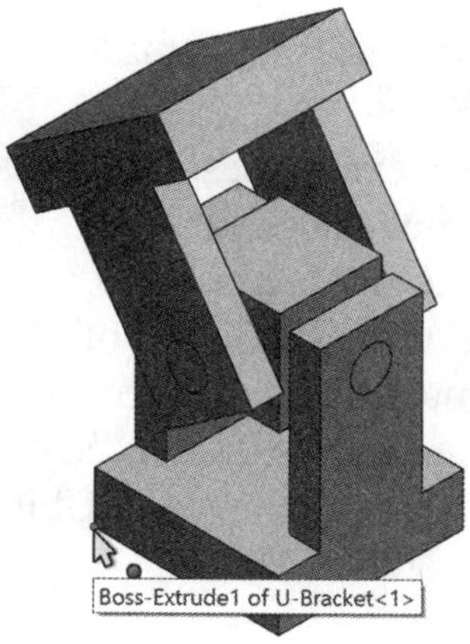

27. **Expand** the Mates folder and the components from the FeatureManager. View the created mates.

Create the coordinate location for the assembly.

28. Select the front **bottom left vertex** of the first U-Bracket component as illustrated.
29. Click the **Coordinate System** tool from the Reference Geometry Consolidated toolbar. The Coordinate System PropertyManager is displayed.
30. Click **OK** from the Coordinate System PropertyManager. Coordinate System1 is displayed.

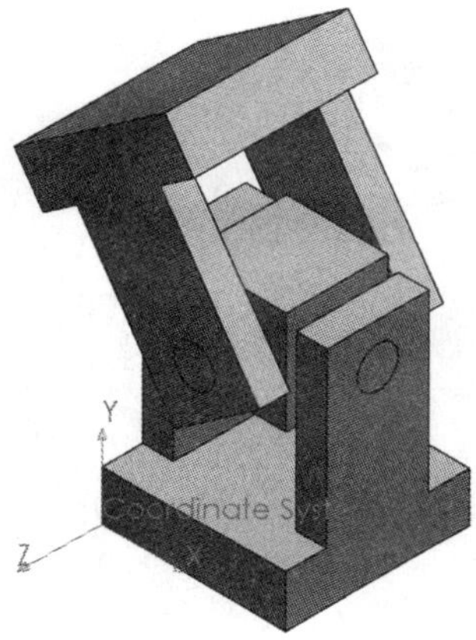

31. **Locate** the Center of mass based on the location of the illustrated coordinate system. Select Coordinate System1.

- X: 31.54 millimeters
- Y: 85.76 millimeters
- Z: -45.00 millimeters

32. **Save** the part and name it Assembly Modeling 3-2.
33. **Close** the model.

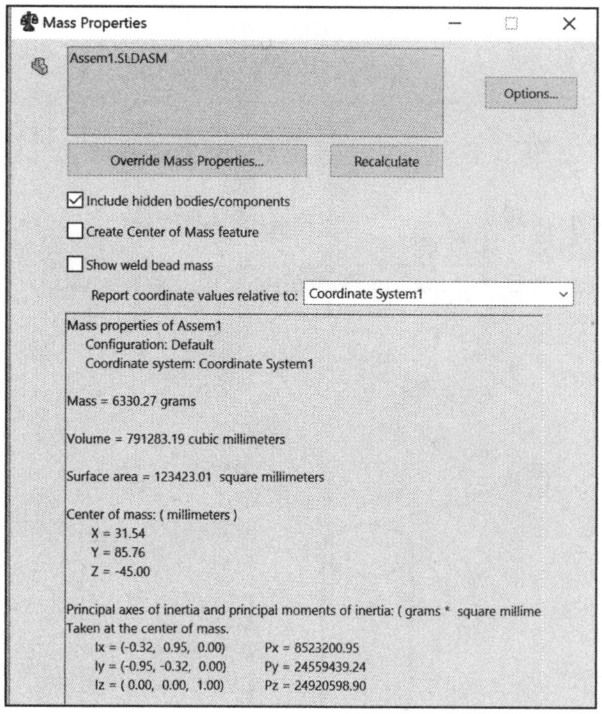

Tutorial: Assembly Model 3-3

An exam question in this category could read: Build this assembly. Locate the Center of mass using the illustrated coordinate system. Set decimal place to 2. Unit system: MMGS.

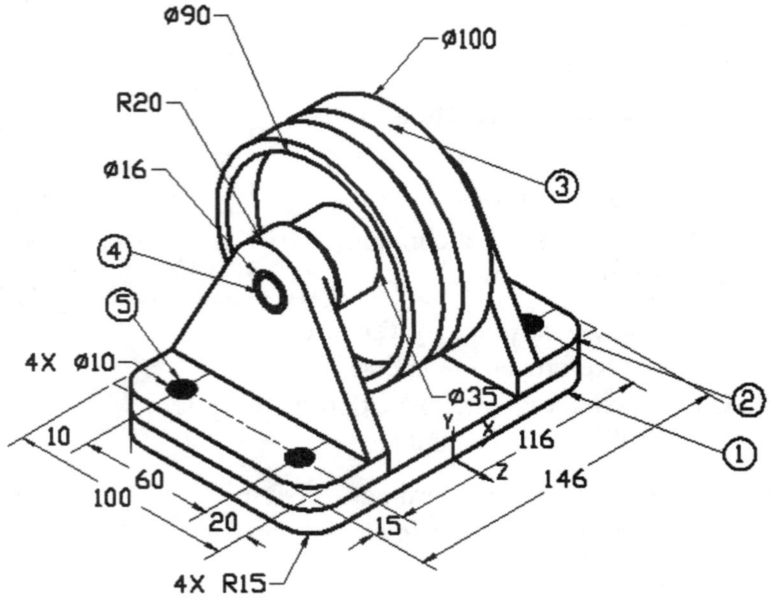

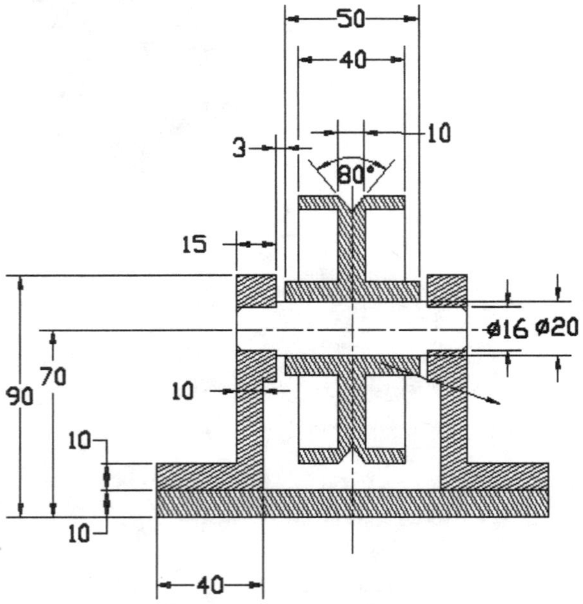

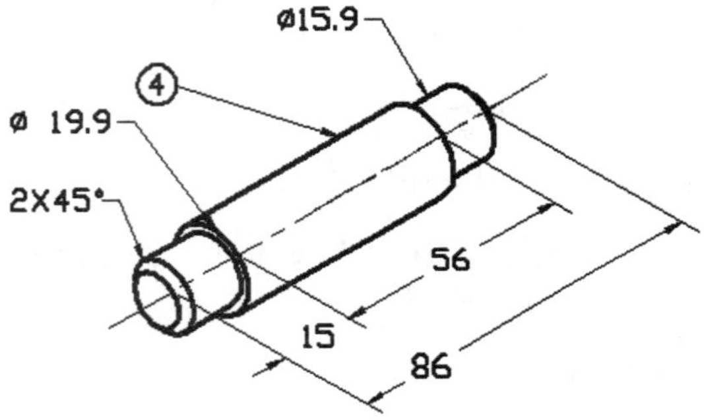

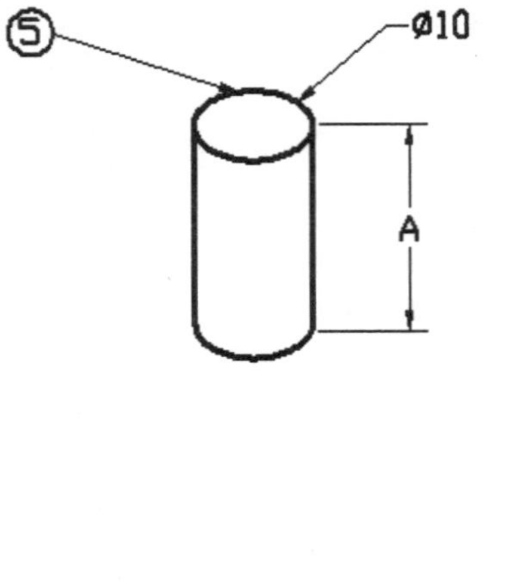

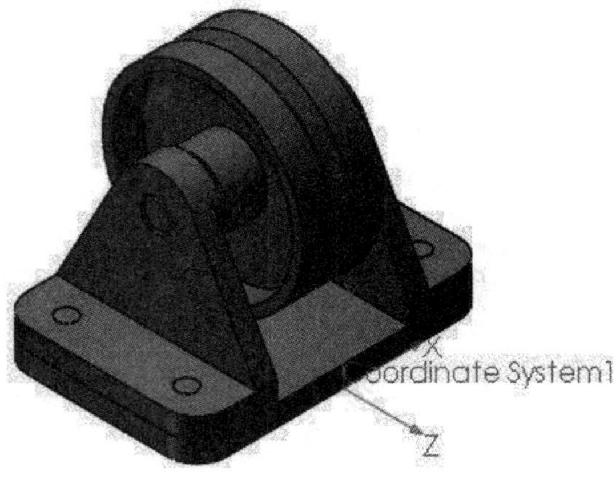

The assembly contains the following: (1) WheelPlate component, (2) Bracket100 components, (1) Axle40 component, (1) Wheel1 component and (4) Pin-4 components.

- WheelPlate (Item 1): Material: AISI 304. The WheelPlate contains 4-Ø10 holes. The holes are aligned to the left Bracket100 and the right Bracket100 components. All holes are THRU ALL. The thickness of the WheelPlate = 10 mm.
- Bracket100 (Item 2): Material: AISI 304. The Bracket100 component contains 2-Ø10 holes and 1- Ø16 hole. All holes are through-all.
- Wheel1 (Item 3): Material AISI 304: The center hole of the Wheel1 component is Concentric with the Axle40 component. There is a 3mm gap between the inside faces of the Bracket100 components and the end faces of the Wheel hub.
- Axle40 (Item 4): Material AISI 304: The end faces of the Axle40 are Coincident with the outside faces of the Bracket100 components.
- Pin-4 (Item 5): Material AISI 304: The Pin-4 components are mated Concentric to the holes of the Bracket100 components (no clearance). The end faces are Coincident to the WheelPlate bottom face and the Bracket100 top face.

Think about the steps that you would take to build the illustrated assembly. Identify the first fixed component. This is the Base component of the assembly. Insert the required Standard mates.

Locate the Center of mass of the illustrated model with respect to the referenced coordinate system.

The referenced coordinate system is located at the bottom, right, midpoint of the WheelPlate. In this example, start with the WheelPlate part.

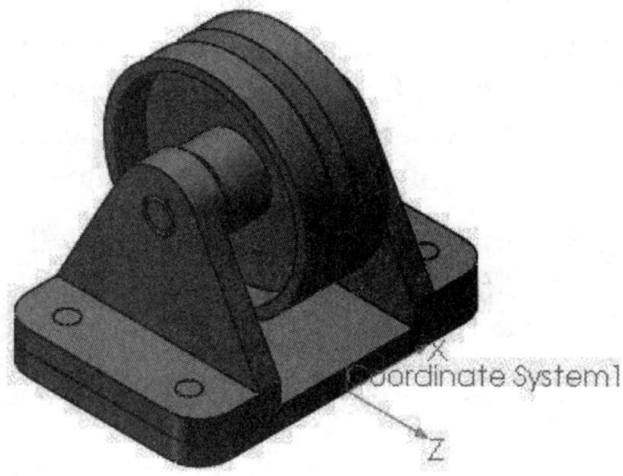

1. **Download** the needed components from the SOLIDWORKS in 5 Hours\Chapter 3 Homework folder to create the assembly.
2. **Create** a new assembly in SOLIDWORKS. The created models are displayed in the Open documents box.

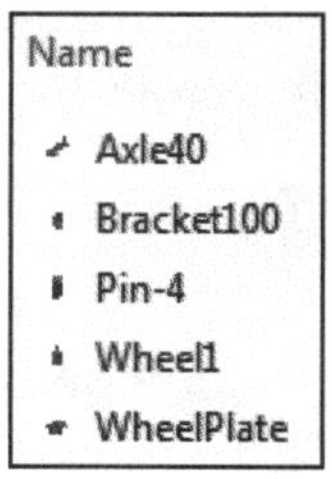

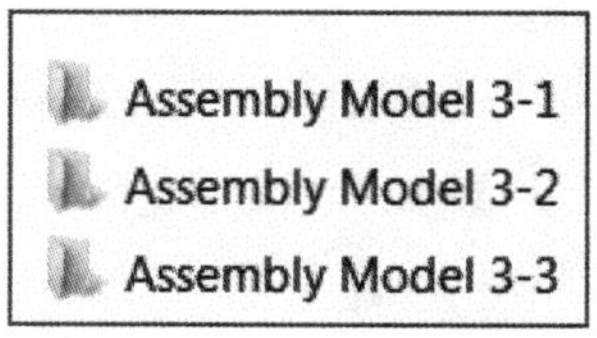

3. Click **Cancel** ✖ from the Begin Assembly PropertyManager.
4. **Set** the document properties for the assembly.

5. **Insert** the first component. Insert the WheelPlate. Fix the component to the assembly Origin. The WheelPlate is displayed in the Assembly FeatureManager and in the Graphics window. The WheelPlate component is fixed.

6. **Insert** the first Bracket100 part above the WheelPlate component as illustrated.
7. **Insert** a Concentric mate between the inside front left cylindrical face of the Bracket100 component and the inside front left cylindrical face of the WheelPlate. Concentric1 is created.
8. **Insert** a Concentric mate between the inside front right cylindrical face of the Bracket100 component and the inside front right cylindrical face of the WheelPlate. Concentric2 is created.
9. **Insert** a Coincident mate between the bottom flat face of the Bracket100 component and the top flat face of the WheelPlate component. Coincident1 is created.

10. **Insert** the Axle40 part above the first Bracket100 component as illustrated.
11. **Insert** a Concentric mate between the outside cylindrical face of the Axle40 component and the inside cylindrical face of the Bracket100 component. Concentric3 is created.
12. **Insert** a Coincident mate between the flat face of the Axle40 component and the front outside edge of the first Bracket100 component. Coincident2 is created.

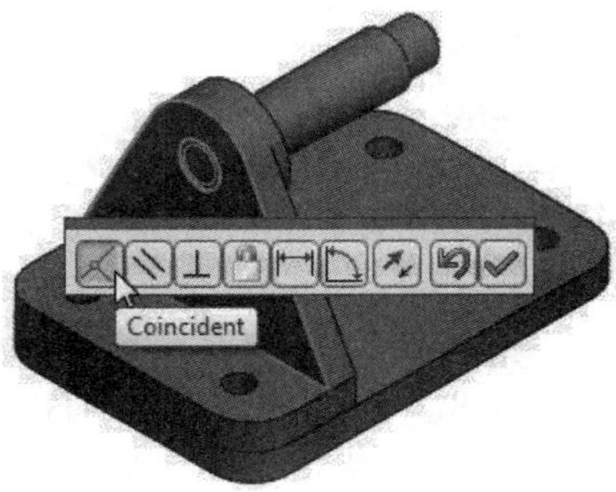

To verify that the distance between holes of mating components is equal, utilize Concentric mates between pairs of cylindrical hole faces.

13. **Insert** the first Pin-4 part above the Bracket100 component.
14. **Insert** the second Pin-4 part above the Bracket100 component.

15. **Insert** a Concentric mate between the outside cylindrical face of the first Pin-4 component and the inside front left cylindrical face of the Bracket100 component. Concentric4 is created.

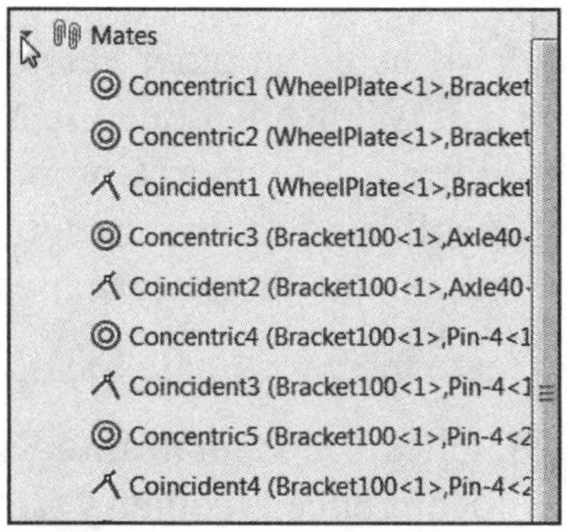

16. **Insert** a Coincident mate between the flat top face of the first Pin-4 component and the top face of the first Bracket100 component. Coincident3 is created.

17. **Insert** a Concentric mate between the outside cylindrical face of the second Pin-4 component and the inside front right cylindrical face of the Bracket100 component. Concentric5 is created.

18. **Insert** a Coincident mate between the flat top face of the second Pin-4 component and the top face of the first Bracket100 component. Coincident4 is created.

19. **Insert** the Wheel1 part as illustrated.

20. **Insert** a Concentric mate between the outside cylindrical face of Axle40 and the inside front cylindrical face of the Wheel1 component. Concentric6 is created.

21. **Insert** a Coincident mate between the Front Plane of Axle40 and the Front Plane of Wheel1. Coincident5 is created.

22. **Mirror** the components. Mirror the Bracket100 and the two Pin-4 components about the Front Plane.

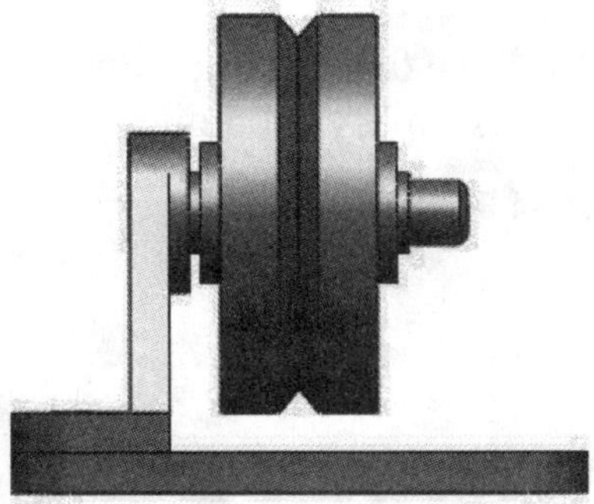

Click **Insert**, **Mirror Components** from the Menu bar menu or click the **Mirror Components** tool from the Linear Component Pattern Consolidated toolbar.

If using an older version of SOLIDWORKS, click the Mirror Component tool from the Linear Component Pattern Consolidated toolbar to activate the Mirror Components PropertyManager.

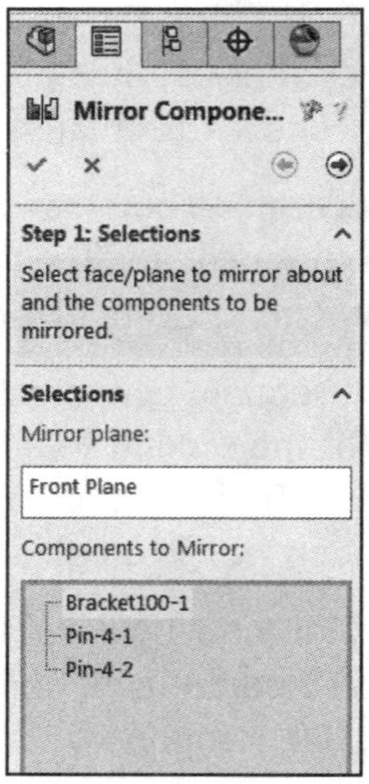

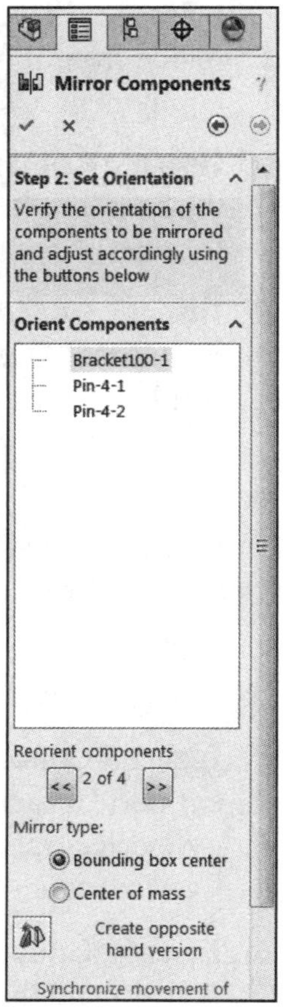

Create the coordinate location for the assembly.

23. Click the **Coordinate System** tool from the Reference Geometry Consolidated toolbar. The Coordinate System PropertyManager is displayed.
24. **Select** the right bottom midpoint as the Origin location as illustrated.
25. **Select** the bottom right edge as the X axis direction reference as illustrated.
26. Click **OK** from the Coordinate System PropertyManager. Coordinate System1 is displayed.
27. **Locate** the Center of mass based on the location of the illustrated coordinate system. Select Coordinate System1.

- X = 0.00 millimeters
- Y = 37.14 millimeters
- Z = -50.00 millimeters

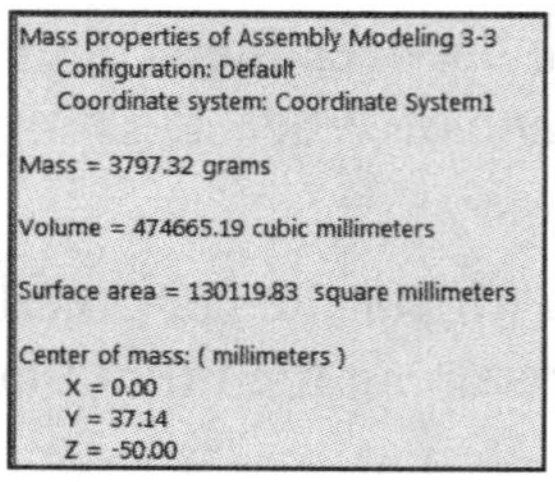

28. **Save** the part and name it Assembly Modeling 3-3.
29. **Close** the model.

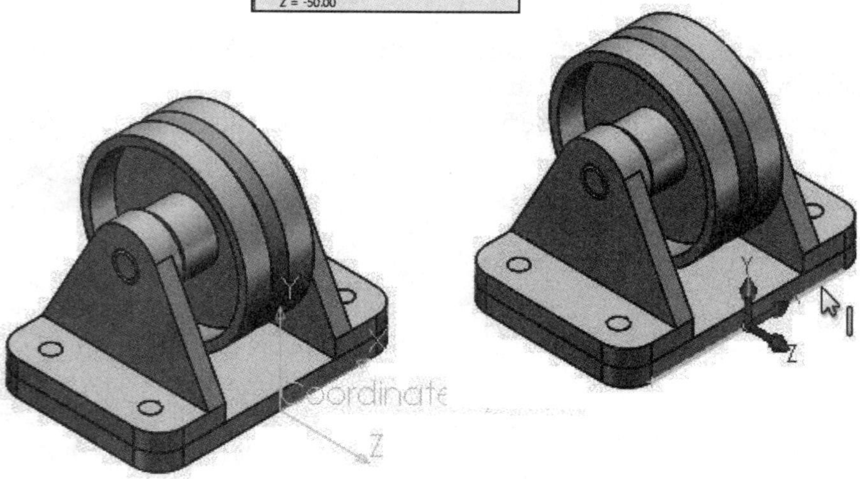

Chapter 4

Design Modifications

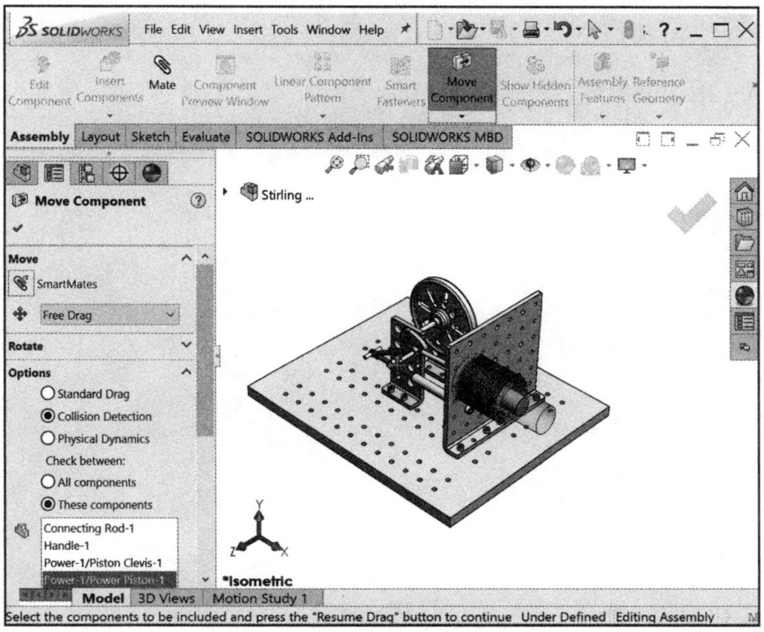

Below are the desired outcomes and usage competencies based on the completion of Chapter 4.

Desired Outcomes:	Usage Competencies:
• Address clearance, interference, static and dynamic behavior of the Stirling Engine Modified Assembly. • Verify behavior between the following components: Power Piston, Power Clevis, Connecting Rod and Handle. • A new Coordinate System. • Run and save a Motion Study AVI file.	• Ability to utilize the following assembly tools: Move, Rotate, Collision Detection, Interference Detection, Selected Components, Edit Feature, Center of Mass and Assembly Visualization. • Comprehend the Interference Detection tool to locate the interference between components in an assembly. • Knowledge to locate and edit the correct mates. • Apply the Measure and Mass Properties tool. • Create a new Coordinate System relative to the origin of the Assembly.

Notes:

Chapter 4 - Design Modifications

Chapter Objective

Before you machine or create a rapid prototype of a part or assembly, you should verify the model for clearance, interference, static and dynamic behavior. Verify behavior between the Power Piston, Power Clevis, Connecting Rod and Handle with Design modifications using the Stirling Engine Modified assembly.

On the completion of this chapter, you will be able to:

- Establish a SOLIDWORKS session.
- Utilize the following assembly tools: Move, Rotate, Collision Detection, Interference Detection, Selected Components, Edit Feature, Center of Mass, Assembly Visualization and Motion Study.
- Utilize the Interference Detection tool to locate the interference between components in an assembly.
- Locate and edit the correct mate.
- Insert a Center of Mass point into the Assembly.
- Modify the Center of Mass point relative to a new Coordinate System.
- Apply the Measure and Mass Properties tool.
- Utilize the Assembly Visualization tool on the Stirling Engine Modified Assembly and sort components by mass.
- Run a Motion Study.
- Create and save the Motion Study AVI file.

Activity: Start a SOLIDWORKS Session

Start a SOLIDWORKS session.

1) Double-click the **SOLIDWORKS icon** from the desktop.

2) **Pin** the Menu bar as illustrated. Use both the Menu bar menu and the Menu bar toolbar in this book.

In the next section, open the Stirling Engine Modified assembly from the SOLIDWORKS in 5 Hours\Design Modifications folder. Verify for clearance, interference, static and dynamic behavior between the Power Piston, Power Clevis, Connecting Rod and Handle with Design modifications using the Stirling Engine Modified assembly.

Activity: Open the Stirling Engine Modified Assembly

Open the Stirling Engine Modified Assembly.

3) Click **File**, **Open** from the Main menu.

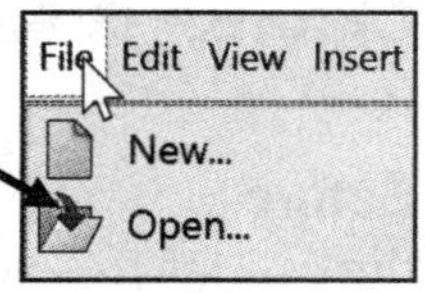

4) Browse to the **SOLIDWORKS in 5 Hours\Design Modifications** folder.

5) Double-click the **Stirling Engine Modified** assembly. The assembly is displayed in the Graphics window.

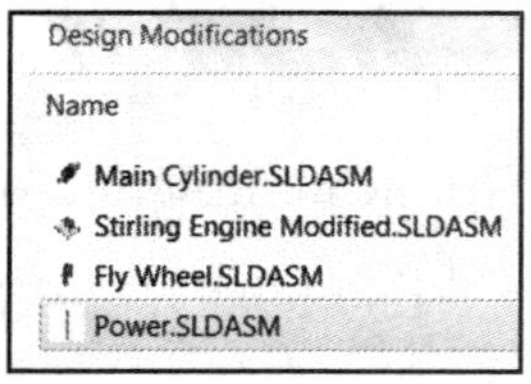

Verify for clearance, interference, static and dynamic behavior between the Power Piston, Power Clevis, Connecting Rod and Handle in the Stirling Engine Modified Assembly.

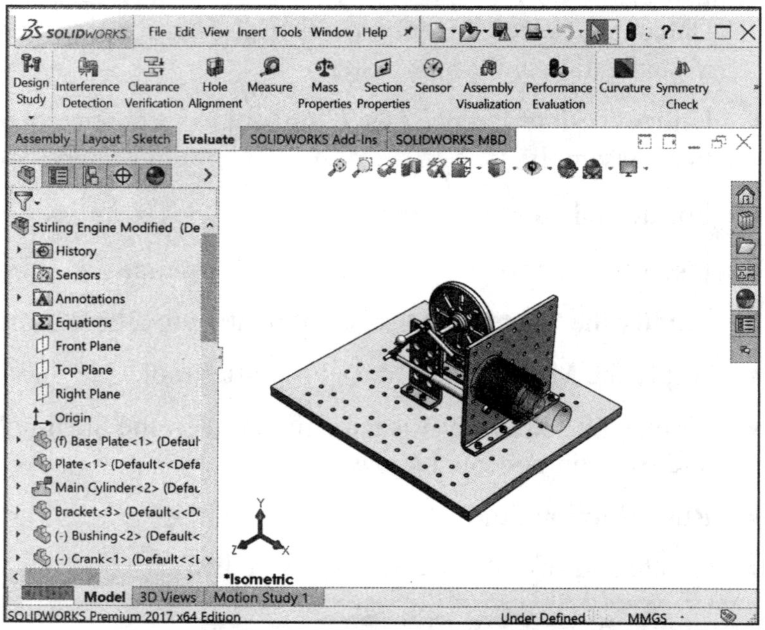

You can detect collisions with other components when moving or rotating a component. The software can detect collisions with the entire assembly or a selected group of components. You can find collisions for either the selected components or for all of the components that move as a result of mates to the selected components.

Physical Dynamics is an option in Collision Detection that allows you to see the motion of assembly components in a realistic way. With Physical Dynamics enabled, when you drag a component, the component applies a force to components that it touches, and moves the components if they are free to translate or rotate.

Activity: Verify Collision between Components in the Assembly

Activate the Collision Detection tool.

6) Click the **Assembly** tab from the CommandManager.

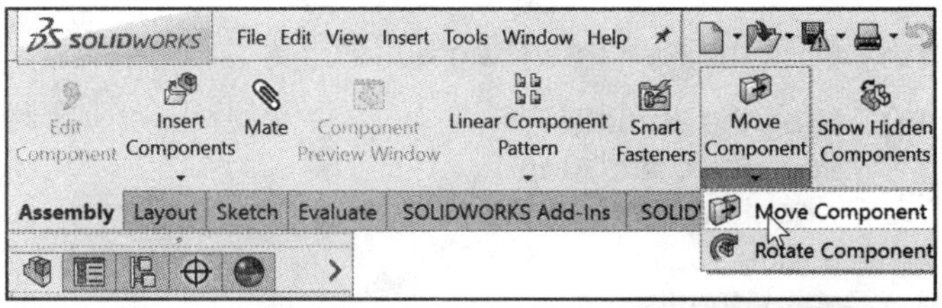

7) Click the **Move Component** icon. The Move Component PropertyManager is displayed.

8) Click the **Collision Detection** button.

9) Check the **Highlight faces, Sound** and **Ignore complex surfaces** box from the Advanced Options section.

10) Uncheck the **Stop at collision** box.

11) Click the **These components** button. If needed Right-click inside the Components for Collision Check box and click **Clear Selections**.

12) Click the **Handle** from the Graphics window. Handle-1 is displayed in the Components for collision Check box.

13) Click the **Connecting Rod** from the Graphics window. Connection Rod-1 is displayed in the Components for Collision Check box.

14) Click the **Piston Clevis** as illustrated from the Graphics window. Power-1/Piston Clevis 1 is displayed in the Components for collision Check box.

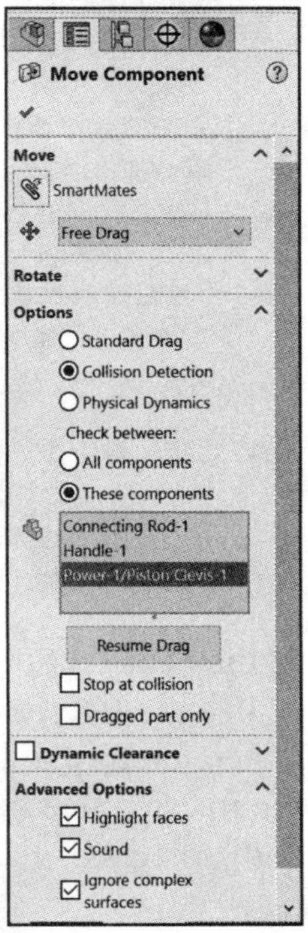

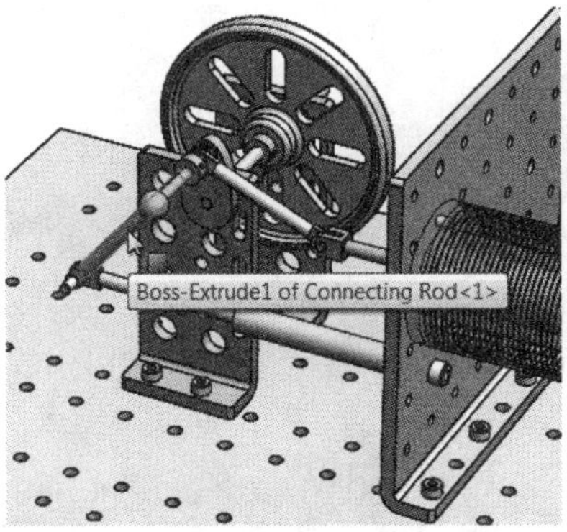

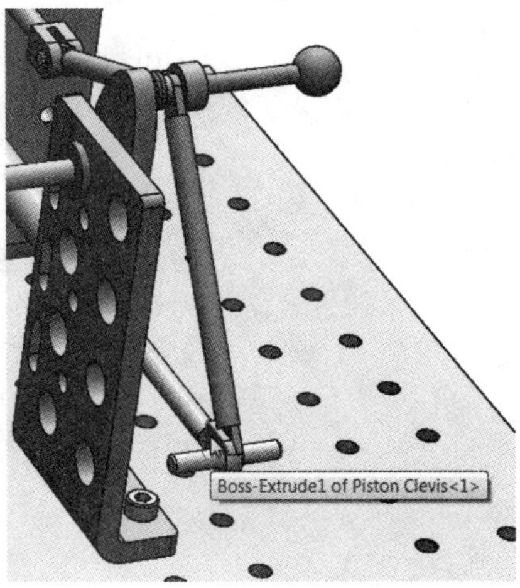

15) Click the **Power Piston** as illustrated from the Graphics window. Power-1/Power Piston-1 is displayed in the Components for Collision Check box.

16) Click the **Resume Drag** button.

17) Drag the **Handle** downward and stop when the components collide. Collision components are displayed in the Graphics window. There are collisions between the Connecting Rod and the Power Piston and the Connecting Rod and the Piston Clevis.

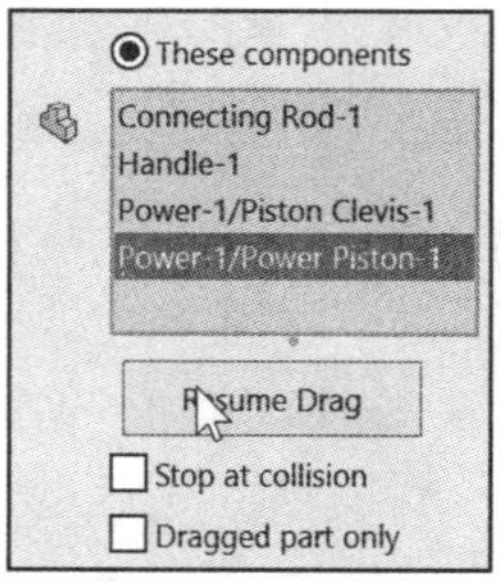

18) Click **OK** ✔ from the Move Component PropertyManager.

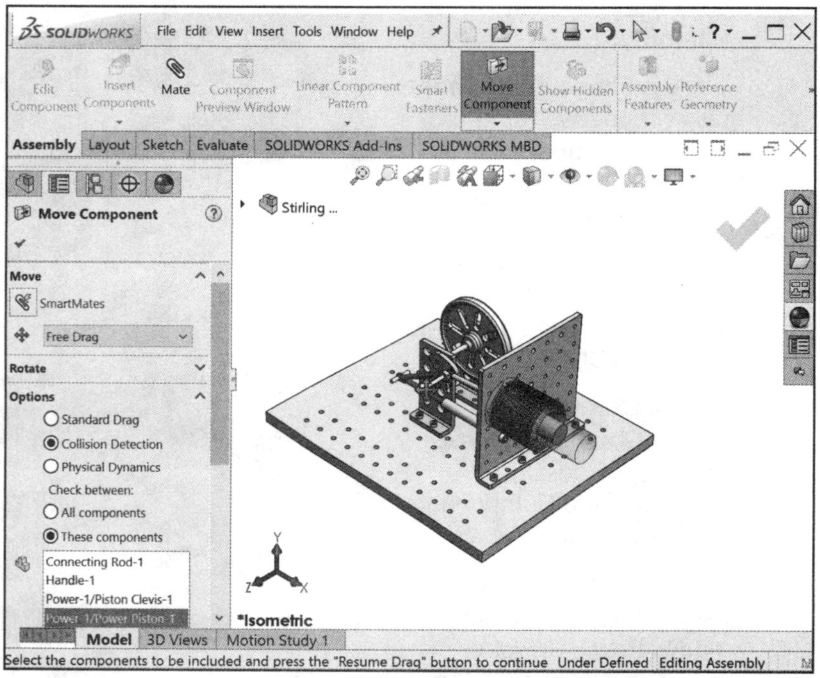

In the next section, utilize the Interference Detection tool to locate the interference between components.

Activity: Utilize the Interference Detection tool

Activate the Interference Detection tool.

19) Click the **Evaluate** tab from the CommandManager.

20) Click the **Interference Detection** icon. The Interference Detection PropertyManager is displayed.

21) Right-click in the **Selected Components** box.

22) Click **Clear Selections**.

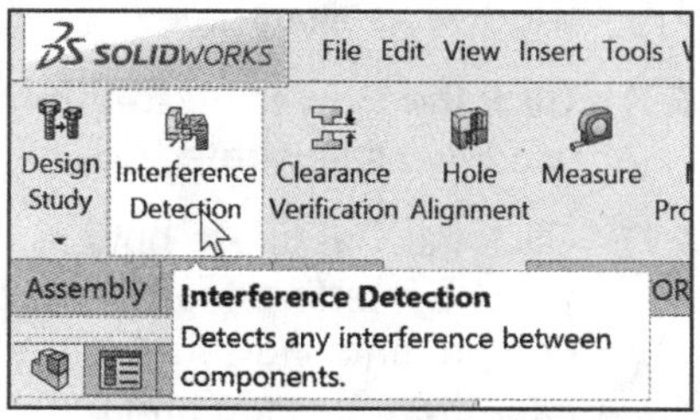

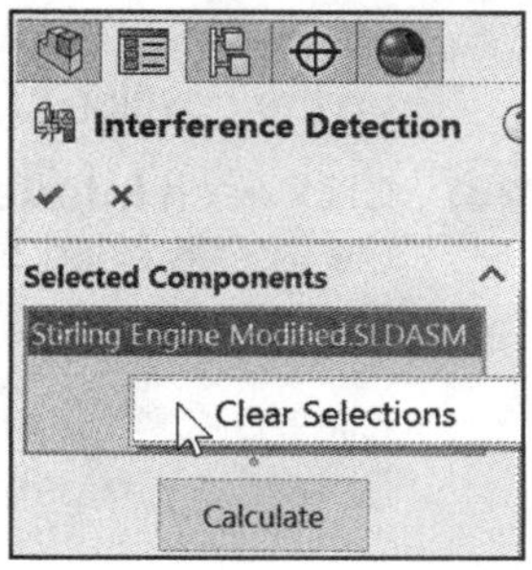

Select component to perform the Interference detection process.

23) Click the **Connecting Rod** from the Graphics window as illustrated. Connection Rod-1 is displayed in the Selected Components box.

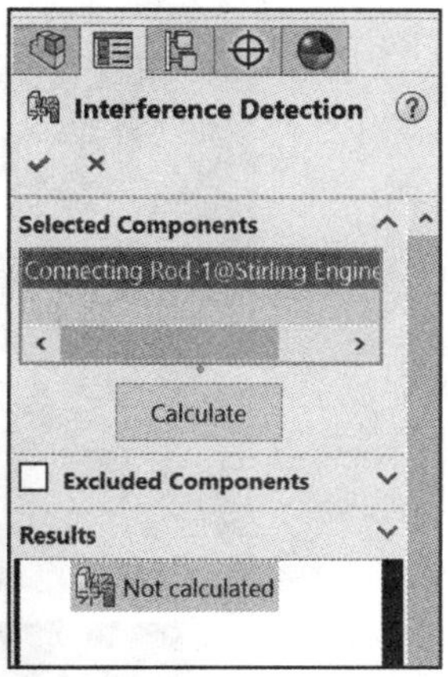

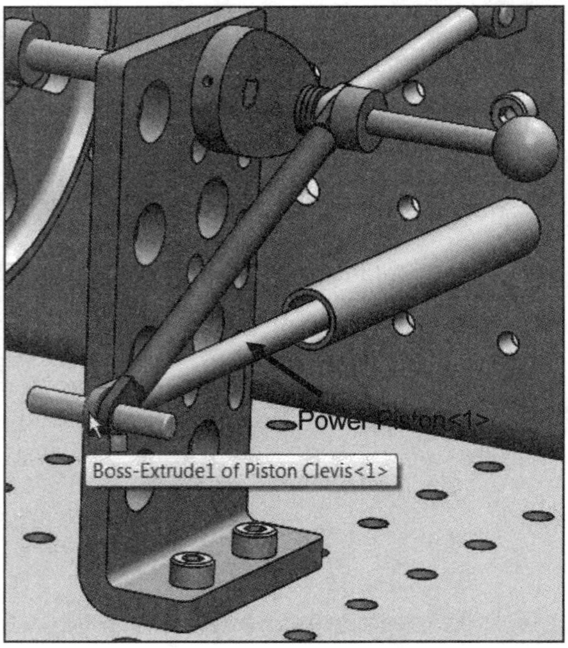

24) **Rotate** the model to view the Piston Clevis.

25) Click the **Piston Clevis** from the Graphics window as illustrated.

26) Click the **Power Piston** from the Graphics window as illustrated.

27) Click the **Calculate** button. There are volume interferences between the components indicated in red. *The volume interference value and the number of interference may be different depending* on the position of the Crank.

28) Click each **Interference Results** to view the interference between the components displayed in red.

29) Click **OK** from the Interference Detection PropertyManager.

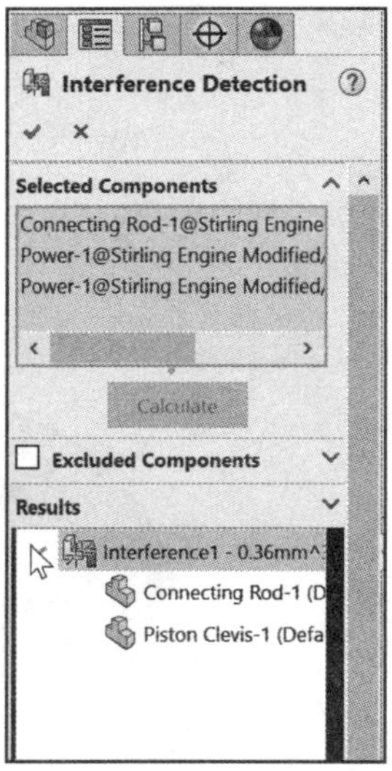

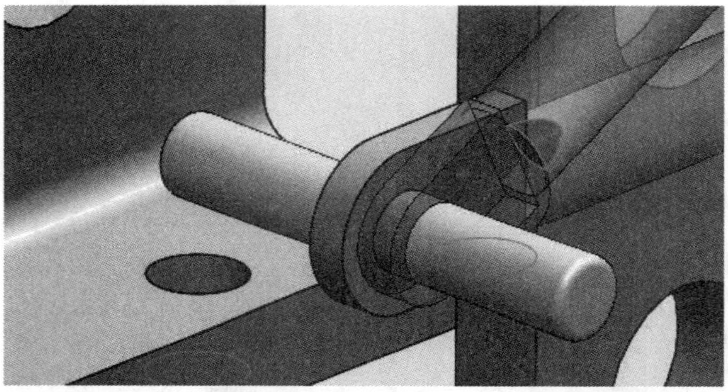

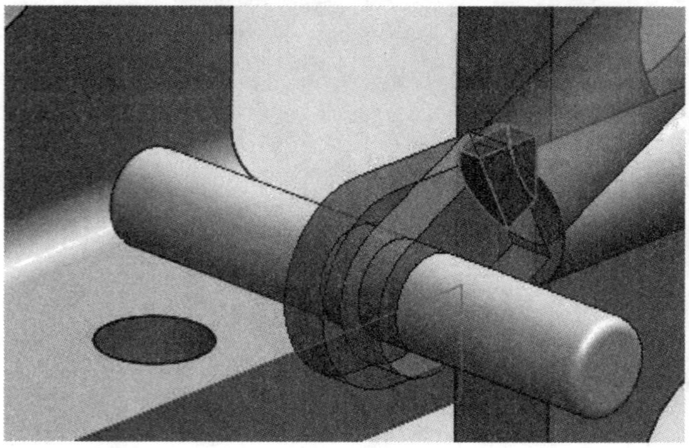

The Interference Detection and Collision Detection results require design changes to the Power Piston, Piston Clevis, Connecting Rod and other components in the Stirling Engine Modified Assembly. Review Assembly and Evaluate tools to modify the design intent.

Activity: Modify the Connecting Distance2 Rod Mate

View the Mates on the Connecting Rod in the Assembly.

30) **Expand** Connecting Rod in the FeatureManager.

31) **Expand** the Mates in Stirling Engine Modified folder as illustrated.

32) Click on each **Mate** to review how the Connecting Rod is constrained in the Stirling Engine Modified assembly.

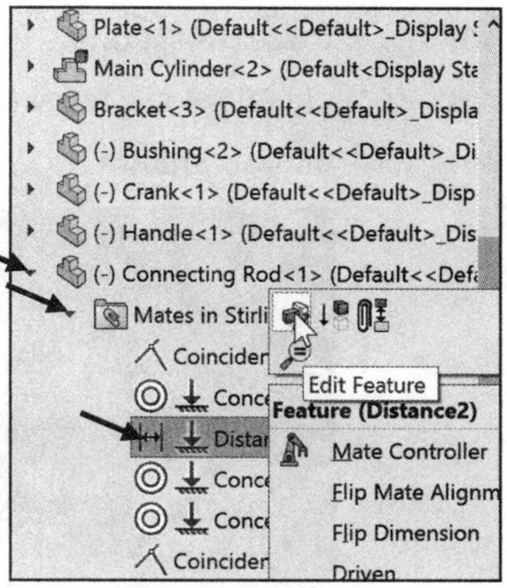

Modify the Distance Mate between the face of the Rod and the face of the Connection Rod.

33) Right-click **Distance2** from the FeatureManager.

34) Click the **Edit Feature** icon from the Context toolbar. The current distance is 0mm.

35) Enter **3mm** for distance.

36) Click **OK** from the Distance2 PropertyManager.

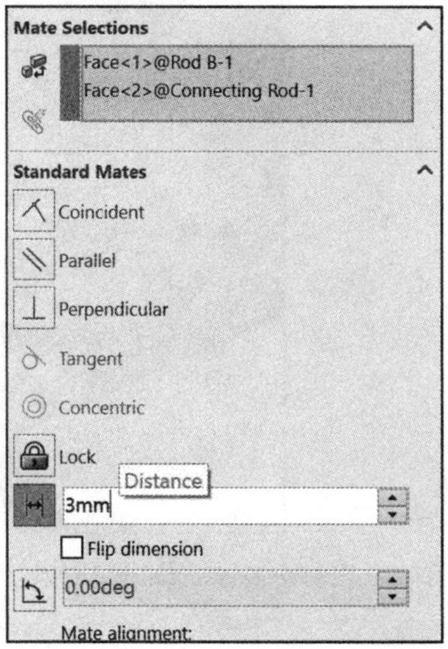

Display a Trimetric view.

37) Click **Trimetric view** from the Heads-up toolbar.

Save the model.

38) Click **Save**.

39) Click **Rebuild and Save the document**.

A Distance Mate of 0mm allows flexibility when you need to vary spacing between components.

If you delete a Mate and then recreate it, the Mate numbers will be different (increase).

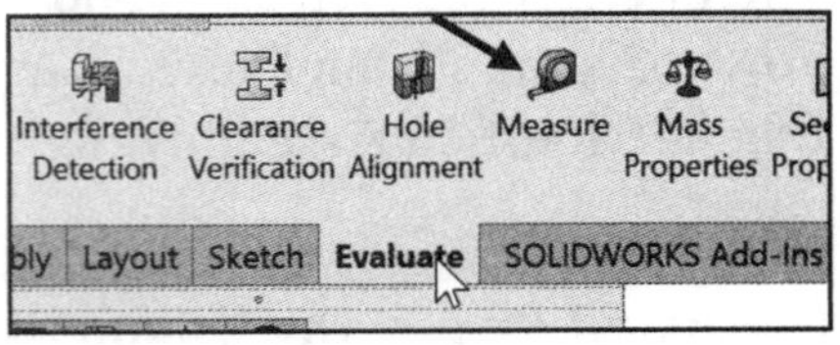

Utilize the Measure tool to check the Distance mate in the Graphics window.

40) Click the **Evaluate** tab in the CommandManager.

41) Click the **Measure** tool. The Measure dialog box is displayed. Click the **Show XYZ Measurements** button.

42) Right-click in the **Selection** box.

43) Click **Clear Selections**.

44) **Zoom in** on the two faces (Rod and Connecting Rod).

45) Click the **two illustrated faces**. The Normal Distance is 3.00mm.

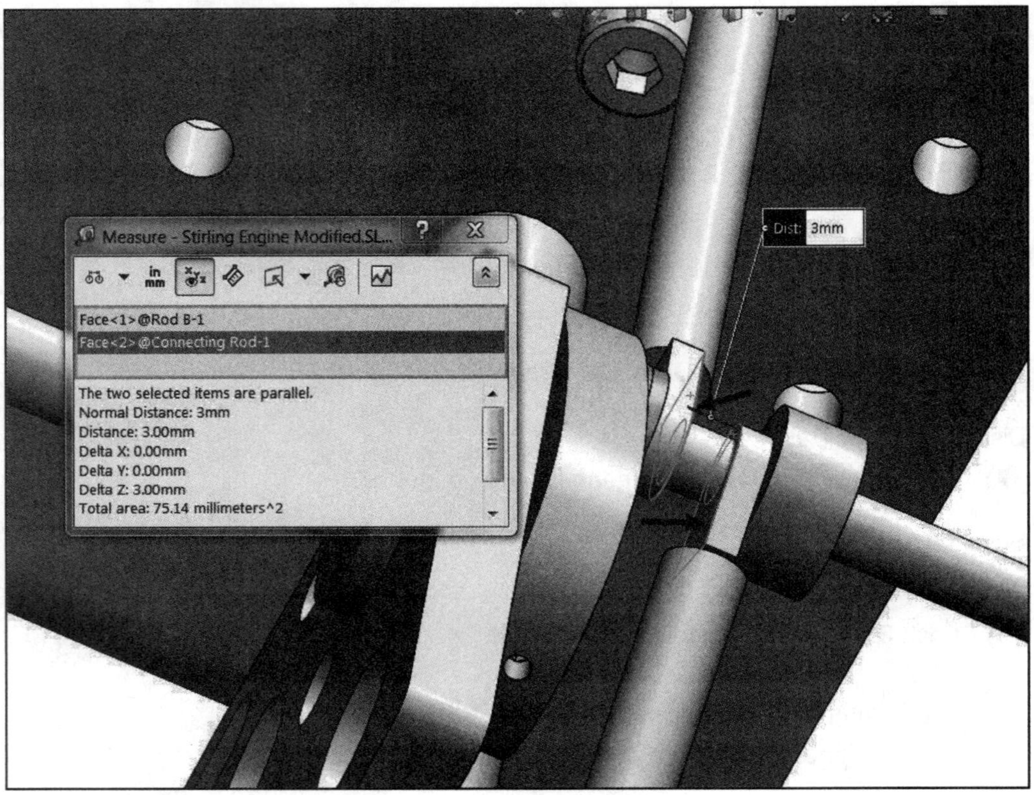

Close the Measure Dialog box.

46) Click **Close**.

Display a Trimetric view.

47) Click **Trimetric view** from the Heads-up toolbar.

Save the model.

48) Click **Save**.

Activity: Utilize the Interference Detection tool - Check the Solution

Activate the Interference Detection tool.

49) Click the **Evaluate** tab from the CommandManager.

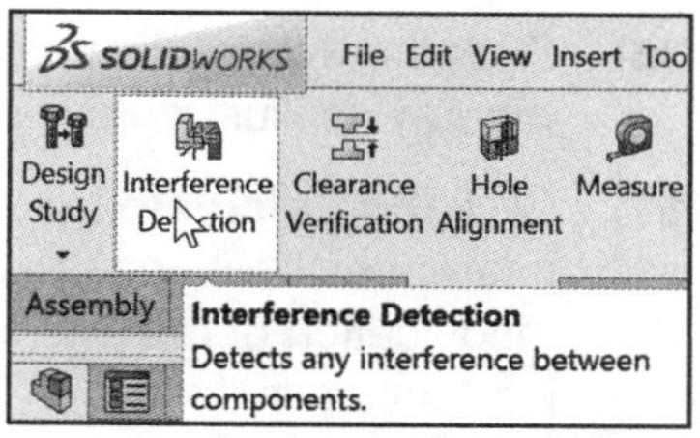

50) Click the **Interference Detection** icon. The Interference Detection PropertyManager is displayed.

51) Right-click in the **Selected Components** box.

52) Click **Clear Selections**.

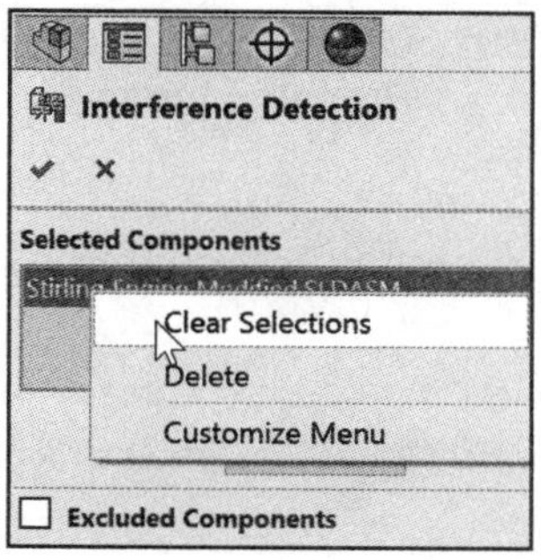

Select component to perform the Interference detection process.

53) Click the **Connecting Rod** from the Graphics window as illustrated. Connection Rod-1 is displayed in the Selected Components box.

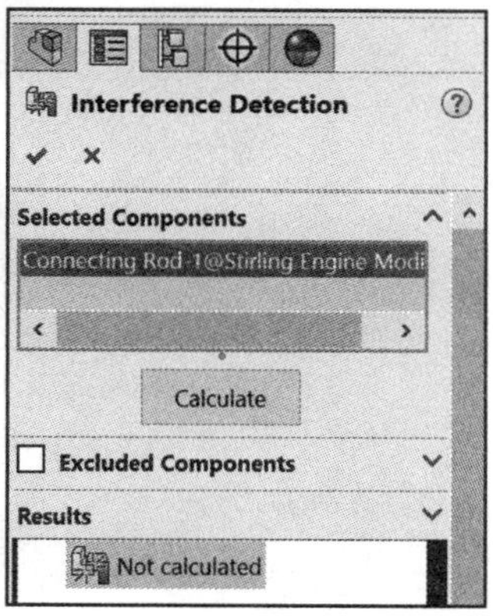

54) **Rotate** the model to view the Piston Clevis.

55) Click the **Piston Clevis** from the Graphics window as illustrated.

56) Click the **Power Piston** from the Graphics window as illustrated.

57) Click the **Calculate** button. There are no Inferences between the components. The modification of the Distance mate resolved the inference issue.

58) Click **OK** from the Interference Detection PropertyManager.

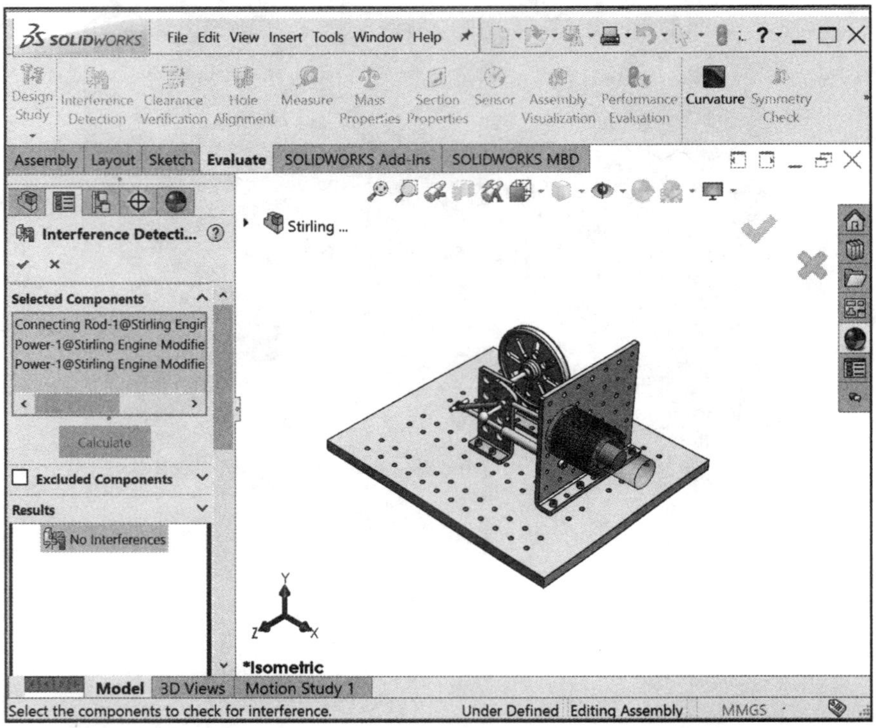

Activity: Locate the Center of Mass of the Assembly

Locate the Center of Mass along with other Mass Properties of the assembly (COM). You can assign values for mass, center of mass and moments of inertia to override the calculated values.

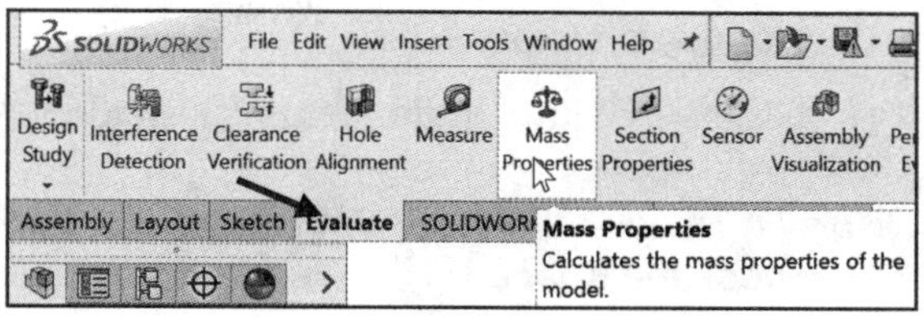

View the Mass Properties of the Assembly.

59) Click the **Evaluate** tab from the CommandManager.

60) Position the **Handle** vertically upward in the assembly.

61) Click the **Mass Properties** icon. The Mass Properties dialog box is displayed. View the results. The total mass is 3447.14 grams. The numbers represent the document properties (2 decimal places). Your Center of mass may be different due to the location of the Handle in the assembly.

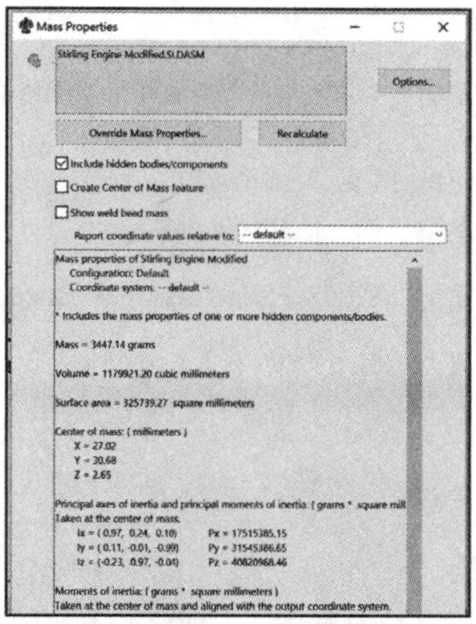

View the Mass Properties of the Plate in the Assembly.

62) Right-click inside the **Selection** box.

63) Click **Clear Selections**.

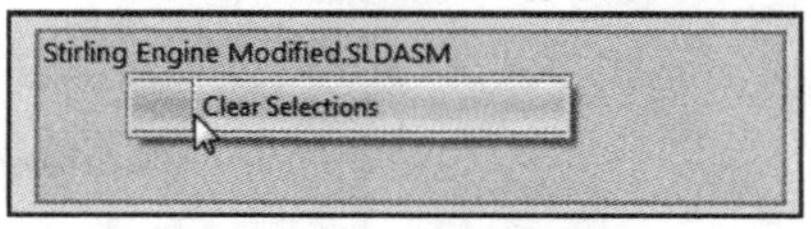

64) Click the **Plate** in the Graphics window as illustrated. Plate-1 is displayed in the Selection box. The Mass is approximately 259.60 grams.

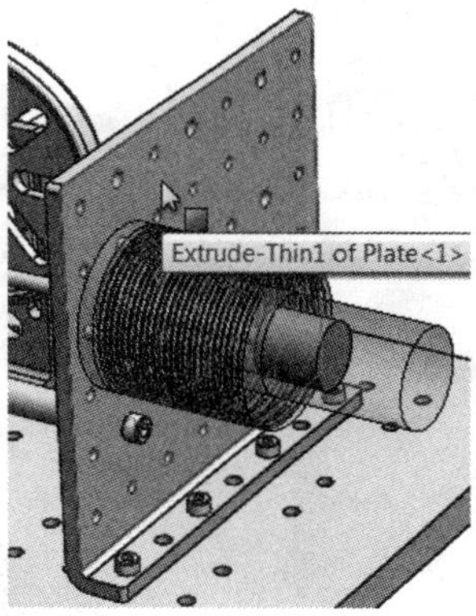

Return to the Mass Properties of the Assembly.

65) Right-click inside the **Selection** box.

66) Click **Clear Selections**.

67) Click **Stirling Engine Modified** from the Assembly FeatureManager as illustrated.

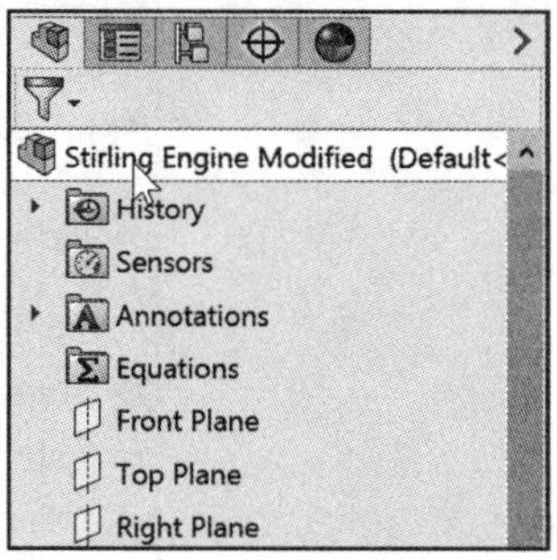

Locate the Center of Mass of the Assembly.

68) Click the **Create Center of Mass feature** box.

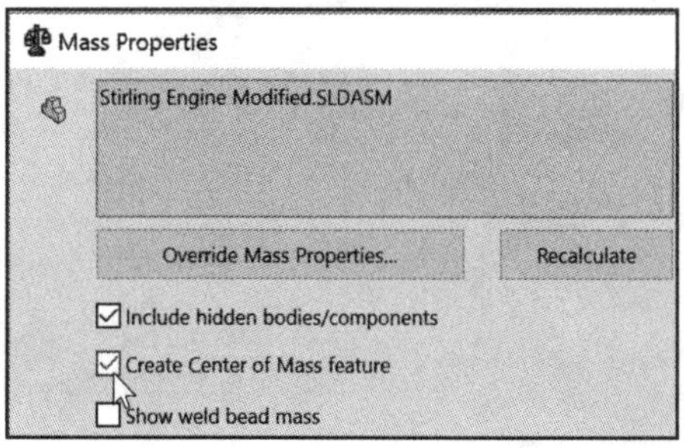

Close the Mass Properties dialog box.

69) Click **Close**.

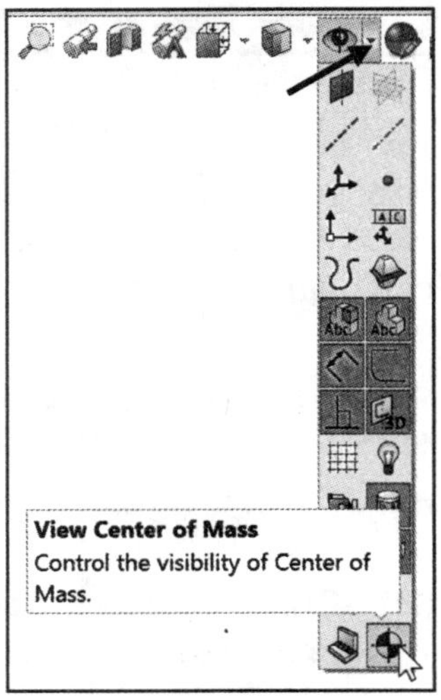

Display the COM point in the Assembly.

70) Click **View Center of Mass** from the Hide/Show Items in the Heads-up toolbar.

71) Click a **position** in the Graphics window. View the results.

Display a Trimetric - Shaded With Edges view.

72) Press the **space bar** to display the Orientation dialog box.

73) Click **Trimetric**. You can also access the Isometric view tool from the Heads-up View toolbar.

74) Click the **Shaded With Edges** icon.

Save the Assembly.

75) Click **Save**.

76) Click **Rebuild** and **save**.

You can add a Center of Mass (COM) point to parts and assemblies. In drawings of parts or assemblies that contain a COM point, you can show and reference the COM point.

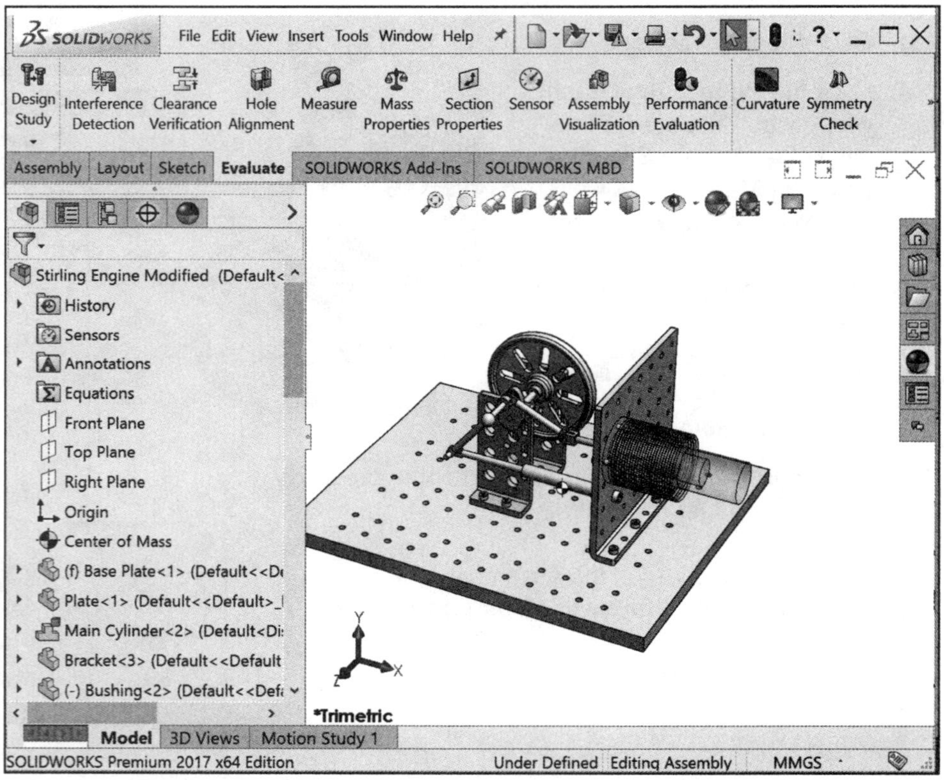

You can define a coordinate system for a part or assembly. Coordinate systems are useful:

- With the Measure and Mass Properties tools.
- When exporting SOLIDWORKS documents to IGES, STL, ACIS, STEP, Parasolid, VRML and VDA.
- When applying assembly mates.

In the next section, create a new coordinate system on the front bottom vertex of the assembly.

Activity: Create a new Coordinate System in the Assembly

View the new Coordinate System on the front bottom vertex of the assembly.

77) Click the **Assembly** tab from the CommandManager.

78) Click **Coordinate System** from the Consolidated Reference Geometry drop-down menu. The Coordinate System PropertyManager is displayed.

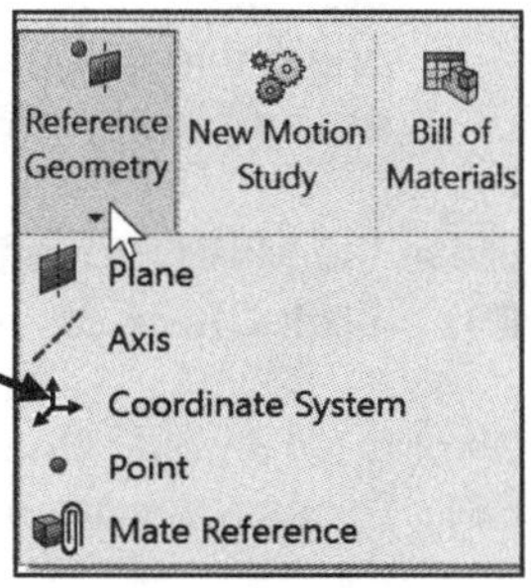

79) Click the **bottom front vertex** of the Assembly Base Plate. Vertex<1> is displayed.

80) Click **OK** from the Coordinate System PropertyManager. Coordinate System1 is displayed in the Assembly FeatureManager.

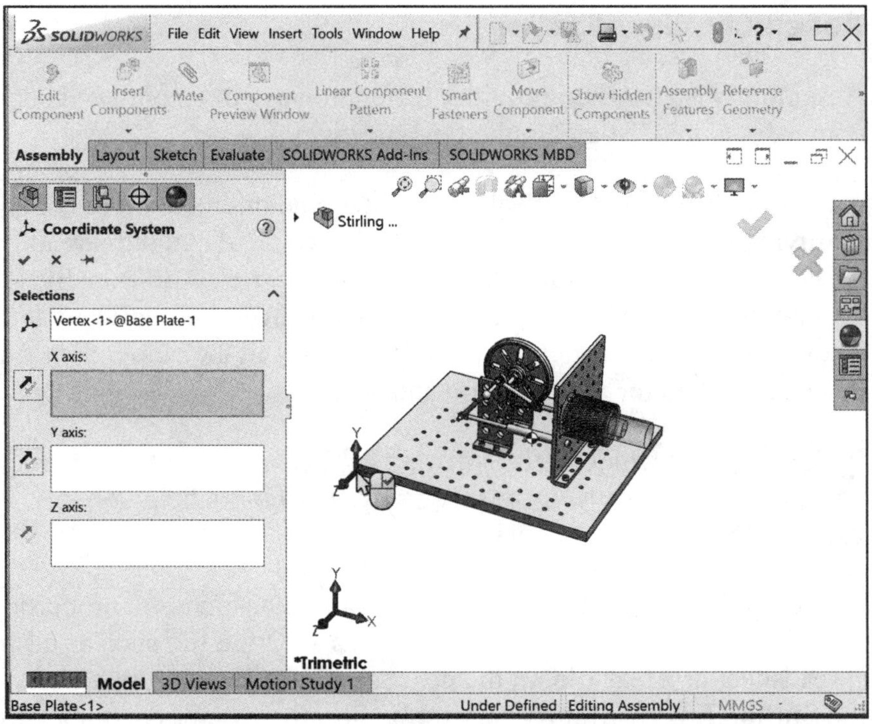

In the next section, display the Mass Properties relative to the new Coordinate system of the assembly.

Activity: Display the Mass Properties relative to the new Coordinate System

View the new Center of Mass point.

81) Click the **Evaluate** tab from the CommandManager.

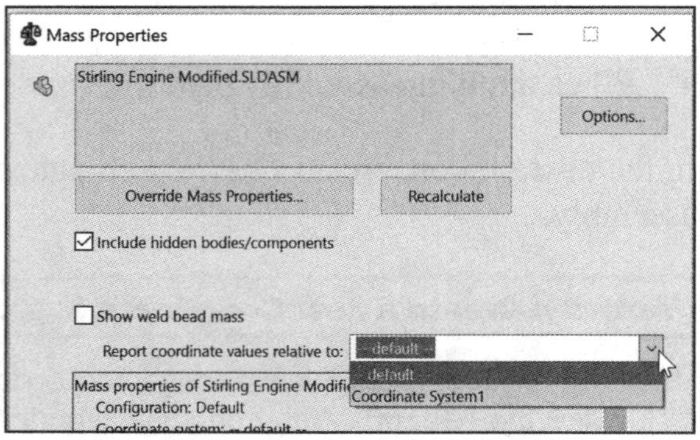

82) Click the **Mass Properties** icon. The Mass Properties dialog box is displayed.

83) Click the **drop-down arrow** for the Report coordinate values relative to:

84) Select **Coordinate System1**. View the updated results (Center of Mass) in the Mass Properties dialog box. Your Center of mass may be different due to the original location of the Handle in the assembly.

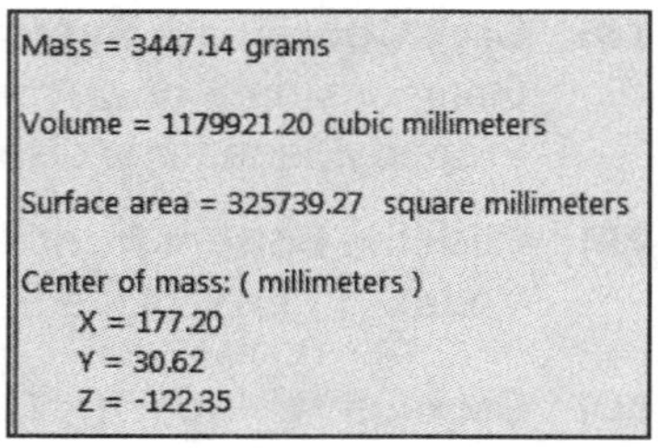

Close the Mass Properties dialog box.

85) Click **Close**.

Display a Trimetric view.

86) Press the **space bar** to display the Orientation dialog box.

87) Click **Trimetric view**. You can also access the Isometric view tool from the Heads-up View toolbar.

Assembly Visualization

Assembly Visualization provides different ways to display and sort an assembly's components in a list and in the Graphics window.

You can sort the list by one property at a time or create more complex sorting scenarios involving several different properties. Basic calculated numerical data such as component mass, density, and volume are available in the tool. Additionally, you can create customized criteria which are dependent on several numerical values. If you defined non-calculated properties such as Vendor or Status in the component files, you can access those properties for modification and sorting.

In the Graphics window, the software applies colors to the components based on the value of the property you are sorting by. The colors help you to visualize the relative value of the property for each component.

You can edit component materials and other non-numeric properties directly from the list. You can save the list information in a separate file such as a Microsoft® Excel® spreadsheet or a text file. In the next section, utilize the Assembly Visualization tool on the Stirling Engine Modify Assembly. Sort the assembly components by mass.

Activity: Assembly Visualization tool - Sort Components by Mass

Apply the Assembly Visualization tool. Sort by mass.

88) Click the **Evaluate** tab from the CommandManager.

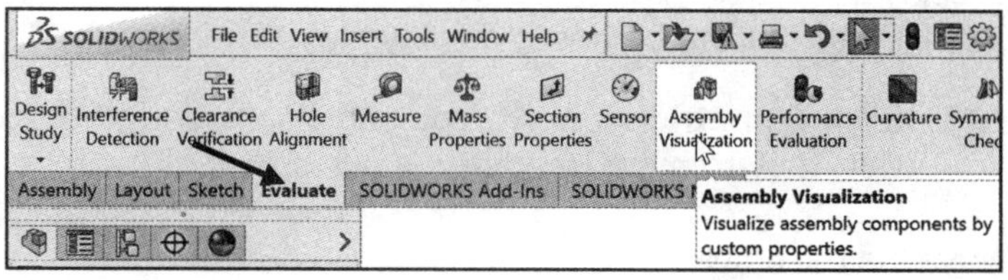

89) Click the **Assembly Visualization** icon. The Assembly Visualization PropertyManager is displayed.

90) Click the **arrow** to the right of the File Name row as illustrated.

91) Select **Mass**.

92) Click the **Mass** column. View the results from low to high or from high to low.

93) Click the **Toggle Slider** to view the color of the components in the Graphics window.

94) Click **OK** from the Assembly Visualization PropertyManager.

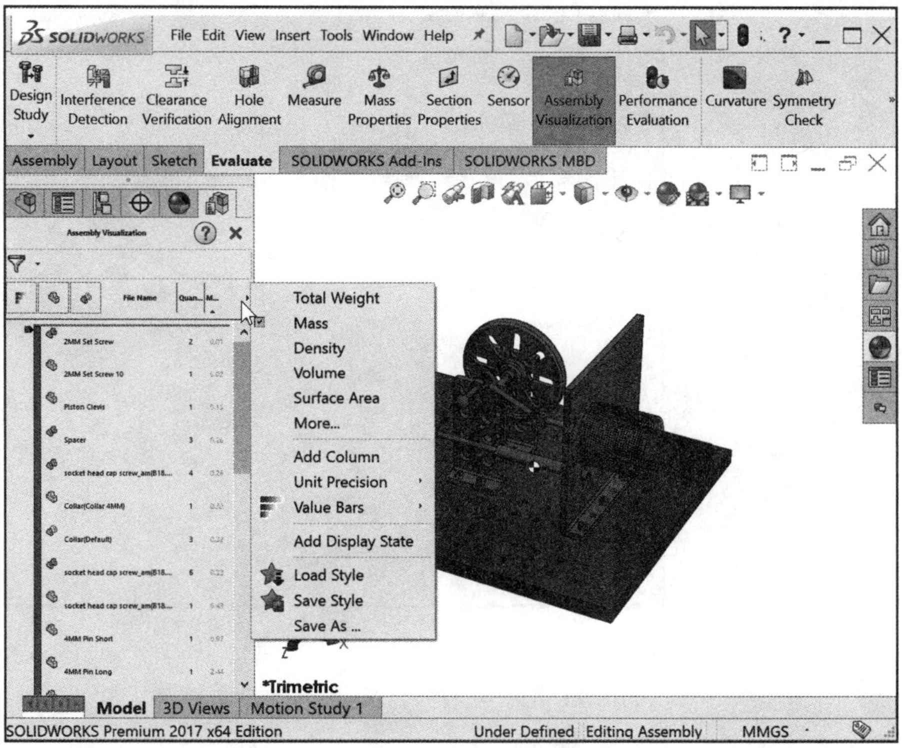

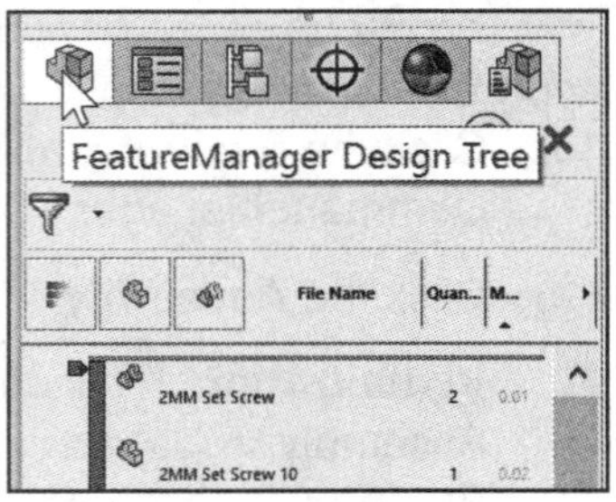

Return to the Assembly FeatureManager.

95) Click the **Assembly FeatureManager Design** icon tree.

Display a Trimetric view.

96) Press the **space bar** to display the Orientation dialog box.

97) Click **Trimetric view**. You can also access the Isometric view tool from the Heads-up View toolbar.

Save the Assembly.

98) Click **Save**.

On your own, insert two Collars and three spacers onto the 4MM Pin Long to complete the assembly.

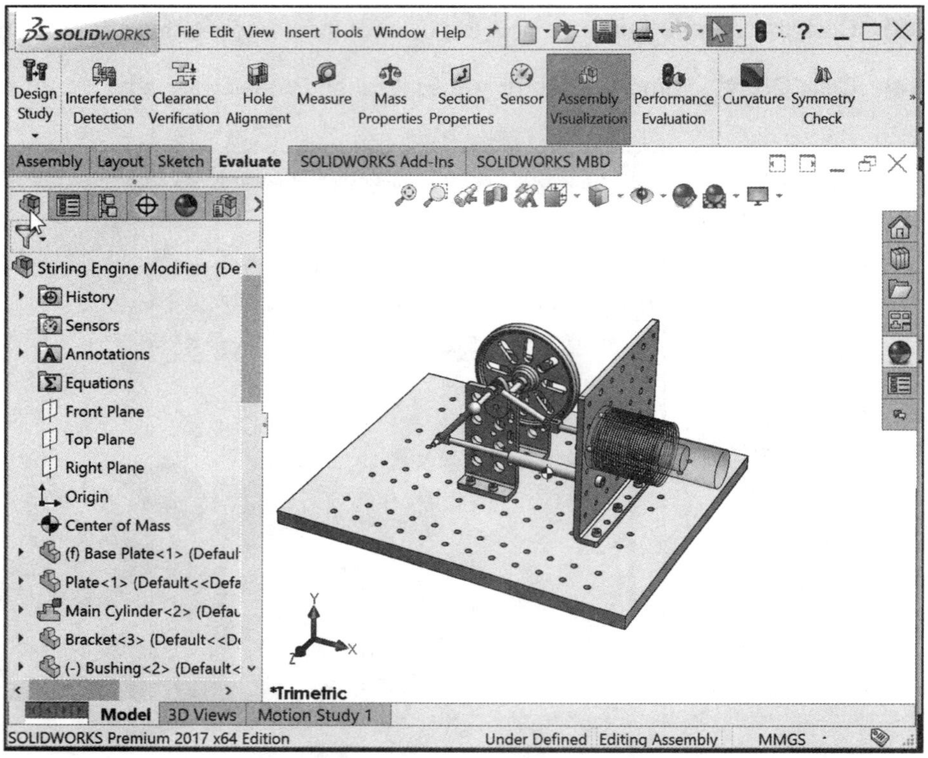

Motion Study

Motion studies are graphical simulations of motion for assembly models. You can incorporate visual properties such as lighting and camera perspective into a motion study.

Motion studies do not change an assembly model or its properties. They simulate and animate the motion you prescribe for a model. You can use SOLIDWORKS mates to restrict the motion of components in an assembly when you model motion.

In the next section, play the Basic Motion study of the final assembly. You can use Basic Motion for approximating the effects of motors, springs, contact and gravity on assemblies. Basic Motion takes mass into account in calculating motion. Basic Motion computation is relatively fast, so you can use this for creating presentation-worthy animations using physics-based simulations. A simple rotary motor was applied to the Handle for movement.

Activity: Play the Basic Motion Study of the Assembly

Play the Basic Motion Study. Access the Motion Manager from the Motion Study tab.

99) Click the **Motion Study 1** tab at the bottom left of the Graphics window. The Motion Manager is displayed.

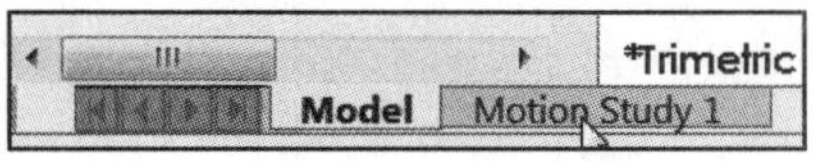

100) Select **Basic Motion** from the Motion Study drop-down menu. A motion study was created using a simple Rotary Motor on the Handle.

101) Click the **Calculate** icon.

102) Click the **Play from Start**. View the Motion Study in the Graphics window.

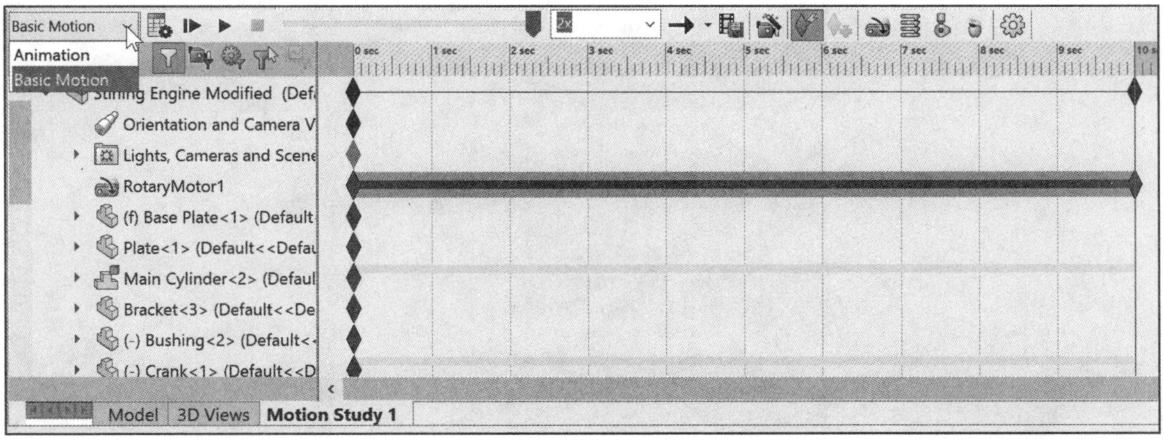

Create an AVI file of the Motion Study.

103) Click the **Save Animation** icon. View the Save Animation to File dialog box.

104) Select a **Save in** location. View your options.

105) Click **Save**. View your options.

106) Click **OK** from the Video Compression dialog box.

Return to the Model.

107) Click the **Model** tab at the bottom left of the Graphics window.

108) **Explore** SOLIDWORKS Help for additional information on Basic Motion using timers and other tools.

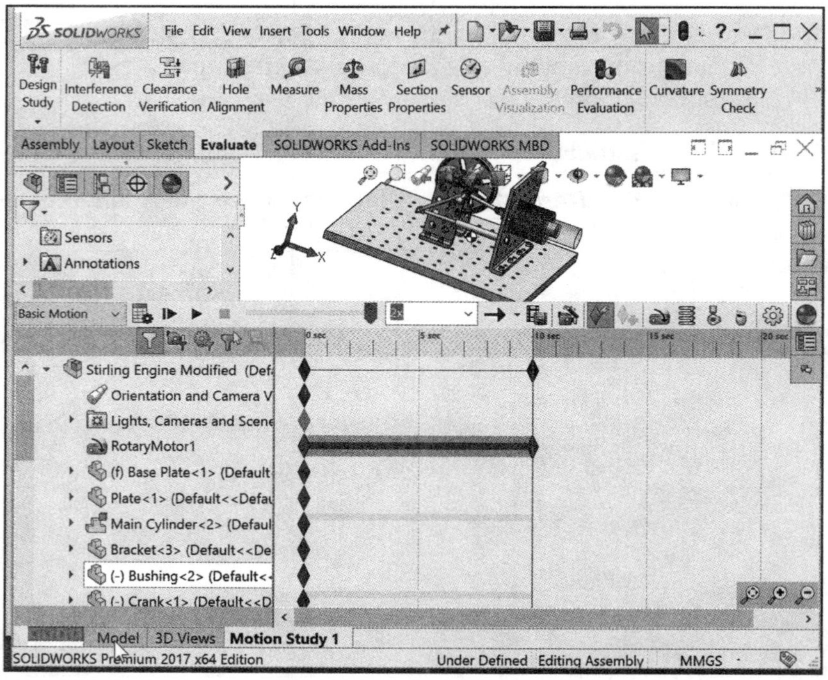

Save the Assembly.

109) Click **Save** .

110) Click **Rebuild** and save.

Close all models.

111) Click **Window**, **Close All** from the Main menu bar.

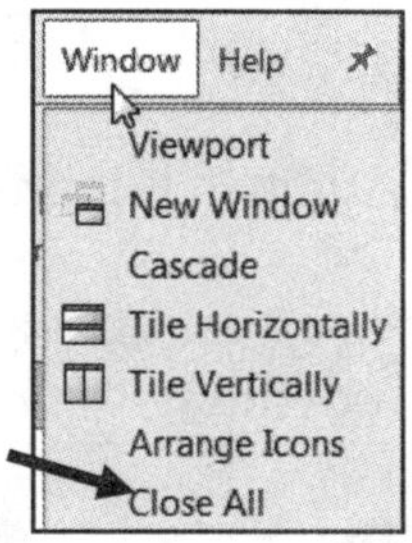

You are finished with this section.

Summary

In this chapter, you addressed clearance, interference, static and dynamic behavior of the Stirling Engine Modified assembly.

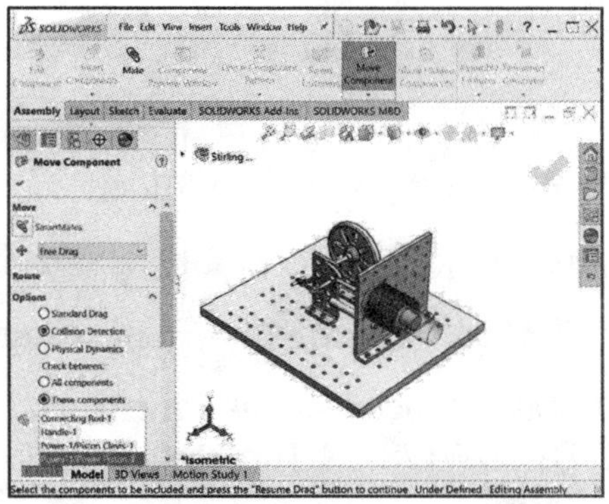

You verified the behavior between the following components: Power Piston, Power Clevis, Connecting Rod and Handle in the assembly.

You applied the following assembly tools: Move, Rotate, Collision Detection, Interference Detection, Selected Components, Edit Feature and Center of Mass along with utilizing the Assembly Visualization tool on the Stirling Engine assembly and sorted by component mass.

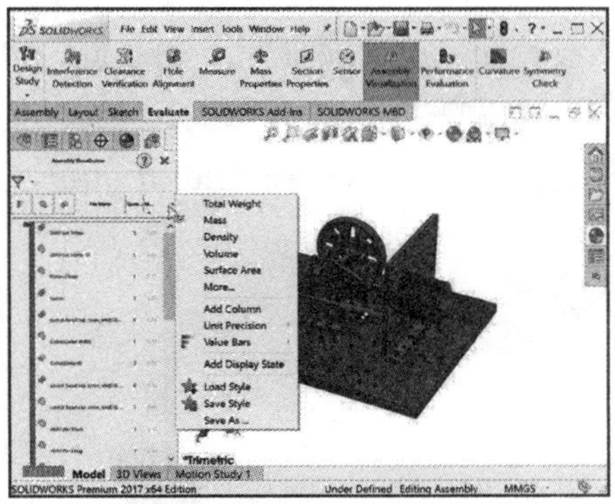

You created a new Coordinate System on the Stirling Engine assembly relative to the default origin, ran a Motion Study and saved the Motion Study AVI file.

In Chapter 5, you will learn about the Drawing and Dimension Fundamentals and create two new drawings with user defined document properties:

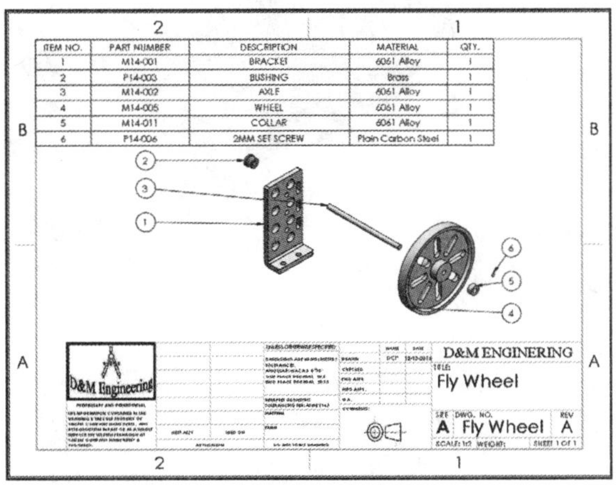

- Fly Wheel Assembly.
- Bushing.

Create the Fly Wheel Assembly drawing with an Exploded Isometric view.

Utilize a Bill of Materials and Balloons.

Learn about Custom Properties and the Title Block.

Create the Bushing Part drawing utilizing Third Angle Projection with two standard Orthographic views: Front, Top and an Isometric view.

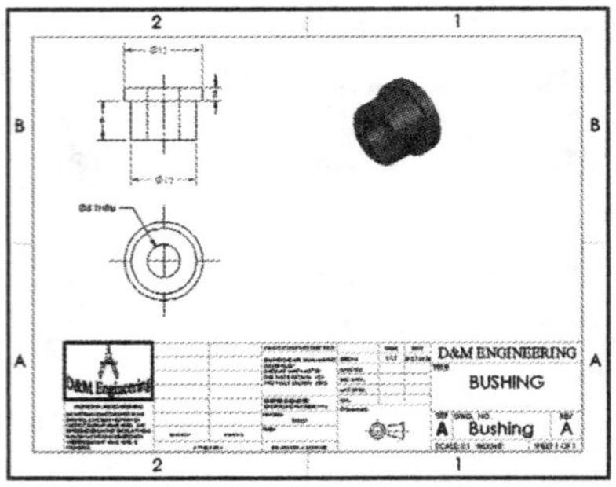

Address imported dimensions from the Model Items tool.

Insert additional dimensions using the Smart Dimension tool along with all needed annotations.

Exercises

Exercise 4.1: Gear Mate (Mechanical mate)

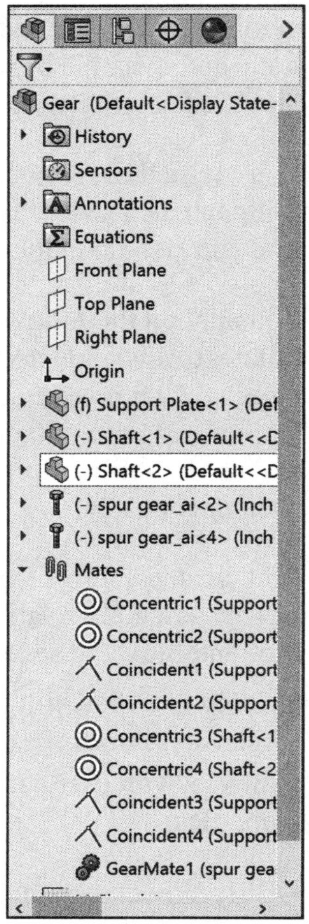

View the provided ppt on Gears located in the Chapter 4 - Homework\Gear Mate folder.

Create the Gear assembly as illustrated.

All needed information is provided in the ppt.

Create all needed components and mates. Use the SOLIDWORKS Toolbox. The SOLIDWORKS Toolbox is an add-in.

View the avi file in the Chapter 4 Homework\Gear Mate folder for proper movement.

Create your own avi file of your assembly.

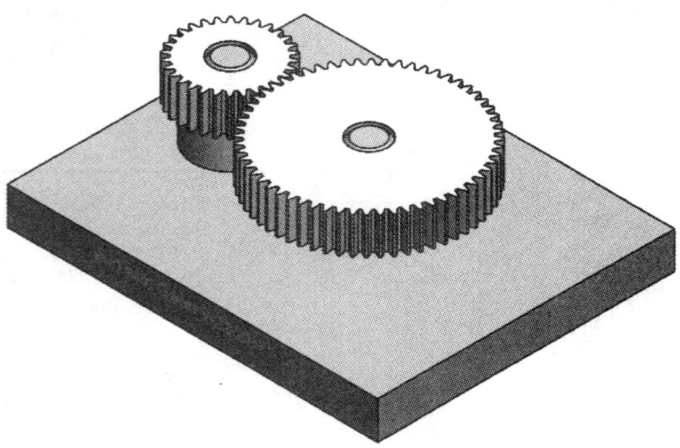

Exercise 4.2: Explicit Equation Driven Curve tool

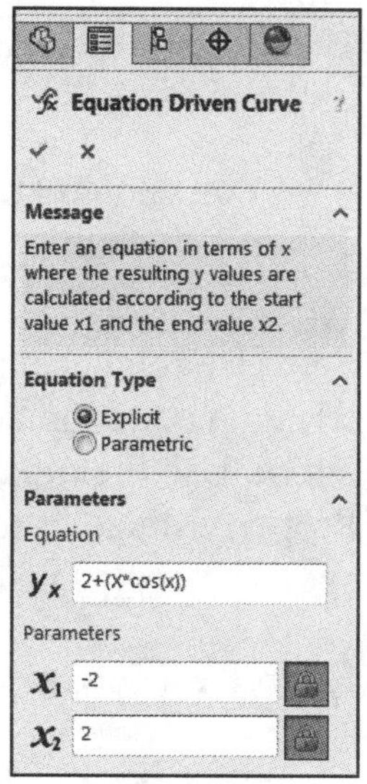

Create an Explicit Equation Driven Curve on the Front plane. Revolve the curve. Calculate the volume of the solid.

Create a New part. Use the default ANSI, IPS Part template.

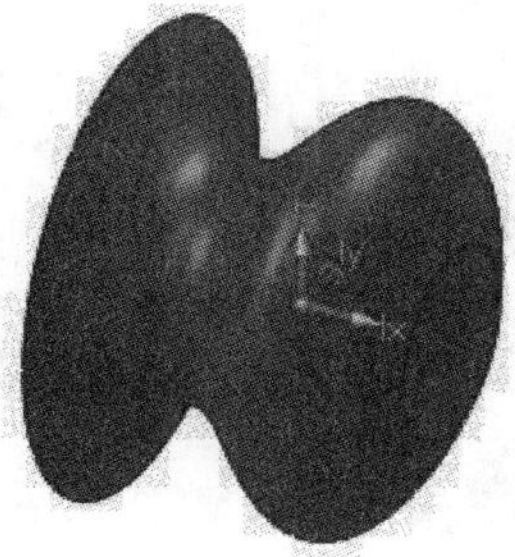

Create a 2D Sketch on the Front Plane.

Activate the Equation Driven Curve Sketch tool from the Consolidated drop-down menu.

Enter the Equation y_x as illustrated.

Enter the parameters x_1, x_2 that define the lower and upper bound of the equation as illustrated. View the curve in the Graphics window.

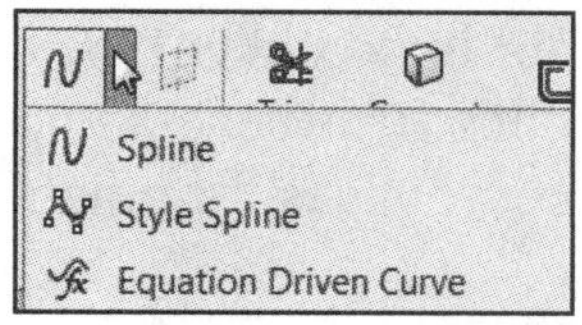

Size the curve in the Graphics window. The Sketch is under defined.

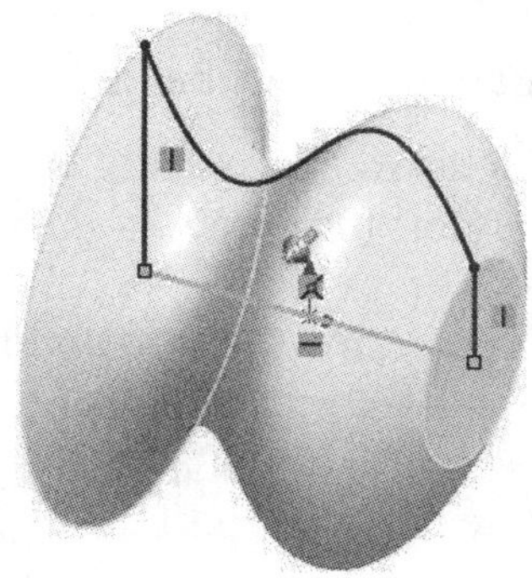

Insert three lines to close the profile as illustrated. Fully define your sketch. Enter dimensions and any needed geometric relation.

Create the Revolved feature. View the results in the Graphics window. Revolve1 is displayed. Utilize the Section tool, parallel with the Right plane, to view how each cross section is a circle.

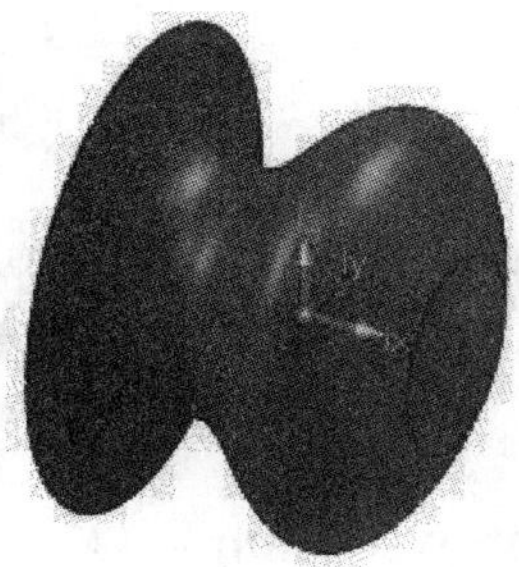

Density = 0.31 pounds per cubic inch

Mass = 16.10 pounds

Volume = 52.43 cubic inches

Surface area = 103.20 square inches

Apply Brass for material.

Precision = 2.

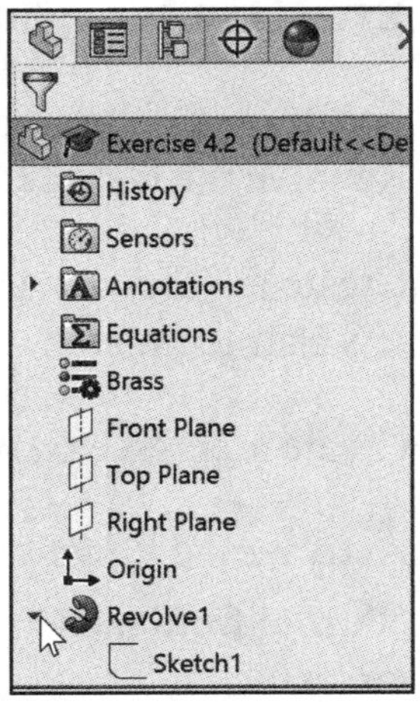

Calculate the volume of the part using the Mass Properties tool. View the results. Also note the surface area and the Center of mass.

You can create parametric (in addition to explicit) equation-driven curves in both 2D and 3D sketches.

Use regular mathematical notation and order of operations to write an equation. x_1 and x_2 are for the beginning and end of the curve. Use the transform options at the bottom of the PropertyManager to move the entire curve in x-, y- or rotation. To specify x = f(y) instead of y = f(x) use a 90 degree transform.

Exercise 4.3: Curve Through XYZ Points tool

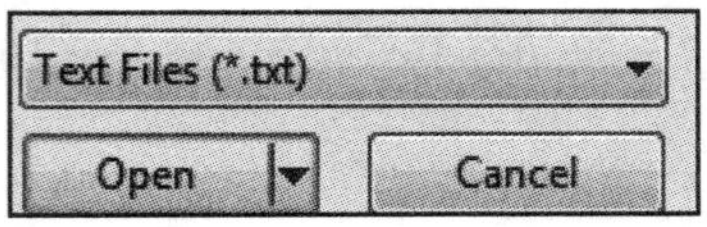

The Curve Through XYZ Points feature provides the ability to either type in (using the Curve File dialog box) or click Browse and import a text file with x-, y-, z-, coordinates for points on a curve.

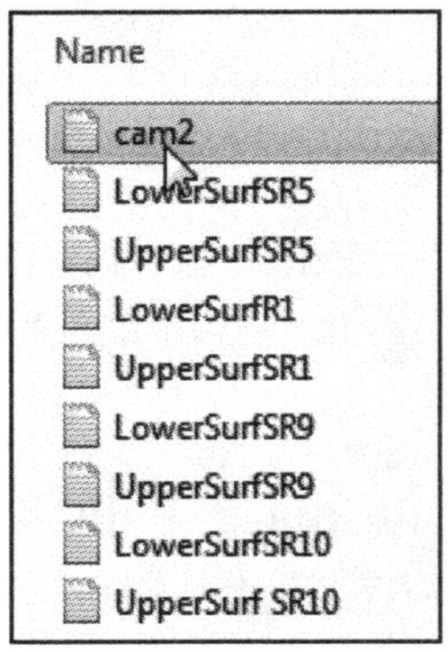

A text file can be generated by any program which creates columns of numbers. The Curve feature reacts like a default spline that is fully defined.

Create a curve using the Curve Through XYZ Points tool. Import the x-, y-, z- data.

Verify that the first and last points in the curve file are the same for a closed profile.

Create a new part.

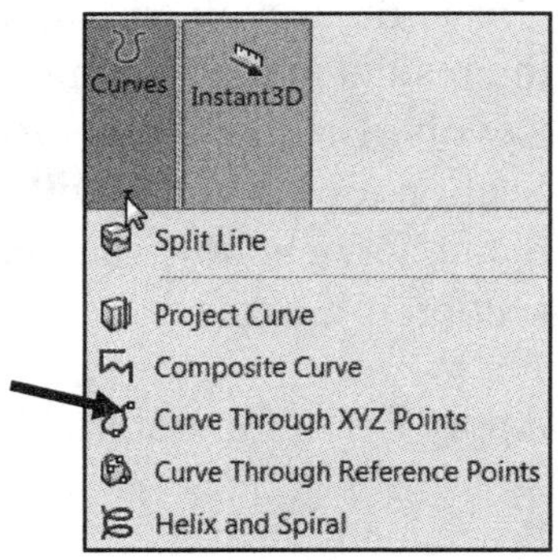

Click the Curve Through XYZ Points tool from the Features CommandManager. The Curve File dialog box is displayed.

Import the curve data. Click Browse from the Curve File dialog box.

Browse to the downloaded folder location: Chapter 4 Homework folder.

Set file type to Text Files.

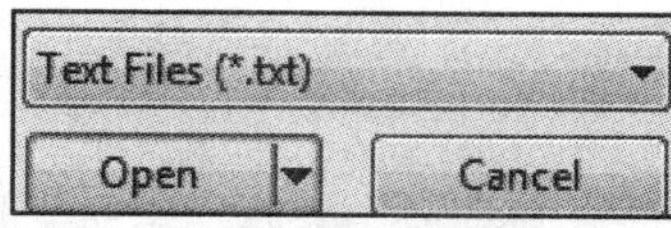

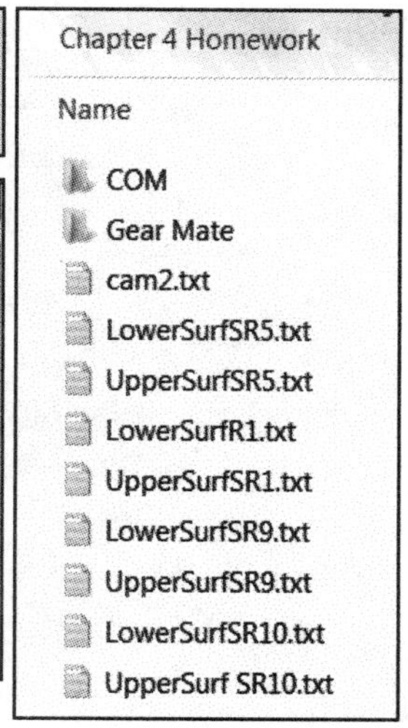

Double-click cam2.text. View the data in the Curve File dialog box. View the sketch in the Graphics window. Review the data points in the dialog box.

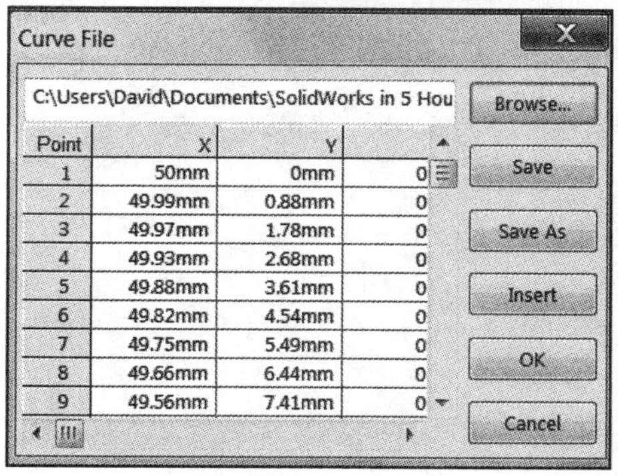

Click OK from the Curve File dialog box.

Fix the Curve to the Graphics window.

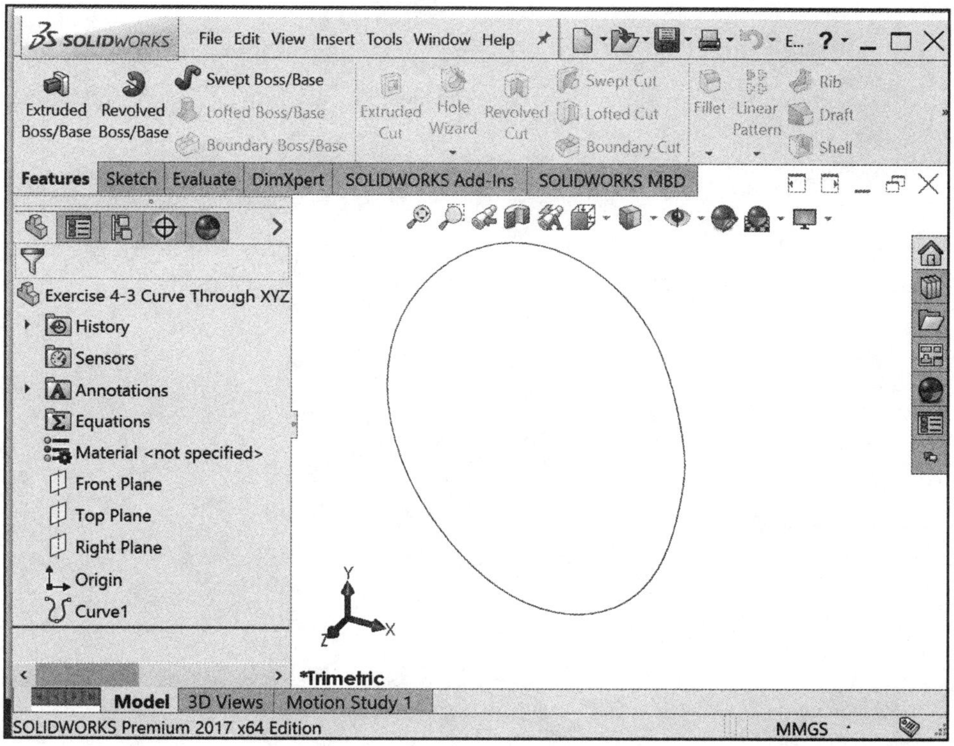

Curve1 is displayed in the FeatureManager. You created a curve using the Curve Through XYZ Points tool with imported x-, y-, z- data from a cam program.

This Curve can now be used to create a sketch (closed profile).

Close the existing model.

Notes:

Chapter 5

Drawing and Dimensioning Fundamentals

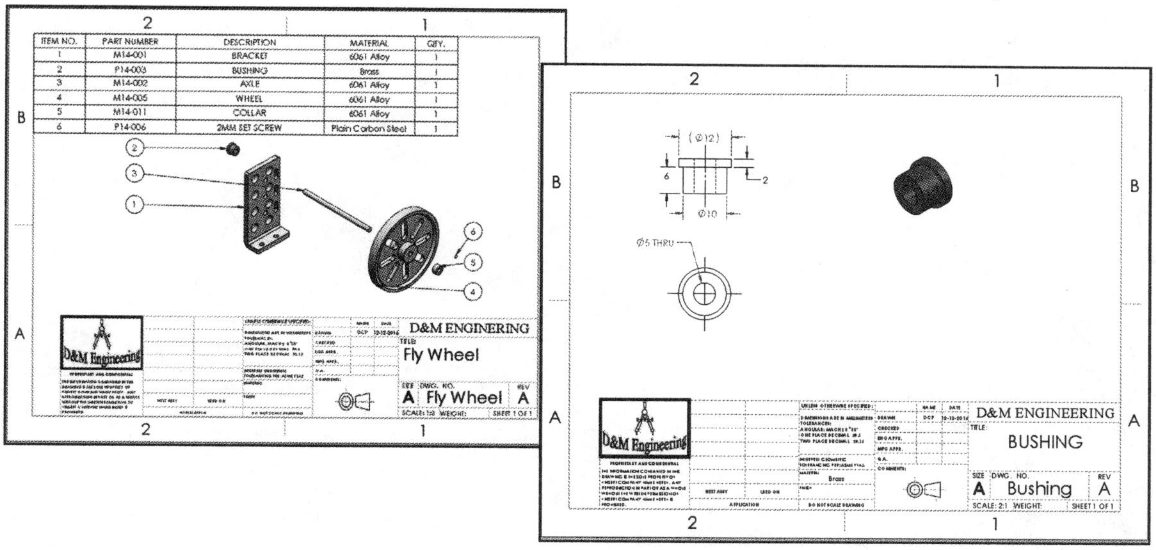

Below are the desired outcomes and usage competencies based on the completion of Chapter 5.

Desired Outcomes:	**Usage Competencies:**

• An Isometric Exploded Fly Wheel Assembly Drawing.
  • Bill of Materials.
  • Balloons.
• A Bushing Drawing.
  • Front, Top, Right and Isometric view.
  • Dimensions.
  • Annotations.
	• Produce a Sheet Format with Custom Sheet Properties, Title block and more.
	• Create an Exploded Isometric Assembly drawing view with a Bill of Materials and Balloons.
	• Create standard Orthographic (Front, Top & Right) views.
	• Aptitude to import dimensions from the Model Items tool.
	• Knowledge to insert additional dimensions using the Smart Dimension toolbar.
	• Ability to insert drawing annotation.

Notes:

Chapter 5 - Drawing and Dimensioning Fundamentals

Chapter Objective

Create two new drawings: Fly Wheel assembly and Bushing part. The first drawing is an Isometric Exploded view of the Fly Wheel assembly. The assembly drawing displays a Bill of Materials at the part level along with Balloons, Magnetic lines and Custom Properties.

The second drawing is a Bushing part. Insert standard Orthographic (Front, Top & Right) views along with an Isometric view. Insert all needed dimensions and annotations.

On the completion of this chapter, you will be able to:

- Create a new SOLIDWORKS drawing.
- Set user defined document properties for a drawing.
- Produce a Sheet Format with Custom Sheet Properties, Title block and more.
- Generate an Exploded Isometric Assembly drawing view.
- Create and insert a Bill of Materials with Auto Balloons in the Assembly drawing.
- Produce a Part drawing with standard Orthographic (Front, Top & Right) views and an Isometric view.
- Address imported dimensions from the Model Items tool.
- Insert additional dimensions using the Smart Dimension toolbar.
- Modify drawing view display styles.
- Insert drawing view annotations.

Activity: Start a SOLIDWORKS Session

Start a SOLIDWORKS session.

1) Double-click the **SOLIDWORKS icon** from the desktop.

2) **Pin** the Menu bar as illustrated. Use both the Menu bar menu and the Menu bar toolbar in this book.

The foundation of a new SOLIDWORKS drawing is the Drawing Template. Drawing size, drawing standards, company information, manufacturing, and/or assembly requirements, units and other properties are defined in the Drawing Template.

Activity: Create a New Drawing Document

Create a New Drawing document.

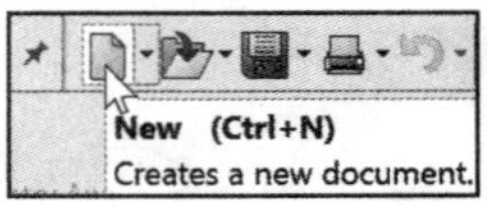

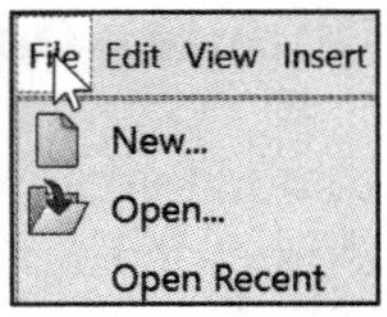

3) Click **New** from the Menu bar or click **File**, **New** from the Menu bar menu. The New SOLIDWORKS Document dialog box is displayed. Advanced mode is used in this book.

4) Double-click **Drawing** from the Templates tab. The Sheet Format/Size dialog box is displayed.

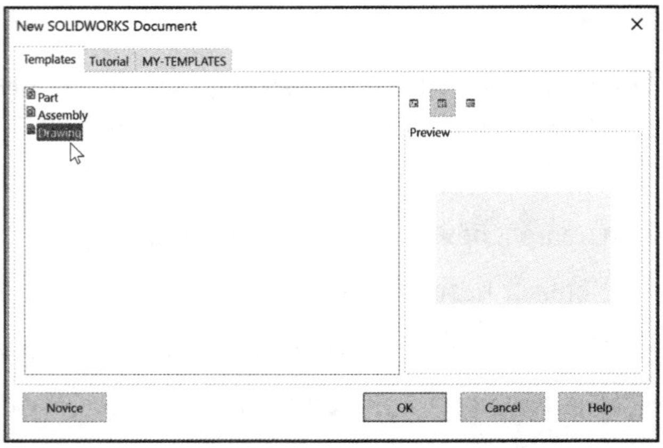

5) If needed, un-check the **Only show standard formats** box.

6) Check the **Display sheet format** box. The default Standard sheet size is A (ANSI) Landscape.

7) Click **OK** from the Sheet Format/Size dialog box.

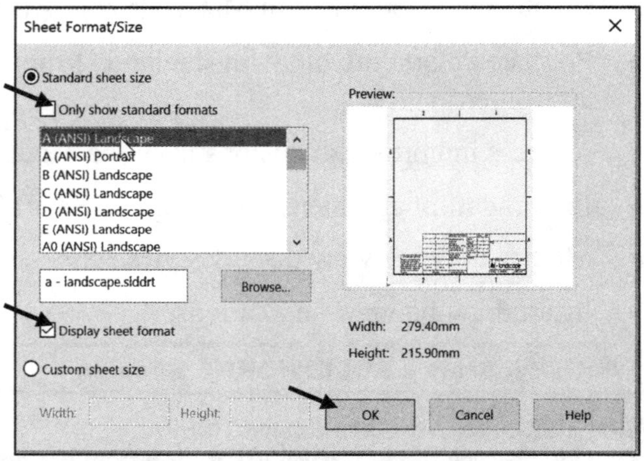

8) Click **Cancel** from the Model View PropertyManager. Draw1 FeatureManager is displayed.

If the Start command when creating new drawing option is checked, the Model View PropertyManager is selected by default.

Draw1 is the default drawing name. Sheet1 is the default first sheet name. The CommandManager alternates between the View Layout, Annotation, Sketch, Evaluate and SOLIDWORKS Add-ins tab.

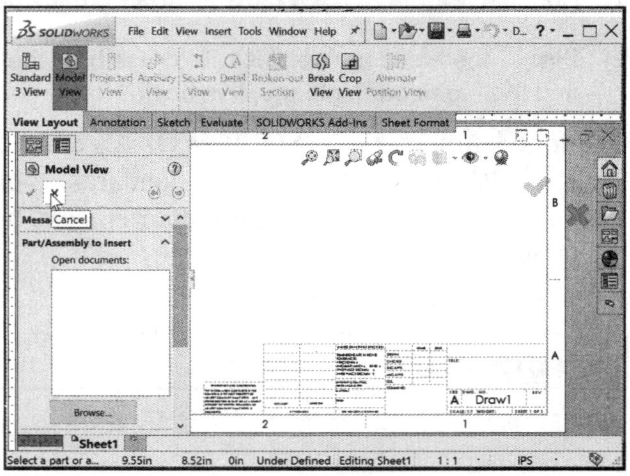

View the provided videos on Drawing Fundamentals to enhance your user experience in this chapter.

The Sheet Format is incorporated into the Drawing Template. The Sheet Format contains the border, Title block information, revision block information, company name, and/or company logo information, Custom Properties, and SOLIDWORKS Properties. Custom Properties and SOLIDWORKS Properties are shared values between documents.

In the next section, set Sheet Properties in the Assembly drawing document.

Activity: Set Sheet Properties for the Drawing

Set Sheet Properties for the Drawing.

9) Right-click on **Sheet1** in the Drawing FeatureManager.

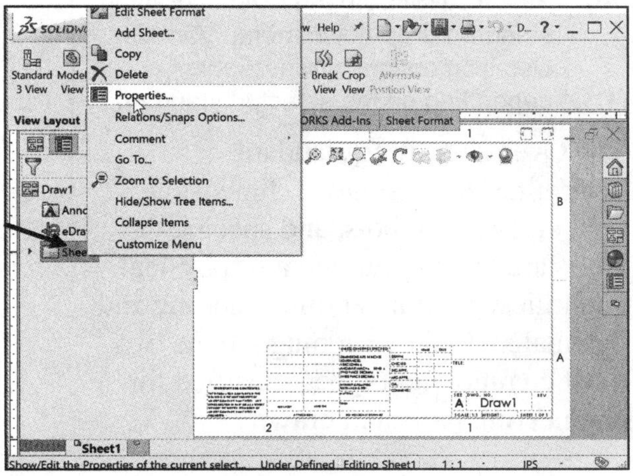

10) Click **Properties**. The Sheet Properties dialog box is displayed.

11) Select **A (ANSI) Landscape** from the Standard sheet size box.

12) Select **Third angle** for Type of projection.

13) Click **Apply Changes** from the Sheet Properties dialog box. The Sheet Properties are set for the drawing document.

There are two different types of Angle Projection: First and Third Angle Projection.

- First Angle Projection is used in Europe, South American and Asia.
- Third Angle Projection is used in the United States.

Both First Angle and Third Angle projections result in the same six principle views (Front, Top, Right, Bottom, Left, and Back); the difference between them is the arrangement of these views.

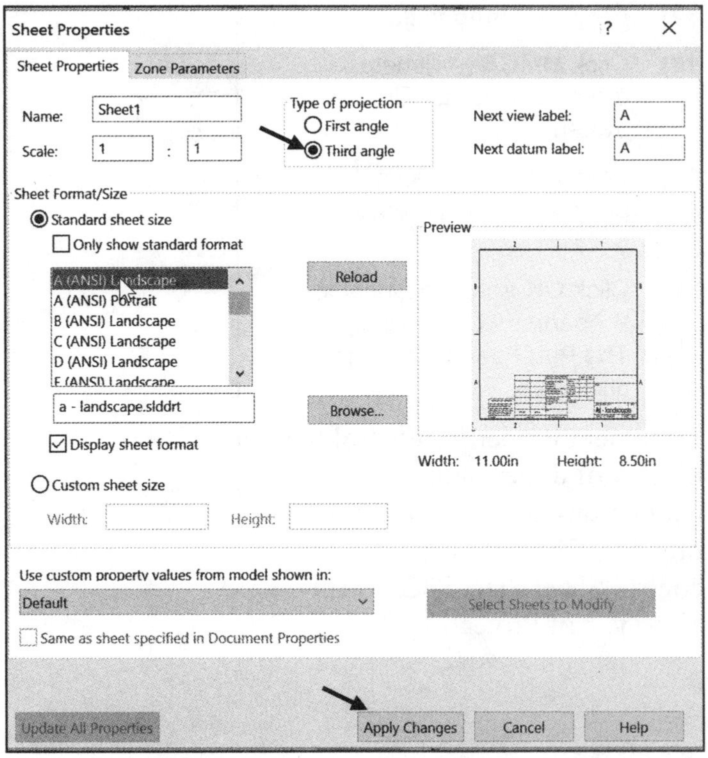

In the next section, set Document Properties in the drawing.

Activity: Set Document Properties for the Drawing

Set Document Properties - Drafting Standard.

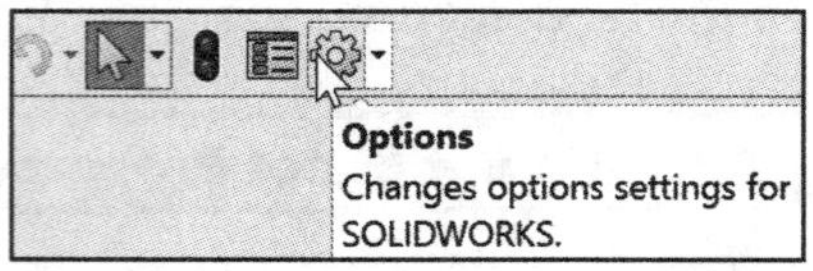

14) Click **Options** from the Menu bar. The System Options General dialog box is displayed.

15) Click the **Document Properties** tab.

16) Select **ANSI** from the Overall drafting standard drop-down menu. Various Detailing options are available depending on the selected standard.

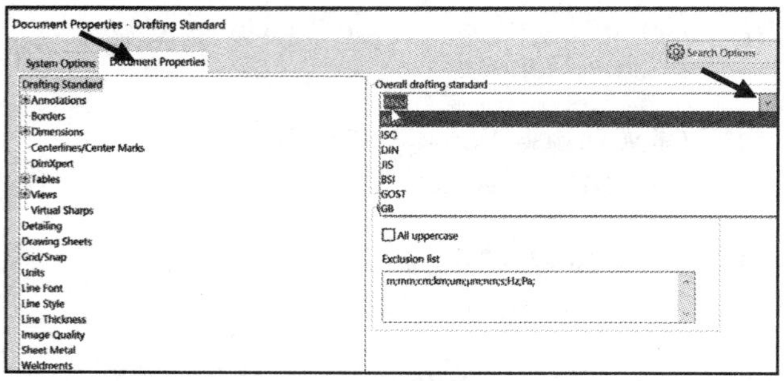

The Overall drafting standard determines the display of dimension text, arrows, symbols, and spacing. Units are the measurement of physical quantities. Millimeter dimensioning and decimal inch dimensioning are the two most common unit types specified for engineering parts and drawings.

Set Document Properties - Units.

17) Click the **Units** folder.

18) Click **MMGS** (millimeter, gram, second) for Unit system.

19) Select **.12** (two decimal places) for Length basic units.

20) Click **OK** from the Document Properties - Units dialog box. The Part FeatureManager is displayed.

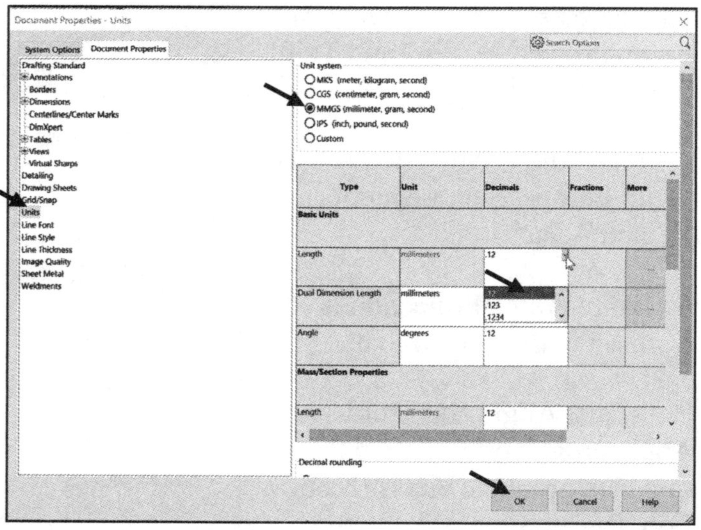

Document Properties control the display of dimensions, annotations and symbols in the drawing. Sheet Properties control Sheet Size, Sheet Scale and Type of Projection.

Title Block

The Title block contains text fields linked to System Properties and Custom Properties. System Properties are determined from the SOLIDWORKS documents. Custom Property values are assigned to named variables. Save time. Utilize System Properties and define Custom Properties in your Sheet Formats.

System Properties and Custom Properties for Title Block:			
System Properties Linked to fields in default Sheet Formats:	**Custom Properties of drawings linked to fields in default Sheet Formats:**		**Custom Properties of parts and assemblies linked to fields in default Sheet Formats:**
SW-File Name (in DWG. NO. field):	CompanyName:	EngineeringApproval:	Description (in TITLE field):
SW-Sheet Scale:	CheckedBy:	EngAppDate:	Weight:
SW-Current Sheet:	CheckedDate:	ManufacturingApproval:	Material:
SW-Total Sheets:	DrawnBy:	MfgAppDate:	Finish:
	DrawnDate:	QAApproval:	Revision:
	EngineeringApproval:	QAAppDate:	

The drawing document contains two modes:

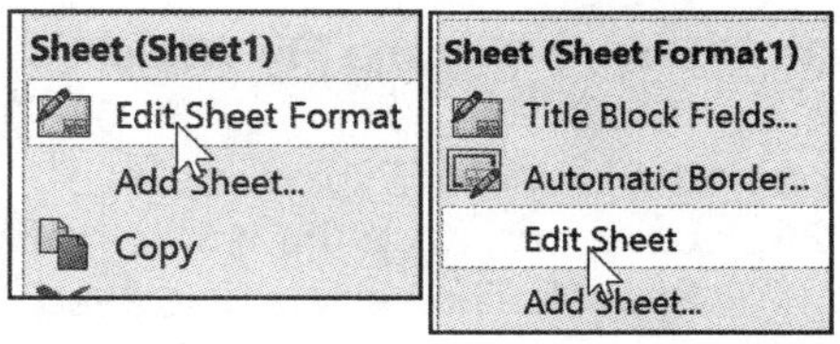

- Edit Sheet Format.
- Edit Sheet.

Insert views and dimensions in the Edit Sheet mode. Modify the Sheet Format text, lines, and the Title block information in the Edit Sheet Format mode. The CompanyName Custom Property is located in the Title block above the TITLE box. There is no value defined for CompanyName. A small text box indicates an empty field. Define a value for the Custom Property CompanyName. Example: D&M EDUCATION LLC. The Tolerance block is located in the Title block.

A part cannot be inserted into a drawing when the Edit Sheet Format mode is selected.

The Tolerance block provides information to the manufacturer on the minimum and maximum variation for each dimension on the drawing.

If a specific tolerance or note is provided on the drawing, the specific tolerance or note will override the information in the Tolerance block. General tolerance values are based on the design requirements and the manufacturing process. Modify the Tolerance block in the Sheet Format for ASME Y14.5 machined parts. Delete unnecessary text. The FRACTIONAL text refers to inches. The BEND text refers to sheet metal parts.

Fly Wheel Assembly Drawing

A drawing contains part views, geometric dimensioning and tolerances, notes, and other related design information. When a part is modified, the drawing automatically updates. When a driving dimension in the drawing is modified, the part is automatically updated.

Drawings consist of one or more views produced from the part or assembly. Create the Fly Wheel Assembly drawing from the Fly Wheel assembly. Utilize the Task Pane to insert an Isometric Exploded drawing view. Create a Bill of Materials at the part level. Unlike a part drawing, no dimensions are required as this time. Utilize the SOLIDWORKS in 5 Hours\Drawing folder for models in the section.

Activity: Create a Fly Wheel Assembly Drawing

Insert the Isometric Exploded Drawing view of the Fly Wheel Assembly.

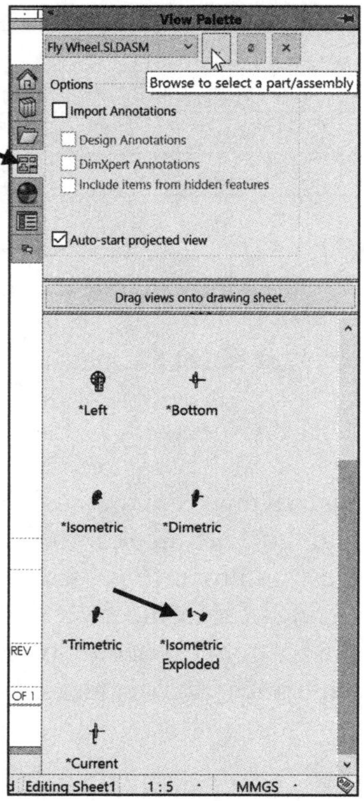

21) Click the **View Palette** icon from the SOLIDWORKS Resource Pane.

22) Click the **Browse** button.

23) Browse to the **SOLIDWORKS in 5 Hours\Drawing** folder.

24) Select **All Files (*.*)** from the drop-down menu.

25) Double-click the **Fly Wheel** assembly.

Insert the Isometric Exploded view.

26) **Drag and drop** the Isometric Exploded view icon into Sheet1. The view is displayed.

Set Sheet Properties for the Drawing.

27) Right-click in the **Graphics window** (not in the Exploded Isometric drawing view).

28) **Expand** the drop-down menu.

29) Click **Properties**. The Sheet Properties dialog box is displayed.

30) Enter Scale: **1:2**.

31) Click **Apply Changes** from the Sheet Properties dialog box. View the results in the Graphics window.

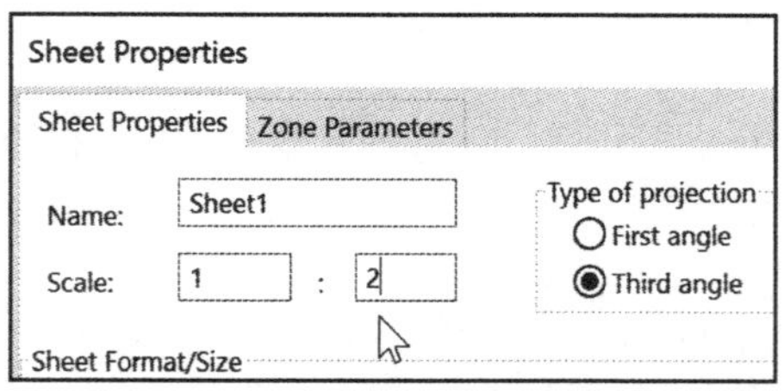

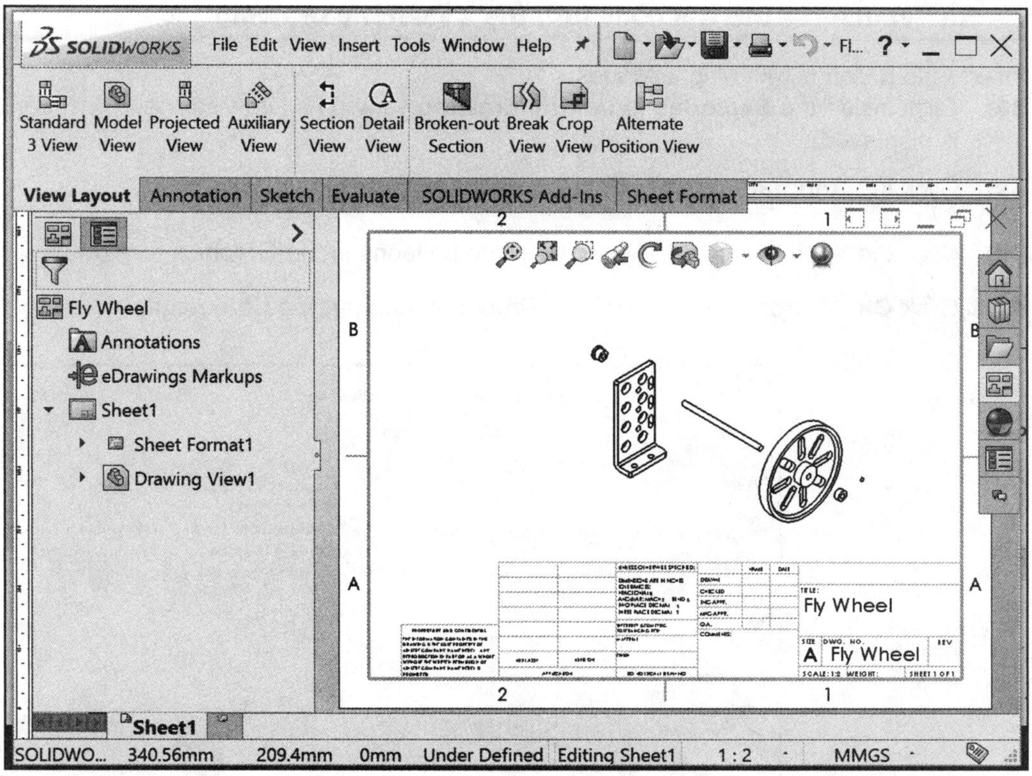

Modify the Display Style.

32) Click **inside** the Exploded Isometric drawing view. The Drawing View1 PropertyManager is displayed.

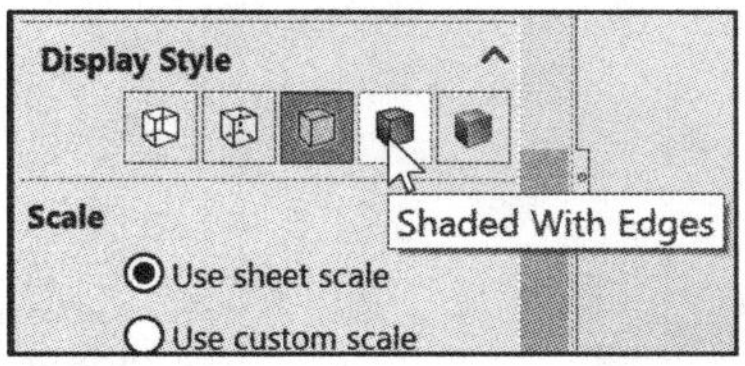

33) Click **Shaded with Edges** for Display Style.

34) Click the **Green Check mark** from the Drawing View1 PropertyManager.

Save the Fly Wheel assembly drawing.

35) Click **Save**. Click **Save All**.

36) **Select** the save in folder.

37) Click **Save**.

Balloons

You do not have to insert a Bill of Materials in order to add balloons. You can use auto balloons to automatically generate balloons in a drawing view.

Insert a set of balloons into one or more drawing views. Balloons are inserted into the appropriate views without duplicates. You can specify that balloons be inserted when creating new drawing views. You can specify that the balloons follow the assembly order or are numbered sequentially. You can automatically insert magnetic lines when using the Auto Balloon command.

In the next section, insert Auto Balloons using Magnetic lines in the assembly.

Activity: Insert Auto Balloons into the Assembly Drawing

Insert Auto Balloons with Magnetic lines.

38) Click inside the **Exploded Isometric drawing** view. The Drawing View 1 PropertyManager is displayed.

39) Click the **Annotation** tab from the CommandManager.

40) Click the **Auto Balloon** icon. View the balloons in the Graphics window.

41) Click **OK** from the Auto Balloon PropertyManager. View the results.

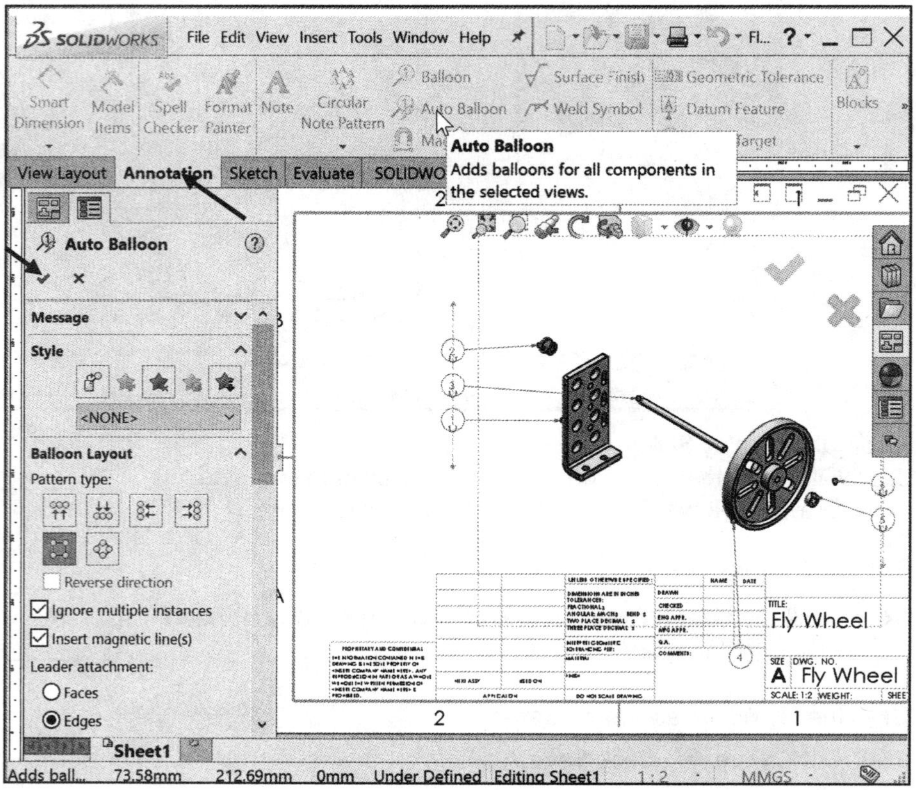

42) Click and **drag** the Balloons as illustrated.

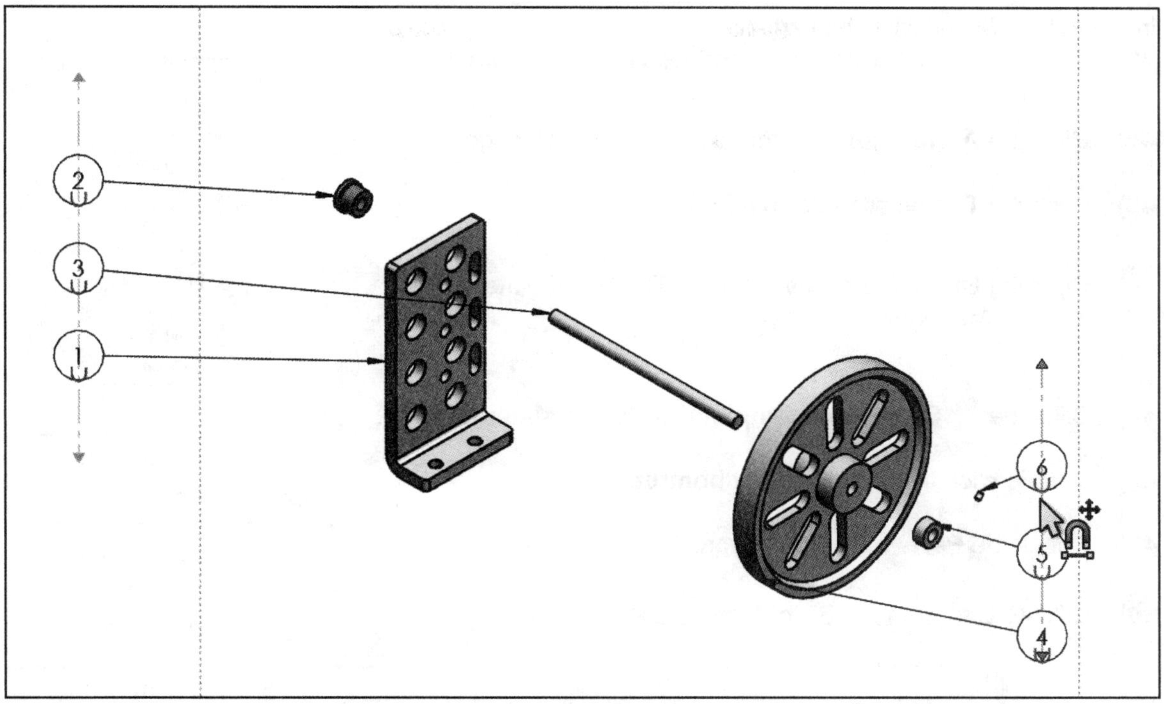

Magnetic lines are a convenient way to align balloons along a line at any angle. You attach balloons to magnetic lines, choose to space the balloons equally or not and move the lines freely at any angle in the drawing.

Bill of Materials

SOLIDWORKS automatically populates a Bill of Materials (BOM) with item numbers, quantities, part numbers, and custom properties in assembly drawings if they are inserted in the proper document. You can anchor, move, edit, and split a BOM.

When you insert balloons into a drawing, the item numbers and quantities in the balloons correspond to the numbers in the Bill of Materials. If an assembly has more than one configuration, you can list quantities of components for all configurations or selected configurations.

You can create BOMs in assembly files and multi-body part files. You can insert a BOM saved with an assembly into a referenced drawing. You do not need to create a drawing first.

In the next section, insert a Bill of Materials (BOM).

Activity: Insert a Bill of Materials

Insert a Bill of Materials at the part level.

43) Click inside the **Exploded Isometric view** in the Graphics window.

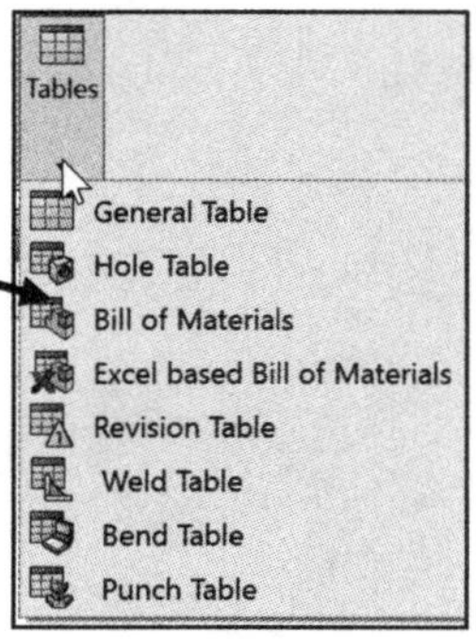

44) Click the **Annotation** tab from the CommandManager.

45) Click the **Tables** drop-down menu.

46) Click the **Bill of Materials** icon. The Bill of Materials PropertyManager is displayed.

47) Click the **Open table template for Bill of Materials** icon.

48) Double-click **bom-material.sldbomtbt**.

49) Check the **Parts only** BOM Type.

50) Click **OK** from the Bill of Materials PropertyManager.

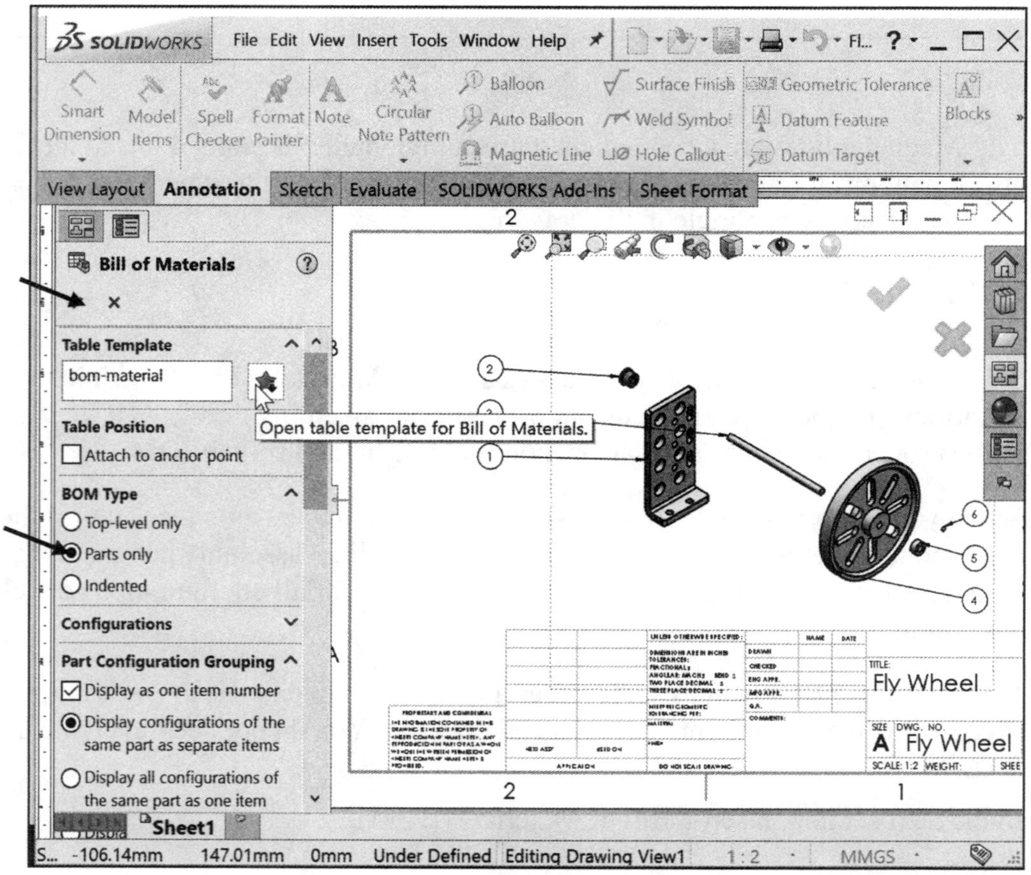

51) Click a **position** in the upper left corner to place the Bill of Material Table.

52) Click **again** in the Graphics window. View the results. Move the Isometric Exploded view if needed.

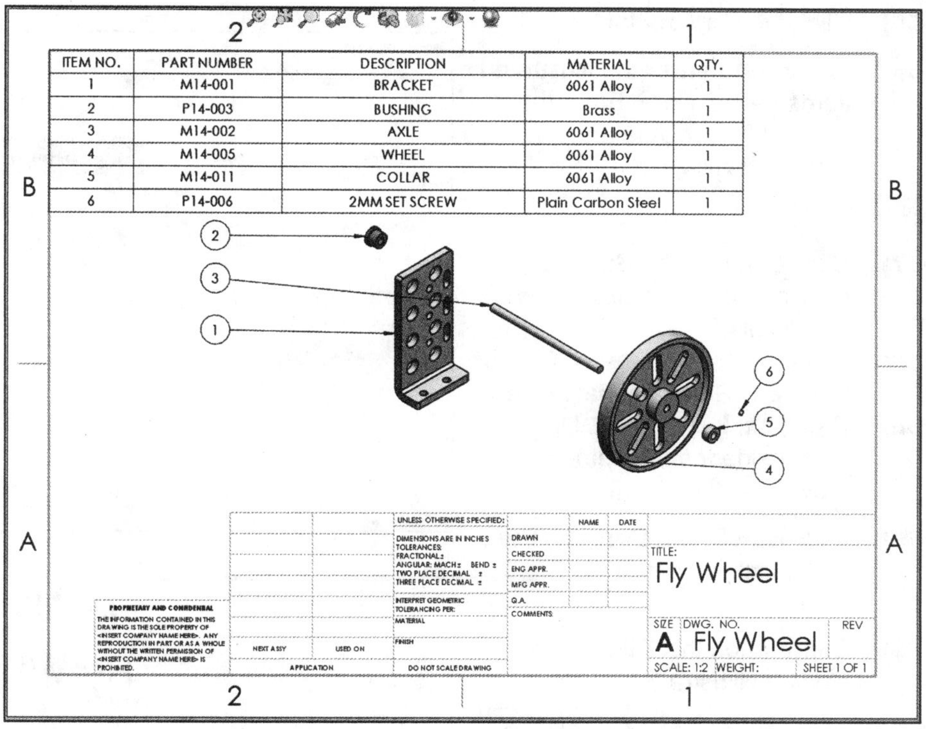

Save the Fly Wheel assembly drawing.

53) Click **Save**.

In the next section we will address Custom Properties and the Title block.

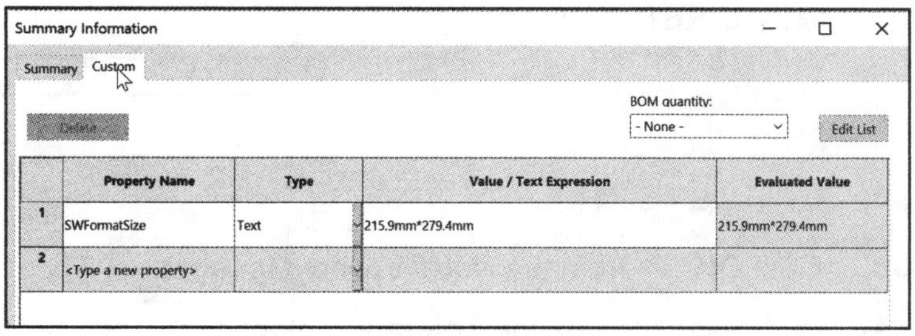

Activity: Address Custom Properties - Modify the Title block

Define Custom Properties in the drawing document.

54) Click **File**, **Properties** from the Menu bar. The Summary Information dialog box is displayed.

55) Click the **Custom** tab.

56) **Select and enter** the illustrated items below. Note: Enter the present DrawnDate and DrawnBy initials.

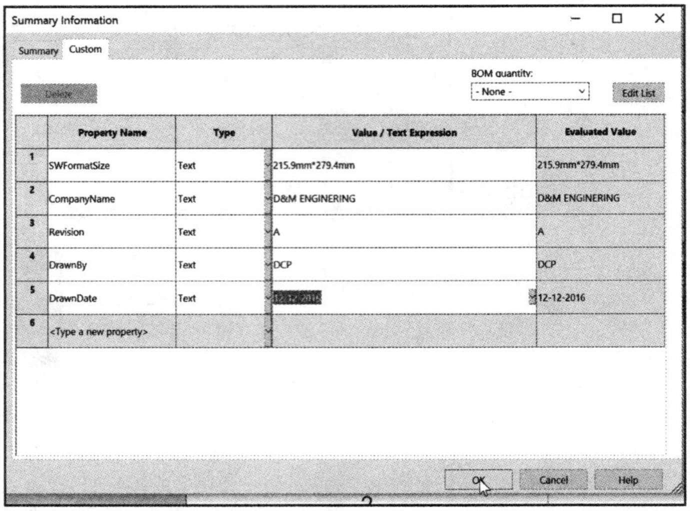

57) Click **OK** from the Summary Information dialog box. View the results.

Activate the Edit Sheet Format mode.

58) **Right-click** in Sheet1. Do not click inside the Isometric drawing view.

59) Click **Edit Sheet Format**. The Title block lines turn blue.

60) **Zoom in** on the Title block as illustrated.

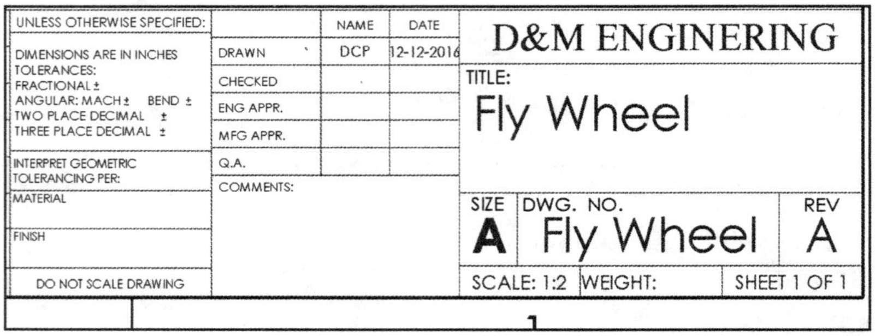

Modify the Tolerance Note.

61) Double-click the text **INTERPRET GEOMETRIC TOLERANCING PER:**.

62) Enter **ASME Y14.5**.

63) Click **OK** ✔ from the Note PropertyManager.

64) Double-click inside the **Tolerance block** text. The Formatting dialog box and the Note PropertyManager is displayed.

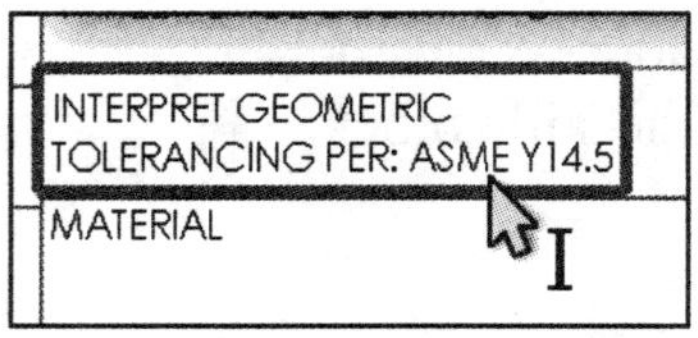

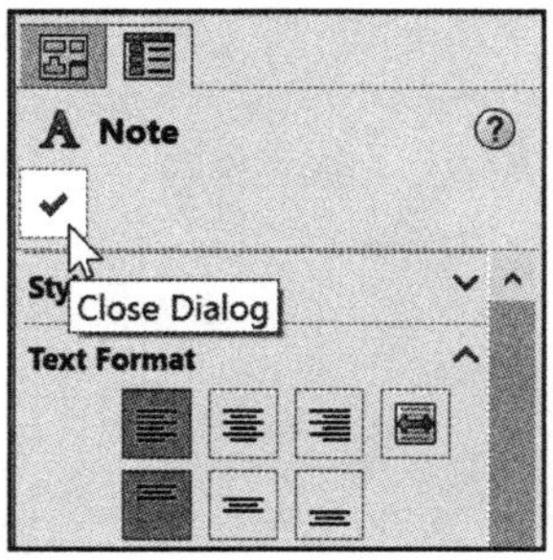

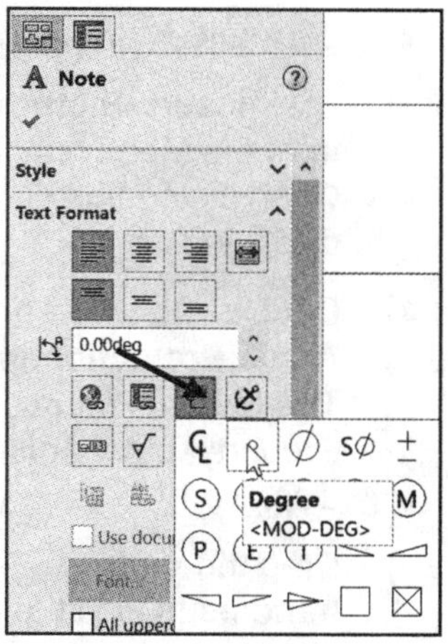

65) Delete the text **INCHES**.

66) Enter **MILLIMETERS**.

67) Delete the line **FRACTIONAL ±** as illustrated.

68) Delete the text **BEND ±** as illustrated.

69) Click a position at the end of the **ANGULAR: MACH ±** line.

70) Enter **0**.

71) Click the **Add Symbol** button from the Text Format box. The Symbols dialog box is displayed.

72) Click **Degree** from the drop-down menu.

73) Enter **30′** for minutes of a degree.

74) Delete the **TWO** and **THREE PLACE DECIMAL** lines.

75) Enter **ONE PLACE DECIMAL ±0.5**.

76) Enter **TWO PLACE DECIMAL ±0.15**.

77) Click **OK** from the Note PropertyManager.

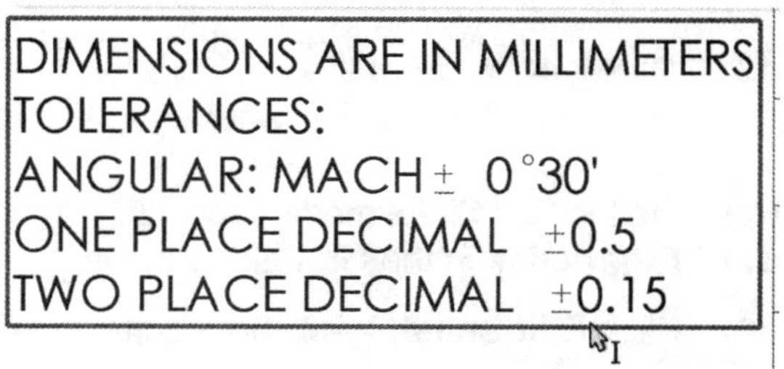

Insert a Company Logo and the Third Angle Projection icon.

78) Click **Insert**, **Picture** from the Menu bar.

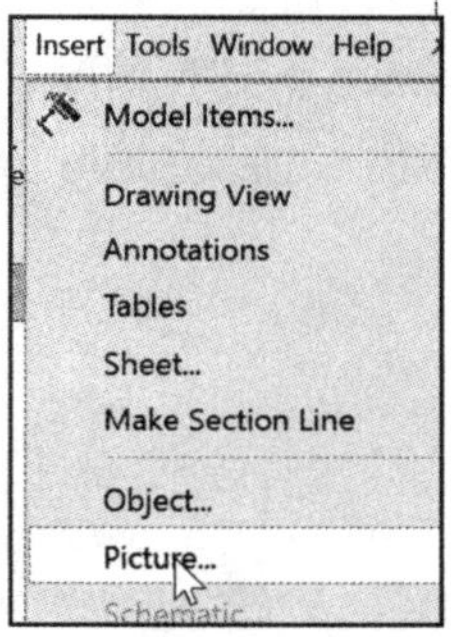

79) Double-click the **LOGO.jpg** from the Drawing folder. Note, if you have your own Logo, use it for the drawing.

80) The Sketch Picture PropertyManager is displayed. Un-check the **Lock aspect ratio** box and the **Enable scale tool** box.

81) Drag the **picture handles** to size the picture to the left of the Title block as illustrated.

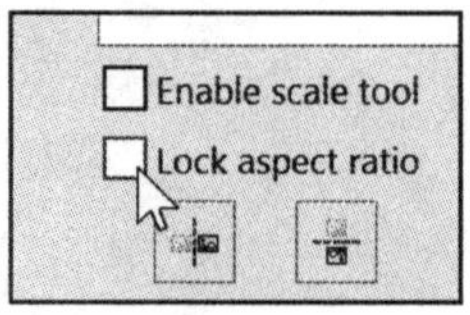

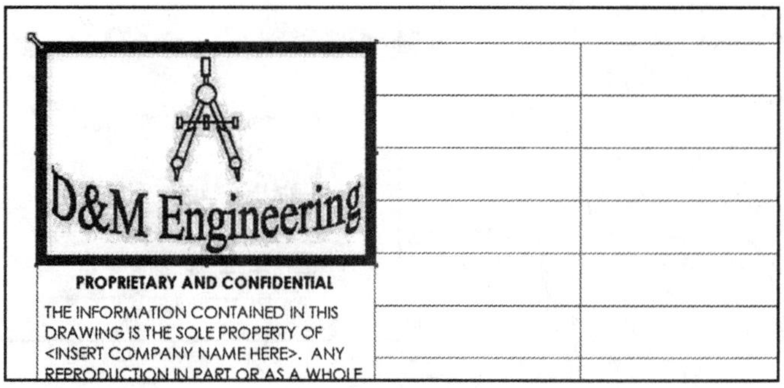

82) Click **OK** from the Sketch Picture PropertyManager.

83) Click **Insert**, **Picture** from the Menu bar. The Open dialog box is displayed.

84) Double-click the **Third Angle Projection.jpg**. The Sketch Picture PropertyManager is displayed.

85) Drag the **picture handles** to size the icon as illustrated.

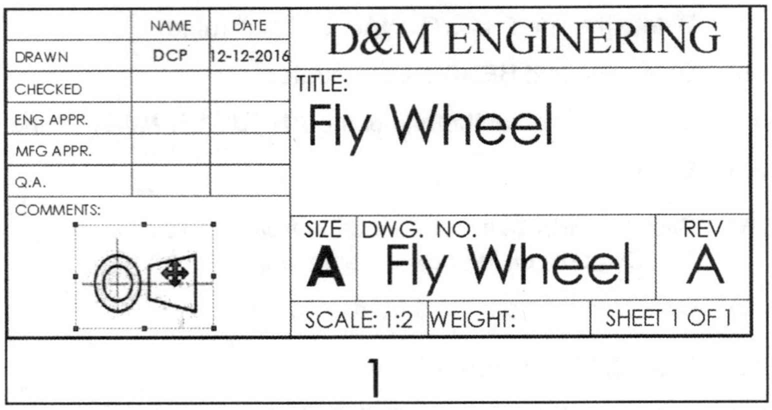

86) Click **OK** from the Sketch Picture PropertyManager.

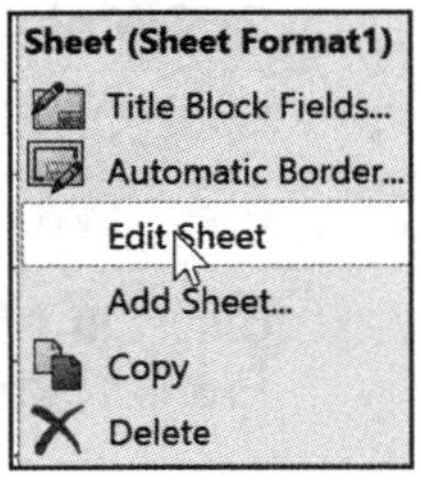

Return to the Edit Sheet mode.

87) **Right-click** in the Graphics window.

88) Click **Edit Sheet**. View the results.

Save the Fly Wheel assembly drawing.

89) Click **Save**.

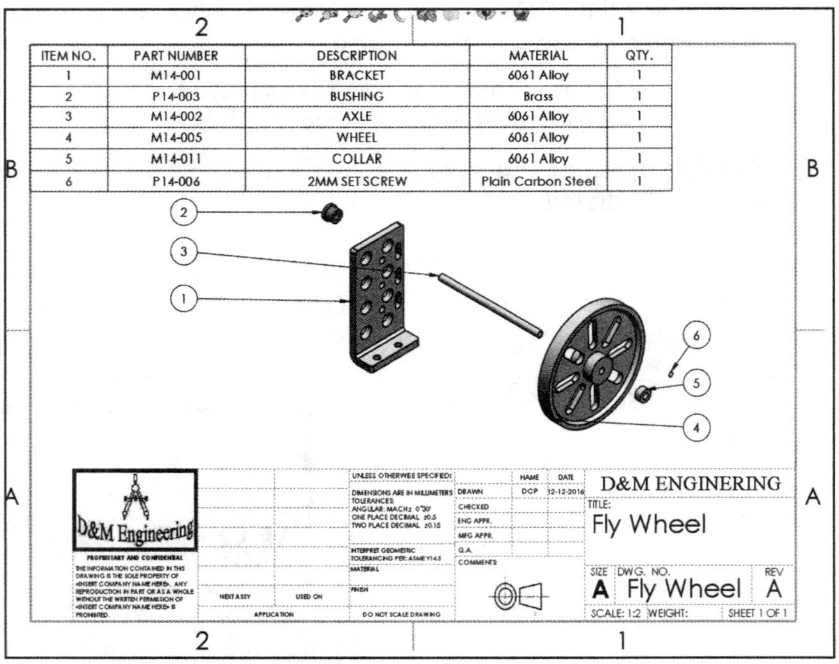

Bushing Part Drawing

A drawing contains part views, geometric dimensioning and tolerances, notes, and other related design information. When a part is modified, the drawing automatically updates. When a driving dimension in the drawing is modified, the part is automatically updated.

Create a Bushing part drawing with inserted dimensions and annotations. Modify the Display mode to show Hidden Lines.

Drawings consist of one or more views produced from the part or assembly. Insert four drawing views: Front, Top, Right and Isometric. Hide any unnecessary drawing views. The Front view should be the most descriptive view. It should be positioned in a natural orientation based on its function.

Open and start the Bushing Drawing with an empty Bushing Drawing document located in the SOLIDWORKS in 5 Hours\Drawing folder.

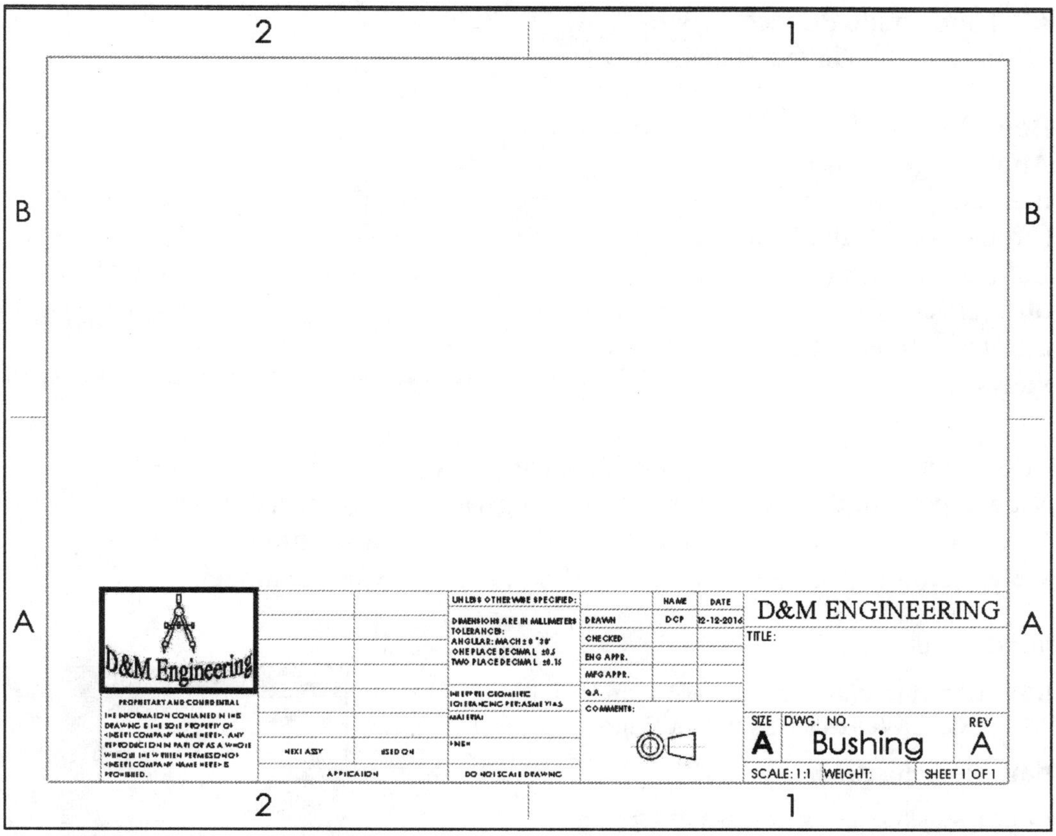

Activity: Open the Empty Bushing Part Drawing

Open the Empty Bushing Part Drawing.

90) Click **File**, **Open** from the Main menu.

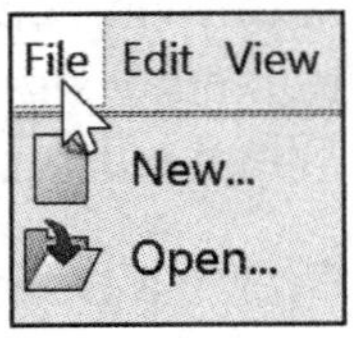

91) Browse to the **SOLIDWORKS in 5 Hours\Drawing** folder.

92) Double-click the **Bushing** part drawing. The empty Bushing part drawing is displayed. Third Angle Projection is selected for Projection type. ANSI is the drafting Standard. MMGS are the units.

There are two different types of Angle Projection: First and Third Angle Projection.

- First Angle Projection is used in Europe, South American and Asia.
- Third Angle Projection is used in the United States.

Both First Angle and Third Angle projections result in the same six principle views (Front, Top, Right, Bottom, Left, and Back); the difference between them is the arrangement of these views.

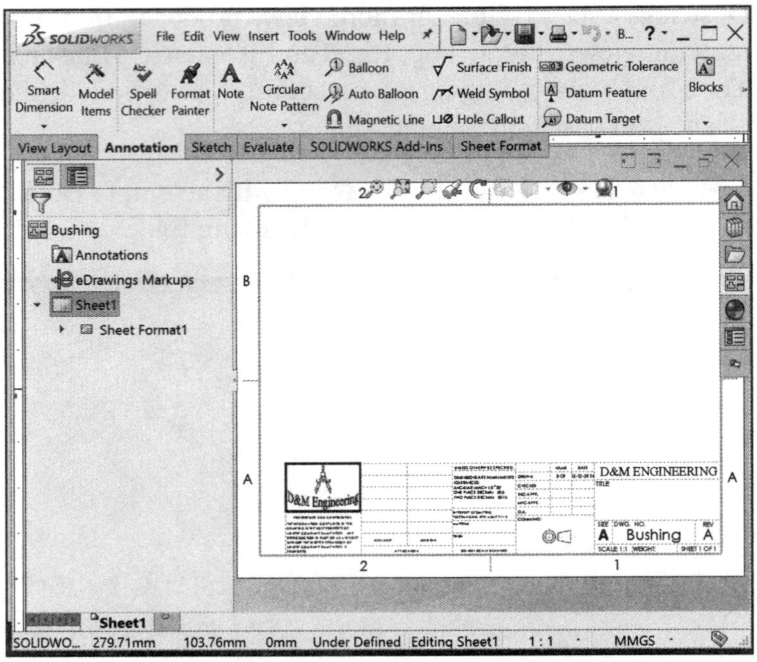

Insert four drawing views: Front, Top, Right and Isometric. Utilize the View Palette in the Task Pane. All drawing views are projected from the Front view. You can place any view in the Front view location. The Front view should be the most natural and descriptive view of the model.

Insert four drawing views.

93) Click the **View Palette** icon from the SOLIDWORKS Resources Pane.

94) Click the **Browse** button.

95) Browse to the **SOLIDWORKS in 5 Hours\Drawing** folder.

96) Double-click the **Bushing** part.

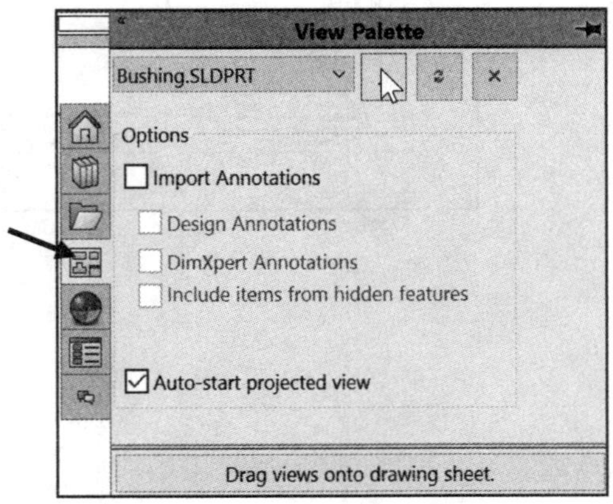

97) **Drag** and **drop** the (A) Right view into the Front view location as illustrated.

98) Click directly **upwards** to create the Top view.

99) Click directly **downward** and to the **right** to create the Right view.

100) Click a location **approximately 45 degrees** to the upper right of the Front view. This is the Isometric view.

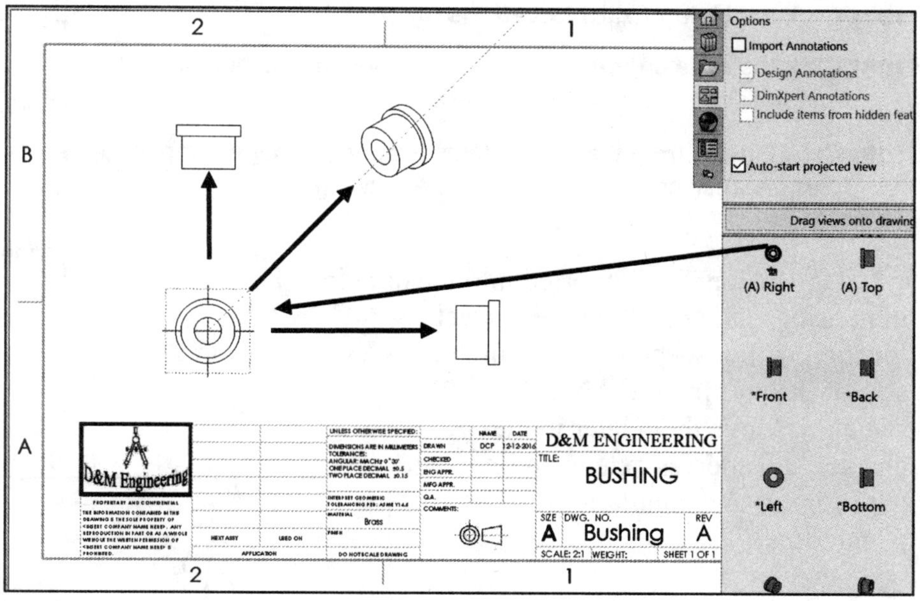

101) Click **OK** from the PropertyManager. View the four views.

102) Click and drag the **drawing views** to space them for dimensions and annotations. The Top and Right view are directly projected from the Front view.

Save the Bushing part drawing.

103) Click **Save**.

Drawing Dimensions

Dimension the part drawing views. Utilize the Model items tool to automatically import model dimensions. Utilize the Smart Dimension tool to insert any additional needed dimensions.

In SOLIDWORKS, inserted dimensions in the drawing are displayed in gray. Imported dimensions from the part are displayed in black.

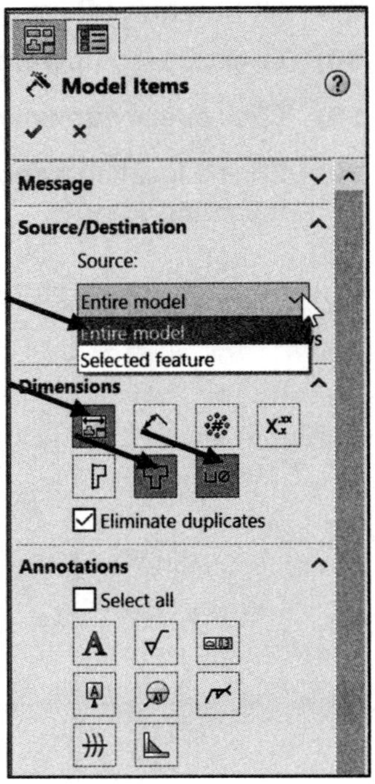

Import Model dimensions using the Model Items tool.

104) Click the **Annotation** tab.

105) Click the **Model Items** tool. The Model Items PropertyManager is displayed. View your options and tool.

106) Select **Entire model** from the Source drop-down menu.

107) Click the **Hole Wizard Locations** icon.

108) Click the **Hole callout** icon. This option inserts hole callout annotations to hole wizard features.

109) Click **OK** from the Model Items PropertyManager. Imported part dimensions are displayed in the drawing.

Dimensions are imported into the drawing. The dimensions may not be in the correct location with respect to the feature or size of the part per the ANSI Y-14.5 standard. Move them later in the chapter and address extension line gaps (5mm) and annotations (Centerline).

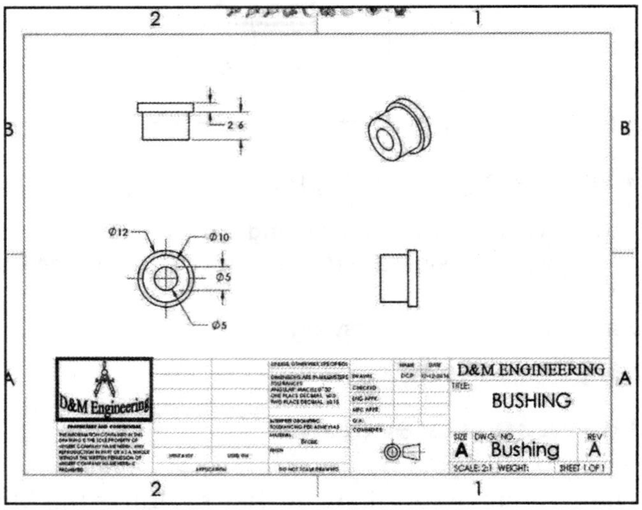

Move parent (Front) and child (Top and Right) views independently by dragging their view boundary. Hold the Shift key down and select multiple views to move as a group.

Third Angle Projection type symbol is illustrated.

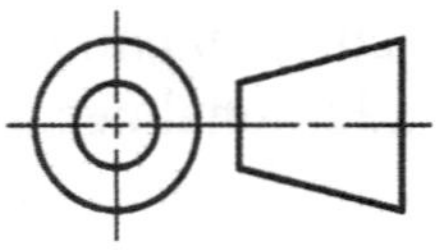

View the provided videos on Drawing Fundamentals to enhance your user experience in this chapter.

The dimensions and text in the next section have been enlarged for visibility. Drawing dimension location is dependent on *Feature dimension creation* and *Selected drawing views.*

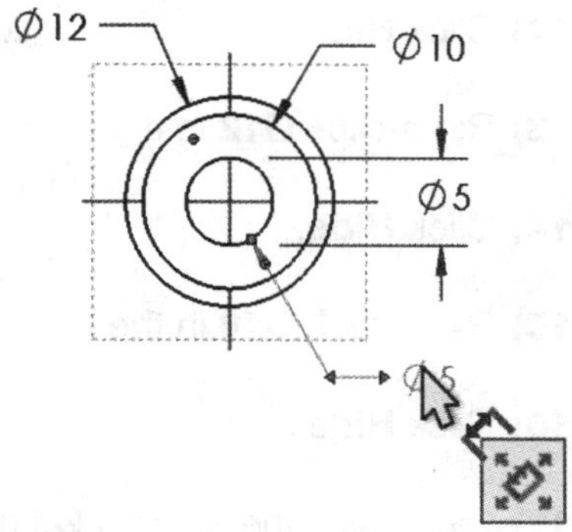

Move dimensions within the same view. Use the mouse pointer to drag dimensions and leader lines to a new location. Leader lines reference the size of the profile. A gap must exist between the profile lines and the leader lines. Shorten the leader lines to maintain a drawing standard. Use the blue Arrow buttons to flip the dimension arrows.

Notes provide relative part or assembly information. Example: Material type, material finish, special manufacturing procedure or considerations, preferred supplier, etc.

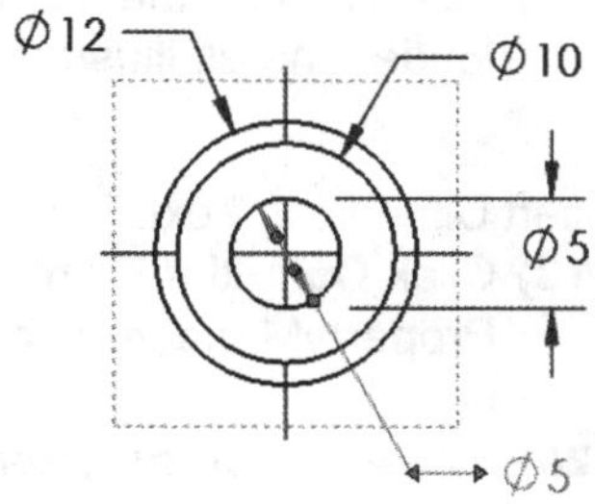

Below are a few helpful guidelines to create general drawing notes:

- Use Upper Case letters.
- Use left text justification.
- Font size should be the same as the dimension text.

Hide superfluous feature dimensions. Do not delete feature dimensions. Recall hidden dimension with the View, Show Annotations command. Move redundant, dependent views outside the sheet boundary or hide redundant views.

Full cylinders (holes and bosses) must always be measured by their diameter. The diameter symbol must precede the numerical value to indicate that the dimension shows the diameter of a circle or cylinder. The symbol used is the Greek letter phi (Ø).

If a hole goes completely through the feature and it is not clearly shown on the drawing, the abbreviation "**THRU**" or "**THRU ALL**" in all upper case follows the dimension.

You should not dimension a hole in a drawing by its radius.

Move and Hide drawing dimensions in the Front view.

110) Zoom-in on the Front view. Right-click and hide all dimensions in the Front view.

111) Right-click **Ø5** as illustrated in the Front view.

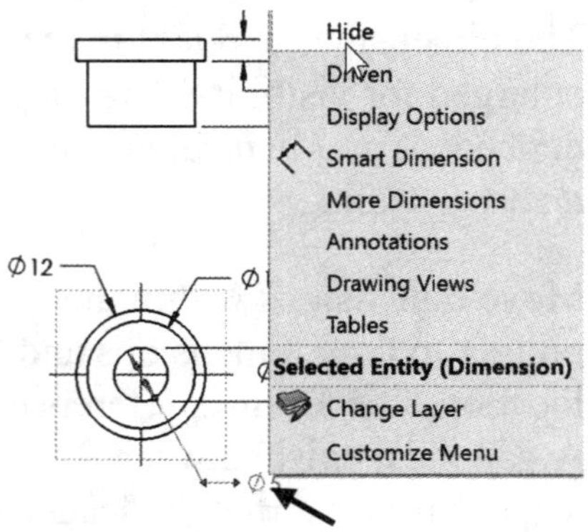

112) Click **Hide**.

113) Right-click **Ø12** in the Front view.

114) Click **Hide**.

115) Right-click **Ø10** in the Front view.

116) Click **Hide**.

117) Right-click the second **Ø5** dimension. Click **Hide.**

118) Insert a **Ø5** dimension in the Front view with a bent leader line as illustrated.

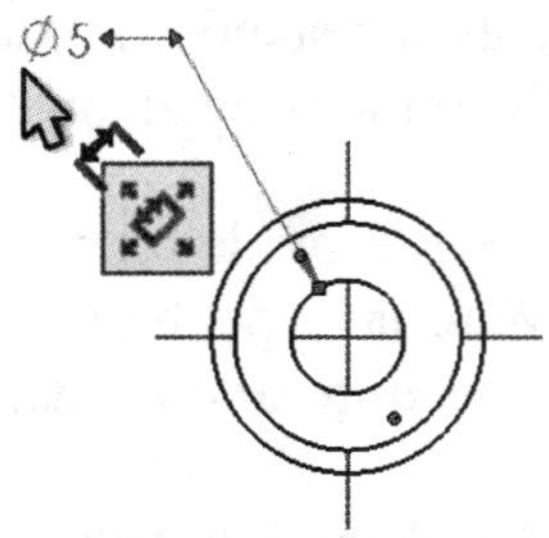

Insert Dimension Text.

119) Click **Ø5** in the Front View. The Dimension PropertyManager is displayed.

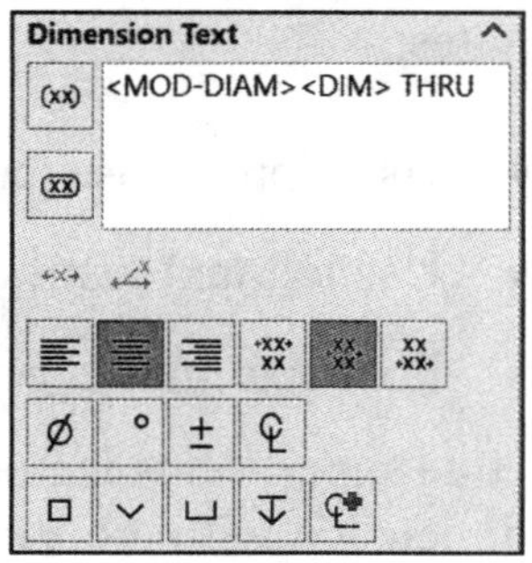

120) Click a **position after** <MOD-DIM><DIM> in the Dimension Text box.

121) Press the **space** key.

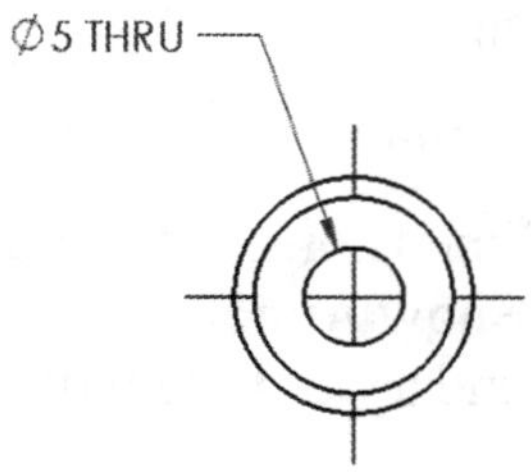

122) Enter **THRU**.

123) Click **OK** ✔ from the Dimension PropertyManager. View the results in Drawing view1.

Display Hidden Lines Visible.

124) Click **inside Drawing View2** as illustrated. The Drawing View2 PropertyManager is displayed.

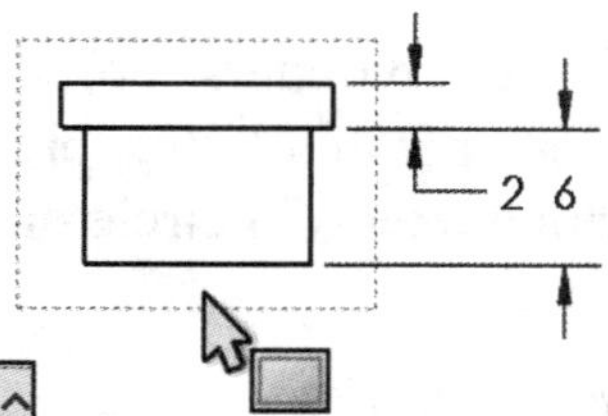

125) Click **Hidden Lines Visible** from the Display Style box.

126) Click **OK** ✔ from the Drawing View2 PropertyManager. View the results.

The general practice is to stagger the dimension text on parallel dimensions (small to large).

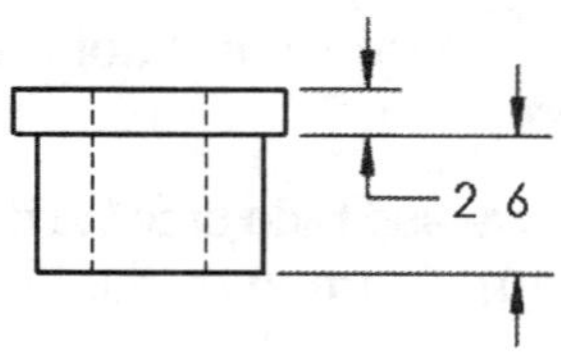

Arrowheads are used to terminate dimension lines.

Insert needed feature and location dimensions in the Top view.

127) Zoom-in on the Top view.

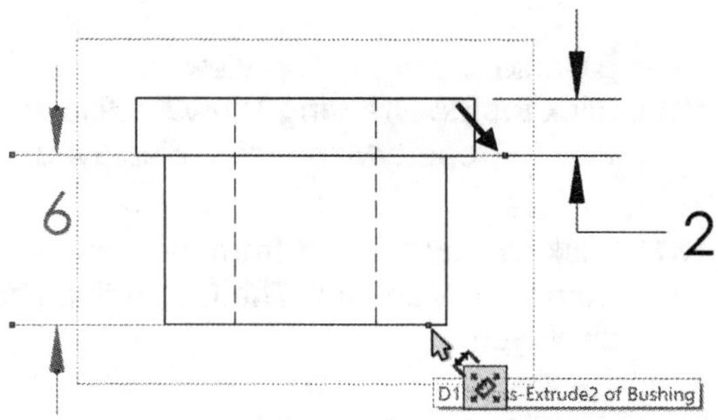

128) Click the **6mm** dimension.

129) Move the 6mm dimension to the left of the drawing view as illustrated.

130) Click the **control points** on the extension lines to create 5mm gaps as illustrated.

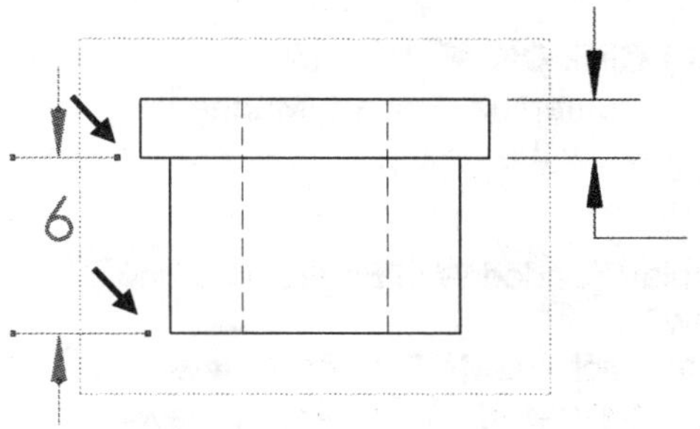

All drawing views with dimensions require gaps (5mm) between the visible feature line and extension lines.

Insert a diameter dimension in the Top View.

131) Click **Smart Dimension** from the CommandManager.

132) Click the **top horizontal line** as illustrated.

133) Click **position** above the model. View the results.

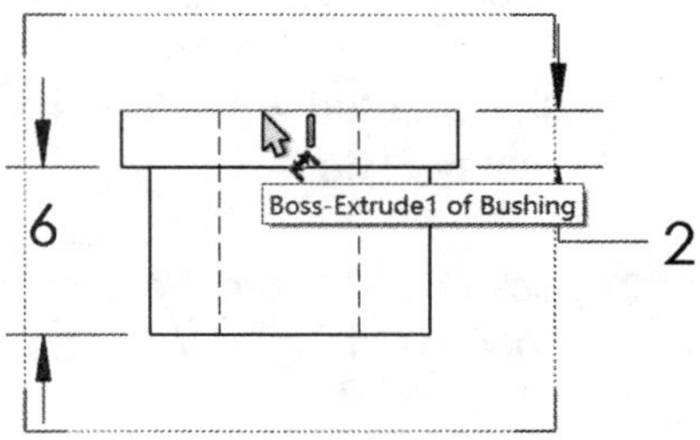

Insert a second diameter dimension in the Top View.

134) Click the **bottom horizontal line**.

135) Click a position **below** the model. View the results.

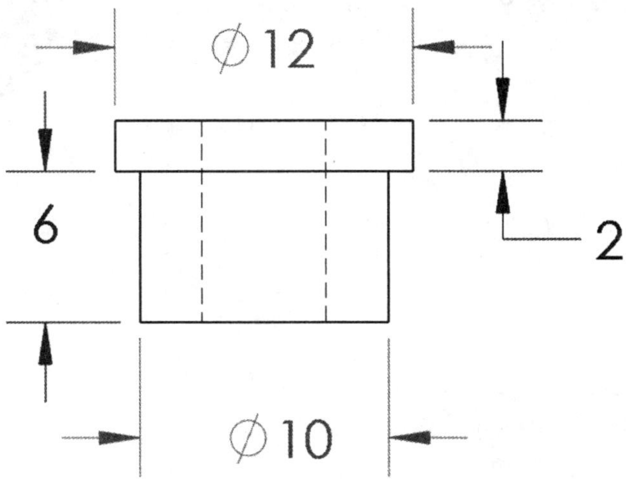

Centerlines or Center marks should be used on all circles, holes and slots.

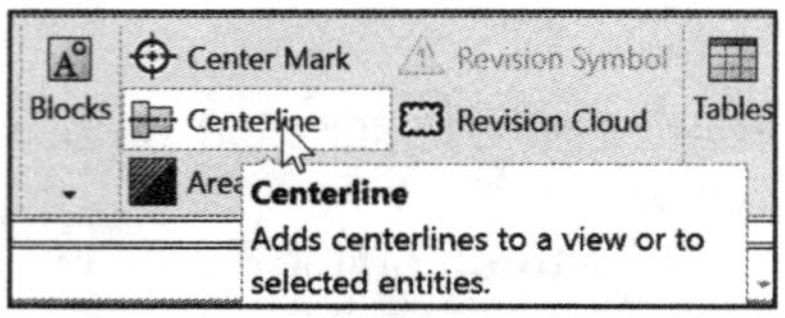

Insert a Centerline in the Top View.

136) Click **inside Drawing View2** as illustrated. The Drawing View2 PropertyManager is displayed.

137) Click **Centerline** from the Annotation CommandManager. The Centerline PropertyManager is displayed.

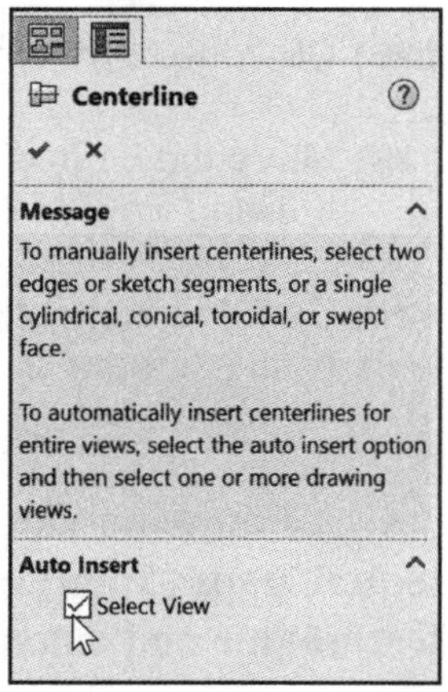

138) Click the **Select View** box.

139) Click **OK** from the Centerline PropertyManager. View the results.

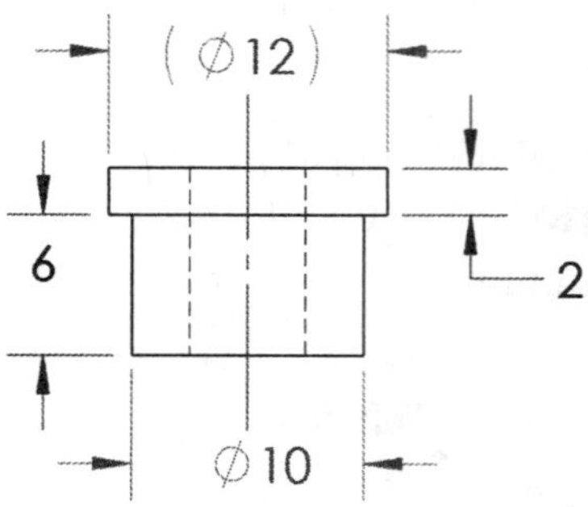

Display Shaded With Edges (Drawing View4).

140) Click **inside Drawing View4** as illustrated. The Drawing View4 PropertyManager is displayed.

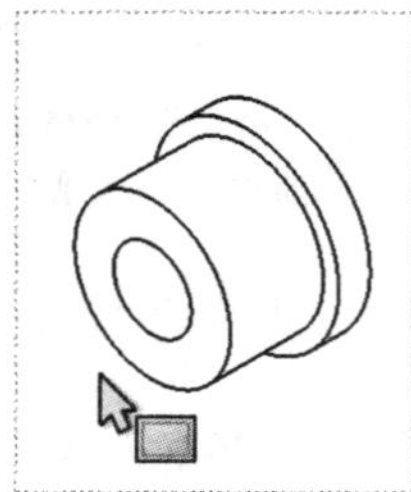

141) Click **Shaded with Edges** from the Display Style box.

142) Click **OK** from the Drawing View4 PropertyManager. View the results.

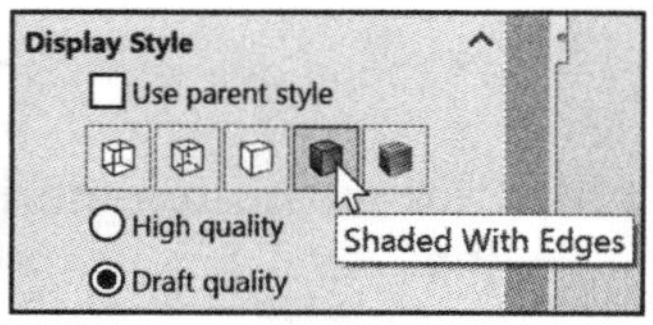

Save the Bushing part drawing.

143) Click **Save**.

Hide the Right View.

144) Right-click in **Drawing View3**.

145) Expand the drop-down menu. Click **Hide**. Hide unneeded drawing views. The Right View is not needed.

146) Click **OK** ✔ from the Drawing View3 PropertyManager. View the results.

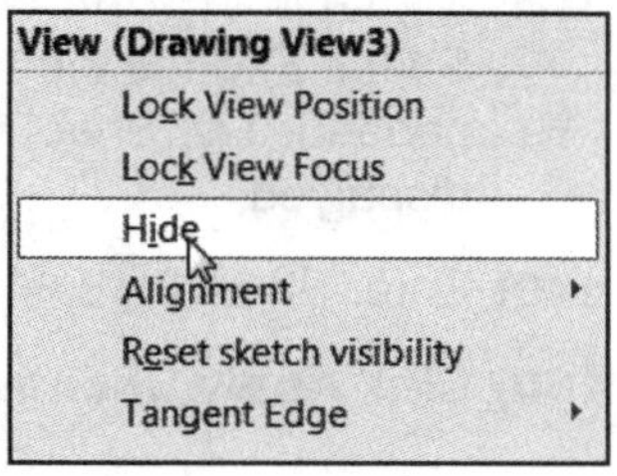

Save the Bushing part drawing.

147) Click **Save**.

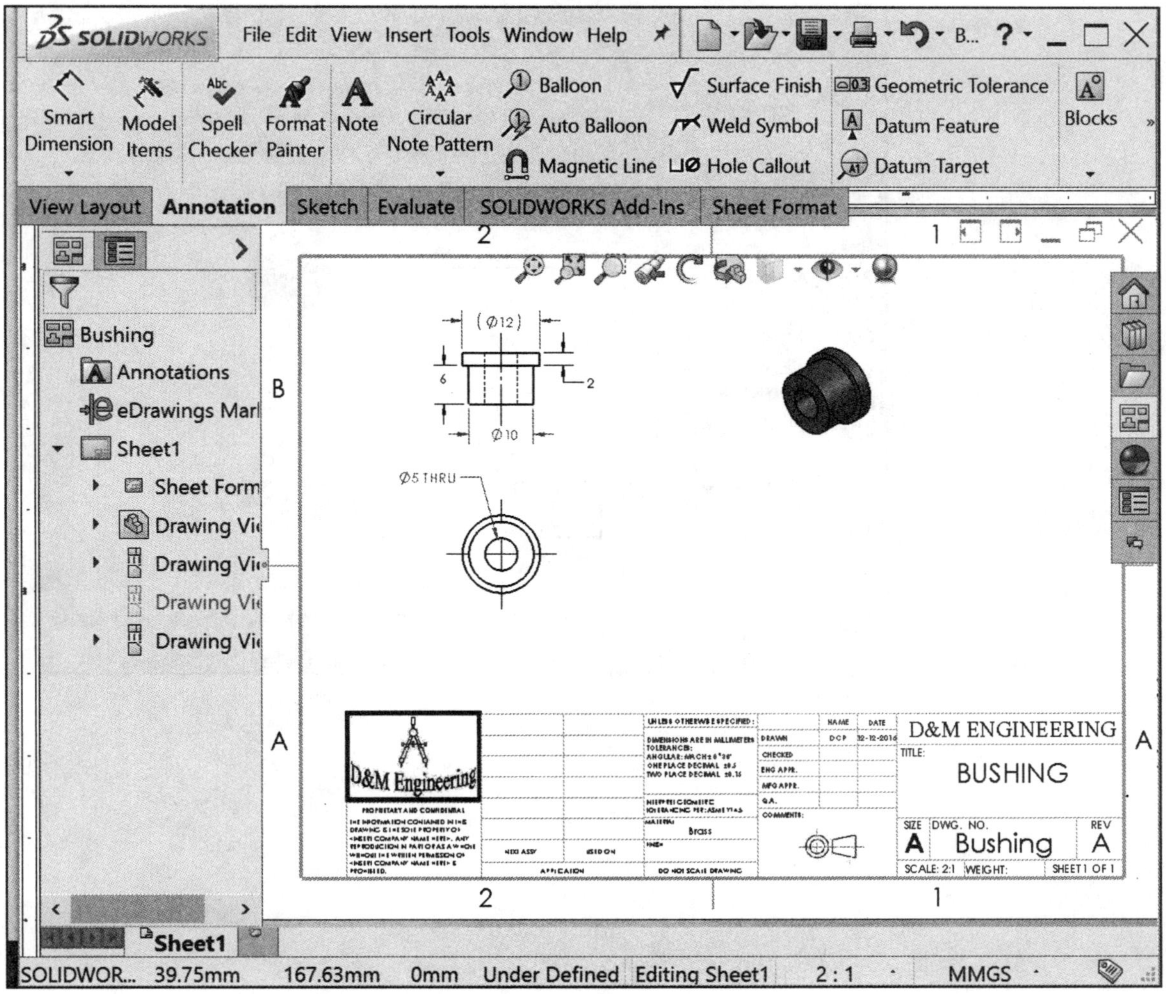

💡 Drawing views and notes outside the sheet boundary do not print.

Modify the Sheet Scale.

148) Right-click **Properties** in the Drawing Sheet. Expand the drop-down menu if needed. The Sheet Properties dialog box is dispalyed.

149) Enter Scale **3:1**.

150) Click **Apply Changes**.

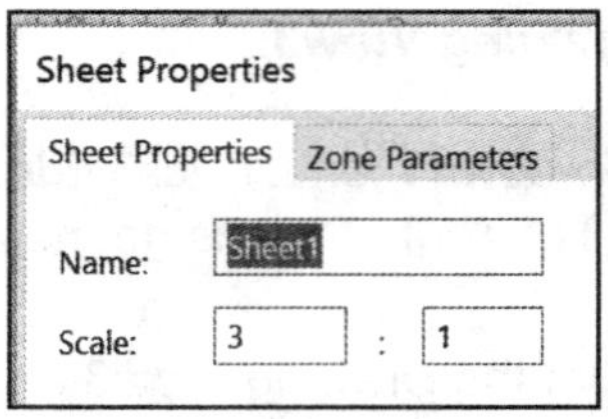

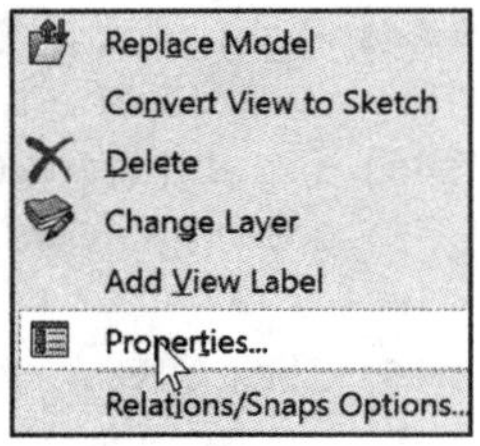

Save the Bushing part drawing.

151) Click **Save**.

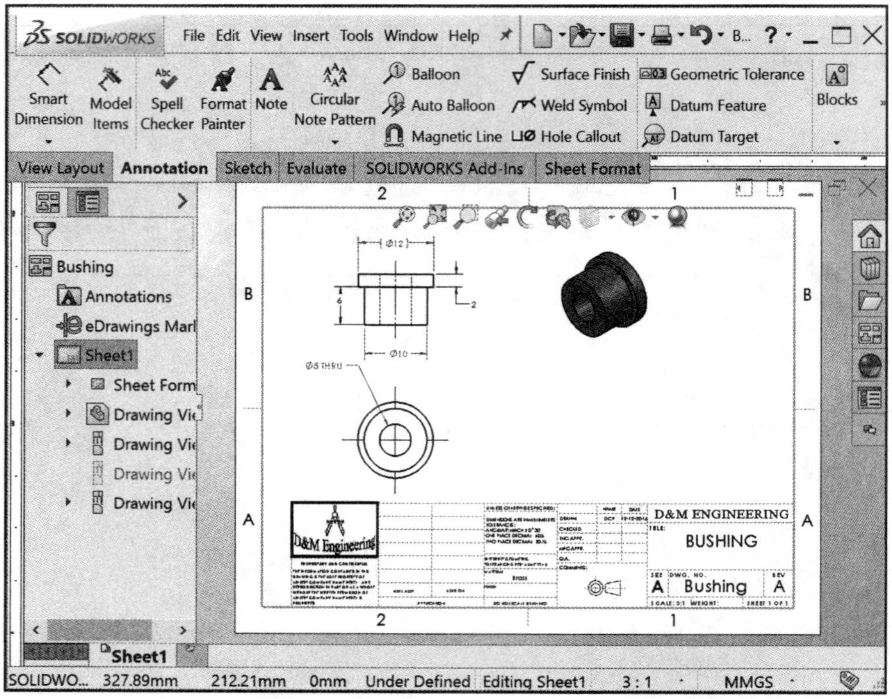

Summary

You learned about the Drawing and Dimension Fundamentals and created two new drawings with user defined document properties:

- Fly Wheel Assembly.
- Bushing.

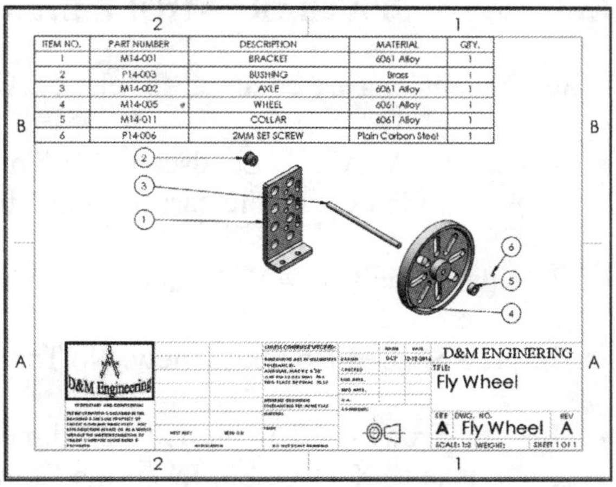

You created the Fly Wheel Assembly drawing with an Exploded Isometric view.

You utilized a Bill of Materials, Magnetic lines, Balloons and learned about Custom Properties and the Title Block.

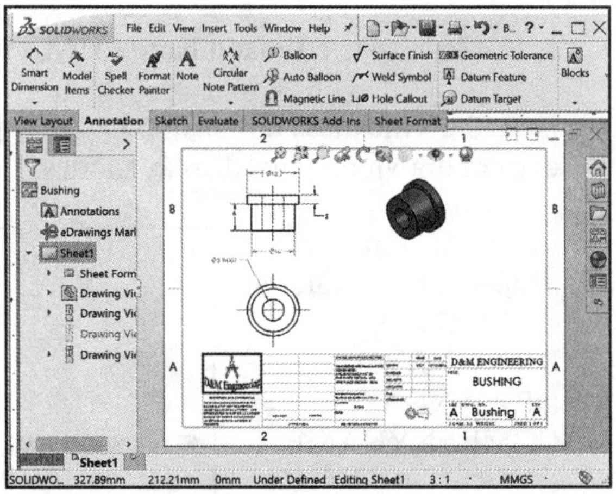

You created the Bushing Part drawing utilizing Third Angle Projection with standard Orthographic views: Front, Top, Right and Isometric.

You addressed imported dimensions from the Model Items tool and then inserted additional dimensions using the Smart Dimension tool along with all needed annotations.

A multi-view drawing should have the minimum number of views necessary to describe an object completely. The most descriptive views are those that reveal the most information about the features, with the fewest features hidden from view.

View the provided videos on Drawing Fundamentals to enhance your experience with this chapter.

Exercises

Exercise 5-1: FLATBAR - 3 HOLE Drawing

Note: Dimensions are enlarged for clarity. Utilize inch, millimeter or dual dimensioning.

- Create the A (ANSI) Landscape IPS Third Angle Projection FLATBAR - 3HOLE drawing. First create the part from the drawing - then create the drawing.
- Use the default A (ANSI) Landscape Sheet Format/Size.
- Insert a Shaded Isometric view. No Tangent Edges displayed.
- Insert a Front and Top view. Insert dimensions. Address all needed extension line gaps. Insert 3X - EQ. SP. Insert the Company and Third Angle Projection icon.
- Add a Parametric Linked Note for MATERIAL THICKNESS.
- Hide the Thickness dimension in the Top view. Insert needed Centerlines. Insert the correct drawing views display modes.
- Insert Custom Properties for Material (2014 Alloy), DRAWNBY, DRAWNDATE, COMPANYNAME, etc.

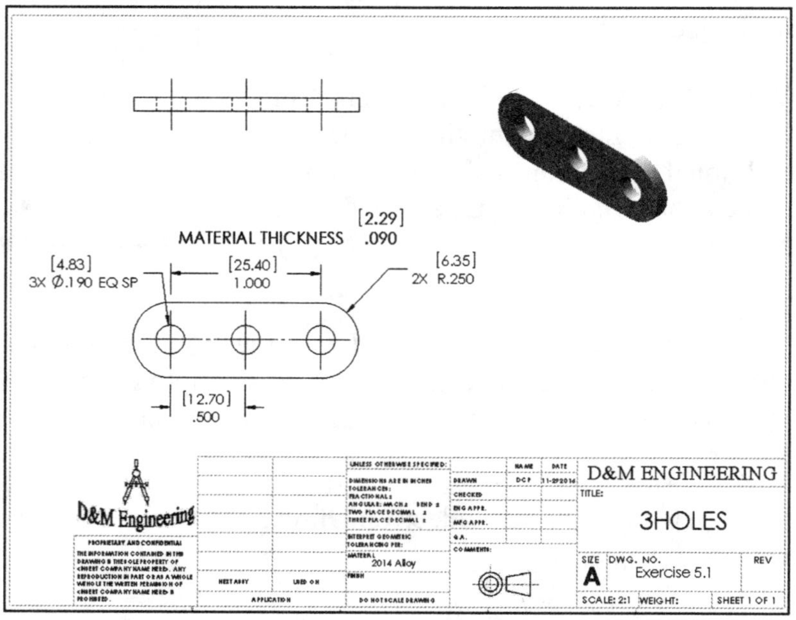

Exercise 5.2: CYLINDER Drawing

Create the A (ANSI) Landscape IPS - Third Angle CYLINDER drawing.

- First create the part from the drawing, then create the drawing. Use the default A (ANSI) Landscape Sheet Format/Size.

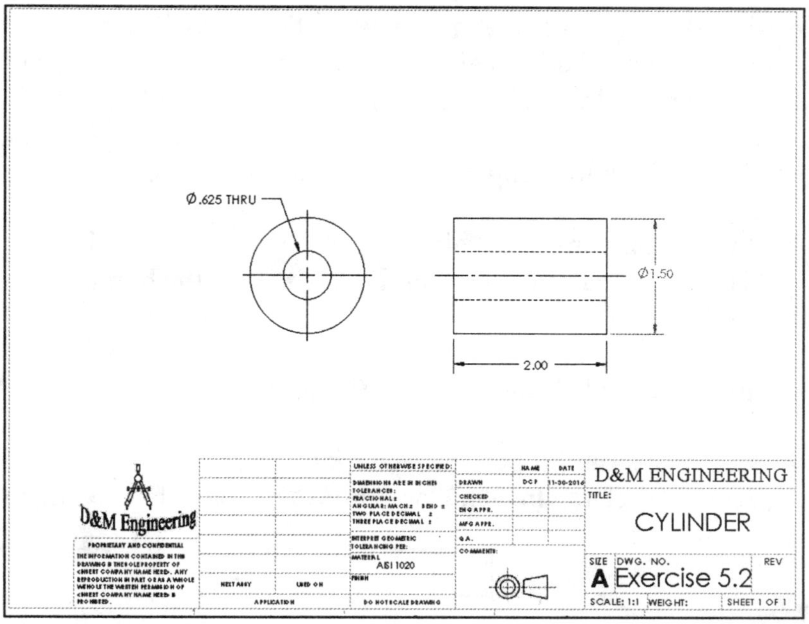

- Insert the Front and Right view as illustrated. Insert dimensions. Address all needed extension line gaps. Think about the proper view for your dimensions.
- Insert Company and Third Angle projection icons. The Third Angle Projection icon is available in the homework folder.
- Insert needed Centerlines and Center Marks. Insert the correct drawing views display modes.

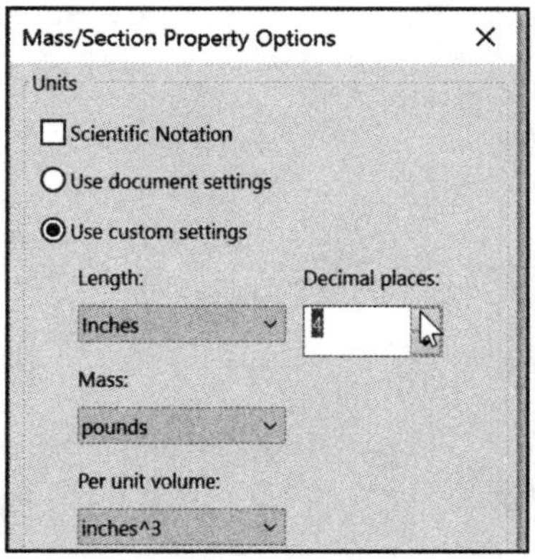

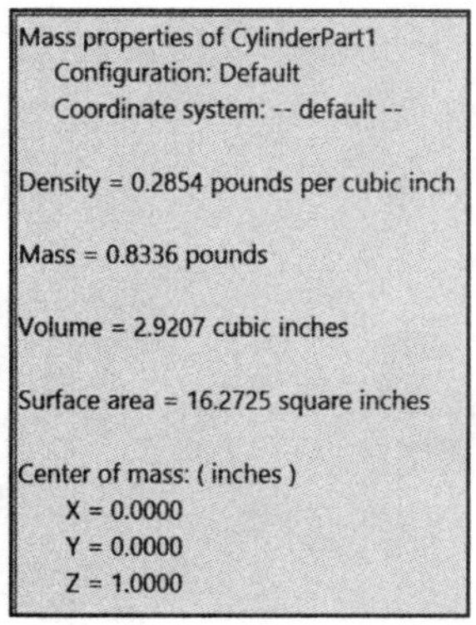

- Insert Custom Properties: Material, Description, DrawnBy, DrawnDate, CompanyName, etc. Note: Material is AISI 1020.
- Utilize the Mass Properties tool from the Evaluate toolbar to calculate the volume and mass of the CYLINDER part. Set decimal places to 4 under the Options button in the Mass Properties dialog box.

Exercise 5.3: PRESSURE PLATE Drawing

Create the A (ANSI) Landscape IPS - Third Angle PRESSURE PLATE drawing.

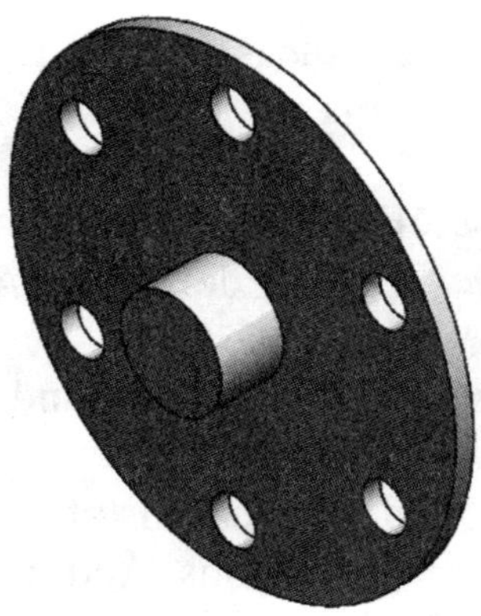

- First create the part from the drawing, then create the drawing. Use the default A (ANSI) Landscape Sheet Format/Size.
- Insert the Front and Right view as illustrated. Insert dimensions. Address all needed extension line gaps. Insert the correct drawing views display modes.
- Think about the proper view for your dimensions.
- Insert Company and Third Angle projection icons. The Third Angle Projection icon is available in the homework folder.
- Insert needed Centerlines and Center Marks.
- Insert Custom Properties: Material, Description, DrawnBy, DrawnDate, CompanyName, etc. Note: Material is 1060 Alloy.

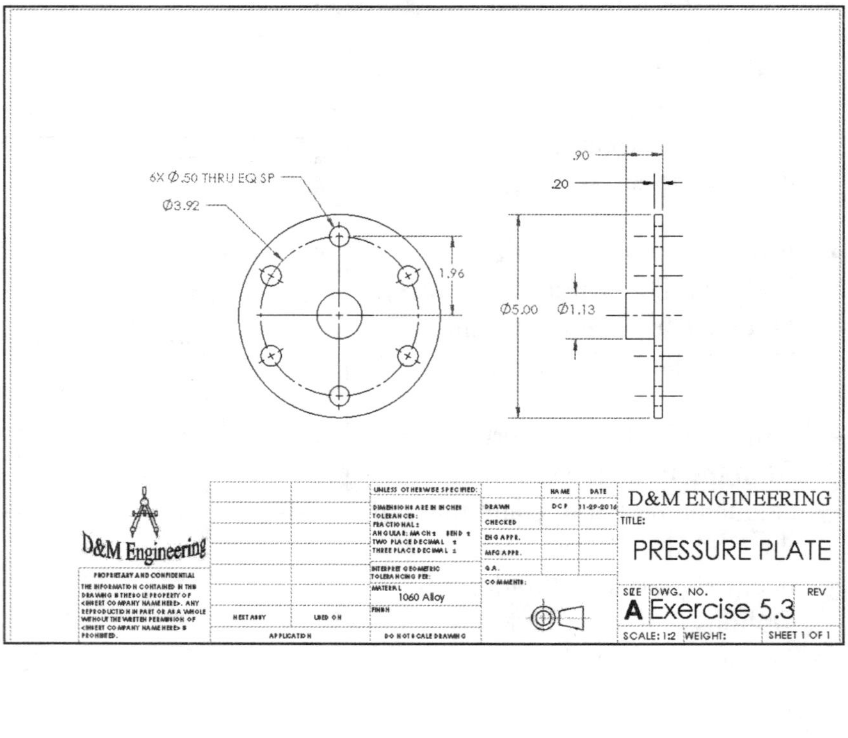

Exercise 5.4: LINKS Assembly Drawing

- Create the LINK A-ANSI assembly. Utilize three different FLATBAR configurations and a SHAFT-COLLAR. The parts are located in the Chapter 5 Homework folder.

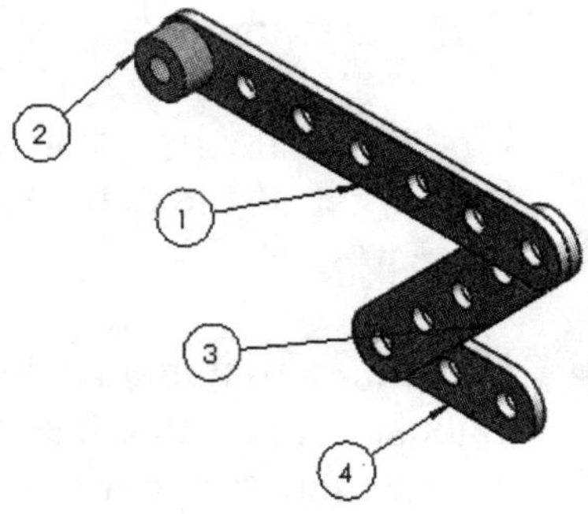

- Create the LINK assembly drawing as illustrated. Use the default A (ANSI) Landscape Sheet Format/Size.
- Insert Company and Third Angle projection icons. The icons are available in the homework folder. Remove all Tangent Edges.
- Insert Custom Properties: Description, DrawnBy, DrawnDate, CompanyName, etc.
- Insert a Bill of Materials as illustrated with Balloons.

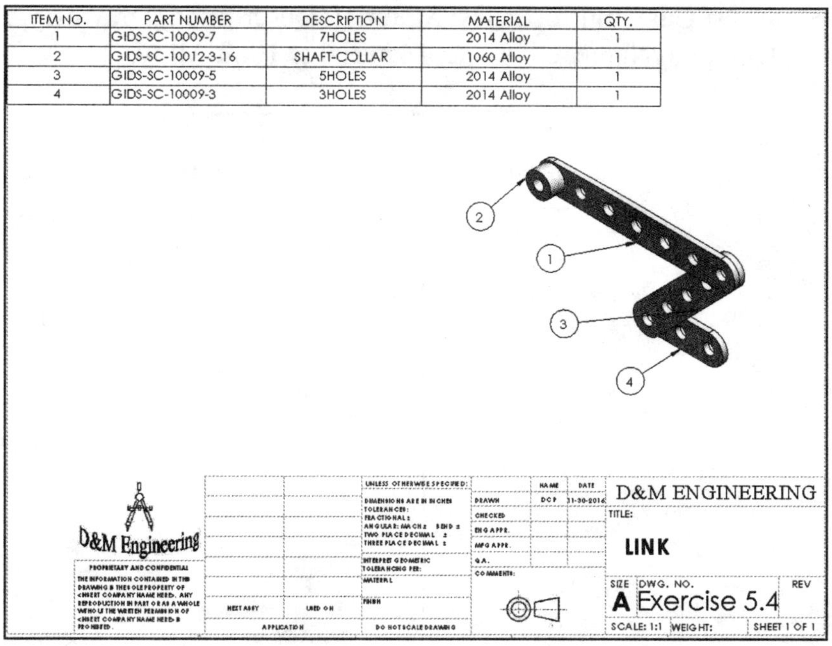

ITEM NO.	PART NUMBER	DESCRIPTION	MATERIAL	QTY.
1	GIDS-SC-10009-7	7HOLES	2014 Alloy	1
2	GIDS-SC-10012-3-16	SHAFT-COLLAR	1060 Alloy	1
3	GIDS-SC-10009-5	5HOLES	2014 Alloy	1
4	GIDS-SC-10009-3	3HOLES	2014 Alloy	1

Exercise 5.5: PLATE-1 Drawing

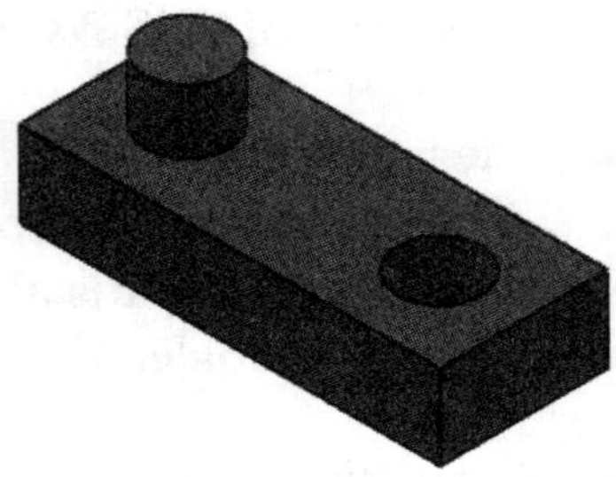

Create the A (ANSI) Landscape MMGS - Third Angle PLATE-1 drawing.

- First create the part from the drawing, then create the drawing. Use the default A (ANSI) Landscape Sheet Format/Size.
- Insert the Front and Right view as illustrated. Insert dimensions. Address all needed extension line gaps. Insert the correct drawing views display modes. Think about the proper view for your dimensions.
- Insert Company and Third Angle projection icons. The icons are available in the homework folder.
- Insert needed Centerlines and Center Marks.
- Insert Custom Properties: Material, Description, DrawnBy, DrawnDate, CompanyName, etc. Note: Material is 1060 Alloy.

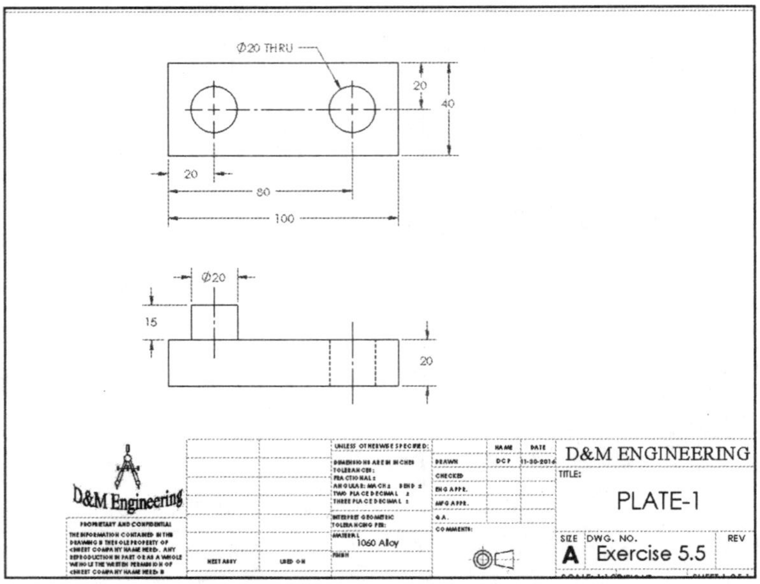

Exercise 5.6: FLATE-PLATE Drawing

Create the A (ANSI) Landscape IPS - Third Angle PLATE-1 drawing.

- First create the part from the drawing, then create the drawing. Use the default A (ANSI) Landscape Sheet Format/Size. Remove all Tangent Edges.
- Insert the Front, Top, Right and Isometric view as illustrated. Insert dimensions. Address all needed extension line gaps. Insert the correct drawing views display modes. Think about the proper view for your dimensions.
- Insert Company and Third Angle projection icons. The icons are available in the homework folder.
- Insert needed Centerlines and Center Marks.
- Insert Custom Properties: Material, Description, DrawnBy, DrawnDate, CompanyName, Hole Annotation, etc. Note: Material is 1060 Alloy.

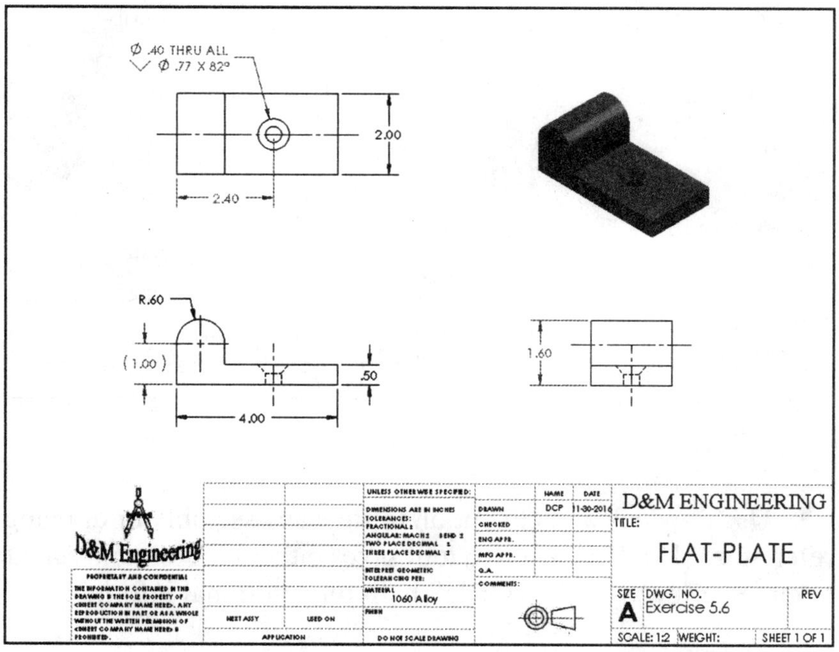

Exercise 5.7: LINKAGE-2 Drawing

- Create a new A-ANSI drawing named LINKAGE-2.
- Insert an Isometric view, shaded view of the LINKAGE-2 Assembly. The Air Cylinder Assembly and all needed parts are located in the Chapter 5 Homework folder.
- Define the PART NO. Property and the DESCRIPTION Property for the AXLE, FLATBAR- 9HOLE, FLATBAR - 3HOLE and SHAFT COLLAR.
- Save the LINKAGE-2 assembly to update the properties. Return to the LINKAGE-2 Drawing. Insert a Bill of Materials with Auto Balloons as illustrated.
- Insert the Company and Third Angle Projection icon. Insert Custom Properties for DRAWNBY, DRAWNDATE and COMPANYNAME.

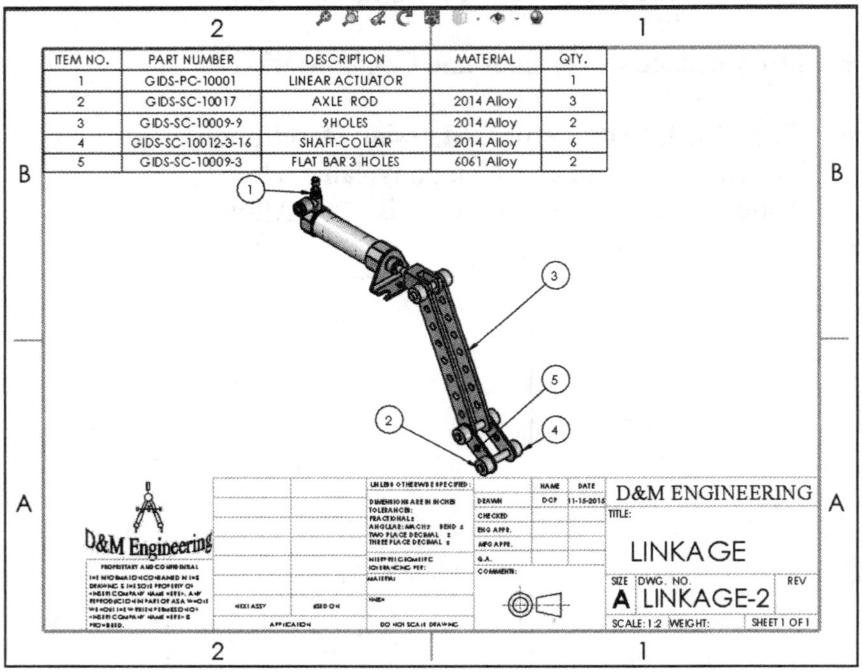

Use the Pack and Go option to save an assembly or drawing with references. The Pack and Go tool saves either to a folder or creates a zip file to email. View SOLIDWORKS help for additional information.

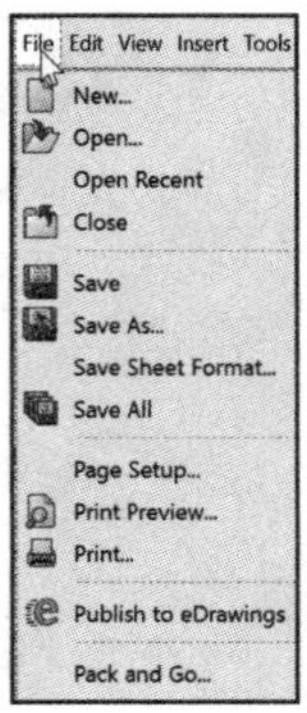

Chapter 6

Additive Manufacturing - 3D Printing

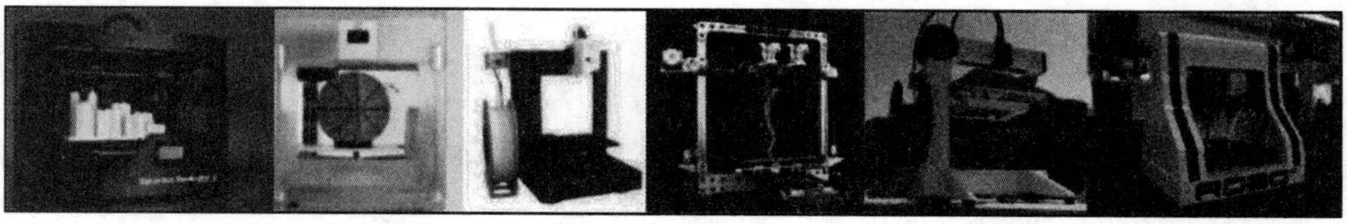

Below are the desired outcomes and usage competencies based on the completion of Chapter 6.

Desired Outcomes:	Usage Competencies:
• Knowledge of Additive Manufacturing. • Identify key features of a low cost \$500 - \$2,000 3D printer. • Create an STL (STereoLithography) file. • 3D Print directly from SOLIDWORKS. • Select the proper Slicer engine and print parameters. • Create a successful print.	• Discuss the advantages and disadvantages of Additive Manufacturing. • Describe the differences between a Cartesian printer and Delta printer. • Explain 3D printer technology: STereoLithography (STL), Fused Filament Fabrication (FFF), Fused Deposition Model (FDM), and Digital Light Process (DLP). • Recognize common 3D printer terminology: Raft, Skirt, Brim, Support, Touching Buildplate, Heated vs. Non-Heated build area. • Choose the proper Slicer and print parameters. • Select the proper filament. • Understand part orientation during the print cycle. • Define general 3D printing tips. • Address fit tolerance for interlocking parts.

Notes:

Chapter 6 - Additive Manufacturing - 3D Printing

Chapter Objective

Provide a basic understanding between the differences of Additive vs. Subtractive Manufacturing. Comprehend 3D printer terminology along with a working knowledge of preparing, saving, and printing a 3D CAD model on a low cost ($500 - $2,000) printer.

On the completion of this chapter, you will be able to:

- Discuss Additive vs Subtractive Manufacturing.
- Determine the differences between a Cartesian printer and a Delta printer.
- Create a STereoLithography (STL) file in SOLIDWORKS.
- 3D print directly from SOLIDWORKS using an Add-In.
  - Save an STL file to G-code.
- Discuss printer hardware.
- Select the correct filament type:
  - PLA (Polylactic acid), ABS (Acrylonitrile butadiene styrene) or Nylon.
- Prepare the G-code.
  - Address model setup, print orientation, extruder temperature, and bed temperature.
- Comprehend the following 3D printer terminology:
  - (STereoLithography) file - STL.
  - Fused Filament Fabrication - FFF.
  - Fused Deposition Model - FDM.
  - Digital Light Process - DLP.
  - Dissolvable Support System - DDS.
  - Fast Layer Deposition - FLD.
  - Raft, Skirt and Brim.
  - Support and Touching Buildplate.
  - Slicer.
  - G-code.
- Address fit tolerance for interlocking parts.
- Define general 3D Printing tips.

Additive vs. Subtractive Manufacturing

In April, 2013, *The Economist* published an article on 3D printing. In the article they stated that this was the "beginning of a third industrial revolution, offering the potential to revolutionize how the world makes just about everything."

Avi Reichental, President and CEO of 3D Systems, stated, "With 3D printing, complexity is free. The printer doesn't care if it makes the most rudimentary shape or the most complex shape, and that is completely turning design and manufacturing on its head as we know it."

Over the past five years, companies are now using 3D printing to evaluate more concepts in less time to improve decisions early in product development. As the design process moves forward, technical decisions are iteratively tested at every step to guide decisions big and small, to achieve improved performance, lower manufacturing costs, delivering higher quality and more successful product introductions. In pre-production, 3D printing is enabling faster first article production to support marketing and sales functions, and early adopter customers. And in final production processes, 3D printing is enabling higher productivity, increased flexibility, reduced warehouse and other logistics costs, economical customization, improved quality, reduced product weight, and greater efficiency in a growing number of industries.

Technology for 3D printing continues to advance in three key areas: **printers** and **printing methods**, **design software**, and **materials** used in printing.

Already, 3D printing is being used in the medical industry to help save lives and in some space exploration efforts. But how will 3D printing affect the average, middle-class person in the future? Low cost 3D printers are addressing this consumer market.

Additive manufacturing is the process of joining materials to create an object from a 3D model, usually adding layer over layer.

Subtractive manufacturing relies upon the removal of material to create something. The blacksmith hammered away at heated metal to create a product. Today, a Computer Numerical Control CNC machine cuts and drills and otherwise removes material from a larger initial block to create a product.

Additive manufacturing, sometimes known as ***rapid prototyping***, can be slower than Subtractive manufacturing. Both take skill in creating the G-code and understanding the machine limitations.

A few advantages of Additive manufacturing:

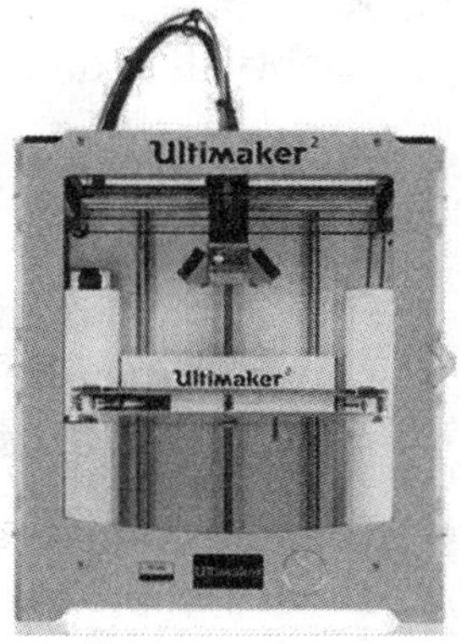

- Lower cost (different entry levels) into the manufacturing environment.
- Lowers the barriers (space, power, safety, and training) to traditional subtractive manufacturing.
- Reduce part count in an assembly from traditional subtractive manufacturing (complex parts vs. assemblies).
- Build complex features, shapes, and objects.
- Reduce prototyping time.
- Faster development cycle.
- Quicker customer feedback.
- Faster product to market.
- Quicker product customization and configuration.
- Parallel verticals: develop and prototype at the same time.
- Open source slicing engines: (Slic3r, Skeinforge, Netfabb, KISSkice, Cura, etc.).

A slicer takes a 3D model (most often in STereoLithography (STL) format and translates the model into individual layers. It then generates the machine code that the printer uses.

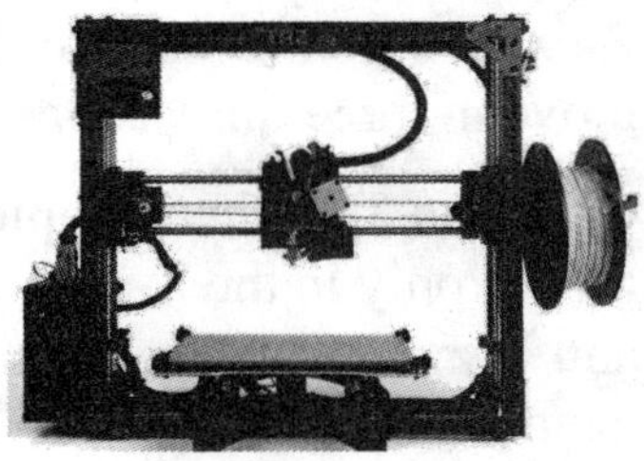

A slicer program allows the user to calibrate printer settings: filament type, part orientation, extruder speed, extruder temperature, bed temperature, cooling fan rate, raft, support, percent infill, infill pattern type, etc.

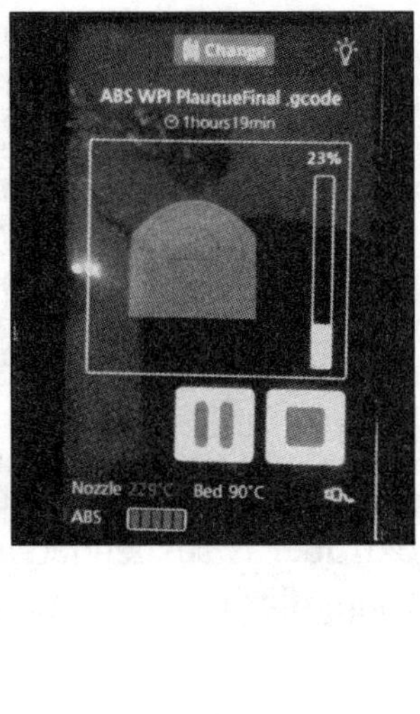

3D printers are controlled either through a small on-board control screen, an external memory device (USB, Sims card, etc.) or through a computer interface. User interface/control software allows a user to generate the needed machine code (G-code, .gcode) file from the computer to the 3D printer.

A few disadvantages of Additive manufacturing:

- Slow build rates. Many printers lay down material at a speed of one to five cubic inches per hour. Depending on the part needed, other manufacturing processes may be significantly faster.

- Requires post-processing. The surface finish and dimensional accuracy may be lower quality than other manufacturing methods.
- Poor mechanical properties. Layering and multiple interfaces can cause defects in the product.
- Frequent calibration is required. Without frequent calibration, prints may not be the correct dimensions, they may not stick to the build surface, and a variety of other not-so-wanted effects can occur.
- Limited component size/small build volume. In most cases, polymer products are about 1 cubic yard in size; metal parts may only be one cubic foot. While larger machines are available, they come at a cost.

Cartesian Printer vs. Delta Printer

Cartesian and Delta style 3D printers are the most common styles of desktop 3D printers currently available. What are the main differences? To understand their unique abilities one first needs to understand the basic technology of a Fused Deposition Model printer.

A Fused Filament Fabrication (FFF) printer takes a filament of a material (usually plastic) and extrudes it through a print-head-like nozzle. This material is then laid down in thin layers to form a 3D object on a platform, built from the bottom up.

Cartesian 3D printers are named after the dimensional coordinate system - the X, Y, and Z-axis - which is used to determine where and how to move in three dimensions.

Cartesian 3D printers typically have a print bed which moves only in the Z-axis. The extruder sits on the X-axis and Y-axis, where it can move in four directions on a gantry. This principle can be seen in action on popular models from Ultimaker, Sindoh, and MakerBot.

Controlling a linear Cartesian system is relatively simple, which is why most low cost 3D printers on the market today use this type of design. The Cartesian coordinate system has long been used for tools like plotters, CNC milling machines, and 2D printers.

Delta 3D printers also work within the Cartesian plane but use a very different approach to getting the print-nozzle where it needs to be.

Identifying characteristics start with the circular print bed. The extruder is suspended above the print bed by three arms in a triangular configuration, thus the name "Delta."

These arms move up and down independently to the print-nozzle keeping it precisely located throughout the print. Delta printers have the advantage in the ability to make taller objects due to the height of the printer and the tall arms.

Rather than using simple Cartesian geometry to calculate where the print-nozzle should go, Delta printers estimate the head position using trigonometric functions.

Create an STL file in SOLIDWORKS

STL (STereoLithography) is a file format native to the Stereolithography CAD software created by 3D Systems. STL has several after-the-fact backronyms such as "Standard Triangle Language" and "Standard Tessellation Language."

An STL file describes only the surface geometry of a three dimensional object without any representation of color, texture, or other common CAD model attributes. The STL format specifies both ASCII and Binary representations.

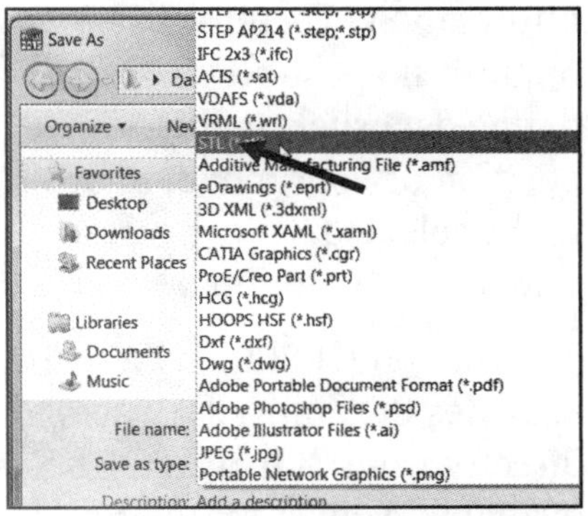

Binary files are more common, since they are more compact. An STL file describes a raw unstructured triangulated (point cloud) surface by the unit normal and vertices (ordered by the right-hand rule) of the triangles using a three-dimensional Cartesian coordinate system.

STL Save options allow you to control the number and size of the triangles by setting the various parameters in the CAD software.

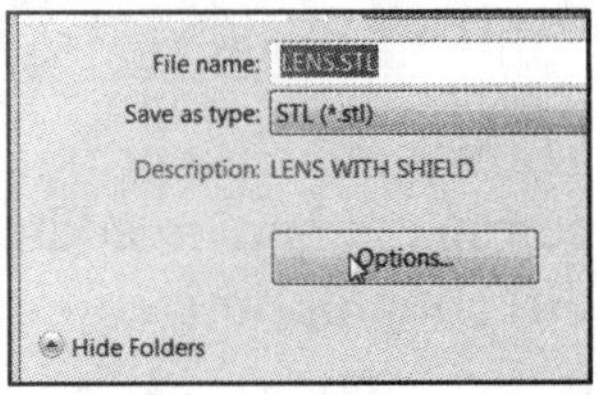

To save a SOLIDWORKS model as an STL file, Click **File**, **Save As** from the Main menu or **Save As** from the Main menu toolbar. The Save As dialog is displayed. Select **STL(*.stl)** as the Save as type.

Click the **Options** button. The Export Options dialog box is displayed. View your options. For most parts, utilize the default setting.

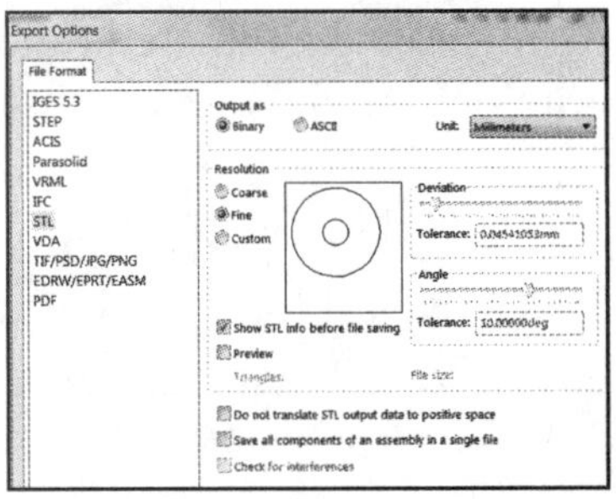

Close the Export Options dialog box. Click **OK**. View the generate point cloud of the part. Click **Yes**. The STL file is now ready to be imported into your 3D printer software.

In SOLIDWORKS for a smoother STL file, change the Resolution to Custom. Change the deviation to 0.0005in (0.01mm). Change the angle to 5. Smaller deviations and angles produce a smoother file but increase the file size and print time.

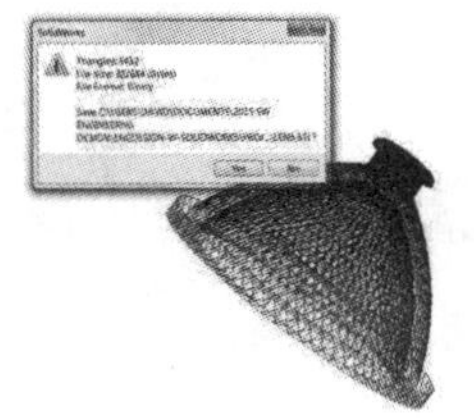

3D Print Directly from SOLIDWORKS

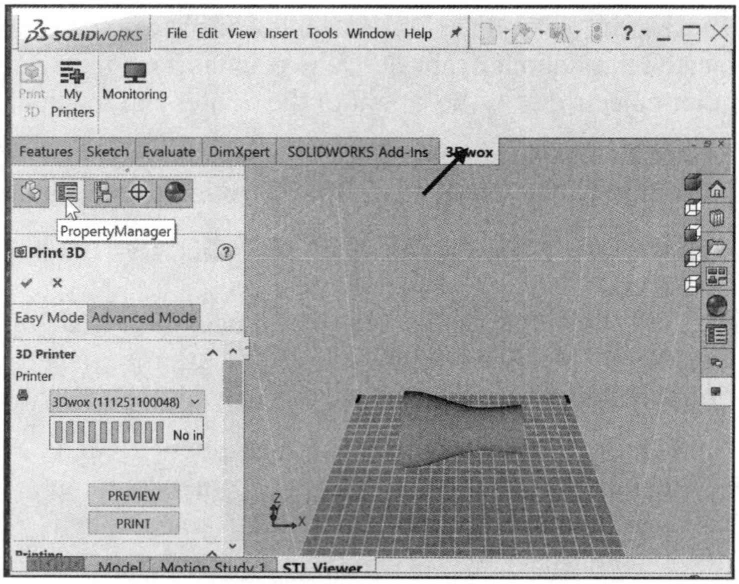

With SOLIDWORKS you can print directly to 3D printers, similar to how you would print a document to your office printer. Although SOLIDWORKS can output .STL, a widely accepted format for 3D printing, the 3MF (3D Manufacturing Format), and AMF (Additive Manufacturing File) formats provide additional model information. Therefore, it requires no post-processing to define data such as the position of your model relative to the selected 3D printer, orientation, color, materials, etc.

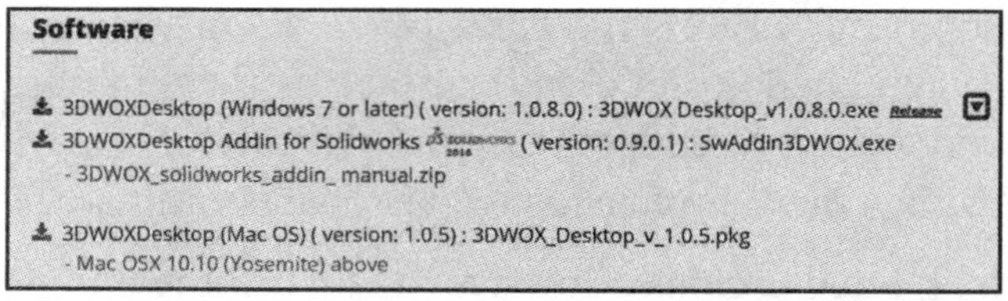

The Sindoh DP200, 3DWox printer provides the ability for users to print directly from SOLIDWORKS with an available Add-In for their printer. Visit http://3dprinter.sindoh.com/Downloads for additional information.

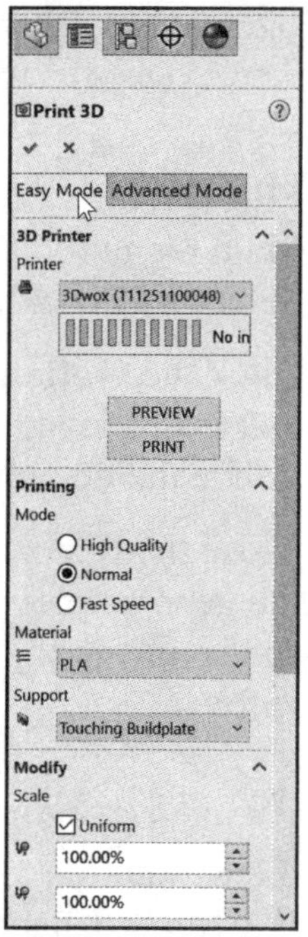

Through the 3D print application, users have access to dedicated command bars to address various print parameters, analysis, print direction optimization, and advanced printer settings.

During the print process, users can monitor the print time, needed filament, and estimated time to completion in the SOLIDWORKS graphics window.

A camera feed can be monitored via an Android smart phone. The 3DWOXDesktop Add-in for SOLIDWORKS is available from http://3dprinter.sindoh.com/Downloads

Print Material

As printed parts cool (PLA, ABS and Nylon), various areas of the object cool at different rates. Depending on the model being printed and the filament material, this effect can lead to warping, curling and or layer delamination.

There are many materials that are being explored for 3D printing; however, you will find that the two dominant plastics are ABS (Acrylonitrile butadiene styrene) and PLA (Polylactic acid). Both ABS and PLA are known as thermoplastics; that is, they become soft and moldable when heated and return to a solid when cooled.

This process can be repeated again and again. Their ability to melt and be processed again is what has made them so prevalent in society and is why most of the plastics you interact with on a daily basis are thermoplastics.

For a material to prove viable for 3D printing, it should pass four general criteria:

- Low cost and easily obtainable.
- Controllable extrusion.
- Second extrusion (two or more heads) and trace-binding during the 3D printing process.
- End use application.

HIPS (High Impact Polystyrene) filament is a soluble support material used with dual head extruders.

ABS - Storage

ABS, PLA, and Nylon do best if, before use or when stored long term, they are sealed off from the atmosphere to prevent the absorption of moisture from the air. This does not mean your material will be ruined by a week of sitting on a bench in the shop, but long term exposure to a humid environment can have detrimental effects, both to the printing process and to the quality of finished parts.

Moisture laden ABS will tend to bubble and spurt from the tip of the extruder nozzle when printing, reducing the visual quality of the part, part accuracy, strength and introducing the risk of a stripping or clogging in the nozzle. ABS can be easily dried using a source of hot (preferably dry) air such as a food dehydrator.

ABS - Part Accuracy

For most, the single greatest hurdle for accurate parts in ABS is a curling upwards off the surface in direct contact with the 3D printer's print bed. A combination of heating the print surface and ensuring it is smooth, flat and clean helps to eliminate this issue. Additionally, some find various solutions can be useful when applied beforehand to the print surface; for example, a mixture of ABS dissolved in Acetone or a shot of hairspray on the build plate. Keep these solutions away from heat.

For fine features on parts involving sharp corners, such as gears, there may be a slight rounding of the corner. A fan, to provide a small amount of active cooling around the nozzle, can improve corners but one does also run the risk of introducing too much cooling and reducing adhesion between layers, eventually leading to cracks in the finished part.

PLA - Storage

PLA responds somewhat differently to moisture. In addition to bubbles or spurting at the nozzle, you may see discoloration and a reduction in 3D printed part properties. PLA (Polylactic acid) is a bioplastic derived from corn and is biodegradable and can react with water at high temperatures and undergo de-polymerization.

PLA can be dried using something as simple as a food dehydrator. It is important to note that this can alter the crystallinity ratio in the PLA and will lead to changes in extrusion temperature and other extrusion characteristics. For many 3D printers, moisture is not a major concern.

PLA - Part Accuracy

Compared to ABS and Nylon, PLA demonstrates much less part warping. For this reason it is possible to successfully print without a heated bed and use more commonly available "Blue" painter's tape as a print surface.

PLA undergoes more of a phase-change when heated and becomes much more liquid. If actively cooled, sharper details can be seen on printed corners without the risk of cracking or warping. The increased flow can also lead to stronger binding between layers, improving the strength of the printed part.

Nylon - Storage

Nylon is very hygroscopic, more so than PLA or ABS. Nylon can absorb more than 10% of its weight in water in less than 24 hours. Successful 3D printing with nylon requires dry filament. When you print with nylon that isn't dry, the water in the filament explodes causing air bubbles during printing that prevents good layer adhesion and greatly weakens the part. It also ruins the surface finish. To dry nylon, place it in an oven at 50 - 60C for 6-8 hours. After drying, store in an airtight container, preferably with desiccant.

Type 6, 6 Nylon requires a higher extruder temperature than ABS. Type 6, 6 Nylon melts at 255-265C (490-510F), type 6 nylon melts at 210-220C (410-428F) and polypropylene melts at 160-175C (320-347F).

Nylon - Part Accuracy

Compared to ABS and PLA, Nylon and ABS warp approximately the same. PLA demonstrates much less part warping. A heated plate (70 - 80C) is required for Nylon printing. It's best to apply a PVA (Polyvinyl acetate) Elmer's or Scotch based glue stick to the bed for adhesion in a cross-hatch pattern. Remember, less is more when using the glue stick on the plate.

Nylon is a flexible, stronger and more durable alternative to PLA and ABS. With Nylon, do not use layer cooling fans and avoid drafty or cool rooms for best results.

Flex PLA - Common flexible filaments are polyester-based (non-toxic) with a low melting point. Print temp: 120C. It is highly recommended to drastically lower your printing speed to around 20% from standard PLA. To take best advantage of the filament's properties, print it with 10% infill or less. Most flexible filament adheres well to acrylic; it does not adhere well to painter's tape and glass.

Build Plates

PLA in general has a lower shrinkage factor than ABS and Nylon. They are common materials which can warp, curl, delaminate and potentially destroy the print. The following equipment and procedures deal with these potential areas.

Non-Heated

People have experimented with different build surfaces such as steel, glass and various kinds of plastic. However, from experience, both ABS and PLA material seem to stick fairly well to any of the above build surfaces when used with a thin even layer of Polymide Kapton tape or a good quality blue painter's tape. It is not recommended to print ABS or Nylon with a non-heated build plate. Using a raft is always a good idea until you fully understand your system limitations.

Some users apply a small amount of acetone to the build plate while rubbing an old print to the plate. This applies a base layer of material to improve adhesion.

Heated

A heated build plate or platform helps keep the lowest levels of a print warm as the higher layers are printed. This allows the overall print to cool more evenly. A heated build plate helps tremendously with most ABS prints and large PLA prints. You need a heated build plate for Nylon. Heated build plate temperatures should range between 90 - 95C for ABS, 60 - 65C for PLA and 70 - 80C for Nylon. Polymide Kapton tape works the best due to its temperature range capabilities for ABS and PLA. For Nylon, it is recommended to use a PVA (Elmer's or Scotch) based glue stick on the bed for adhesion in a cross-hatch pattern. Remember, less is more when applying the glue stick on the plate.

Ultimaker 3D printer with a heated build plate.

Polymide Kapton tape used in 3D printing.

Some users apply a small amount of acetone to the build plate while rubbing an old print to the plate. This applies a base layer of material to improve adhesion.

Most PSUs (power supply units) supplied with non-heated build plate printers need to be upgraded to handle a heated plate upgrade.

Clean

Print materials stick better to a clean build plate. Clean your build plate after every build. Remove any build up material (hairspray, glue, old print residue, etc.). Replace needed tape (blue, Kapton, etc.).

Level

Level the build plate after every build. Do not print with a badly calibrated printer.

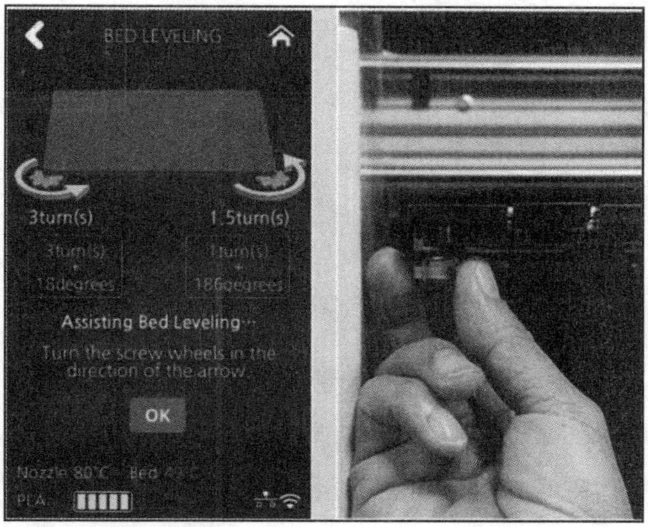

A level printing surface means every thin trace of support will be laid down at the intended height. A slope can cause some traces to be laid down too high from the print bed and prevent them from adhering.

Rule of thumb: For a low cost 3D printer, place the print surface (Z axis) approximately 0.1mm away from the nozzle at six points around the print bed.

Control Temperature

Eliminate all drafts (air conditioner, heater, windows) and control air flow that may cause a temperature gradient within the build area. Changes in temperature during a build cycle can cause curling, cracking and layer delamination, especially on long thin parts. Below are five fully enclosed 3D printers: A modified MakerBot Replicator 2, an Ultimaker 2 Go, a bq witbox, a Sindoh DP200 3DWox and an XYZ da Vinci.

PLA in general is more forgiving to temperature fluctuations and moisture than ABS and Nylon during a build cycle.

Filament Storage

Below is a filament roll. The filament roll is packed with a package of desiccant. A desiccant is a hygroscopic substance that induces or sustains a state of dryness (desiccation) in its vicinity. Do not open filament packages before you need them. Moisture is your enemy. The filament will swell with moisture and can be an issue (size and temperature) in the extruder head during the print cycle.

Darker colors in general (PLA and ABS) often require higher extruder temperatures. Extruding at higher temperatures may help prevent future delamination if you do not have a heated build plate or control build area.

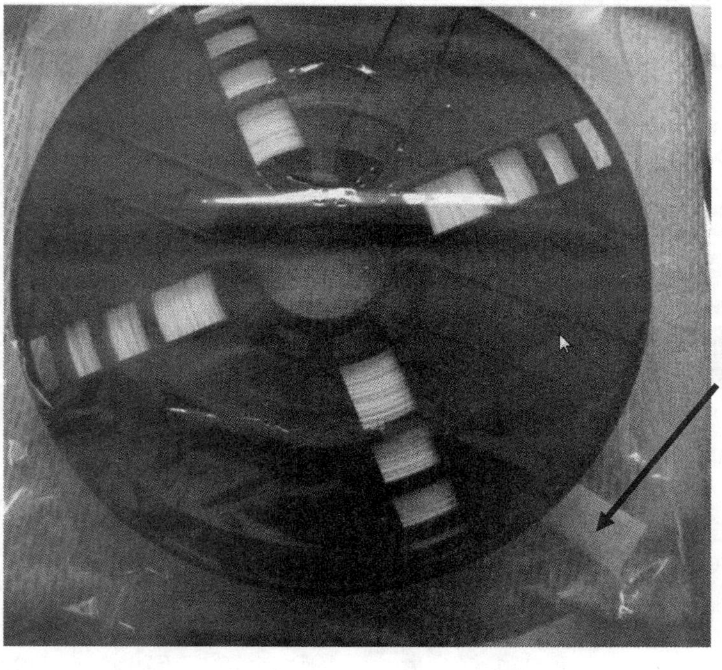

Desiccant package

There are set defaults that come in many low cost printers. The default setting for the diameter of the filament in the Replicator G software is 1.85mm. If you are having build/extruder problems, use a pair of calipers to measure the diameter of the filament. Most calipers will have measurements down to .01mm. To measure your filament, take an average reading of at least three readings and re-set the default filament setting if needed.

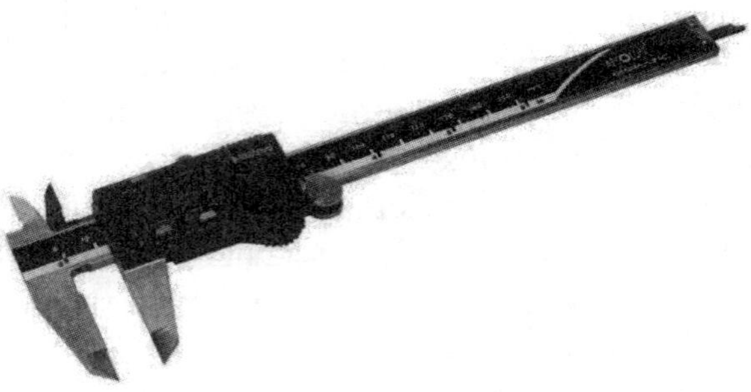

Never focus too much on one single issue. These machines are complex, and trouble often arises from multiple reasons. A slipping filament may not only be caused by a bad gear drive, but also by an obstructed nozzle, a wrong feed value, a too low (or too high) temperature or a combination of all these.

The following images and models were created on the MakerBot Replicator 2 and the Sindoh DP200 3DWox 3D printer. Table 1 below displays a general comparison of the two machines.

Table 1: Sindoh DP200 vs. MakerBot Replicator 2

Manufacturer	Sindoh	MakerBot
Model	Sindoh DP200	Replicator 2
Print Technology	FFF	FDM
Printer Type	Cartesian	Cartesian
Extruder	Single Head	Single Head
Nozzle Diameter	0.4mm [0.015in]	0.4mm[0.015in]
Open Filament System	No	Yes
Print Material	PLA, ABS	PLA
Filament Diameter	1.75mm [0.069in]	1.75mm [0.069in]
Resolution	1mm (100-micron)	1mm (100-micron)
Build Plate	Heated Aluminum	Non-heated
Removable Print Platform	Yes	Yes
Self-Leveling	Yes	No
Self-Cleaning	Yes	No
Build Volume	8.3in L x 7.9in W x 7.7in H (210mm x 200mm x 195mm)	11.2in L x 6.0in W x 6.1in H (285mm x 152mm x 155mm)
Frame Design	Enclosed	Open
Supported File Types	STL, G-Code	STL, OBJ, Thing

Prepare the Model

There are many available open source software packages for preparing your model in an STL file format. To turn the .STL file into code for your printer, you'll need a slicing program. The MakerWare software (slicing program) for the MakerBot Replicator 2 Desktop and the Sindoh DP200 3DWox is displayed in this section.

The first action is to add/insert or load your STL file using the slicing program in the build area.

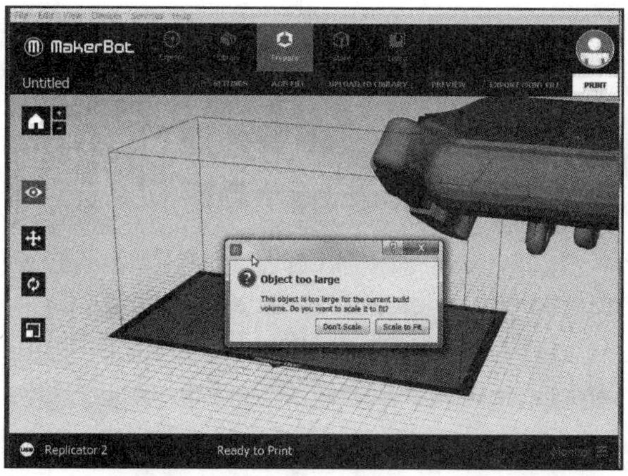

Depending on your printer "slicing program," you may or may not receive a message indicating your object is too large for the current build volume. If the object is too large, then you will need to scale it down or to redesign it into separate parts.

Use caution when scaling if you require fasteners or a minimum wall thickness.

You should center the part and have it lay flat on the build plate.

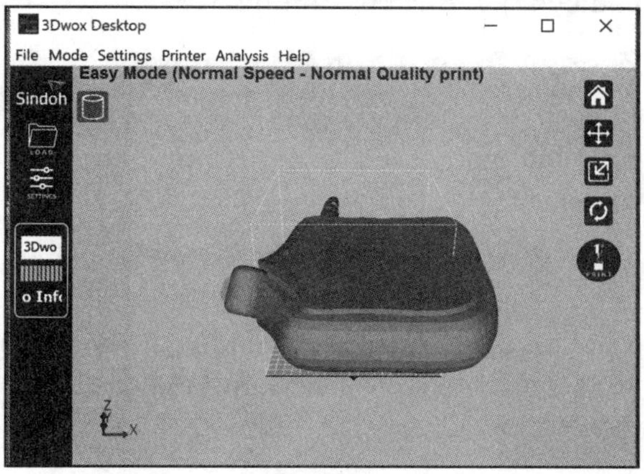

If you are printing more than one part, space them evenly on the plate or position them for a single build.

In SOLIDWORKS, lay the parts out in an assembly. Save the assembly as a part. Save the part file as an STL file. Open the STL in the printer using your slicer.

Consideration should be used when printing an assembly. If the print takes 20 hours, and a failure happens after 19 hours, you just wasted a lot of time versus printing each part individual.

Example 1: Part Orientation

Part orientation is very important on build strength and the amount of raft and support material required for the build. Part orientations can also be related to warping, curling, and delamination.

If maximizing strength is an issue, select the part orientation on the build plate so that the "grain" of the print is oriented to maximize the strength of the part.

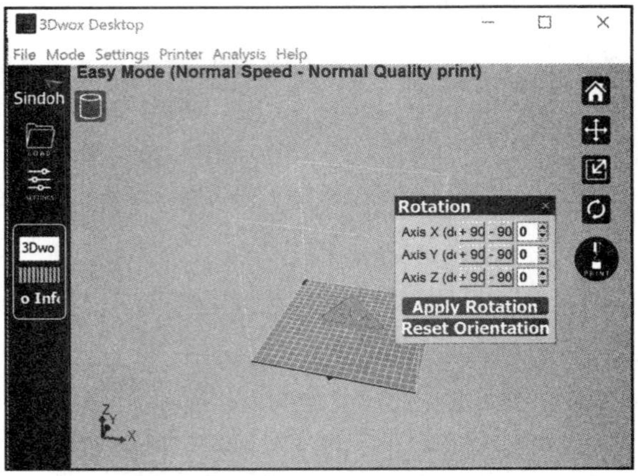

First orientation - vertical

First Orientation - Vertical

In the first orientation (vertical), due to the number of holes and slots, additional support material is required (with minimum raft material) to print the model.

Removing this material in these geometrics can be very time consuming.

Second Orientation - Horizontal

In the second orientation (horizontal), additional raft material is used, and the support material is reduced.

The raft material can be easily removed with a pair of needle-nose pliers and no support material clean-up is required for the holes and slots. Note: In some cases, raft material is not needed.

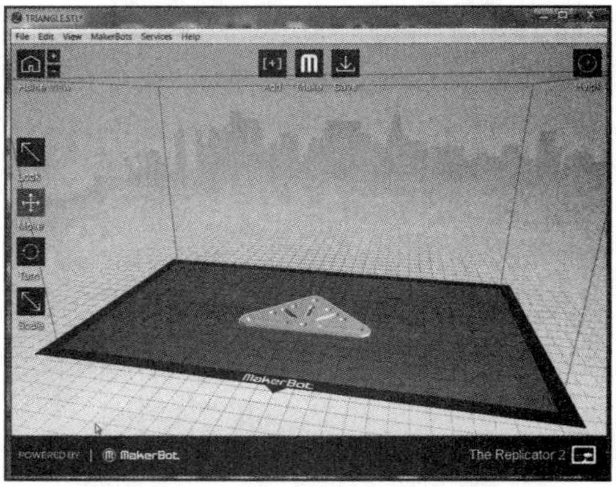

Second orientation - horizontal

Example 2: Part Orientation

The lens part is orientated in a vertical position with the large face flat on the build plate. This reduces the required support material and ensures proper contact with the build plate.

The needed support material is created mainly internal to the part to print the CBORE feature. Note: There is some outside support material on the top section of the part.

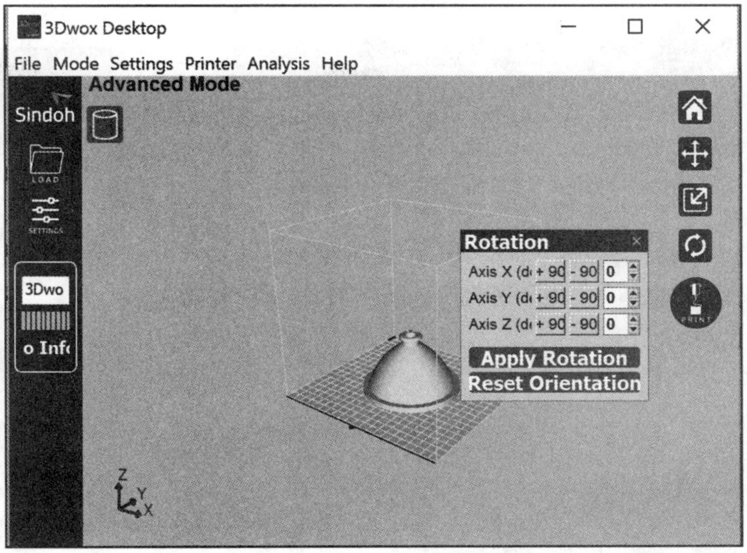

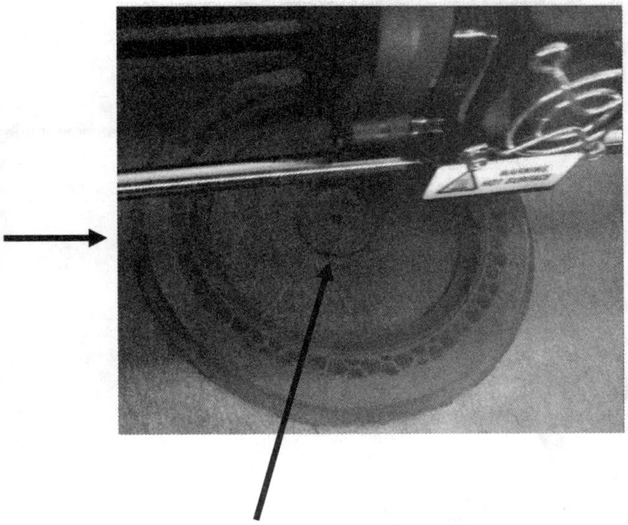

Raft material

Internal support material for the CBORE

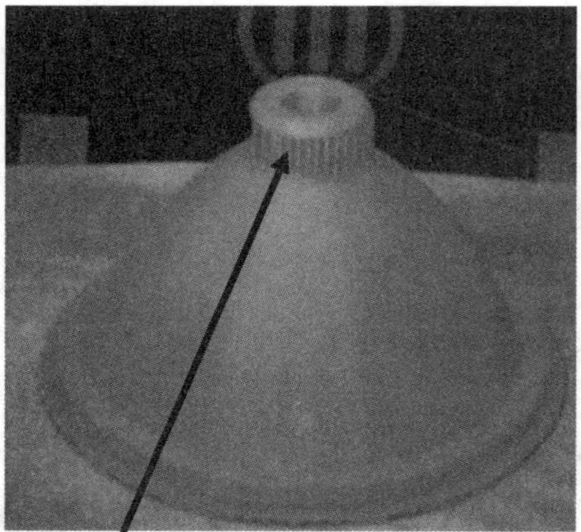

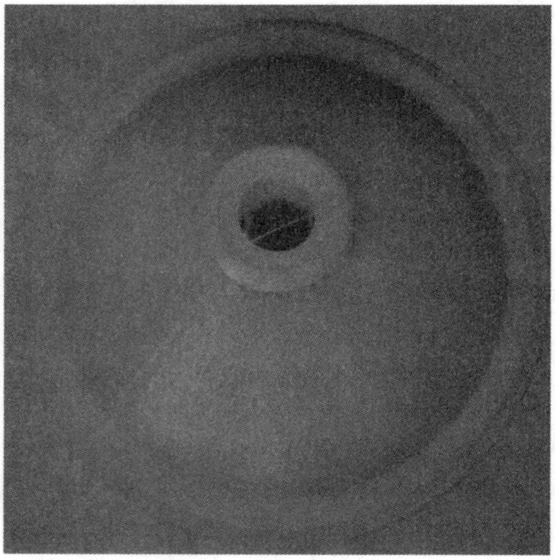

Outside support material for the CBORE

3D Print Terminology

Stereolithography (SL or SLA)

Stereolithography (SL or SLA) is one of several methods used to create 3D printed objects. This is a liquid-based process that consists in the curing or solidification of a photosensitive polymer when an ultraviolet laser makes contact with the resin.

The process was patented as a means of rapid prototyping in 1986 by Charles Hull, co-founder of 3D Systems, Inc.

The process starts with a model in a CAD software and then it is translated to a STL (STereoLithography) file in which the pieces are "cut in slices" containing the information for each layer.

Fused Filament Fabrication (FFF)

Fused Filament Fabrication (FFF) is an additive manufacturing technology used for building three-dimensional products, prototypes or models. It is a rapid prototyping and manufacturing technique that adds layer after layer of molten plastic to create a model or product.

Typically, the FFF mechanism consists of a nozzle that emits material and deposits it onto a moving table. The FFF machine takes input from G-code and starts moving the nozzle and build plate to the needed coordinates. The material is heated in the nozzle to form liquid, which solidifies immediately when it is deposited onto the layer surface. The nozzle works layer-by-layer until the product is finished.

Fused Deposition Fabrication (FDM)

Fused Deposition Modeling (FDM) is an additive manufacturing technology that builds parts up layer-by-layer by heating and extruding thermoplastic filament. Ideal for building durable components with complex geometries in nearly any shape and size, FDM is the only 3D printing process that uses materials like ABS, PC-ISO polycarbonate, and ULTEM 9085. The actual term "Fused Deposition Modeling" and its abbreviation "FDM" are trademarked by Stratasys Ltd.

Digital Light Process (DLP)

Digital Light Processing (DLP) is a form of Stereolithography (SL, or SLA) that is used in Additive Manufacture or rapid prototyping. The main difference between DLP and SLA is the use of a projector light rather than a laser to cure photo-sensitive polymer resin. A DLP 3D printer projects the image of the object's cross section onto the surface of the resin. The exposed resin hardens while the machine's build platform descends, setting the stage for a new layer of fresh resin to be coated to the object and cured by light. Once a complete object is formed, additional post processing may be required such as removal of support material, chemical bath, and UV curing.

An example of a DLP 3D printer is the Formlabs Form1 printer as shown.

Raft, Skirt and Brim

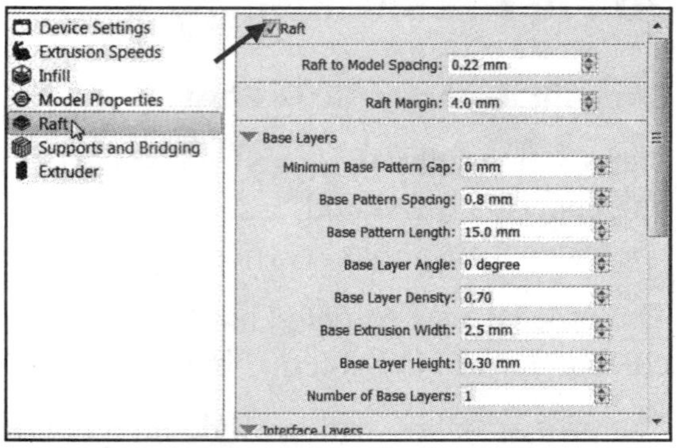

A Raft is a horizontal latticework of filament located underneath the part. A Raft is used to help the part stick to the build plate (heated or non-heated).

Rafts are also used to help stabilize thin tall parts with small build plate footprints.

When the print is complete, remove the part from the build plate. Peel the raft away from the part. If needed, use a scraper or spatula.

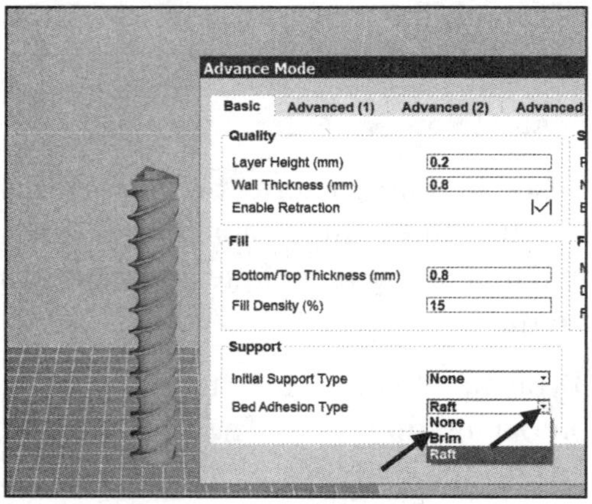

The Raft Settings dialog box illustrates numerous settings and options.

A Skirt is a layer of filament that surrounds the part with a 3-4mm offset. The layer does not connect the part directly to the build plate. The Skirt primes the extruder and establishes a smooth flow of filament. In some slicers, the skirt is added automatically when you select None for Bed Adhesion Type.

A Brim is basically like a Skirt for the part. A Brim has a zero offset from the part. It is a layer of filament that is laid down around the base of the part to increase its surface area. A Brim, however, does not extend underneath the part, which is the key difference between a brim and a raft.

Proper part orientation for thin parts will make the removal of the raft easier.

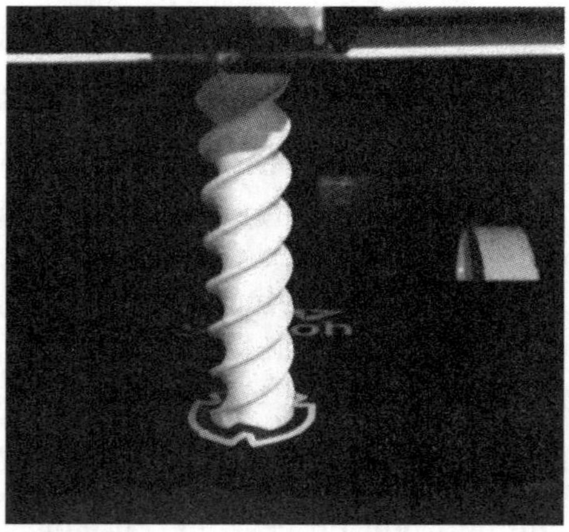

Part with a Skirt on the Build plate

Part with a Raft on the Build plate

Support and Touching Buildplate

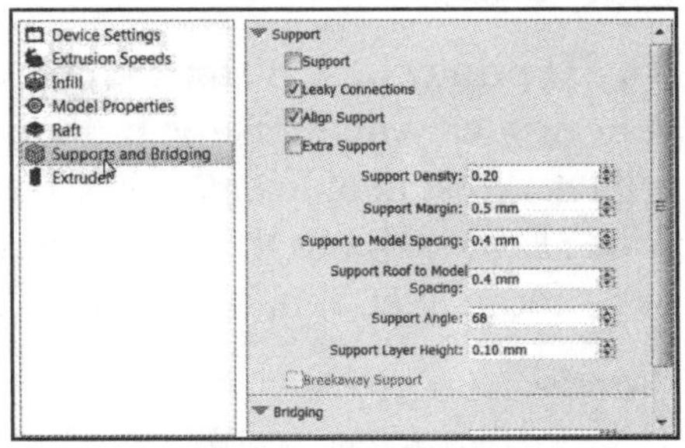

Printing with support is required when material must be deposited on a layer where there is no or insufficient material on the previous layer. This includes steep overhanging surfaces, straight overhangs, and fully suspended islands. Learning to print objects on a 3D Printer that require support structures will dramatically expand the potential of your printer and give you the confidence to undertake printing tasks that perhaps you had previously avoided.

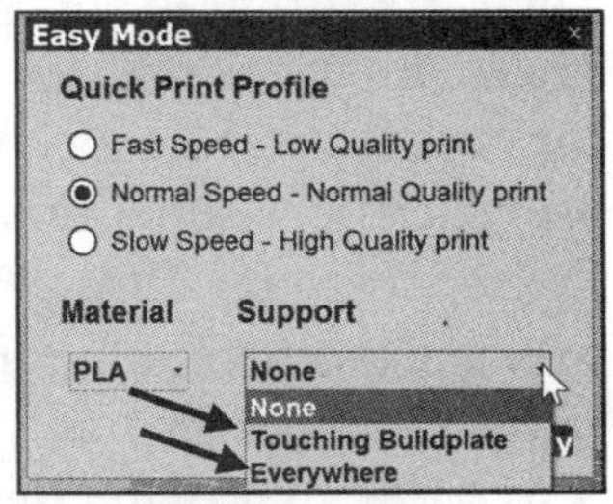

You can remove supports after building the object, but be careful in the initial orientation of the part.

If the part has numerous holes, sharp edges, steep angles or thin bodies, additional support will be added and can make it difficult to remove cleanly.

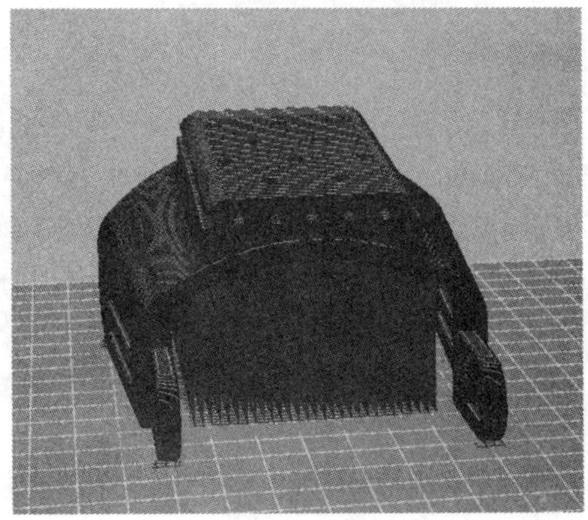

In some slicers, there is a Touching Buildplate option. This option provides supports only where the part touches the build plate. This reduces build time, clean up and support build material. Use this option when you have overhangs and tricky angles toward the bottom of a design, but do not wish to plug up holes, hollow spaces, or arches in the rest of the design.

See the below illustration of a support material example.

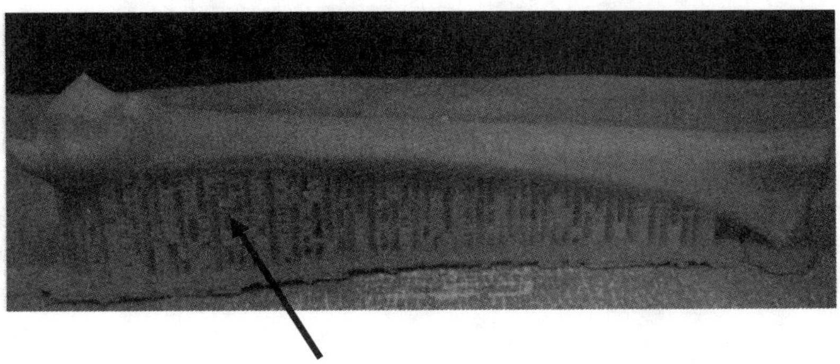

Support material

My favorite tools to remove support and raft material are a good pair of needle nose pliers, angle tweezers and a small flat head screwdriver.

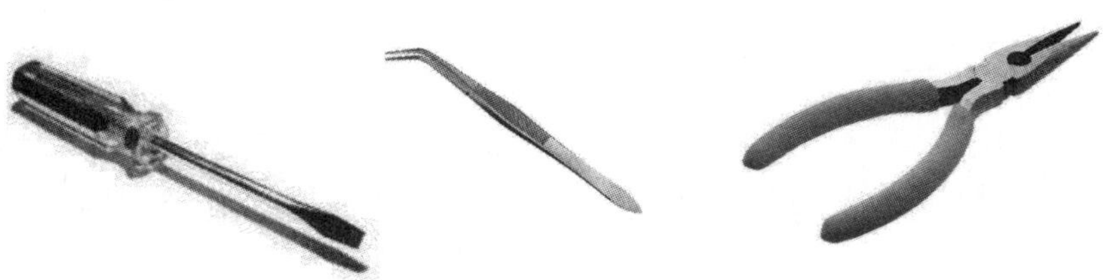

Slicer Engine

All 3D printers use a slicer engine. Slicing generates the G-code necessary to feed into your printer. Slicing is the process of turning your 3D model into a toolpath for your 3D printer. Most people call it slicing because the first thing the slicing engine does is cut your 3D model into thin horizontal layers. Open source slicing engines include Slic3r, Skeinforge, Netfabb, KISSkice, Cura, etc. to name a few.

G-code

There are different ways to prepare G-code for a printer. One is to use a slicer engine. These programs take a CAD model, slice it into layers, and output the G-code required for each layer. Slicers are an easy way to go from a 3D model to a printed part, but the user sacrifices some flexibility when using them. Another option for G-code generation is to use me-code, a lower level open source library. Me-code libraries give precise control over the toolpath providing a solution for a complex print that is not suitable for slicing. If you need to run a few test lines while calibrating your 3D printer, then the final option is to write your own G-code.

Infill

Infill is the internal structure of your object, which can be as sparse or as substantial as you would like it to be. A higher percentage will result in a more solid object, so 100% infill will make your object completely solid, while 0% infill will give you something completely hollow. The higher the infill percentage, the more material and longer the print time required. In general, use a 10% - 15% infill.

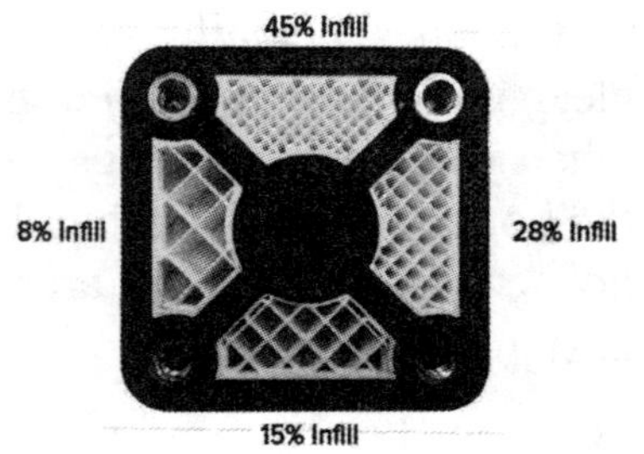

Infill Pattern/Shape

When using any infill percentage, a pattern is used to create a strong and durable structure inside the print. A few standard patterns are Rectilinear, Honeycomb, Circular and Triangular.

Shells/Parameters

The number of shells on the object refers to the number of times the outline of the model is retraced. Shells are the outer most layer of the object, the part of the object you see and interact with.

More shells result in a stronger object but longer printing time and more material.

Shells are also referred to as perimeters in some software and documents.

Do not use additional shells on fine featured models, such as small text. It will obscure the detail.

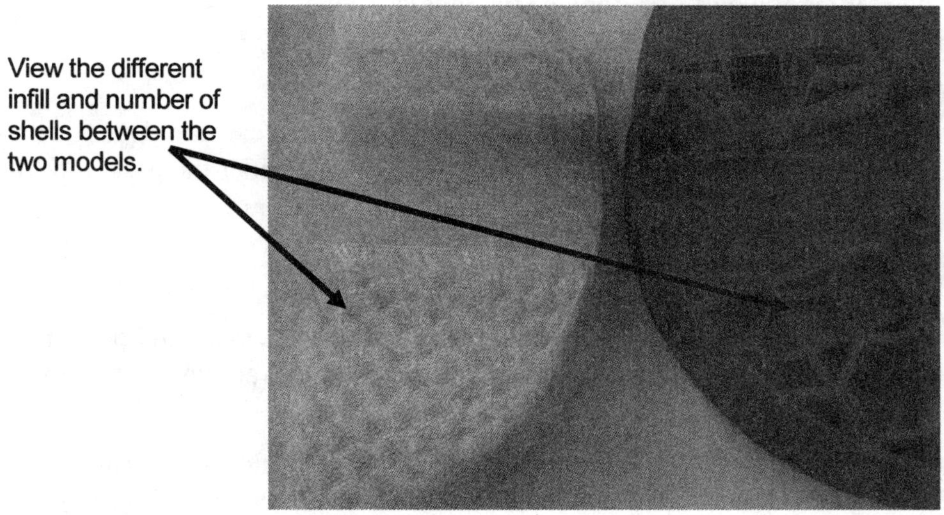

Layer Height

Traditionally, extrusion-based 3D printers have emphasized the layer height (such as 0.1mm or 0.3mm) as the main indicator of accuracy or quality. One reason for this may be that 3D prints made with this technology typically have visible ridges between different layers.

Layer height has a significant effect on the resolution of organic (curvy) parts. In general use 0.3mm for fast draft quality, 0.25mm for medium draft quality, 0.2mm for standard quality, and 0.1mm for high quality.

(1micron = 1μm = 0.001mm).

Remove the Model from the Build Plate

If you have a non-heated build plate with a sheet of good quality blue painter's tape, it is not too difficult to remove the part. Utilize a flat edge tool (a thin steel spatula), gently work under the part, and lift the raft or the part directly on the tape. You may rip the tape when taking the part off. Replace the tape. Re-level your build plate after every build.

If you have a heated build plate your temperatures can range between 60 - 90C (Kapton tape) depending on the material, so be careful. Again, as above, utilize a flat edge tool (a thin steel spatula), gently work under the part, and lift the part directly from the plate. Re-level your build plate after every build.

Know the Printer's Limitations

There are features that are too small to be printed in plastic on a desktop 3D printer. An important, but often overlooked, variable in what your printer can achieve is thread width.

Thread width is determined by the diameter of your printer's nozzle. Most printers have a 0.4mm or 0.5mm nozzle. Practically, this means that a circle drawn by a 3D printer is always two thread widths deep: 0.8mm thick with a 0.4mm nozzle to 1mm thick for a 0.5mm nozzle. A good rule of thumb is "The smallest feature you can create is double the thread width."

Tolerance for Interlocking Parts

For objects with multiple interlocking parts, design in your fit tolerance. Getting tolerances correct can be difficult. Typical minimum wall thickness for a model is roughly 1mm, and printed part accuracy is ±0.2mm. It is recommended to use a ±0.2mm offset for tight fit (press fit parts, connectors) and use a ±0.4mm offset for loose fit (hinges, box lids).

Keep in mind the underlying problems with low cost 3D printers. The same 3D model will produce prints with varying part tolerances when printed on different types and brands of 3D printers. Users need to check the specifications from the 3D printer and filament manufacturer and then adjust the model geometries accordingly. Also, with any 3D printer, make sure the printer is calibrated to ensure the resolution will be the same across multiple prints.

Test the fit yourself with the particular model to determine the right tolerance for the items you are creating and material you are using.

General Printing Tips

Reduce Infill

When printing a model, you can choose to print it hollow or completely solid, or some percentage between 0 and 100. Infill is a settable variable in most Slicer engines. The material inside the part exerts a force on the entire printed part as it cools. More material increases cost of the part and build time.

Parts with a lower percentage of Infill should have a lower internal force between layers and can reduce the chance of curling, cracking, and layer delamination along with a low build cost and time.

Control build area temperature

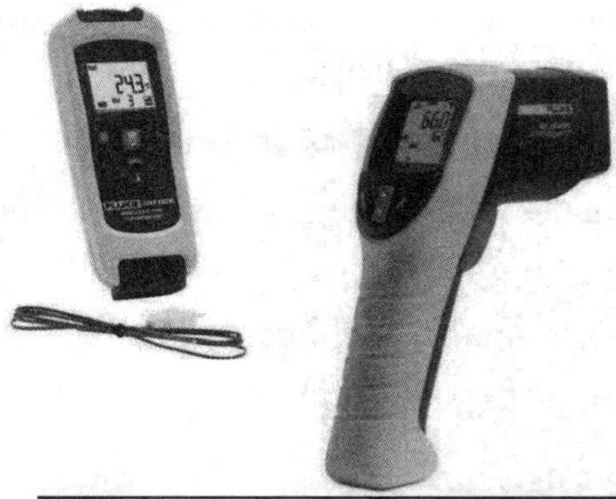

For a consistent quality build, control your build area and environment temperature. Eliminate all drafts and control air flow that may cause a temperature gradient within the build area.

Changes in temperature during a build cycle can cause curling, cracking and layer delamination, especially on long thin parts. From 1000s of hours in 3D printing experience, having a top cover, sides and a heated build plate along with a consisted room temperature provides the best and repeatable builds.

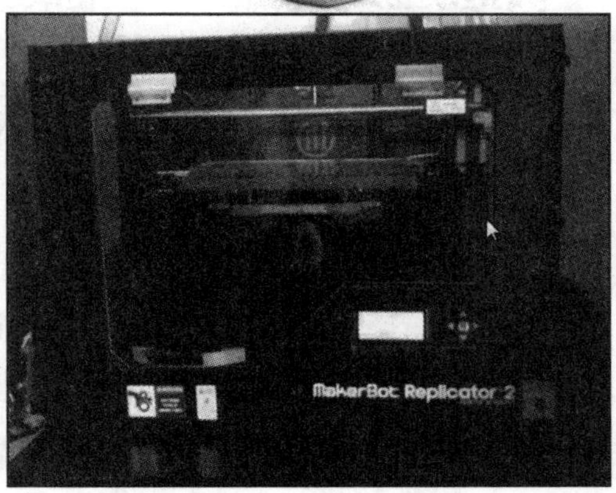

When troubleshooting issues with your printer, it is always best to know if the nozzle and heated bed are achieving the desired temperatures. A thermocouple and a thermometer come in handy. I prefer a Type-K Thermocouple connected to a multi-meter. But a non-contact IR or Laser-based thermometer also works well.

One important thing to remember is that IR and Laser units are not 100% accurate when it comes to shiny reflective surfaces. A Type-K thermocouple can be taped to the nozzle or heated bed using Kapton tape, for a very accurate temperature measurement.

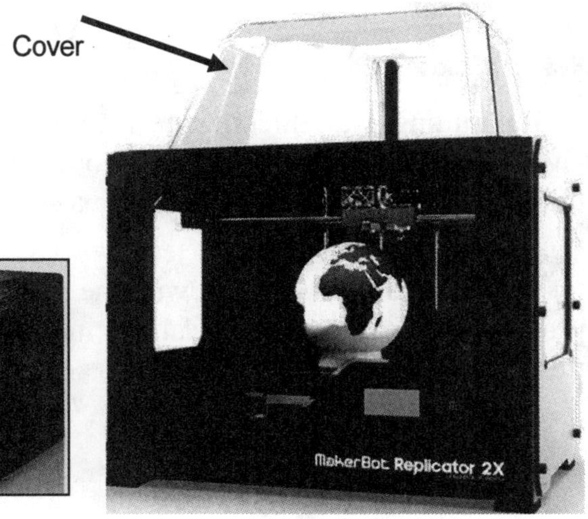

Add Pads

Sometimes, when you are printing a large flat object, such as a simple box container or a very long thin feature, you may view warping at the corners or extremities. One way to address this is to create small pads to your part during the modeling process. Create the model for the print. Think before you print and know your printer limitations. The pads can be any size and shape, but generally, diameter 10mm cylinders that are 1-2 layers thick work well. After the part is printed, remove them.

Makerbot Image

Unique Shape or a Large Part

If you need to make parts larger than your build area or create parts that have intricate projections, here are a few suggestions:

- Fuse smaller sections together using acetone (if using ABS). Glue if using PLA.
- Design smaller parts to be attached together (without hardware).
- Design smaller parts to be screwed together (with hardware).

Safe Zone Rule

Parts may have a safe zone. The safe zone is called "self-supporting" and no support material is required to build the part.

The safe zone can range between 30° to 150°. If the part's features are below 30° or greater than 150°, it should have support material during the build cycle. This is only a rule. Are there other factors to consider? Yes. They are layer thickness, extrusion speed, material type, length of the overhang along with the general model design of features.

Design your part for your printer. Use various modeling techniques (ribs, fillets, pads, etc.) during the design process to eliminate or to minimize the need for supports and clean up.

Wall Thickness

In 3D printing, wall thickness refers to the distance between one surface of your model and the opposite sheer surface. A model made in stereolithography with a minimal wall thickness of 1mm provides you with a strong solid surface.

If you scale your model with the 3D printer software, the wall thickness also scales proportionally. Make modifications in the CAD model to ensure the minimal wall thickness of 1mm.

Extruder Temperature

When working with a new roll of filament for the first time, I generally start out printing at about 200 - 210C (heated plate) and 225 - 230C (non-heated plate) for PLA and then adjust the temperature up or down by a few degrees until I obtain the quality of the print and the strength of the part to be in good balance with each other.

If the temperature is too high, you will see more strings between the separate parts of your print and you may notice that the extruder leaks out material while moving between separate areas of the print.

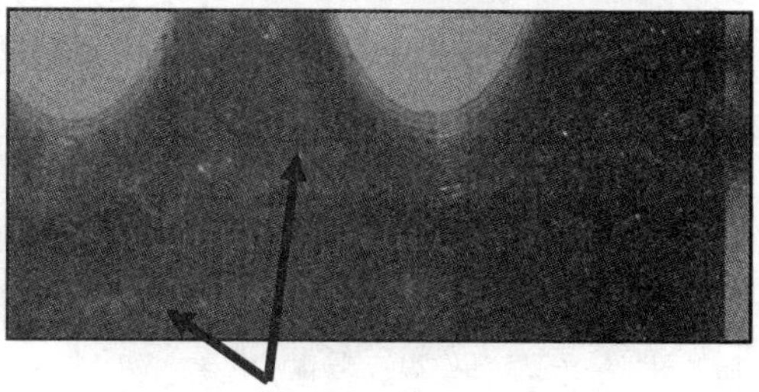

Too cold – rough surface

If the temperature is too cold, you will either see that the filament is not sticking to the (non-heated build plate) or the previous layer and you are getting a rough surface. You will get a part that is not strong and can be pulled apart easily.

The extruder temperature for PLA ranges between 200C - 215C (heated bed 60C - 65C), 225C - 230C (non-heated bed). For ABS they are 225C - 240 (heated bed 90C - 95C).

Various factors can influence the optimal extruding temperature:

- Moisture content.
- Temperature of the printing environment.
- Color.
- Glow in the dark ability.
- Elevation (from sea level) of the printing environment.

First Layer Not Sticking

One of the toughest aspects of 3D printing is to get your prints to stick to the build surface or bed platform. Investigate the following:

- Make sure the bed is level.
- Make sure the bed is hot enough. Do not use blue painter's tape with a heated plate.
- Make sure that the ambient temperature of the print environment isn't too hot or cold (or else adjust accordingly).
- Make sure you put the adhesive on the bed.
- Make sure the print head is close enough to make a nice squished first layer.
- Make sure you run the extruder enough before your print starts so there is filament going onto the bed during the entire first layer.

- Kapton/PET tape is a great way to print ABS. It makes a great shiny bottom layer and the heated bed ensures that your parts stay nice and flat.

Level Build Platform

An unleveled build platform will cause many headaches during a print. You can quickly check the platform by performing the business card test: use a single business card to judge the height of your extruder nozzle over the build platform. Achieve a consistent slight resistance when you position the business card between the tip of the extruder and the platform for all leveling positions.

Minimize Internal Support

Design your part for your printer. Use various modeling techniques (ribs, fillets, pads, etc.) during the design process to eliminate or to minimize the need for support and final clean up.

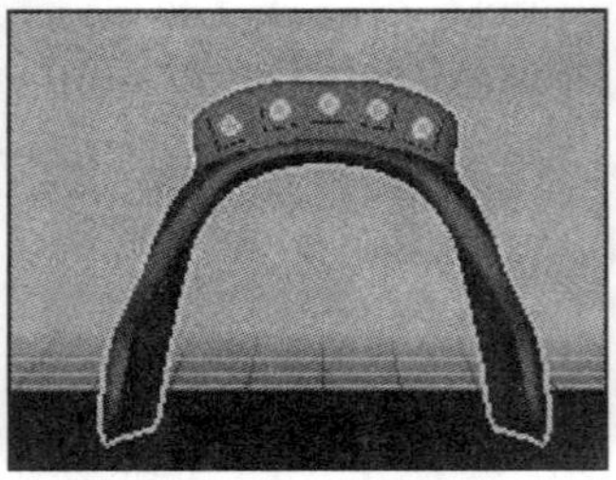

Water Tight Mesh

A water-tight mesh is achieved by having closed edges creating a solid volume. If you were to fill your geometry with water, would you see a leak? You may have to clean up any internal geometry that could have been left behind accidentally from Booleans.

Clearance

If you are creating separate or interlocking parts, make sure there is a large enough distance between tight areas. 3D Printing production, such as Selective Laser Sintering (SLS), makes moving parts without assembly a possibility that was not there before. Take advantage of this strength by creating enough clearance that the model's pieces do not fuse together or trap support material inside.

In General

- Keep your software and firmware up to date.
- Think before you print. Design your model for your printer.
- Understand the printer's limitations. Adjust one thing at a time between prints and keep notes about the settings and effect on the print. Label test prints with a Sharpie and take photographs.
- Always level and clean the build plate before a build.
- Select the correct material (filament) for the build and application. Materials are still an area of active exploration. Use ABS, PLA and Nylon, each of which has specific printing requirements.
- Select the correct part orientation on the build plate. Many of these devices require some attention when printing. 3D printers fabricate objects from thin layers of material; there is a grain to the structure of the printed parts, much like there is grain in wood. Try to print in an orientation so that the "grain" of the print is oriented to maximize the strength of the part.
- Make sure that the bottom surface of each part of the print is firmly secured to the build platform, both for the success of the print and for the surface finish on the bottom face of the object.
- Select the correct Slicing engine settings. Models go through two software processes on their way to becoming finished prints: slicing and sending. Slicing divides a model into printable layers and plots the toolpaths to fill them in. The printer client then sends these movements to the hardware and provides a control interface for its other functions.
- Control the environment for the filament and build area (temperature, humidity, etc.).
- If in doubt, create your first build with a raft and support.
- 3D printers cannot print perfectly, so there will always be a bit of variation between the model and the output. If you make a round hole that's 10mm in diameter and a 10mm diameter drive shaft to fill that hole, it won't have enough clearance to fit into the hole. The best current commercially available printers have a resolution of 0.1mm. This means there could be up to 0.2mm difference between the actual surface of your print and the 3d model. Models also shrink a little after being printed.
- The best thing to do after a print has been completed is to cool down your machine entirely before switching it off. But, if you are in a rush, make sure to at least get it under 100C before switching it off.

Summary

With 1000s of hours using multiple low cost 3D printers, learning about additive print technology is a great experience. Students face a multitude of obstacles with their first 3D prints. Understanding what went wrong and knowing the capabilities of the 3D printer produces positive results.

Never focus too much on one single issue. These machines are complex, and trouble often arises from multiple reasons. A slipping filament may not only be caused by a bad gear drive, but also by an obstructed nozzle, a wrong feed value, a too low (or too high) temperature or a combination of all these.

As printed parts cool (PLA, ABS and Nylon), various areas of the object cool at different rates. Depending on the model being printed and the filament material, this effect can lead to warping, curling and or layer delamination.

Design your part for your printer. Use various modeling techniques (ribs, fillets, pads, etc.) during the design process to eliminate or to minimize the need for supports and clean up.

Technology for 3D printing continues to advance in three key areas: **printers** and **printing methods**, **design software**, and **materials** used in printing.

Additive manufacturing or sometimes known as ***rapid prototyping*** can be slower than Subtractive manufacturing. Both take skill in creating the G-code and understanding the machine limitations.

Appendix

Engineering Changer Order (ECO)

D&M

Engineering Change Order

ECO # ____________
Page 1 of __

	☐	Hardware		Author
	☐	Software		Date
Product Line	☐	Quality		Authorized Mgr.
	☐	Tech Pubs		Date
Change Tested By				

Reason for ECO(Describe the existing problem, symptom and impact on field)

D&M Part No.	Rev From/To	Part Description	Description	Owner

ECO Implementation/Class		Departments	Approvals	Date
All in Field	☐	Engineering		
All in Test	☐	Manufacturing		
All in Assembly	☐	Technical Support		
All in Stock	☐	Marketing		
All on Order	☐	DOC Control		
All Future	☐			
Material Disposition		ECO Cost		
Rework	☐	DO NOT WRITE BELOW THIS LINE(ECO BOARD ONLY)		
Scrap	☐	Effective Date		
Use as is	☐	Incorporated Date		
None	☐	Board Approval		
See Attached	☐	Board Date		

This text follows the ASME Y14 2009 Engineering Drawing and Related Documentation Practices for drawings. Display of dimensions and tolerances are as follows:

TYPES of DECIMAL DIMENSIONS (ASME Y14.5 2009)			
Description:	**UNITS: MM**	**Description:**	**UNITS: INCH**
Dimension is less than 1mm. Zero precedes the decimal point.	0.9 0.95	Dimension is less than 1 inch. Zero is not used before the decimal point.	.5 .56
Dimension is a whole number. Display no decimal point. Display no zero after decimal point.	19	Express dimension to the same number of decimal places as its tolerance. Add zeroes to the right of the decimal point. If the tolerance is expressed to 3 places, then the dimension contains 3 places to the right of the decimal point.	1.750
Dimension exceeds a whole number by a decimal fraction of a millimeter. Display no zero to the right of the decimal.	11.5 11.51		

TABLE 1 **TOLERANCE DISPLAY FOR INCH AND METRIC DIMENSIONS (ASME Y14.5 2009)**		
DISPLAY:	**UNITS: INCH:**	**UNITS: METRIC:**
Dimensions less than 1	.5	0.5
Unilateral Tolerance	$1.417^{+.005}_{-.000}$	$36^{\ 0}_{-0.5}$
Bilateral Tolerance	$1.417^{+.010}_{-.020}$	$36^{+0.25}_{-0.50}$
Limit Tolerance	.571 .463	14.50 11.50

SOLIDWORKS Keyboard Shortcuts

Listed below are some of the pre-defined keyboard shortcuts in SOLIDWORKS:

Action:	Key Combination:
Model Views	
Rotate the model horizontally or vertically	**Arrow** keys
Rotate the model horizontally or vertically 90 degrees	**Shift** + **Arrow** keys
Rotate the model clockwise or counterclockwise	**Alt** + left of right **Arrow** keys
Pan the model	**Ctrl** + **Arrow** keys
Magnifying glass	**g**
Zoom in	**Shift + z**
Zoom out	**z**
Zoom to fit	**f**
Previous view	**Ctrl + Shift + z**
View Orientation	
View Orientation menu	**Spacebar**
Front view	**Ctrl + 1**
Back view	**Ctrl + 2**
Left view	**Ctrl + 3**
Right view	**Ctrl + 4**
Top view	**Ctrl + 5**
Bottom view	**Ctrl + 6**
Isometric view	**Ctrl + 7**
NormalTo view	**Ctrl + 8**
Selection Filters	
Filter edges	**e**
Filter vertices	**v**
Filter faces	**x**
Toggle Selection Filter toolbar	**F5**
Toggle selection filters on/off	**F6**
File menu items	
New SOLIDWORKS document	**Ctrl + n**
Open document	**Ctrl + o**
Open From Web Folder	**Ctrl + w**
Make Drawing from Part	**Ctrl + d**
Make Assembly from Part	**Ctrl + a**
Save	**Ctrl +s**
Print	**Ctrl + p**
Additional shortcuts	
Access online help inside of PropertyManager or dialog box	**F1**
Rename an item in the FeatureManager design tree	**F2**
Rebuild the model	**Ctrl + b**
Force rebuild - Rebuild the model and all its features	**Ctrl + q**
Redraw the screen	**Ctrl + r**

Cycle between open SOLIDWORKS documents	**Ctrl + Tab**
Line to arc/arc to line in the Sketch	**a**
Undo	**Ctrl + z**
Redo	**Ctrl + y**
Cut	**Ctrl + x**
Copy	**Ctrl + c**
Additional shortcuts	
Paste	**Ctrl + v**
Delete	**Delete**
Next window	**Ctrl + F6**
Close window	**Ctrl + F4**
View previous tools	**s**
Selects all text inside an Annotations text box	**Ctrl + a**

In a sketch, the **Esc** key un-selects geometry items currently selected in the Properties box and Add Relations box. In the model, the **Esc** key closes the PropertyManager and cancels the selections.

Use the **g** key to activate the Magnifying glass tool. Use the Magnifying glass tool to inspect a model and make selections without changing the overall view.

Use the **s** key to view/access previous command tools in the Graphics window.

Windows Shortcuts

Listed below are some of the pre-defined keyboard shortcuts in Microsoft Windows:

Action:	Keyboard Combination:
Open the Start menu	Windows Logo key
Open Windows Explorer	Windows Logo key + E
Minimize all open windows	Windows Logo key + M
Open a Search window	Windows Logo key + F
Open Windows Help	Windows Logo key + F1
Select multiple geometry items in a SOLIDWORKS document	Ctrl key (Hold the Ctrl key down. Select items.) Release the Ctrl key.

Helpful Online Information

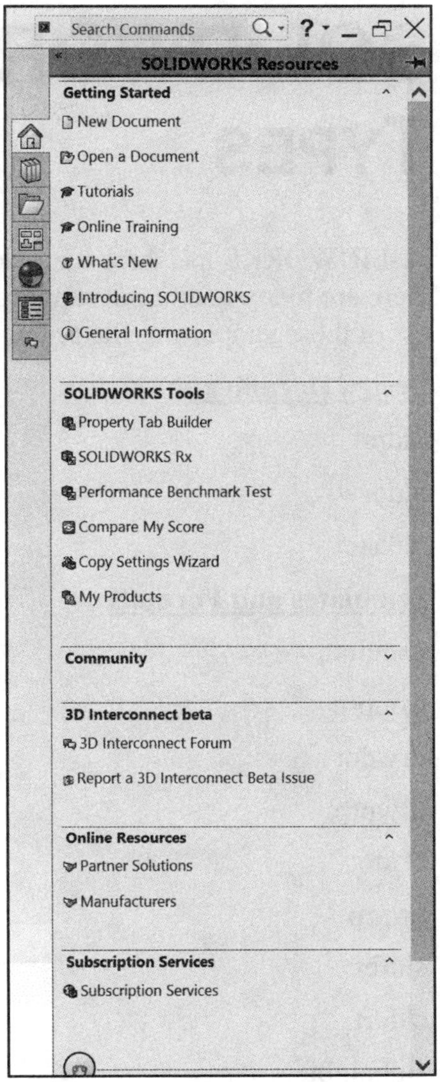

The SOLIDWORKS URL: http://www.SOLIDWORKS.com contains information on Local Resellers, Solution Partners, Certifications, SOLIDWORKS users groups and more.

Access 3D ContentCentral using the Task Pane to obtain engineering electronic catalog model and part information.

Use the SOLIDWORKS Resources tab in the Task Pane to obtain access to Customer Portals, Discussion Forums, User Groups, Manufacturers, Solution Partners, Labs and more.

Helpful on-line SOLIDWORKS information is available from the following URLs:

- http://www.mechengineer.com/snug/.

  News group access and local user group information.

- http://www.swugn.org/.

  List of all SOLIDWORKS User groups.

- http://www.caddedge.com/SOLIDWORKS-user-group-calendar-for-CT-MA-ME-NH-NJ-NY-PA-RI-VT/.

  Updated SOLIDWORKS information and user group calendar for New England and surrounding areas.

- http://www.SOLIDWORKS.com/sw/engineering-education-software.htm.

  SOLIDWORKS in Academia. Information on software, support, tutorials, blog and more.

*On-line tutorials are for educational purposes only. Tutorials are copyrighted by their respective owners.

SOLIDWORKS DOCUMENT TYPES

SOLIDWORKS has three main document file types: Part, Assembly and Drawing, but there are many additional supporting types that you may want to know. Below is a brief list of these supporting file types:

Design Documents	Description
.sldprt	SOLIDWORKS Part document
.slddrw	SOLIDWORKS Drawing document
.sldasm	SOLIDWORKS Assembly document
Templates and Formats	**Description**
.asmdot	Assembly Template
.asmprp	Assembly Template Custom Properties tab
.drwdot	Drawing Template
.drwprp	Drawing Template Custom Properties tab
.prtdot	Part Template
.prtprp	Part Template Custom Properties tab
.sldtbt	General Table Template
.slddrt	Drawing Sheet Template
.sldbombt	Bill of Materials Template (Table-based)
.sldholtbt	Hole Table Template
.sldrevbt	Revision Table Template
.sldwldbt	Weldment Cutlist Template
.xls	Bill of Materials Template (Excel-based)
Library Files	**Description**
.sldlfp	Library Part file
.sldblk	Blocks
Other	**Description**
.sldstd	Drafting standard
.sldmat	Material Database
.sldclr	Color Palette File
.xls	Sheet metal gauge table

GLOSSARY

Alphabet of Lines: Each line on a technical drawing has a definite meaning and is drawn in a certain way. The line conventions recommended by the American National Standards Institute (ANSI) are presented in this text.

Alternate Position View: A drawing view superimposed in phantom lines on the original view. Utilized to show range of motion of an assembly.

Anchor Point: The origin of the Bill of Material in a sheet format.

Annotation: An annotation is a text note or a symbol that adds specific information and design intent to a part, assembly, or drawing. Annotations in a drawing include specific note, hole callout, surface finish symbol, datum feature symbol, datum target, geometric tolerance symbol, weld symbol, balloon and stacked balloon, center mark, centerline marks, area hatch and block.

ANSI: American National Standards Institute.

Area Hatch: Apply a crosshatch pattern or solid fill to a model face, to a closed sketch profile, or to a region bounded by a combination of model edges and sketch entities. Area hatch can be applied only in drawings.

ASME: American Society of Mechanical Engineering, publisher of ASME Y14 Engineering Drawing and Documentation Practices that controls drawing, dimensioning and tolerancing.

Assembly: An assembly is a document in which parts, features and other assemblies (sub-assemblies) are put together. A part in an assembly is called a component. Adding a component to an assembly creates a link between the assembly and the component. When SOLIDWORKS opens the assembly, it finds the component file to show it in the assembly. Changes in the component are automatically reflected in the assembly. The filename extension for a SOLIDWORKS assembly file name is *.sldasm.

Attachment Point: An attachment point is the end of a leader that attaches to an edge, vertex, or face in a drawing sheet.

AutoDimension: The AutoDimension tool provides the ability to insert reference dimensions into drawing views such as baseline, chain, and ordinate dimensions.

Auxiliary View: An Auxiliary View is similar to a Projected View, but it is unfolded normal to a reference edge in an existing view.

AWS: American Welding Society, publisher of AWS A2.4, Standard Location of Elements of a Welding Symbol.

Axonometric Projection: A type of parallel projection, more specifically a type of orthographic projection, used to create a pictorial drawing of an object, where the object is rotated along one or more of its axes relative to the plane of projection.

Balloon: A balloon labels the parts in the assembly and relates them to item numbers on the bill of materials (BOM) added in the drawing. The balloon item number corresponds to the order in the Feature Tree. The order controls the initial BOM Item Number.

Baseline Dimensions: Dimensions referenced from the same edge or vertex in a drawing view.

Bill of Materials: A table inserted into a drawing to keep a record of the parts and materials used in an assembly.

Block: A symbol in the drawing that combines geometry into a single entity.

BOM: Abbreviation for Bill of Materials.

Broken-out Section: A broken-out section exposes inner details of a drawing view by removing material from a closed profile. In an assembly, the Broken-out Section displays multiple components.

CAD: The use of computer technology for the design of objects, real or virtual. CAD often involves more than just shapes.

Cartesian Coordinate System: Specifies each point uniquely in a plane by a pair of numerical coordinates, which are the signed distances from the point to two fixed perpendicular directed lines, measured in the same unit of length. Each reference line is called a coordinate axis or just axis of the system, and the point where they meet is its origin.

Cell: Area to enter a value in an EXCEL spreadsheet, identified by a Row and Column.

Center Mark: A cross that marks the center of a circle or arc.

Centerline: An axis of symmetry in a sketch or drawing displayed in a phantom font.

CommandManager: The CommandManager is a Context-sensitive toolbar that dynamically updates based on the toolbar you want to access. By default, it has toolbars embedded in it based on the document type. When you click a tab below the Command Manager, it updates to display that toolbar. For example, if you click the Sketch tab, the Sketch toolbar is displayed.

Component: A part or sub-assembly within an assembly.

ConfigurationManager: The ConfigurationManager is located on the left side of the SOLIDWORKS window and provides the means to create, select and view multiple configurations of parts and assemblies in an active document. You can split the

ConfigurationManager and either display two ConfigurationManager instances, or combine the ConfigurationManager with the FeatureManager design tree, PropertyManager or third party applications that use the panel.

Configurations: Variations of a part or assembly that control dimensions, display and state of a model.

Coordinate System: SOLIDWORKS uses a coordinate system with origins. A part document contains an original origin. Whenever you select a plane or face and open a sketch, an origin is created in alignment with the plane or face. An origin can be used as an anchor for the sketch entities, and it helps orient perspective of the axes. A three-dimensional reference triad orients you to the X, Y, and Z directions in part and assembly documents.

Copy and Paste: Utilize copy/paste to copy views from one sheet to another sheet in a drawing or between different drawings.

Cosmetic Thread: An annotation that represents threads.

Crosshatch: A pattern (or fill) applied to drawing views such as section views and broken-out sections.

Cursor Feedback: The system feedback symbol indicates what you are selecting or what the system is expecting you to select. As you move the mouse pointer across your model, system feedback is provided.

Datum Feature: An annotation that represents the primary, secondary and other reference planes of a model utilized in manufacturing.

Depth: The horizontal (front to back) distance between two features in frontal planes. Depth is often identified in the shop as the thickness of a part or feature.

Design Table: An Excel spreadsheet that is used to create multiple configurations in a part or assembly document.

Detail View: A portion of a larger view, usually at a larger scale than the original view. Create a detail view in a drawing to display a portion of a view, usually at an enlarged scale. This detail may be of an orthographic view, a non-planar (isometric) view, a section view, a crop view, an exploded assembly view or another detail view.

Detailing: Detailing refers to the SOLIDWORKS module used to insert, add and modify dimensions and notes in an engineering drawing.

Dimension Line: A line that references dimension text to extension lines indicating the feature being measured.

Dimension Tolerance: Controls the dimension tolerance values and the display of non-integer dimensions. The tolerance types are *None*, *Basic*, *Bilateral*, *Limit*, *Symmetric*, *MIN*, *MAX*, *Fit*, *Fit with tolerance* or *Fit (tolerance only)*.

Dimension: A value indicating the size of the 2D sketch entity or 3D feature. Dimensions in a SOLIDWORKS drawing are associated with the model, and changes in the model are reflected in the drawing, if you DO NOT USE DimXpert.

Dimensioning Standard - Metric: - ASME standards for the use of metric dimensioning require all the dimensions to be expressed in millimeters (mm). The (mm) is not needed on each dimension, but it is used when a dimension is used in a notation. No trailing zeros are used. The Metric or International System of Units (S.I.) unit system in drafting is also known as the Millimeter, Gram Second (MMGS) unit system.

Dimensioning Standard - U.S: - ASME standard for U.S. dimensioning uses the decimal inch value. When the decimal inch system is used, a zero is not used to the left of the decimal point for values less than one inch, and trailing zeros are used. The U.S. unit system is also known as the Inch, Pound, Second (IPS) unit system.

DimXpert for Parts: A set of tools that applies dimensions and tolerances to parts according to the requirements of the ASME Y.14.41-2009 standard.

DimXpertManager: The DimXpertManager lists the tolerance features defined by DimXpert for a part. It also displays DimXpert tools that you use to insert dimensions and tolerances into a part. You can import these dimensions and tolerances into drawings. DimXpert is not associative.

Document: In SOLIDWORKS, each part, assembly, and drawing is referred to as a document, and each document is displayed in a separate window.

Drawing Sheet: A page in a drawing document.

Drawing Template: A document that is the foundation of a new drawing. The drawing template contains document properties and user-defined parameters such as sheet format. The extension for the drawing template filename is .DRWDOT.

Drawing: A 2D representation of a 3D part or assembly. The extension for a SOLIDWORKS drawing file name is .SLDDRW. Drawing refers to the SOLIDWORKS module used to insert, add, and modify views in an engineering drawing.

Edit Sheet Format: The drawing sheet contains two modes. Utilize the Edit Sheet Format command to add or modify notes and Title block information. Edit in the Edit Sheet Format mode.

Edit Sheet: The drawing sheet contains two modes. Utilize the Edit Sheet command to insert views and dimensions.

eDrawing: A compressed document that does not require the referenced part or assembly. eDrawings are animated to display multiple views in a drawing.

Empty View: An Empty View creates a blank view not tied to a part or assembly document.

Engineering Graphics: Translates ideas from design layouts, specifications, rough sketches, and calculations of engineers & architects into working drawings, maps, plans and illustrations which are used in making products.

Equation: Creates a mathematical relation between sketch dimensions, using dimension names as variables, or between feature parameters, such as the depth of an extruded feature or the instance count in a pattern.

Exploded view: A configuration in an assembly that displays its components separated from one another.

Export: The process to save a SOLIDWORKS document in another format for use in other CAD/CAM, rapid prototyping, web or graphics software applications.

Extension Line: The line extending from the profile line indicating the point from which a dimension is measured.

Extruded Cut Feature: Projects a sketch perpendicular to a Sketch plane to remove material from a part.

Face: A selectable area (planar or otherwise) of a model or surface with boundaries that help define the shape of the model or surface. For example, a rectangular solid has six faces.

Family Cell: A named empty cell in a Design Table that indicates the start of the evaluated parameters and configuration names. Locate Comments in a Design Table to the left or above the Family Cell.

Fasteners: Includes Bolts and nuts (threaded), Set screws (threaded), Washers, Keys, and Pins to name a few. Fasteners are not a permanent means of assembly such as welding or adhesives.

Feature: Features are geometry building blocks. Features add or remove material. Features are created from 2D or 3D sketched profiles or from edges and faces of existing geometry.

FeatureManager: The FeatureManager design tree located on the left side of the SOLIDWORKS window provides an outline view of the active part, assembly, or drawing. This makes it easy to see how the model or assembly was constructed or to examine the various sheets and views in a drawing. The FeatureManager and the Graphics window are dynamically linked. You can select features, sketches, drawing views and construction geometry in either pane.

First Angle Projection: In First Angle Projection the Top view is looking at the bottom of the part. First Angle Projection is used in Europe and most of the world. However, America and Australia use a method known as Third Angle Projection.

Fully defined: A sketch where all lines and curves in the sketch, and their positions, are described by dimensions or relations, or both, and cannot be moved. Fully defined sketch entities are shown in black.

Foreshortened radius: Helpful when the centerpoint of a radius is outside of the drawing or interferes with another drawing view: Broken Leader.

Foreshortening: The way things appear to get smaller in both height and depth as they recede into the distance.

French curve: A template made out of plastic, metal or wood composed of many different curves. It is used in manual drafting to draw smooth curves of varying radii.

Fully Defined: A sketch where all lines and curves in the sketch, and their positions, are described by dimensions or relations, or both, and cannot be moved. Fully defined sketch entities are displayed in black.

Geometric Tolerance: A set of standard symbols that specify the geometric characteristics and dimensional requirements of a feature.

Glass Box method: A traditional method of placing an object in an *imaginary glass box* to view the six principle views.

Global Coordinate System: Directional input refers by default to the Global coordinate system (X-, Y- and Z-), which is based on Plane1 with its origin located at the origin of the part or assembly.

Graphics Window: The area in the SOLIDWORKS window where the part, assembly, or drawing is displayed.

Grid: A system of fixed horizontal and vertical divisions.

Handle: An arrow, square or circle that you drag to adjust the size or position of an entity such as a view or dimension.

Heads-up View Toolbar: A transparent toolbar located at the top of the Graphic window.

Height: The vertical distance between two or more lines or surfaces (features) which are in horizontal planes.

Hidden Lines Removed (HLR): A view mode. All edges of the model that are not visible from the current view angle are removed from the display.

Hidden Lines Visible (HLV): A view mode. All edges of the model that are not visible from the current view angle are shown gray or dashed.

Hole Callouts: Hole callouts are available in drawings. If you modify a hole dimension in the model, the callout updates automatically in the drawing if you did not use DimXpert.

Hole Table: A table in a drawing document that displays the positions of selected holes from a specified origin datum. The tool labels each hole with a tag. The tag corresponds to a row in the table.

Import: The ability to open files from other software applications into a SOLIDWORKS document. The A-size sheet format was created as an AutoCAD file and imported into SOLIDWORKS.

Isometric Projection: A form of graphical projection, more specifically, a form of axonometric projection. It is a method of visually representing three-dimensional objects in two dimensions, in which the three coordinate axes appear equally foreshortened and the angles between any two of them are 120°.

Layers: Simplifies a drawing by combining dimensions, annotations, geometry and components. Properties such as display, line style and thickness are assigned to a named layer.

Leader: A solid line created from an annotation to the referenced feature.

Line Format: A series of tools that control Line Thickness, Line Style, Color, Layer and other properties.

Local (Reference) Coordinate System: Coordinate system other than the Global coordinate system. You can specify restraints and loads in any desired direction.

Lock Sheet Focus: Adds sketch entities and annotations to the selected sheet. Double-click the sheet to activate Lock Sheet Focus. To unlock a sheet, right-click and select Unlock Sheet Focus or double click inside the sheet boundary.

Lock View Position: Secures the view at its current position in the sheet. Right-click in the drawing view to Lock View Position. To unlock a view position, right-click and select Unlock View Position.

Mass Properties: The physical properties of a model based upon geometry and material.

Menus: Menus provide access to the commands that the SOLIDWORKS software offers. Menus are Context-sensitive and can be customized through a dialog box.

Model Item: Provides the ability to insert dimensions, annotations, and reference geometry from a model document (part or assembly) into a drawing.

Model View: A specific view of a part or assembly. Standard named views are listed in the view orientation dialog box such as isometric or front. Named views can be user-defined name for a specific view.

Model: 3D solid geometry in a part or assembly document. If a part or assembly document contains multiple configurations, each configuration is a separate model.

Motion Studies: Graphical simulations of motion and visual properties with assembly models. Analogous to a configuration, they do not actually change the original assembly model or its properties. They display the model as it changes based on simulation elements you add.

Mouse Buttons: The left, middle, and right mouse buttons have distinct meanings in SOLIDWORKS. Use the middle mouse button to rotate and Zoom in/out on the part or assembly document.

Oblique Projection: A simple type of graphical projection used for producing pictorial, two-dimensional images of three-dimensional objects.

OLE (Object Linking and Embedding): A Windows file format. A company logo or EXCEL spreadsheet placed inside a SOLIDWORKS document are examples of OLE files.

Ordinate Dimensions: Chain of dimensions referenced from a zero ordinate in a drawing or sketch.

Origin: The model origin is displayed in blue and represents the (0,0,0) coordinate of the model. When a sketch is active, a sketch origin is displayed in red and represents the (0,0,0) coordinate of the sketch. Dimensions and relations can be added to the model origin but not to a sketch origin.

Orthographic Projection: A means of representing a three-dimensional object in two dimensions. It is a form of parallel projection, where the view direction is orthogonal to the projection plane, resulting in every plane of the scene appearing in affine transformation on the viewing surface.

Parametric Note: A Note annotation that links text to a feature dimension or property value.

Parent View: A Parent view is an existing view on which other views are dependent.

Part Dimension: Used in creating a part, they are sometimes called construction dimensions.

Part: A 3D object that consist of one or more features. A part inserted into an assembly is called a component. Insert part views, feature dimensions and annotations into 2D drawing. The extension for a SOLIDWORKS part filename is .SLDPRT.

Perspective Projection: The two most characteristic features of perspective are that objects are drawn smaller as their distance from the observer increases and foreshortened: the size of an object's dimensions along the line of sight are relatively shorter than dimensions across the line of sight.

Plane: To create a sketch, choose a plane. Planes are flat and infinite. Planes are represented on the screen with visible edges.

Precedence of Line Types: When obtaining orthographic views, it is common for one type of line to overlap another type. When this occurs, drawing conventions have established an order of precedence.

Precision: Controls the number of decimal places displayed in a dimension.

Projected View: Projected views are created for Orthogonal views using one of the following tools: Standard 3 View, Model View or the Projected View tool from the View Layout toolbar.

Properties: Variables shared between documents through linked notes.

PropertyManager: Most sketch, feature, and drawing tools in SOLIDWORKS open a PropertyManager located on the left side of the SOLIDWORKS window. The PropertyManager displays the properties of the entity or feature so you specify the properties without a dialog box covering the Graphics window.

RealView: Provides a simplified way to display models in a photo-realistic setting using a library of appearances and scenes. RealView requires graphics card support and is memory intensive.

Rebuild: A tool that updates (or regenerates) the document with any changes made since the last time the model was rebuilt. Rebuild is typically used after changing a model dimension.

Reference Dimension: Dimensions added to a drawing document are called Reference dimensions, and are driven; you cannot edit the value of reference dimensions to modify the model. However, the values of reference dimensions change when the model dimensions change.

Relation: A relation is a geometric constraint between sketch entities or between a sketch entity and a plane, axis, edge or vertex.

Relative view: The Relative View defines an Orthographic view based on two orthogonal faces or places in the model.

Revision Table: The Revision Table lists the Engineering Change Orders (ECO), in a table form, issued over the life of the model and the drawing. The current Revision letter or number is placed in the Title block of the Drawing.

Right-Hand Rule: Is a common mnemonic for understanding notation conventions for vectors in 3 dimensions.

Rollback: Suppresses all items below the rollback bar.

Scale: A relative term meaning "size" in relationship to some system of measurement.

Section Line: A line or centerline sketched in a drawing view to create a section view.

Section Scope: Specifies the components to be left uncut when you create an assembly drawing section view.

Section View: You create a section view in a drawing by cutting the parent view with a cutting, or section line. The section view can be a straight cut section or an offset section defined by a stepped section line. The section line can also include concentric arcs. Create a Section View in a drawing by cutting the Parent view with a section line.

Sheet Format: A document that contains the following: page size and orientation, standard text, borders, logos, and Title block information. Customize the Sheet format to save time. The extension for the Sheet format filename is .SLDDRT.

Sheet Properties: Sheet Properties display properties of the selected sheet. Sheet Properties define the following: Name of the Sheet, Sheet Scale, Type of Projection (First angle or Third angle), Sheet Format, Sheet Size, View label, and Datum label.

Sheet: A page in a drawing document.

Silhouette Edge: A curve representing the extent of a cylindrical or curved face when viewed from the side.

Sketch: The name to describe a 2D profile is called a sketch. 2D sketches are created on flat faces and planes within the model. Typical geometry types are lines, arcs, corner rectangles, circles, polygons, and ellipses.

Spline: A sketched 2D or 3D curve defined by a set of control points.

Stacked Balloon: A group of balloons with only one leader. The balloons can be stacked vertically (up or down) or horizontally (left or right).

Standard views: The three orthographic projection views, Front, Top and Right, positioned on the drawing according to First angle or Third angle projection.

Suppress: Removes an entity from the display and from any calculations in which it is involved. You can suppress features, assembly components, and so on. Suppressing an entity does not delete the entity; you can unsuppress the entity to restore it.

Surface Finish: An annotation that represents the texture of a part.

System Feedback: Feedback is provided by a symbol attached to the cursor arrow indicating your selection. As the cursor floats across the model, feedback is provided in the form of symbols riding next to the cursor.

System Options: System Options are stored in the registry of the computer. System Options are not part of the document. Changes to the System Options affect all current and future documents. There are hundreds of Systems Options.

Tangent Edge: The transition edge between rounded or filleted faces in hidden lines visible or hidden lines removed modes in drawings.

Task Pane: The Task Pane is displayed when you open the SOLIDWORKS software. It contains the following tabs: SOLIDWORKS Resources, Design Library, File Explorer, Search, View Palette, Document Recovery and RealView/PhotoWorks.

Templates: Templates are part, drawing and assembly documents that include user-defined parameters and are the basis for new documents.

Third Angle Projection: In Third angle projection the Top View is looking at the Top of the part. First Angle Projection is used in Europe and most of the world. America and Australia use the Third Angle Projection method.

Thread Class or Fit: Classes of fit are tolerance standards; they set a plus or minus figure that is applied to the pitch diameter of bolts or nuts. The classes of fit used with almost all bolts sized in inches are specified by the ANSI/ASME Unified Screw Thread standards (which differ from the previous American National standards).

Thread Lead: The distance advanced parallel to the axis when the screw is turned one revolution. For a single thread, lead is equal to the pitch; for a double thread, lead is twice the pitch.

Tolerance: The permissible range of variation in a dimension of an object. Tolerance may be specified as a factor or percentage of the nominal value, a maximum deviation from a nominal value, an explicit range of allowed values, be specified by a note or published standard with this information, or be implied by the numeric accuracy of the nominal value.

Toolbars: The toolbar menus provide shortcuts enabling you to access the most frequently used commands. Toolbars are Context-sensitive and can be customized through a dialog box.

T-Square: A technical drawing instrument, primarily a guide for drawing horizontal lines on a drafting table. It is used to guide the triangle that draws vertical lines. Its name comes from the general shape of the instrument where the horizontal member of the T slides on the side of the drafting table. Common lengths are 18", 24", 30", 36" and 42".

Under-defined: A sketch is under defined when there are not enough dimensions and relations to prevent entities from moving or changing size.

Units: Used in the measurement of physical quantities. Decimal inch dimensioning and Millimeter dimensioning are the two types of common units specified for engineering parts and drawings.

Vertex: A point at which two or more lines or edges intersect. Vertices can be selected for sketching, dimensioning, and many other operations.

View Palette: Use the View Palette, located in the Task Pane, to insert drawing views. It contains images of standard views, annotation views, section views, and flat patterns (sheet metal parts) of the selected model. You can drag views onto the drawing sheet to create a drawing view.

Weld Bead: An assembly feature that represents a weld between multiple parts.

Weld Finish: A weld symbol representing the parameters you specify.

Weld Symbol: An annotation in the part or drawing that represents the parameters of the weld.

Width: The horizontal distance between surfaces in profile planes. In the machine shop, the terms length and width are used interchangeably.

Zebra Stripes: Simulate the reflection of long strips of light on a very shiny surface. They allow you to see small changes in a surface that may be hard to see with a standard display.

INDEX

U & V

W & X & Y

Z

About Us

SDC Publications specializes in creating exceptional books that are designed to seamlessly integrate into courses or help the self learner master new skills. Our commitment to meeting our customer's needs and keeping our books priced affordably are just some of the reasons our books are being used by nearly 1,200 colleges and universities across the United States and Canada.

SDC Publications is a family owned and operated company that has been creating quality books since 1985. All of our books are proudly printed in the United States.

Our technology books are updated for every new software release so you are always up to date with the newest technology. Many of our books come with video enhancements to aid students and instructor resources to aid instructors.

Take a look at all the books we have to offer you by visiting SDCpublications.com.